STUDYING PUBLIC POLICY

Edited by Michael Hill

First published in Great Britain in 2014 by

Policy Press
University of Bristol
6th Floor
Howard House
Queen's Avenue
Clifton
Bristol BS8 1SD
UK
Tel +44 (0)117 331 5020
Fax +44 (0)117 331 5369
e-mail pp-info@bristol.ac.uk
www.policypress.co.uk

North American office:
Policy Press
c/o The University of Chicago Press
1427 East 60th Street
Chicago, IL 60637, USA
t: +1 773 702 7700
f: +1 773-702-9756
e:sales@press.uchicago.edu
www.press.uchicago.edu

British Library Cataloguing in Publication Data
A catalogue record for this book is available from the British Library

Library of Congress Cataloging-in-Publication Data
A catalog record for this book has been requested

ISBN 978 1 44731 107 2 paperback
ISBN 978 1 44731 106 5 hardcover

Cover design by Robin Hawes
Front cover image: www.istock.com
Printed and bound in Great Britain by TJ International, Padstow

MIX
Paper from
responsible sources
FSC® C013056

Contents

List of contributors

Chloe A. Vlassopoulos, University of Picardie

Gyu-Jin Hwang, University of Sydney

Pei-Yuen Tsai, National Chengchi University

Daniel Nohrstedt, University of Uppsala

Gregory P. Marchildon, University of Regina

Kristin O'Donovan, Wayne State University

Naonori Kodate, University College, Dublin

Jennifer Curtin, University of Auckland

Michael J. Prince, University of Victoria

Anna Zachrisson and Katarina Eckerberg, University of Umea

Corinne Larrue, University of Paris Est

Marie Fournier, University of Mulhouse

Sonia Exley, London School of Economics

René Torenvlied, University of Leiden

Anna Coleman, Kath Checkland and Stephen Harrison, University of Manchester

Turo Virtanen, University of Helsinki

Srinivasa Vittal Katikireddi, University of Glasgow

Katherine E. Smith, University of Edinburgh

Mairéad Considine and Fiona Dukelow, University College, Cork

Paul Burton, Griffith University

Dorte Sindbjerg Martinsen and Nikolay Vasev, University of Copenhagen

Preface

What is very evident to anyone who has participated in, or observed, policy processes is an absence of shape. While participants (just as much as academic observers) attempt to explain what they do in terms of notions about a desirable pattern regarding ideals of 'rational' or 'democratic' decision making, their activities do not conform well to any attempt to provide a textbook account. Within the literature on studying the policy process there are disagreements about the feasibility of generalisation from, at one extreme, a view that with more and better research a 'policy science' can be developed with hypotheses to test based on established theories to, at the other, a view that all that can be done is to tell carefully documented 'stories'. My own position lies somewhere between those extremes, but quite close to the latter end. This means that I regard the careful analysis of real world examples as of great importance for teaching. I have always aimed to make my teaching about the making of public policy as grounded as possible, both by illustrating concepts and theories from my own experience and by requiring students to analyse examples for themselves. Hence, as a textbook writer, whose main contribution on this subject is now in its sixth edition, I have long wanted to supplement what I have written with a book that examines specific examples of the policy process.

My first plan for such a book was to write it on my own, working through a number of cases. Such cases would need to be drawn from material available to me, and easily interpreted by me. That meant in practice they would almost certainly have to be based on processes occurring in the United Kingdom. I designed a book proposal along those lines, indicating that I would aim to compensate for the ethnocentric shortcomings of the examples with commentary that would adopt a wider, potentially comparative, perspective. My idea was well received by the Policy Press, but Alison Shaw persuaded me that it would be much better to produce an edited book in which contributions were provided from a wide range of countries, linked by my commentary.

Having agreed to this task my main worry was that my contacts across the world were too limited to provide a really wide-ranging book. While there were some people I knew I could depend on for good contributions, I knew I would have to research widely, and I sent requests to many people I had never met. I was apprehensive about an activity likely to be full of frustrations. I was wrong. Clearly I had underrated the importance of emails for modern academic activities. In fact, I have enjoyed sitting in my office emailing the 'world', and respondents have been wonderfully helpful. At the very least most people I contacted came back with negative but supportive responses. Many said 'yes'. Of course I do not need to acknowledge them in person since they are the contributors to this book, but many who felt unable to contribute themselves made helpful suggestions of others I might contact. I am particularly grateful, in this respect, to Daniel Béland, Tom Birkland, Anders Lidstrom, Peter May and Christopher Pollitt.

I was similarly apprehensive that once the process of putting the book together started, I would encounter difficulties in persuading contributors to deal with the issues in the way I wanted. In practice everyone was flexible, although some flexibility was also necessary on my side to mould the structure of the book to recognise that the shapelessness of the subject meant that I had to make changes to my original design. I also worried about deadlines, as I always do. When you recruit strangers to work on a project you have no idea of the others' pressures they may be experiencing. I want therefore to offer warm thanks to all the contributors for their timely responses to my various demands.

Alison Shaw in effect commissioned the book, and has supported its realisation, offering a sounding board at various stages. A very special thanks therefore to her. Thank you also to the rest of the team at Policy Press, Dave Worth, Jo Morton, Kathryn King and Ruth Harrison, and to the copy editor, Dawn Rushen.

Part One
Introduction

1.1
Introduction

The origins of this book lie in long experience of teaching and writing about the public policy process. While there is plenty of theoretical and conceptual material around, in order to bring this to life for students, illustrations must be used. The argument for this is not simply one about the understanding of abstract ideas, an accusation that students cannot cope without having these grounded in real world examples. It is that exploring the policy process is about using tools that help with understanding the real world. Moreover, these tools do not come in some coherent theoretical 'kit' that has to be mastered before applying it to the real world. Rather, the tools comprise a range of often-contestable propositions derived from empirical studies. In order to explain such propositions, it is necessary to work through the evidence used to develop them, and then to discuss their application outside the context in which they were developed in order to establish their wider relevance.

Policy process analysis sits, sometimes uncomfortably, between scholarship that offers a deductive approach enabling real world events to be explained by abstract theory (as is sometimes claimed by economists) and scholarship that insists that little more can be done than the presentation of an accurate account of those events (as is often claimed by historians). I accept the case for this uncomfortable position. I do not think that this is a temporary condition of an embryonic science, before a coherent theoretical edifice can be erected. Nor do I reject efforts to study the policy process systematically. My perspective is one that has been described as 'critical modernist', explained by Pollitt and Bouckaert as still holding to 'the importance of the empirical testing of theories and hypotheses, although accepting that this is only one kind of test, and that arguments concerning whether the appropriate conditions for falsification will be met will never cease' (2011, quote from the 2000 edition, p 23). They go on to emphasise that 'reality is socially constructed, but not all constructions have equal claim to our credulity', and that there is a need to 'discriminate between more – and less – adequate descriptions and explanations' (Pollitt and Bouckaert, 2011, quote from the 2000 edition, p 23).

No attempt is made here to justify that editorial perspective. Contributions to this book have come from a range of scholars from all over the world – and in choosing them no attempt was made to see if they agreed with that perspective. It is, however, one that, broadly speaking, allows many 'flowers to bloom'. In that sense the aim of this book is to demonstrate how many of the key contemporary ideas (that word is used deliberately instead of theories) may be applied to the analysis of the policy process. In the early planning for this book it was described as an attempt to assemble 'case studies'. That description was subsequently rejected, since it implies a methodological stance, and perhaps an effort to achieve greater coherence in the whole book than is in fact the aim. Rather, we have here a collection of empirical studies (featuring one or sometimes two nation states) that contribute through their detailed analysis to the advancement of the understanding of the policy process. These studies were chosen to illustrate issues about the analysis, using various methods, of the policy process. Some use material that is quite old, while others deal with what were, at the time of writing, contemporary events. All may be in some respects dated by the time the book is read, and should be valued for the light they throw on the process rather than as analyses *of* policy.

A teacher's reaction to the need for illustrations is likely to involve the provision of a combination of repetition of ones used in textbooks, brief descriptions of leading studies (many of which are likely to be rather old) and more or less top of the head references to current news items. Efforts may be made to go beyond the last kind of response by deeper reflections. In this respect it helps if the lecturer has substantive expertise on some current policy issues, although the problem may then be that students get a lot of attention given to the policy process in a limited range of policy fields. In any case, these processes of illustrating an argument are likely to be very constrained by the need to have a strong grasp of the institutional and cultural context within which the policy process is occurring. In short, the lecturer (and for that matter, the textbook writer) is unlikely to find it easy to go outside his or her own country for illustrations. This book therefore does that, through a collective enterprise in which scholars from a wide variety of countries have contributed accounts of policy processes they have studied.

It would be dishonest to try to hide the fact that my motivation in producing this book stems from my interest in building on my own textbook, *The public policy process* (6th edition, Pearson, 2013). That book grew steadily in size across successive volumes, and much of that growth occurred because of more extensive use of illustrative examples. There were, however, always difficulties in making good use of examples from outside the UK.

While the connection between this book and *The public policy process* is acknowledged, it is hoped that this book will be regarded as valuable supplementary reading to accompany other textbooks in this field. The key examples here are Howlett, Ramesh and Perl's *Studying public policy* (2009), Hudson and Lowe's *Understanding the policy process* (2009), John's *Analyzing public policy* (2012), Knoepfel, Larrue, Varone and Hill's *Public policy analysis* (2007) and Knill and Tosun's *Public policy: A new introduction* (2012).

There is then a subsidiary point, in respect of teaching, that can be made about the provision of a book like this: that students are often expected to carry out small studies of their own. My experience here ranges from undergraduate courses in which mini-projects have been required of students, through Master's courses where quite substantial project work is required to preparatory training before students engage in research for doctoral theses. In all these cases students are likely to want to ask questions about what a project might look like. It is hoped that this book will help to answer these questions.

Hence this is a book of specific empirical studies, diverse in respect of both the countries to which they relate and to the policy issues they consider, linked together by a commentary that draws attention to the theories and concepts used in the study of the policy process and cross-references to other empirical studies available in books and articles.

Studying the policy process

The study of the public policy process is located where policy and politics intersect. The study of policy alone is about the examination of what governments do. Policies may be described and evaluated and alternatives explored. To look at why some policies are accepted and others rejected, or at why some succeed and others fail, consideration has to be given to politics (in the widest possible sense): the factors that affect policy adoption, elaboration and implementation. A great deal of discussion of policy involves concerns about what *should* be done. The injection of political realism shifts that discussion rather towards what *could* be done.

However, to put the issues in that way makes the study of the policy process sound very much an applied discipline. It certainly has its roots in concerns to give realistic advice to policy activists. Taking a step back from that it is possible to construct a view of the study of the policy process that is concerned with more than just what works in a practical sense. That is the wish for a wider understanding of how the system works. This may or may not lead to practical conclusions to help policy makers. It may lead to deep cynicism or pessimism about policy change. Or indeed it may contribute to a view that only a revolution can effect desired changes.

It is tempting, in looking at the relationship between any attempt to develop an overall understanding of the policy process and the practical concerns about making policy, to use the analogy of the relationship between physics and engineering. The problem is, however, that it is unlikely that policy studies will evolve much towards a systematic body of theory comparable to that of physics. Schlager has defined the state of the discipline as having 'mountain islands of theoretical structure ... occasionally attached together by foothills of shared methods and concepts, and empirical work ... surrounded by oceans of descriptive work' (Schlager, 1997, p 14). The implication is that it can do better, but how much better?

The alternative, as already suggested, is to see the discipline as closer to history. There is a substantial literature from historians trying to answer the question, 'what is the use of history?' (see Evans, 1997). Historians have more or less abandoned heroic efforts to generalise about the future from the past (as in the work of Karl Marx or Arnold Toynbee, for example). Those who therefore come closest to the concerns of this book offer tentative answers in terms of the need to learn from experience. The interesting issue here is the confidence with which historians defend their discipline in terms of the advancement of knowledge in its own right.

It is not appropriate here to go further into these issues about the nature of academic disciplines. The point is that we may defend the study of the policy process both in terms of practical contributions to policy making and in terms of the intellectual case for trying to make sense of questions about the way it is made. There is, moreover, a case to be made for it as a discipline that contributes shared concepts which help with the understanding of the policy process despite the fact that generalisation is difficult.

At the core of the latter arguments are issues about the transferability of knowledge derived in one context to another. These are, in a broad sense, comparative questions: about transferability between contexts (particularly different policy areas), transferability in time and transferability between nations. The premise on which this book is based is that all these forms of transferability are possible. It is of course not alone in this respect – all the textbooks quoted above make such an assumption, and most, if not all, of the theorists whose work is used in this book. But in this respect the comments already made about the limitations of the discipline suggest a need for caution.

It must be said that this book does not in any formal sense claim to be comparative. The editorial introductions to each part aim to point out connections between the contributions and between them and other published work, but this must not be seen as more than making appropriate connections. The systematic comparative study of public policy is very much in its infancy. The main areas of achievement tend to involve quantitative comparisons of nations with particular policy outputs as dependent variables and very broad political and institutional differences as independent variables. They tend to be organised around typologies: perhaps the three most widely used examples of these are Lijphart's 'patterns of democracy' (1999), Hall and Soskice's 'varieties of capitalism' (2001) and Esping-Andersen's 'regime theory' (1990). What can be seen in these is largely comparison between nation states, with comparisons between policy areas rare. There is a strong case for further developments, but these face considerable methodological and practical difficulties.

In selecting contributions to this book no attention was paid to comparative theory. Nor was there any attempt to select policy areas to be covered in terms of types of policy. I have argued elsewhere (Hill, 2013, Chapters 7 and 8) that while the characteristics of a policy analysis activity will obviously be affected by the type of policy involved, there are no satisfactory policy typologies. Rather than following the lead of the best known attempt to develop a typology, that of Lowi (1972), there is a need to recognise differences in the interest conflicts around policy issue and variations in policy complexity. This is perhaps best captured in Matland's (1995) analysis of the importance of these two dimensions for policy implementation (discussed in the Introduction to Part Five). What has been done in selecting contributions has simply been a pragmatic approach, ensuring that a range of different policy areas are featured alongside differences in theoretical focus and countries covered. Undoubtedly the result is evidence on the relevance of Matland's dimensions, particularly policy complexity.

One way to try to secure shared theoretical development is to attempt to develop what are sometimes called middle-range theories. This implies a need to segment the policy process into identifiable parts. Hypotheses may be developed and tested that apply only to those parts. Perhaps the most evident development in this respect concerns implementation studies. It has become accepted, however, that there are difficulties about separating implementation from other parts of the policy process (a point discussed further in the Introduction to Part Five). The notion of separating parts of the policy process is embodied in what has been called 'the stages model' of the policy process (sometime also referred to as 'the policy cycle'). While it may be argued that in teaching about or researching the policy process there is a need to divide up the topic, the problem is that, as John puts it:

> Policy is by definition complex and changeable, and political actors who recognize its nature are likely to be more successful than those who uphold rational procedures. The linear model is more relevant for elucidating the presentation of policy than in detecting the reality of bargaining. (1998, p 27)

John's references to 'rational procedures' and the 'linear model' refer to the simplistic notion of a completed decision followed by action, and implicitly to a model of democratic politics in which there is a simple follow through from an originating decision by elected representatives. The 'reality' he refers to is the frequency of more complex interactions through the history of the development of this policy. This adds to the difficulty of working with simple testable generalisations about the policy process.

Departures from a staged model of the policy process are well illustrated in many of the contributions to this book. In determining the contents of the book a balance had to be struck between the need for what may be called a 'textbook' structure, with discussions of separate issues about the study of the policy process, in which acceptance of the idea of 'stages' presented the simplest option, and the fact that the presentation of real cases would be likely to need to range widely across any divisions chosen. What was chosen was a mixture of topics headings related to the stages model and others emphasising aspects of complexity. The end result is, however, that in some cases contributions fit quite well within their designated part while others do not. There are discussions introducing the parts, and brief introductions to each contribution, to help the reader identify these issues.

Structure of the book

The topic for Part Two cuts across the stages model, focusing on 'policy stability and policy change'. A great deal of recent policy process analysis has involved the use of institutional theory to deal with the related issues about the factors that contribute to policy stability and the circumstances under which that stability is disturbed.

This is followed by three parts in which a stages approach has been used to separate 'agenda setting', 'policy formulation' and 'implementation'. Here readers will find evidence of the point made above, that this separation is often unclear in practice.

Within the policy studies literature there is a substantial body of work on agenda setting. Inasmuch as this looks to the factors that start off a policy process, particularly the way that 'problems' become the subjects of political attention, this is perhaps the stage most easily subjected to policy process analysis.

In contrast to agenda setting, policy formulation, that is, the processes of settling the details of policy, has been relatively neglected in the literature. This is obviously partly a consequence of the difficulties in determining where this middle stage between agenda setting and implementation begins and ends. A typical problem is posed by theory about 'instrument choice', on the one hand dealing with how policy goals are established and on the other with the way policy is to be implemented. Fully formulating any complex policy involves the setting of an elaborate rule framework. Such activities are likely to involve a combination of political and pressure group participation with administrative action by civil servants. While the substantive policy issues influence how this formulation process occurs, so do national institutional and cultural factors.

The problem then about giving separate attention to the topic of Part Five, 'implementation', is the way in which interactive processes – between detailed rule making and the putting of those rules into practice – are particularly salient. In the past much was made of the distinction between a top-down approach to the examination of implementation and a bottom-up one. This distinction concerned not just issues about how the implementation process should be perceived or studied, but also assumptions about who should be in control of policy delivery. While this debate is now rather dated, resolutions having been achieved between the extreme positions, there is still a tendency for the extensive literature on implementation to be divided between those who find it feasible to separate this stage from those that went before and those who, as noted above, highlight the interactions between this and earlier stages. The latter emphasis is particularly evident in the contributions in Part Five.

The final part, 'governance and globalism', further develops the concern to stress complexity. The starting point here is the literature on the shift from 'government' to 'governance' which highlights several phenomena: institutional complexity within nation states, complexity arising from nation state participation in supranational governments and (cutting across both of those issues) complexity arising from the increasing participation of non-governmental actors as decision makers rather than simply sources of pressure on governments.

The book does not end with a concluding part. The issues addressed by the contributions are highlighted both in introductions to each part and in introductions to the individual contributions, with the latter emphasised by the use of a separate typeface. It would be unnecessarily repetitive to revisit them again. No special concluding messages are appropriate for a book designed simply to extend understanding of the complex world in which policy is made.

Part Two
Stability and change

2.1
Introduction

There is a considerable literature on the extent to which policies remain stable over time and on the factors that contribute to change. In many respects this is a reflection at the policy level of a wider literature on stability in political systems and indeed in societies. While it is possible to identify theoretical contributions that focus on stability and others that focus on change, these are essentially about the same thing with simply a difference in terms of the extent of emphasis on one or other end of a continuum. A theory stressing stability has to deal with exceptions where this does not apply and vice versa. In fact it may be asserted that the extremes in this continuum rarely exist. The analysis below offers evidence on why complete stability is rare. Total instability in societies, on the other hand, may be identified, but as far as public policy is concerned, this is likely to involve an ambience in which the establishment of secure policies is very difficult. It is in the latter context that people have written of 'stateless societies' and the 'ungovernability' of societies. Hence in most cases in which we explore stability and change we are looking at cases that sit somewhere around the middle of the continuum between them.

If almost all policy systems involve some degree of change there is no easy way of making distinctions between high and low levels of change. Dunleavy, in a discussion of British policy disasters, wrote of Britain as 'the fastest law in the West' (1995, p 60), suggesting that only New Zealand was comparable in this respect. An important part of his argument draws on institutional theory, the extent to which there are institutions that facilitate or constrain policy change. Some wider considerations along this line are provided by the comparative institutional analysis in the work of Lijphart (1999) and others in which the checks on change provided by electoral systems that typically deliver coalition government, corporatist consultative mechanisms and the division of power implicit in federalism are seen as sources of policy stability. However, it is not easy to apply this rather high-level comparative work – about policy systems – to actual policy processes.

It may be that the most important point is not so much that different rates of change may be observed but that changes in the rate of change are significant. This is crucial for one of the key approaches to this issue, Baumgartner and Jones' (1993) notion of 'punctuated equilibrium' to capture 'the tendency of political systems to drift incrementally most of the time, only to be roused to major action when collective attention became galvanised around an issue' (Baumgartner et al, 2006, p 962). Note 'systems drifting incrementally', not simply stable. Punctuated equilibrium implies acceleration of change, implicitly then followed by deceleration. But there is also something more complicated here: that incremental drift implies some notion of consistent direction while the punctuation of that implies not merely the speeding up of change but also a change of direction.

This is a notion that is particularly salient in another approach to the analysis of change, the notion of 'paradigm shift', where ideological change is involved. Hence in the work in which Hall (1986, 1993) pioneered the use of this concept, the ideological shift involved the rejection of Keynesian approaches to economic policy in favour of monetarist ones.

However, change may at one and the same time be both fundamental and slow. In this respect Pollitt and Bouckaert introduce (2009, p 18, building on work by Streeck and Thelen, 2005) a geological analogy, distinguishing slow drip-like change, stalactite formation, from earthquakes. Or to complicate this even further it may be that there is a steady process of change that nevertheless follows predictable 'pathways' (Pierson, 2000). These pathways may involve both institutionalised policy delivery systems and the establishment of interests in stable policy outcomes (pensions policy provides particularly strong illustrations of this; see Bonoli and Shinkawa, 2005). These issues are explored in the contributions in this part, particularly that by Pei-Yuen Tsai (Chapter 2.4) on work–family balance policies in Taiwan.

Moving on now to explanations of stability and change, the divisions identified above in terms of which of these is the starting point for efforts to theorise, is apparent again. In respect of stability a variety of approaches to explanation can be found in forms of institutional theory. Knoepfel et al's (2007, p 93) categorisation of modern institutional theory as sociological ('cultural approach'), historical ('structuralist approach') and economic ('calculating approach') represents a useful way to summarise the strands in the literature. Of course these approaches get mixed together in specific writings. However, the sociological approach highlights what may be called institutionalisation: the tendency for social practices ('this is the way we do things') to solidify over time. In the writings of Max Weber, 'the routinisation of charisma' (Weber, 1947, pp 363-73) highlights this process in both politics and religion. The way in which this sort of approach embraces cultural practices within the notion of institutions has been called 'the big tent theory of institutions' (Frederickson and Smith, 2003, p 69) for its all-embracing approach. Historical institutionalism tends in practice to lay stress on the formal aspects of this process, from the writing of constitutions through to the making of laws and the setting up of the organisations of government. These generate continuities in the policy process, establishing the rules within which policy 'games' are played. Economic institutionalism stresses the extent to which these formal arrangements then entrench interests, advantaging some players in these games and disadvantaging others. Seen together these may be seen as forces for continuity and policy stability. When new issues arise on the agenda (a topic explored further in Part Three), policy-making activities do not normally occur 'on a desert island' where nothing is already in place.

Much contemporary theory about change starts from institutional theory, exploring – as already noted in respect of Baumgartner and Jones' work – ways in which the emphasised stability may be punctuated. It is important to note that before this modern emphasis on relative stability, there were influential theories of long-run historical change, within which policy change explanations were likely to be located. Theories of modernisation, generally located in the optimistic view of the growth of enlightenment, saw the growth of government activity (particularly the growth of the welfare state) in terms of progressive problem solving. Interestingly the main counter to this point of view, Marxist theory, broadly accepted the progressive view but saw that occurring by way of recurrent crises and consequent revolutions (for a modern exposition of this view, see Harvey, 2011). Ideas about, on the one hand, new problems to be solved and, on the other, crises to be resolved are still relevant, although not necessarily explored in the broad terms of these theories. It is important not to see the relationship between social problems and policy responses as a straightforward one (see Vlassopoulou's contribution to this part, Chapter 2.2).

Exploration of the 'punctuation' of stability is sometime categorised in terms of exogenous and endogenous factors (see Surel, 2000). There are influences on policy change that are clearly exogenous (the impact of 'focusing events' such as environmental disasters is explored in Part Three). But there are two problems about this distinction. One is that what is or is not exogenous is likely to depend on the focus of the policy analysis. For example, entry to the European Union (EU) can be seen as an exogenous event for a specific policy area within a nation state, but hardly so for a national policy system as a whole. The other point is that it is very often the interaction between the exogenous and the endogenous that is important. This can be seen particularly in Bovens and 't Hart's (1996) analysis of 'policy fiascos' where the incapacity of institutions to cope with specific occurrences exposes their inadequacy and then leads to policy change. It is explored further by Nohrstedt and Weible (2010) in an article that links crisis explanations of change to policy subsystem structures.

However, the more general point about the exogenous/endogenous distinction is that policies may be seen as responses to situations at one point in time which then prove to be in need of change as situations change (see Hwang, Chapter 2.3). While this seems to be an exogenous cause of change, what is then crucial is the reaction within the system (see Tsai, Chapter 2.4). Thus we see in usages of Sabatier's notion of 'advocacy coalitions' (Sabatier and Weible, 2007) exploration of the way in which coalition memberships change as situations change. The economics approach to this topic is interesting in this respect (see the discussion of this by Pierson, 2000). Some of the theory concerns the advantages accruing to early entrants to a market that sustains monopoly or oligopoly for a while but then decays over time. Applied to the policy process the argument about decay runs rather differently, either seeing the problem-solving capacity of established institutions as decaying over time or their activities as generating the emergence of new political interest groups.

Another approach to the explanation of change involves a stress on the role of ideas. Béland (2005, drawing on the work of Blyth, 2002) suggests that ideas have an impact on political decisions in three ways:

- 'as "cognitive locks" that help reproduce existing institutions and policies over time' (as in Hall's policy paradigms perspective);
- 'as policy blueprints that provide political actors with a model for reform';
- 'as powerful ideological weapons' that allow actors to challenge existing policies (2005, p 125).

There is an important challenge to positivist approaches to the study of the policy process here, as there is in theories that see events depending on accidental conjunctions (the 'garbage can' model of the policy process; see Cohen et al, 1972). It is very hard to model how such influences on policy will occur, or to make predictive statements based on them. However, particularly when viewed retrospectively, the rise and fall of dominant ideas does seem to offer an important way of accounting for change in otherwise comparatively stable policy systems.

To conclude, issues about the relative importance of stability and change are explored in a variety of ways in the policy process literature. There is a need to recognise that there is a continuum between stability and change, and that policy systems vary in respect of where they may be placed along this. What are likely to be the subjects of attention are changes in the rate of change, particularly when they are dramatic or involve changes in the direction of policy? Institutional theory provides reasons for expecting high levels of stability in well-established policy systems, with change as slow incremental drift. What is then likely to be significant is the emergence of contradictions as the relationships change between policies on the one hand, and social demands and needs on the other.

2.2

We start in this part with Chloe Vlassopoulos' exploration of what may be meant by policy change and its connections to problem change. Policy analyses have repeatedly shown that the policy process is far from constituting an ordered phenomenon, as presumed by the sequential approach specified in the 1970s (Jones, 1970). The study of policy change shows the same complexity, making it difficult to model. Various explanatory models have been proposed but their comparability remains rather low. Authors do not always engage at the same level of analysis, and the way in which the notion of 'policy change' should be conceived is rarely discussed. Indeed, the unit of analysis varies from one case to another without an explanation of the preferred choice. This subject must be considered seriously because, depending on that choice, the way of perceiving the process of change differs strongly. Further, studies of change often give little attention to the definition of the term 'policy change'. However, specifying its components (that is, the elements that one must observe to confirm or not the presence of policy change) appears a necessary preliminary stage before trying to qualify the process of change.

Hence the first part of this contribution seeks to identify the various units of analysis usually employed for the study of policy change, and argues for the relevance of the choice of 'public problems' as the most pertinent unit of analysis. The second part proposes a specific definition of the notion of policy change that serves as a basis for the development of an analytical framework respectful of the complexity of the phenomenon. This framework is based on post-positivist approaches to public action (Edelman, 1991; Rochefort and Cobb, 1994; Stone, 2012), and puts the process of problem definition at the heart of the analysis. The last part presents the main results of the application of this framework to a comparative and historical analysis of clean air policy in France and Greece (Vlassopoulos, 1999, 2000, 2003).

This study makes it possible to note that the components of policy change do not evolve at the same tempo, or with the same intensity. This phenomenon can be described as 'double-speed policy change'. This perspective results from the analysis of a specific empirical setting, and to this end cannot claim generalisation before it is tested in other cases. Nevertheless, the comparative and historical dimensions of the analysis and the choice of two countries differing considerably in their social, political and economic structure strengthen the validity of the results.

How policies change: clean air policy in France and Greece

Chloe A. Vlassopoulos

Looking for policy change: methodological considerations

A survey of the literature shows that there is no consensus on the level to choose in order to theorise the process of change. The most commonly selected unit is 'public policy'. The choice of public policy as the unit of analysis presents, however, certain disadvantages that are discussed here first. Second, it is proposed that if one moves the attention from public policies to 'public problems', this can moderate these disadvantages and create new perspectives for the study of policy change. Last, it is important to define what policy change might mean in order to propose a framework for the analysis of clean air policy change.

Limits of the 'policy' choice

Public policies constitute the most often used unit of analysis for research, but there has never been consensus on the definition of 'policy'. It is used to describe various forms of public action that are not without effects on the observation of policy change. Moreover, public policies are temporarily and spatially situated. The limited lifetime of a policy does not allow a longitudinal analysis and prevents the discovery of policy inheritance. Further, since public problems are multisectoral, the examination of any single policy provides only a limited account of the story. In the study of policy change what is interesting, however, is to study how various policies merge or separate themselves over time in response to a given problem.

It is possible to present policies like Russian dolls enclosed within one another. Let's take the example of the environment that is often used as a case study for 'policy changes'. What is called 'environmental policy' represents a *sectoral policy* made up of a series of *issue policies* such as clean air policy, water quality policy, waste management policy, and so on. An issue policy can also be divided into more restricted *sub-issue policies*, such as motor vehicle pollution policy or industrial pollution policy. Further, the policy to promote clean motor vehicle technology is a component (or measure) of motor vehicle pollution policy. In short, the term 'public policy' concerns very different levels of public interventions.

In his presentation of the advocacy coalition model, Sabatier (1988, p 138) explores an issue policy (clean air) but uses subsectoral and sectoral examples without distinction. Sabatier and Brasher's (1993) article covers the impact of the new environmental policy on a series of issue policies in the basin of Lake

Tahoma. What the authors call a 'policy subsystem' comprises a large number of actors coming from all the issue policies under examination (water, air, town planning) to form a new environmental policy coalition. Jenkins-Smith (1988) analyses a series of very restricted measures related to US energy policy such as the size of the petroleum reserve, the price of natural gas or the organisation of the refinery market. For him the term 'policy subsystem' refers to a rather narrow configuration of actors that is relatively homogeneous because it is composed of energy experts in each one of these issues. Hall (1993) studies a paradigmatic change within a policy sector, that of British economic policy, and its impact on issue policies that compose the sector (inflation policy, unemployment policy, monetary policy, fiscal policy, and so on).

The choice of a sectoral or subsectoral unit of analysis is not without importance for the study of policy change because it has implications for the way in which this change is perceived. The sectoral level is a much more crowded space than the subsectoral. For example, the environmental sector includes all the actors concerned with soil pollution, sea, air problems, and so on. This overload of actors with different perceptions and interests make changes and policy learning more rare than changes exclusively concerning a policy issue or sub-issue. These changes, when they occur, cover the theoretical foundation of public action (their intensity is discussed below). Thus Hall describes the passage from Keynesianism to the monetarism of British economic policy as a paradigmatic change. Muller and Jobert (1987) speak about the change of *référenciel global* within the French agricultural sector of the 1980s. Sabatier and Brasher refer to major changes of the belief system (deep core) to describe the impact of the environmental sector on a series of pre-existing public policies. However, these large-scale sectoral changes cover only one dimension of the process of change and risk under-estimating the importance of subsectoral changes. Issue policy changes are more diversified. These policies can undergo the effects of the paradigmatic change that affects the sector to which they belong (as in the case examined by Hall). They can also undergo internal modifications that are often of lower importance, that Sabatier describes as 'near core' or 'secondary aspects', and Hall as change of first and second order. These changes mostly concern the adjustments of current programmes. Lastly, issue policies can undergo more important changes affecting not only policy instruments but also the perceptions and beliefs of policy actors. In that case, as the example of clean air policy shows, new programmes can emerge without any large-scale sectoral change.

The study of a sectoral policy with simultaneous analysis of a series of representative issue policies can give a rich image of the process of change, but the choice of public policies as a unit of analysis is likely to prove temporally and spatially restrictive. First, the temporality of public policies does not coincide with that of the problem that they deal with. To take up again the example of clean air, an ad hoc policy on the matter began in France with the 1961 law and in Greece with the programme of 1982. This does not mean, however, that before these dates the problem was not known – it was dealt with within other policies. To fix attention on a public policy runs the risk of ignoring the period preceding its emergence, which is highly important for the comprehension of its inheritance. Further, the appearance of a new policy does not inevitably eliminate the other policies that coped with the problem up to that point. The actors in place fight in order not to lose the budgets they control and the influence they exert over the matter. For example, after the appearance of an ad hoc clean air policy, industrial policy continued managing part of the problem.

The choice of public policy as a unit of analysis therefore leaves certain dimensions of the process of change in the shade. The shift of attention from policies to public problems seems to deal better with the complexity of the phenomenon.

The 'public problem' choice: a post-positivist approach

Public problems (or policy problems) can be defined as social problems dealt with by the public authorities. This first definition requires better specification because the concept of a 'public problem' has as many meanings as the concept of public policy and can cover different realities. To take up again the previous example, environmental degradation is a public problem as well as air pollution, motor vehicle pollution or pollution by lead emissions. All these problems take the form of the same Russian doll evoked above: air pollution is an environmental problem, motor vehicle pollution a component of air pollution and lead emissions a component of motor vehicle pollution. Is there a most pertinent level for the study of policy change?

The post–positivist approach can help to answer this question. Post–positivist sociology, and in particular the influential work of Spector and Kitsuse (1987), covers primarily the construction of social problems. When these studies refer to the public authorities, they are perceived as an additional actor in the current definitional process. However, when a social problem is transformed into a public problem, its definition follows a specific process which has to be connected to the fact that the entry of a problem within the public sphere places the official authorities in the position of orchestrator of this process: social actors can negotiate only via the official authorities. What is the impact of this situation on the definitional process?

In the case of a social problem, negotiations between actors primarily cover the causes of the problem and marginally its consequences. The importance attached to the causes is obvious since these distribute the cost of the resolution of the problem (who will pay and who will benefit) between the different actors. The reference to the consequences of the problem has only a symbolic impact: justifying to the other participants the perception that certain actors have of a given situation. Whatever the justifications are, it is up to the actors concerned to solve the problem while agreeing on its causes and therefore, on the solutions to apply. On the contrary, in the case of public problems, the evocation of the consequences has a symbolic and a concrete impact. This difference is related to the fact that those who are concerned with the problem do not coincide with those who are responsible for solving it, namely, a public authority.

Each reference to the consequences of the problem constitutes, in the case of public problems, not only a justification legitimising to differing degrees the intervention of political leaders ('we act to protect the citizens' health', 'we act to guarantee safety', and so on), but also a means of the distribution of authority within the state. In this sense, Edelman (1991, p 50) writes that the construction of a problem invites the recognition of authority to those who claim various types of competence. In that sense, air pollution can be defined as an industrial problem or as a motor vehicle problem. This determines the causes of the problem. It can also be defined as a public health risk or as an environmental problem. This determines the consequences produced by the presence of the problem. As will be seen below, the distribution of authority between administrations changes according to whether the definition covers health protection or environmental protection.

It is then possible to claim that the definition of a public problem is carried out through a double-definitional process: the first determines the causes of the problem and answers the question 'what is the problem?'; the second determines the consequences of the problem and answers the question 'why does this situation constitute a problem?'.

To reveal this double process a specific separation of public action must be performed. One could choose to study environmental degradation, but the environment does not generate a definitional debate on its consequences. Environmental protection is a 'self-justified' question in that it constitutes an accepted social value (to say that one must protect the environment does not require any additional justification). In order to be able to identify the double definition of a public problem, a 'hetero-justified' problem must be chosen, namely, a problem that necessitates a broader justification to be admitted as indisputable. This is the case of air pollution which has to be justified with reference to environmental quality, public health, quality of life, and so on. Simultaneously the selected problem must be sufficiently broad to be able to generate a debate on its causes. For example, Gusfield's (1984) study of drinking and driving constitutes a mono-causal problem linked to alcoholism. The quality of the roadways, the driver's age, young drivers' training, and so on, can also cause accidents but are not discussed. To obtain a multicausal problem one must therefore climb up a level and choose the problem of road accidents.

According to what precedes, various arguments can be put forward to support the relevance of the choice of the public problem as a unit of analysis in the study of change:

• In order to reconstruct the process of problem definition and redefinition, this choice invites us to adopt a longitudinal viewpoint. During this process the problem can pass through different sectors and be the subject of various public policies. Thus the analyst must go beyond the narrow borders of a sector and/or of a public policy to study their inheritance and thus better appreciate the weight of the past and the innovative elements introduced in each definitional stage. This also makes it possible to identify within the same study the different dimensions of policy change: the impact produced when the problem penetrates a new sector, the effects of the emergence of a new programme or the adding of new measures into current programmes.

- As an issue of power, problem definition divides the actors into winners and losers and legitimates certain courses of action to the detriment of others. Thus, the reconstitution of the definitional process has to go together with the identification of the 'problem subsystem' (preferred to the term 'policy subsystem' because it refers to all actors mobilised about a public problem and participating more or less actively to successive formulations of policies in order to cope with the problem) and of the programmes of action. The analytical framework proposed below is based on the interaction between these three variables and their evolution throughout the definitional process.

- The distinction between the definition of the consequences and the definition of the causes of the problem makes it possible to specify better the relationship between changes of ideas, changes of actors and changes of policy content programmes/measures, and thereby to evaluate better the tempo and intensity of the process of change.

Variables and dimensions of policy change

As Bosso suggests (1994, p 201), the effort to understand better the process of problem definition helps to answer in a more relevant way the 'why' and 'how' of policy change. More than just a question of 'why public policies change?' it is a question about 'how this change is carried out?' that is privileged here. Because public policies always generate winners and losers, change is always possible. The dissatisfied are in search of favourable conditions enabling them to improve their position by modifying the dominant definition of the problem and the policy action.

Policy change is an eminently complex phenomenon and its study requires not only the specification of its components (the elements that must be analysed to affirm the presence, or not, of change) but also the consideration of its tempo (the rapidity with which the change occurs) and its importance (the modifications produced in relation to the previous state balance).

In a more or less explicit way, policy change is recognised when a new programme emerges. Sabatier (1988, p 1) explicitly refers to change as a change in governmental programmes. He relates this change to modifications of the belief system within a 'policy subsystem'. Rose and Davies (1994) evaluate the rhythm of policy change in terms of the number of new programmes voted in the space of a century in the UK. Hall (1993, p 279) identifies three orders of change covering various components of current programmes (the organisation of the instruments, the instruments themselves and the hierarchy of goals behind policy).

Baumgartner and Jones (1993, pp 132-3) remain less precise in their definition, and evoke alternatively change in 'policy outcomes', 'policy enactments', 'policy action' or 'programme creation'. The two independent variables mainly underlined as being at the origin of policy change are actors (policy venue) and ideas (policy image). According to changes in ideas and actors, policy change can be more or less important. Simultaneous changes in ideas and actors should generate rapid and paradigmatic policy change.

There are two criticisms of this correlation between actors, ideas and programmes. First, the analysis seldom goes beyond the obviousness of the appearance of a new actor, a new idea and/or a new programme. This is more often the case when the analysis is longitudinal and multisectoral. The scale of the data pushes toward the choice of quantitative rather than qualitative analysis. For example, the very interesting analyses of Baumgartner and Jones and of Rose and Davies do not seek to appreciate the concrete impact of the change on the studied reality. The analysis of air pollution in France and Greece set out below makes it possible to note that the appearance of a new actor and new programme can be less innovative than it appears at first sight. Consequently the study of policy change does not have to be limited to the identification of innovative elements. It has to seek to evaluate the importance of change: to what extent does the emergence of a new actor disturb the previous balances, and to what extent does the content of a new policy programme modify the pre-established method of problem regulation? In this case a quantitative approach is important as an entry to identify the periods of upheaval and the emergence of new actors, new ideas and new programmes likely to challenge the status quo. But in order to study the extent of change, the simultaneous use of qualitative longitudinal analysis, especially discourse and content analysis, is equally necessary.

Second, as Dudley and Richardson remark (1998, p 731), 'a paradigmatic shift in terms of ideas and values may not be immediately expressed in terms of policy outcomes.' Indeed, the case of air pollution contests the correlation between change in actors and ideas and change in the policy content. As will be shown, the appearance of new actors and/or of new perceptions of the problem may not generate changes in the content of policy. However, all these partial changes must be considered seriously because they can introduce important modifications. The change of discourse and problem definition can, for example, influence the balance of power between policy actors and transform the nature of the subsystem. This was the case in France at the beginning of the 1970s: the subsystem became less pluralist and more homogeneous and made it possible to limit the visibility of the problem and to prevent the emergence of new measures.

From what precedes, it is relevant to consider policy change as *the result of changes in all or some of three interactive variables: ideas (problem definition), actors (public and private) and policy content (measures).* Further there is no reason to consider *a priori* that these variables evolve inevitably at the same tempo and with the same intensity. Last, the distinction between the definition of consequences and the definition of causes can serve as a means to specify better the relationship between the changes of the above three variables and therefore to better evaluate the tempo and intensity of policy change.

Since the determination of the causes influences the actors that have to assume the cost of problem resolution, the study of the causal definition should allow the identification of the private actors mobilised around the problem. The definition of the consequences should make it possible to identify the institutional actors and the way authority is distributed between policy sectors. It should therefore be possible to connect changes of the causal definition with changes in the balance of power between private actors and changes in the definition of the consequences with institutional restructurings. The following analysis shows that the definition of air pollution as a motor vehicle problem actively mobilised car manufacturers within the problem subsystem. At the same time, the industrial lobby became less visible and positioned at the margin of the subsystem. The definition of air pollution as an environmental problem transferred, in both France and Greece, the attribution of the political and administrative responsibility for policy making to the environmental sector. The changes in the perception of the consequences and/or causes of the problem should, in addition, modify current programmes in order to adapt them to the new definition. Like any attempt to model reality, this analytical framework schematises the complexity of the process of change. Air pollution shows, for example, that the public and private actors do not act independently of one another: the interpenetration between the public and private spheres and the close relations established between public agencies and organised interest groups means that the mobilisation of a private actor often involves the implication of the corresponding administration, and vice versa (Chevallier, 1994, p 373).

The longitudinal study of the double-definitional process signifies reconstituting the genealogy of the policy problem, that is, the stages through which it passed until arriving at its current definition. Moreover, it is important to juxtapose the phases of redefinition of the causes and consequences with the chronological listing of the programme set up. The study of air pollution does not always show a coincidence between the two processes: there can be definitional change without the appearance of a new programme. Lastly, around each period of redefinition and emergence of new programmes it is important to locate and identify the actors present and the balance of power between them. After this preliminary work the tempo and intensity of change can be appreciated. Therefore discourse analysis is an important source of information. Do all the actors accept the dominant definition of the problem? Do some actors take a less active part in the debates? Do they remain vague in the way that they evoke the problem? Content analysis of the current programme constitutes a second major source of information. Do programmes comprise clear objectives? Do they define precise and feasible means different from those employed up until now? What is the margin of action they give to policy actors?

Two-speed policy change in clean air policy in France and Greece

The double-definitional process of air pollution since the beginning of industrialisation covers the period from the beginning of the 19th century in France and the beginning of 20th century in Greece. As it is impossible to present in detail this long definitional story, certain major changes that demonstrate the specificity of each case are selected here. Despite the social, political and economic differences between the two countries, the comparison reveals certain regularities in their policy change process.

Redefining consequences and institutions

For almost two centuries air pollution in France has known only one redefinition in terms of the consequences that it generates. The discourse that developed around the Napoleonic Law of 1810 to justify the intervention of the state in the domain of air quality perceived air pollution as a public health risk. This definition had a direct impact on the institutional organisation of clean air action. The principal 'expert' heard on this matter was the hygienist corps present within the public service and in Parliament. Hygiene science emerged in the 18th century and is based on a neo-Hippocratic perception of human health: environmental conditions are considered to have a major influence on human health. A healthy society is one that lives in a clean environment. The hygienists' approach consists of studying the environment (air, soil, water) in order to combat its deterioration that is at the origin of sickness. This broad environmental vision of health problems was initially dominated by what is called the 'aerist' approach: the air was considered to have a direct influence on the body and health because it was carrying miasmas seen as the main cause of the transmission of diseases. Until the mid-19th century the indicator used to measure the quality of the air was odour. Disseminated through the air, odours were considered as the main pathogenic factor to combat. Progressively, smog and other substances were taken into consideration. The 'aerist' approach led hygienists to base their expertise on a thorough analysis of the composition of the atmosphere. The city, as the most important space of interaction between individuals and the environment, became the privileged laboratory for studying and acting on public health. Throughout the 19th century hygienists gradually affirmed their position within the new problem subsystem.

During the same period the new *grand corps d'état* of the mining engineers was created and charged with promoting industrialisation. The mining engineers also looked at controlling the problem and imposing their technocratic vision of pollution over the health vision. As their main concern was to support manufacturing initiatives, they combated the hygienist perception that pointed at the harmfulness of industrial emissions. This confrontation between engineers and hygienists within the state led to a specific division of authority, reflecting the balance between contradictory visions and interests. This compromise was given concrete expression by the 1961 law on air pollution and odours. Air pollution was defined as a public health problem and the Ministry of Health was named the official authority responsible for the coordination of clean air policy. However, the law did not give the Ministry any possibility for autonomous action: measures to combat industrial pollution were elaborated and applied by the mining engineers within the Ministry of Industry, and measures concerning motor vehicle emissions remained the responsibility of the Ministry of Transport in direct collaboration with car manufacturers. The new law tried to assemble in only one text the various components of the problem, managed until then within various public policies. But the administrations competent in this field, with the support of the polluters' lobbies, succeeded in maintaining their competencies, confining the Ministry of Health to the role of a simple supervisor.

The environmental era in the 1970s marked an important change in the previous equilibrium: air pollution was no longer discussed as a health risk but defined as an environmental problem. This definitional change can be described as rapid to the extent that the discussions on environmental degradation started officially in France in 1969, and two years later the first programme for the protection of the environment emerged. Since then, air pollution has been transferred into the new policy sector. This change can be also described as radical because the nature of the problem changed as it started to be discussed in new terms. At first sight it could be said that this redefinition produced important modifications to the problem's subsystem. First of all, the new Ministry of the Environment emerged in 1971. In 1973, by simple decree and without any public debate, the Ministry of Health was deprived of its competences that were then transferred to the new Ministry. But was this change as radical as it initially appears?

The French Ministry of the Environment was made up by the transfer of civil servants and of competences from pre-existing administrations. In the case of air pollution, the issue was taken over within the new Ministry by the mining engineers transferred from the Ministry of Industry. In a sense, the environmental era served as a window of opportunity for the mining engineers to impose themselves as the most competent body to deal with the problem. With this reorganisation they also took charge of motor vehicle pollution, although they did not contest the authority of the Ministry of Transport and of car manufacturers that continued to decide on the policy to be followed on the matter. In other words, after the 1970s, the polluters and their administrations managed to exclude health authorities from the subsystem and to monopolise clean air policy (Vlassopoulos, 2007). In the light of the role that the hygienists and the mining engineers had played for one-and-a-half centuries previously, the changes that occurred in the 1970s appear minor insofar as they rather confirm the persistent incapacity of the health specialists to impose themselves within the problem subsystem, and the capacity of the polluters to control the domain. Thus the conditions of policy making and implementation remained fragmented and controlled by the actors hostile to clean air policy objectives. The preservation of the established balance of power explains why the redefinition of air pollution as an environmental problem did not give rise to a new governmental programme. The 1961 law stayed active for another 25 years after the creation of the Ministry of the Environment.

The case of Greece reveals certain similarities that confirm the capacity of actors to contain the process of change. For historical, political and economic reasons the first national public debate on cities' air quality emerged in Greece a century later (in 1911). Pollution was not defined as a public health problem but rather as an urban problem. From 1909, the E.Venizelos progressive party placed the country's modernisation at the centre of its political project (Mavrogordatos and Hatziiossif, 1992). To carry out this modernisation project the new political class represented by the Venizelian party was supported by a new technocratic elite trained in civil engineering at the new Polytechnic School of Athens. All modernisation policies drawn up by this elite of town civil planning engineers concerned the organisation and rationalisation of urban space. Whereas there was neither real industrialisation nor car traffic at the beginning of the 20th century, the debate on air pollution covered above all motor vehicle pollution that was better integrated into the urban dimension of the modernisation project. The absence of car manufacturers in Greece also facilitated the development of a rigorous political discourse against the new means of transport. Since the first parliamentary debate of 1911, motor vehicles were presented practically as an enemy of the society: 'the society must fight against these inconsiderate modes of transport', 'all we say on the risk generated by cars cannot reflect the true danger that these means of transport involve for the citizens [...] cars are like trains that run off the railway'. In a climate of panic the Greek Parliament didn't hesitate to denounce these 'dangerous machines', according to one deputy, as being the origin of four problems requiring the intervention of public authorities: accidents, noise, roadway erosion and pollution: 'the state of the roadway, dust, and odours constitute social damages caused by the cars'. This speech went even further by accusing this means of transportation as a factor of social discrimination and expensive for public finances: 'it refers to social class which rolls for its pleasure and by vanity and puts the life of all society in danger [...] social damage goes further if we consider that we export funds to buy these vehicles' ((Vlassopoulos, 2005, p 253, see also 1999)). From this moment and until the environmental era in the 1970s all legislative initiatives in the field of air pollution were taken by the technocratic elite within the Ministry of Public Works and the Ministry of Transport. Here air pollution was perceived not as a health problem but as a problem of quality of life in the cities. Further, the creation in 1923 of the Technical Chamber of Greece, which played the double role of representative of the engineers' interests and of official adviser to the government on development policies, gave scientific validation to this perception and support to the ministerial initiatives.

As was the case in France, at the beginning of the environmental era, air pollution was redefined as an environmental problem. After the end of the dictatorship in 1975 a new Ministry of the Environment took charge of the problem. Even more so than in France, the appearance of this Ministry did not mark any rupture in relation to the past. The new Ministry of the Environment consisted of a reinforced

Ministry of Public Works promoted to a Ministry of the Environment, of Town Planning and of Public Works. As in the French case, this definitional change did not give birth to new clean air measures.

The above analysis shows that in both countries, the redefinition of the consequences of the problem marked some changes, but their tempo and intensity varied according to the variables under consideration (see Table 2.2.1).

Table 2.2.1: Redefinition of the consequences and policy change

Variable / Type	Tempo		Intensity	
	France	Greece	France	Greece
Ideas	Rapid	Rapid	Radical	Radical
Actors	Rapid	Rapid	Weak	Weak
Programme	None	None	None	None

Only the way of representing the problem changed radically and rapidly. Immediately after the beginning of the environmental era in the 1970s it started being discussed in new terms and presented as a 'new' problem: from a health or quality of life problem it became an environmental problem. A new institutional actor quickly appeared (the Ministry of the Environment in 1971 in France and in 1975 in Greece) during this period, and authority was redistributed within the state. But the analysis of this change using an historical approach makes it possible to appreciate the weight of policy inheritance: the actors already involved in the administration of the problem had sufficient legitimacy and authority to allow them to contain the change. Thus, the appearance of the Ministry of the Environment did not trouble the established equilibrium. Further, this definitional change did not modify the measures set up to deal with the problem.

Redefining causes and polluters

In France air pollution was initially defined as a problem that was due to industrialisation. Some rare debates mentioned other sources of pollution such as cars or central heating, but they received little publicity. Until the 1990s (with an exception at the beginning of the 1980s marked by the European debate on acid rain) all public debates put the emphasis on industry. This remark confirms Stone and Edelman's analysis when they note that in the public sphere problems are always defined in a simplified way. The first causal redefinition took place in 1996 with the enactment of the law on air pollution and the rational use of energy. Since then air pollution has been redefined as a motor vehicle problem.

The powerful lobby of car manufacturers, with the intimate collaboration of the Ministry of Transport, succeeded for nearly a century in keeping the question of motor vehicle pollution off the political agenda. A public policy monopoly was thus created around motor vehicle policy that maintained this source of pollution at the periphery of the clean air subsystem in order to preserve the agenda denial. Three factors (conjunctural, political and strategic) met to make it possible to break this balance. First, a confidential study on the harmfulness of motor emissions was published in the daily press. Second, the Minister for the Environment was seeking an issue to mark her political career. Third, the mining engineers of the Ministry of the Environment supported their Minister's initiative because they perceived her legislative project as an opportunity to discharge industry of the blame that had hung over it since the 19th century (Vlassopoulos, 1999).

What was the impact of this new causal definition on the actors involved? This redefinition did not mobilise new actors. It did, however, redistribute power between existing actors. For the first time, the Minister of the Environment played an active role in clean air policy. Further, the balance of power between polluters was reconfigured. The industrialists who were until this moment very active within the subsystem fell back to the periphery of the subsystem, hoping to be forgotten. On the other hand, car manufacturers became much more active and placed themselves at the heart of the subsystem in order to protect their interests and to prevent blame. Thus it is not surprising to observe that the former were almost absent from the negotiations of the 1996 law while the representatives of car manufacturers intervened vigorously.

Was there an impact on the policy content? This time a new programme was set up aiming, for the first time, at motor vehicles and car traffic. The enactment of this law, the causal redefinition of the problem and the redistribution of power between the actors lead us to suppose the presence of a major change. This first estimation is moderated, however, after analysis of the preparatory debates and of the content of the 1996 law. The radical change envisaged initially by the Minister for the Environment did not take place. The pressure exerted by the motor lobby was very high, obliging the Minister to progressively remove from her project the most radical and innovative measures (for example, the one concerning the prohibition of car traffic in case of a high air pollution incident). The document finally enacted constitutes a vague text full of wishes without regulatory measures and requiring a considerable number of decrees for its application. This observation also makes it possible to nuance the importance of the changes concerning policy actors. The reinforcement of the Ministry for the Environment within the subsystem was real, but its autonomy remained limited because the other actors did not lose all their resources. If car manufacturers lost the symbolic definitional battle, they succeeded in imposing their limits regarding the content of the new law. The traditional fragmented way of dealing with the problem also remained unchanged, and the Ministry of Transport continued to exert its control over decisions concerning motor vehicles.

In contrast to the French case, air pollution in Greece has mainly been discussed as a car traffic problem, and industrial pollution has been left out of the political discourse. A law was passed in 1912 concerning the rationalisation of industrial facilities, but it did not generate public debate. The second attempt to define industry as an important polluter by the dictators at the beginning of the 1970s consisted of a demagogic effort to condemn capital in the name of public interest. Otherwise all the history of air pollution in Greece has been marked by the clear condemnation of car traffic. During parliamentary debates motor vehicles have been constantly presented as an enemy of society, even in periods where car traffic was almost non-existent in the cities. This made possible the adoption of rather strict and innovatory regulations. For example, in 1911, a law was enacted on civil and penal liability for drivers followed by a protectoral decree forbidding trucks from crossing the town centre of Athens. In 1930, the Highway Code condemned drivers whose vehicles emitted noxious fumes. While in France the problem of fumes emitted by diesel engines is just beginning to be discussed officially, in Greece, a 1937 prescription stipulates that: 'all types of diesel vehicles which emit smoke and odours [...] will be penalised by a withdrawal of their licence for between two and ten days'. Thus, in Greece we do not note any major redefinition of the causes of the problem. The political changeover with the arrival of socialists in power in 1981, and the great publicity given to the problem during the electoral period, made it possible, however, to set up in 1982 the first ad hoc clean air programme. This generated for the first time the mobilisation of new categories of actors such as the car importers' and taxi drivers' trade unions, but with weak negotiating capacity. Like past initiatives, this programme was quite strict, proving the autonomy of the Greek government in dealing with this dimension of the problem because of the absence of an automobile industry in the country. Indeed, the attention paid to automobile pollution in Greece should not be interpreted as due to the specific demographic and climatic situation of the cities. The first debate in 1911 on car traffic took place while there were practically no cars in the streets of the city of Athens. In recent times, urban concentration has certainly aggravated automobile pollution, but industrial pollution is equally serious (and even more serious during the first half of the 20th century), although it has not attracted the attention of the authorities.

From what precedes, it appears that, as was the case in the redefinition of the consequences (see Table 2.2.2), in both countries the redefinition of the causes of the problem marked some changes, but their tempo and intensity varied according to the variables under consideration. In France the way of representing the problem changed radically and rapidly. After one year of debate, air pollution was transformed from an industrial problem to a car traffic problem. In Greece, no definitional change has been observed – car traffic has always been considered as the main source of pollution. As far as the actors involved are concerned, in France there was no change concerning their identity, but the distribution of power between them changed quickly during the car traffic debate in the 1990s. In Greece, only after the publicity given to air pollution in the 1980s did some new actors emerge within the problem subsystem, but their capacity to intervene remained weak. Last, in both cases, this definitional change modified the measures set up to deal with the problem, but the content of the new programmes of action adopted produced rather a weak break in comparison to the past: in France, the 1996 law remains eminently vague and consequently difficult to implement; the

1982 Greek programme is as rigorous as past initiatives and continues to focus on the same pollution source. However, in the Greek case it seems more difficult to appreciate the connection between the way the problem is defined and the actors mobilised in a historical perspective. This is due to the fact that in the absence of a welfare state at the beginning of the 20th century, the political and social spheres were disconnected and policy initiatives did not respond to publicly expressed social needs. Thus a series of initiatives (such as the 1912 law) remained confined within the government space, and the mobilisation of the actors concerned was very superficial or null.

Table 2.2.2: Redefinition of the causes and policy change'

Variable \ Type	Tempo		Intensity	
	France	Greece	France	Greece
Ideas	Rapid	None	Radical	None
Actors	Rapid	Slow	Weak	Weak
Programme	Rapid	Slow	Weak	Weak

Conclusions

Both definitional processes of air pollution in France and Greece show that with each redefinition the subsystem undergoes modifications. Changes in the perceptions of the consequences primarily have an impact on the institutional actors responsible for problem solving, while changes in the definition of causes influence the identity and position of private actors. Policy content does not change with each change of definition.

In the two cases studied, the only change that marks a rupture with the past is in the definition of the problem. In each redefinition a new perception of the problem is promoted: the nature of the problem changes in the sense that it is mentioned and discussed in new terms. Changes (even rapid) concerning the configuration of actors and the policy content appear much less radical. This phenomenon is described here as 'double-speed policy change'. This is related to the policy inheritance, that is, to agreements and practices contained in the way of dealing with the problem that reduce the rupture introduced by changes in the definition of the problem. When the battle over symbols and representations is lost, actors can mobilise other means to preserve their interests, position and values.

Even if these changes do not mark a rupture and do not succeed in breaking the established methods of problem administration, they open prospects for further modifications in policy variables. Baumgartner and Jones (1993, p 16) claim that 'issue redefinition and institutional control combine to make possible the alteration between stability and rapid change that characterizes political systems'. Paraphrasing this statement it is claimed here that *problem definition and the configuration of actors combined with the policy contents make possible simultaneous changes of variable tempo and intensity.*

Does clean air policy tell us something about endogenous and exogenous determinants of change? No regularity appears on this subject. There is generally a combination of external and internal elements to the subsystem that combine to produce the change. This is the case with the transfer of air pollution policy into the environmental sector that coincided both in France and in Greece with the international imposition of new environmental values at the end of the 1960s. By appropriating these new values, actors already involved in clean air policy succeeded in consolidating their position within the subsystem. Motor vehicle pollution policy is related to the European debate on acid rain and NOx emissions, but also to research conducted within some French scientific communities and to the ministerial initiative for agenda setting. In Greece, the character of motor vehicle pollution policy is primarily due to internal elements (the town planner's sovereignty and the absence of a motor vehicle lobby).

Actors in search of opportunities to modify the existing equilibrium as well as actors looking to preserve it are always present within the problem subsystems. This seems, however, more the case for the French clean air problem subsystem than for the Greek one, which is monopolised by a community of experts and lacks strong interest groups potentially hostile to the policy content. The plurality within the French problem subsystem has prohibited any possibility for a common base to build a consensus and thus for policy-oriented learning (Jenkins-Smith, 1988, p 199).

The results regarding the analysis of clean air policy change can be valid only for the cases studied. Nevertheless the thesis of 'double-speed policy change' can take the form of a 'proposal for generalisation' to be tested in other case studies. The analytical framework for observing policy change can take the form of a 'formal theory' (Boudon, 1991, p 76) that does not aim to explain the policy change process but to underline the usefulness of considering certain variables in the study of policy change.

2.3

The next contribution focuses on situations in which efforts are made to effect change in established policies. As has been noted in the Introduction to this part, elements in institutional theory that stress difficulties in securing change focus not just on formal arrangements but also on cultural and ideational notions that support them. Hence, even in the face of strong advocacy of the need for policy change, policy reversal may be difficult. Here, Gyu-Jin Hwang examines attempts to reverse policies about pensions and population control in Japan and Korea in the face of demographic changes that have led politicians to argue that policy changes are needed.

In democratic electoral competition, it is often the case that political parties with attractive policy propositions appeal better to the electorate. The opposition candidates who challenge existing provisions often promise to repeal them in order to serve the interests they represent. Indeed, the primacy of interest figures prominently in almost any events of policy change. Policy change also occurs as the newly arrived ideas successfully upset the status quo, as was the case in the shift from Keynesian demand management policy to monetarism. Policy reversal comes from changes in social habitat too, by making old policies obsolete in the face of new conditions. The very successful population control policy of Korea in the past has now been seen as completely inappropriate under more recent conditions of a consistent below-replacement fertility rate. This has led to calls for a dramatic policy reversal. Policy reversal also comes from inside, with policies and institutions destroying themselves rather than being destroyed from the outside. The early exit programmes of the 1980s in many industrialised countries grew to become seen as a cause of the problem in dealing with the issues of an increasing old-age population. In short, as an impetus for policy change, these analytically distinctive variables are closely interlocked to provide explanatory accounts for why policy change occurs.

While policies change all the time, policy change and reversal is also fraught with difficulties. In fact, in the past few decades the academic literature has moved from the question of why policy change occurs to that of why policy change is so difficult, and what makes some policies more enduring and resistant to change than others. Part of the answer has been found in the discussion of path dependency and policy feedback effect. Once policies have been committed to, it is argued, they may be difficult to reverse, especially when they become mature enough to create their own constituencies. If this path dependency is significant, it is reasonable to expect that policy inertia is more likely. However, as the following two cases illustrate, it is not simply the maturity and the enduring effects of existing policies that create policy inertia. The existing and established social policy institutions can also bring about a significant change in people's value systems, thereby influencing not only people's preferences over particular policy choices, but also their priority over life choices. This often goes beyond the intended consequences of the very policy itself, which is arguably becoming increasingly important in the contemporary design of social provisions.

Both Korea and Japan face what are seen as serious problems of population ageing. The issue here is, of course, picking up on Chloe Vlassopoulos' discussion in the last contribution, on the complex relationship between problem definition and policy action, not whether or not the problem definition activity is correct, but about its dominance among key policy makers. Korea has one of the lowest fertility rates in the Organisation for Economic Co-operation and Development (OECD) while Japan has the highest proportion of elderly people. Interestingly, Korea used to implement a population control policy to lower its birth rate while Japan has long implemented a mandatory retirement age, set at one of the earliest ages by international standards. In both cases, these policies have been an integral part of their modernisation process. In the case of Korea, having fewer children was a symbol of modernity. In Japan, early mandatory retirement was central to maintaining its lifetime employment practices. Recently, however, attempts have been made to reverse these policies. Once seen as a great success story, population control policy in Korea has now shifted the way people see the ideal size of family so fundamentally that new family policy initiatives are facing great difficulties in reversing the trend. A strong top-down initiative that had driven the course of policy development eventually led to a significant shift in people's preference of life choices, while dominant cultural values in employment practices have not changed much. In Japan, the idea of abolishing the early mandatory retirement age has disrupted the longstanding social custom of lifetime employment, thereby resulting in an increase in the mandatory retirement age instead. These two cases highlight the complex issues and difficulties involved in the reform process of public policy against the norms and values attached to existing practices.

When a solution becomes the problem: policy reversals in Korea and Japan

Gyu-Jin Hwang

Policy reversal of population control in Korea

In 2012, Korea became the seventh country in the world to be a member of '20-50 club' which refers to countries that have a population of over 50 million with US$20,000 GNP (gross national product) per head. Japan joined this club in 1987, followed by the USA (1988), France (1990), Italy (1990), Germany (1991) and the UK (1996). Although the population of Korea doubled between 1960 and 2012, its membership of the 20-50 club is expected to be short-lived as its population is projected to drop below 50 million around 2045. At the same time, Korea is now the fastest ageing nation in the OECD, with its working-age population (aged 15 to 64) to begin a downward trend after reaching a peak in 2016 (KNSO, 2010).

The reasons why Korea is now facing this unprecedented level of an ageing society are often related to a number of factors including, but not limited to, the increasing level of female labour force participation, urbanisation and child-rearing and education costs. For instance, education expense as a proportion of total household expenditure grew from 5.5 per cent in 1963 to 6.9 in 1983 to 12.6 in 2008 (KOSIS database). In 2009, Korea was the second biggest spender on education. While its share of public spending on tertiary education was much lower than the OECD average, the proportion of private expenditure on tertiary education was 73.9 per cent compared to the OECD average of 30 per cent. This is particularly significant given the fact that 65 per cent of population aged between 25 and 34 has attained tertiary education (OECD average: 38 per cent), the highest out of 37 countries (OECD, 2012a). At the same time, Korea's household net saving rates as a percentage of household disposable income has dropped substantially, from 16.1 per cent in 1997 to 3.6 in 2009 (OECD, 2011). In an ever more competitive environment, it is argued, 'the average Korean parents are often willing to forgo their ideal family size for fewer children so that they can maximize their children's success later in life' (Anderson and Kohler, 2012, p 20). Here, one's success in life is often equated with securing a top job. On the one hand, the high level of education costs discourages families from having more children. On the other hand, the idea of having fewer children drives parents to concentrate their resources more and more on their children.

On top of these factors the current low fertility rate has also resulted from Korea's deliberate attempt to curb population growth. As one of the very early global social policy interventions, population control appeared on the international agenda in the 1950s and 1960s, particularly for developing countries, not least because over-population was largely seen as a major cause of poverty and environmental threat (cf Yeates, 2002, p 119). As one of the poorest countries, Korea remained primarily rural, with its total fertility rate (TFR) exceeding six children per woman in the early 1950s. Neither demographic knowledge nor strong recognition of the issue existed until the top decision-making body of the military junta, the Supreme Council for National Reconstruction, set the agenda for a nationwide effort to reduce birth rates, one of their imperatives to achieve economic growth and modernisation. Supported by foreign aid, the newly set family planning programme became an integral part of each successive national five-year economic development plan (Kim, 2009, p 61). A series of policy measures was introduced over three decades. In the 1960s, Korea signed the United Nations (UN) Population Declaration and abolished the laws that prohibited the importation and production of contraceptives. In the 1970s, it revised income tax law to limit personal deductions to two children, and permitted sterilised couples with two children to apply for public housing. In the 1980s, the government announced that it would levy extra healthcare contributions and residential tax on households with three children or more (Kwon, 2001). As a result, it achieved the target of lowering the fertility rate below the replacement level earlier than planned, as the TRF was down to 1.96 by 1984 (The World Bank, various years). Since then the TFR has remained below 2 per cent, while the process of fertility reduction continued into the early 1990s.

As previously noted, it is rather difficult to establish exactly what caused this dramatic reduction in fertility rates. Indeed, Korea's population control policy might not have been the direct cause of this, as early research indicates that women in the 1960s wanted to limit their pregnancies due to widespread poverty and destitution. In fact, the fertility decline of the early 1960s was not the result of Korea's population control policy as the family planning programme did not even begin to operate nationwide until 1965. The growth of the national economy and the process of urbanisation and modernisation might equally have influenced the decline of fertility rates, especially during the 1960s. Yet there is little doubt that this population control policy was one of the very few 'strong' programmes ever implemented (Ross and Finnigan, 1968). In addition to socioeconomic pressures, the authoritarian governments that initiated and continued the family planning programme were extremely effective in mobilising resources, implementing policies and directing the campaign without being consultative and inclusionary.

Particularly significant was the fact that this family planning programme contributed to more than simply reducing fertility rates. Table 2.3.1 presents the trend of fertility decline both in terms of TFR and the desired number of children (DNC). With little doubt, the decline of TFR has been dramatic, although the possibility of change may be anticipated based on the slight rise of DNC. The figures for 2010 are particularly low as it only represents Seoul, which has the lowest fertility rate in Korea.

Table 2.3.1: Total fertility rates (TFR) and the desired number of children (DNC) in Korea

	1960	1965	1971	1976	1982	1985	1990	1996	2001	2010ᵃ
TFR	6.0	5.2	4.5	3.1	2.4	1.7	1.6	1.6	1.3	1.02
DNC	5.0	3.9	3.7	2.8	2.5	2.0	2.1	2.4	2.4	1.96

Note: ᵃ Seoul only.

Sources: World Bank (various years); Kwon (2001); World Values Survey (1982, 1990, 1996, 2001); SFWF (2011)

Despite the fact that the TFR began to drop to the level below the desired number from the early 1980s, it was only in 2002 that the population control policy began to be reversed following the warning the National Pensions Corporation (NPC) think tank made: the pension fund would soon be exhausted because of a decline in the working-age population vis-à-vis the number of retirees. The problems that low fertility rates may cause had been already been raised before. Yet the responsible Ministry of Health and Welfare ignored this, stating that 'nothing specific about promoting childbirth has been pursued, nor has there been any policy orientation on this' (*Women's News*, 3 August 2001). The NPC's warning, however, worked as a critical catalyst, pressing the immediate reform of the national pension programme on the one hand, signalling the urgency of reversing the previous population control policy on the other. The number of women of child-bearing age was declining fast. By 2005, the TFR reached a historic low of 1.07, following the below-replacement rate of two children over 20 years (The World Bank, various years).

In 2005, an advisory committee to the President was formed and a law passed to provide the basic legal framework for a new pro-natalist policy. Known as the New Beginning Plan for 2006 to 2010 it included provisions to provide a more favourable environment for child-bearing such as tax incentives, priority for the purchase of a new flat, support for childcare including a 30 per cent increase in facilities, childcare facilities at work, support for education and assistance for infertile couples. The committee identified the conflict in work and family balance as one of the core reasons for low fertility. To this end, the reconciliation of work–family balance has been sought through a dramatic increase in the total number of childcare centres as well as in the enrolment rate in formal care or early education services (Michel and Peng, 2012, p 409). Subsequently, the government introduced compulsory corporate nurseries for companies with over 300 female workers, or over 500 of all workers. In June 2006, it announced the Vision 2020 Plan to raise fertility and to prepare for a society with a much larger number of older people. Each of the local governments has also introduced a range of financial incentives to boost the fertility rate.

It is perhaps too soon to make any judgement about whether any of these policy measures have made any significant impact on fertility rates. According to Peng (2011), however, they have succeeded in achieving the goal of promoting married women's employment but not the fertility rate. Indeed, compared to the process of population control policy adoption, the course of its reversal has been very slow as well as unremarkable, despite some notable developments in family policy, such as the extended paid parental leave scheme, the expansion of childcare benefit and the introduction of child allowance. For instance, the lack of coordinated nationwide plans has had unequal consequences for many localities that already have very unequal financial resources. And some crucial provisions, such as parental leave, have failed to achieve high enough take-up rates to be effective. In fact, albeit increasing, the take-up of parental leave remains low, and men's share of parental leave remains almost negligible (see Table 2.3.2).

Central to this low use of the parental leave scheme among women lies the fear of being unable to return to work. In fact, according to Lee et al (2004), potential disadvantages in the workplace were the most important reason why they do not take up the scheme. This indicates a substantial gap between the social policy institutions and people's value systems that are often developed in the context of workplace culture. Clearly, the level of financial support is critical as the costs of children are influential in child-bearing decisions (d'Addio and d'Ercole, 2005). Indeed, the governments' response to the low fertility crisis has been geared towards reducing the financial burden of caring. Here, the newly introduced universal free childcare services (and a non–means-tested allowance for those who stay at home) for children under five is expected to relieve the financial burden. The introduction of long-term care insurance in 2008 was also an important step towards socialising the family responsibility of care. Yet businesses largely remained opposed to family policy expansion, consenting only to the policies that were to be funded by general revenue (Fleckenstein and Lee, 2012, p 21). Given the fact that work–life balance was at the heart of the conflict, any attempt to achieve reconciliation between the two without taking businesses on board was deemed limited.

Equally importantly, unless this policy reversal leads to some notable transition in values, it is unlikely to achieve the similar result of Korea's extraordinarily successful population control policy. For instance, the New Beginning Plan set out to remove obstacles that would prevent promoting work and life balance by introducing the 40-hour week working hours. As of 2008, however, the average annual hours actually worked per worker were 2,246, the second highest in the OECD). As Table 2.3.3 demonstrates, opinion surveys show that women would like to have more children if possible. However, even this desired level of fertility is low, suggesting that a social norm regarding the acceptable number of children for a family has experienced a noticeable shift. At the same time, marriage rates have dropped to an all-time low, recording 10.6 per 1,000 people in 1989 dropping to

Table 2.3.2: Take-up rate of the parental leave scheme

	2004	2005	2006	2007	2008	2009	2010	2011
Total	24.14	26.03	27.91	36.29	42.50	50.17	55.09	64.38
Men's share	1.9	1.9	1.7	1.5	1.2	1.4	1.9	2.4

Source: Ministry of Labour, Employment Insurance database (www.index.go.kr/egams/stts/jsp/potal/stts/PO_STTS_IdxMain.jsp?idx_cd=1504)

Table 2.3.3: The attitude of female spouses aged between 15 and 44 towards the question of 'It is necessary to have children' (% and number of people)

	Necessary	Total	Good to have them	Okay not to have them	Don't know	Total
1991	90.3	8.5	–	–	1.2	100.0 (7,448)
1997	73.7	26.0	16.6	9.4	0.3	100.0 (5,409)
2000	58.0	41.5	31.5	10.0	0.5	100.0 (6,363)
2003	54.5	44.9	32.3	12.6	0.6	100.0 (6,593)
2006	53.8	46.2	34.1	12.1	–	100.0 (5,386)
2009	55.9	44.1	32.7	11.4	–	100.0 (4,867)

Note: 1991 refers to married women aged between 15 and 49.

Sources: Kim et al (2004, 2009)

6.2 in 2009 (KOSIS database). As marriage rates are positively related to higher birth rates, this indicates the likelihood of a further drop in fertility. Table 2.3.3 shows that women's attitudes towards births have changed dramatically.

All in all, a series of pro-natalist policies that were introduced have not addressed organisational culture in the workplace. Among the OECD members, the gender wage differences in median earnings of full-time employees remain largest in Korea, while the incidence of long hours among women is highest. Despite this, the New Beginning Plan identifies the dominance of a full-time employment culture as one of the work environment-related reasons undermining work and life balance. Indeed, the incidence of part-time employment (part-time employment as a proportion of total employment) in Korea is below the OECD average. Yet Korean women have the highest incidence of temporary employment in the OECD. This raises the question of whether it is the lack of part-time jobs that discourages women from entering the labour market or the temporary nature of employment available for them. At the same time, public spending on families increased the least in Korea between 1980 and 2003 (OECD, 2007). In fact, Korea, along with Japan, has been recognised as a country where workplace practices are the least family-friendly, greatly restricting maternal employment and contributing to low fertility rates. There is also a great deal of gender inequality in the home. Korean men with non-employed spouses contribute about 31 minutes per day to housework and care, while their spouses spend about 6 hours and 25 minutes each day on those tasks. In dual-earner households, men spend 32 minutes while women spend 3 hours and 28 minutes per day (KNSO, 2005). This strong male breadwinner model is exacerbated by a discriminatory workplace culture that demands longer working hours and socialising after work with other colleagues. In addition, the seniority-based remuneration systems punish any worker who takes time off to care for children by way of reduced responsibility and earning power, thereby making it very difficult to balance work and caring activities (OECD, 2007, p 24).

Policy reversal of mandatory retirement in Japan

Against the backdrop of high unemployment in the 1970s, many developed nations adopted early exit programmes to provide more employment opportunities for young jobseekers (Hartlapp and Kemmerling, 2008, p 367). The exact shape of early exit strategies varies widely, ranging from explicit early retirement programmes to many functional equivalents such as disability schemes, a lowered regular retirement age or long-term unemployment benefits for older workers. From the employers' point of view, early retirement was considered to be a peaceful means to restructuring their workforce, as older workers were deemed less productive. Bernhard Ebbinghaus (2006, p 3) refers to this as, 'not only a case of politics *against* markets ... but also that it functions as politics *for* markets, facilitating the restructuring of production systems' (emphasis in original) (cf Esping-Andersen, 1985).

Partly because of this, the decline in labour force participation among older people has been widespread around OECD countries (Auer and Fortunny, 2000). At the same time, a combination of the 'demographic time bomb' and earlier exits from the labour market has led to the dramatic rise in social expenditure for inactive older people. The early exit route was thought of as a partial cure for the modern ills of large-scale redundancy and mass unemployment. But today these passive labour market policies are being publicly criticised as the wrong medicine. The early exit route sought to reduce the supply of labour and thereby lower unemployment. Instead, it became a very costly passive labour market policy resulting in insufficient use, if not active disregard, of human capital and expertise. Hence, most countries have engaged in reversing this by controlling the increasingly costly early exit routes and shifting towards policies better attuned to an active ageing society. Some of the examples that have been tried include: postponing statutory retirement; reforming disability insurance; closing special pre-retirement schemes; activating older workers; and fostering gradual retirement.

Of the rich industrialised countries, Japan stands out not only because it has undergone the least dramatic shift in the labour force participation rates of older people (see Figure 2.3.1), but also because it has maintained one of the lowest early mandatory retirement ages until very recently. Despite its low mandatory retirement age, however, Japan has maintained one of the highest labour market participation rates of male workers aged between 60 and 64 by international standards. In the form of implicit as well as long-standing re-employment practices, the low mandatory retirement age has avoided its extinction. Yet this has received a renewed challenge in recent years not least because there has been some notable decline of the participation rate of male workers, dropping from 85.8 per cent in 1970, through 78.9 per cent in 1995 and to 76.4 per cent in 2008 (International Labour Organization Statistics). This is at odds with its lowest mandatory retirement age. Unlike those countries where mandatory retirement is not permitted at any age (for example, the USA, Canada, New Zealand and Australia), the use of mandatory retirement with a minimum permitted age

Figure 2.3.1: Labour force participation rate (for those aged between 60 and 64)

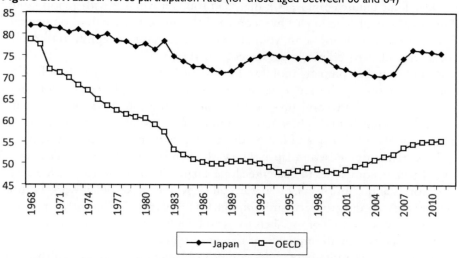

Source: Online OECD employment database (www.oecd.org/employment/employmentpoliciesanddata/
onlineoecdemploymentdatabase.htm#unr)

was always lawful and almost universal in Japan. In 2008, for instance, nearly all companies had a mandatory retirement age system in place (Duell et al, 2010, p 137). The age of 55 was taken as the end point of men's lifetime commitment in the sense that their children would have grown up and been out 'on their own'. Under *nenko* rules (the seniority wage system), wages tended to rise with age and seniority while promotions tended to be automatic. This in effect served the purpose of the 'living wage' as it was expected that wages would have to rise as the average worker's needs arose until their major needs were met. The employees' salary at this age was deemed to be much higher than their productivity. According to Robert Evans, Jr (1991), this explains why Japanese workers' earnings peak at an earlier age than in other countries, and why the company-specific training models dominant in Japan do not reap benefits over a number of years.

Against the backdrop of a rise in unemployment in the 1950s and when the Japanese economy was heavily dependent on exports to the US associated with the Korean War, labour relations in Japan involved a combination of a long-term employment commitment for regular workers and the extensive use of temporary and subcontract employees. Unexpectedly, however, when the Japanese economy began to take off and to record remarkable growth rates, the institutionally embedded labour patterns began to be established that involved employer commitment to sustained employment for regular workers, age- and tenure-based wages, the widespread use of bonus income and low levels of inter-company mobility up to the mandatory retirement age (Gordon, 1985). Indeed, Japanese workers tend to stay with the same employer longer than any other country, while Japanese companies tend to provide a higher incidence of formal on-the-job training for their workers than elsewhere (Casey, 1998). What is also uniquely Japanese is the practice that involves, if layoffs cannot be avoided, layoffs of older, long-tenure employees, rather than younger workers with a short tenure. This may be explained in part by a company's desire to replace overcompensated older workers with low-cost younger personnel. A more significant account comes from Japan's employment structure that stresses years of company loyalty and inhibits inter-company mobility. In this context, the long-run health of the enterprise required the securing of qualified senior employees by equipping young workers with company-specific skills on the job. Mid-career re-entry was highly unlikely in this hierarchical employment structure with strong ties to kinship. Much of this was in line with the employment patterns of mandatory early retirement practised in Japan. The early mandatory retirement age allowed large Japanese companies to guarantee long-term employment, age-related career trajectories and seniority pay structure, all of which make older workers more expensive. According to Bernhard Ebbinghaus (2006, p 187) 'this early retirement practice relies on a web of social customs and public policies which allows larger firms to maintain their employment tenure system.'

So, a mandatory retirement age is common employment practice. At the same time, the fact that it is set at an early age allows young workers to enter the labour market. Yet from the mid-1980s the rate of youth unemployment began to exceed that of prime-aged workers (see Figure 2.3.2), while the working-age population went into serious decline (see Figure 2.3.3). A massive upward trend of old-age related social expenditure also occurred at the same time (see Figure 2.3.4). Part of the response to this has been the prevention of withdrawal from employment and the promotion of re-employment of older workers. Government subsidies introduced in the 1990s were targeted specifically at protecting older workers by paying employers to retain or employ older workers (Grenda and Rebick, 2000). Indeed, about 71 per cent of companies had a re-employment system in 2008, although in many cases 'employment contracts of older workers are changed, even if they perform the same tasks and continue to work full-time' (Duell et al, 2010, p 137). With a very low fertility rate of 1.39 in 2010, the declining number of the working-age population has been seen as the 'biggest single cause' of Japan's declining share of world gross domestic product (GDP) (Krugman, 2010). This decline of working-age population was particularly important for the need to reverse the trend towards earlier retirement (Yashiro and Oshio, 1999, p 242). Along with the existence of the early mandatory retirement age, a series of employment policies have therefore been adopted for older workers. In addition to the initial efforts that 'encouraged' private companies to employ older workers and to increase the mandatory retirement age (Kajitani, 2006, p 51), there have been enhanced financial incentives for the re-employment of older jobseekers this time.

At the same time, a series of policy measures have been introduced to keep elderly people in the labour market. For instance, in 2000, public pensions were reformed to phase out the 'specially-provided' employees' pension benefits to those aged between 60 and 64, which amounted to an equivalent of benefits for those

Figure 2.3.2: Male unemployment rates in Japan

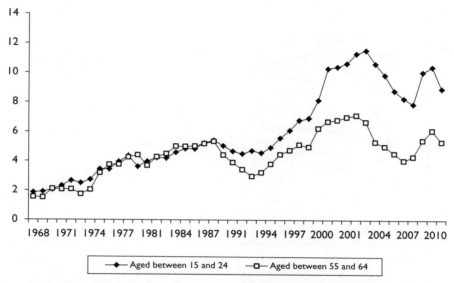

Source: Online OECD employment database (ww.oecd.org/employment/employmentpoliciesanddata/onlineoecdemploymentdatabase.htm#unr)

Figure 2.3.3: Percentage of the population aged between 15 and 64

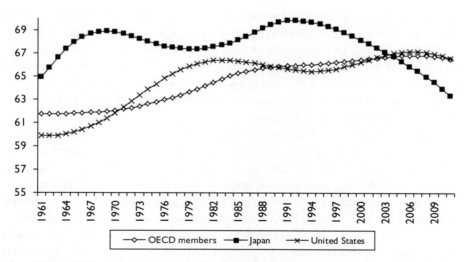

Source: Online OECD employment database (www.oecd.org/employment/employmentpoliciesanddata/onlineoecdemploymentdatabase.htm#unr)

Figure 2.3.4: Old-age expenditure (public and private mandatory) (% of GDP)

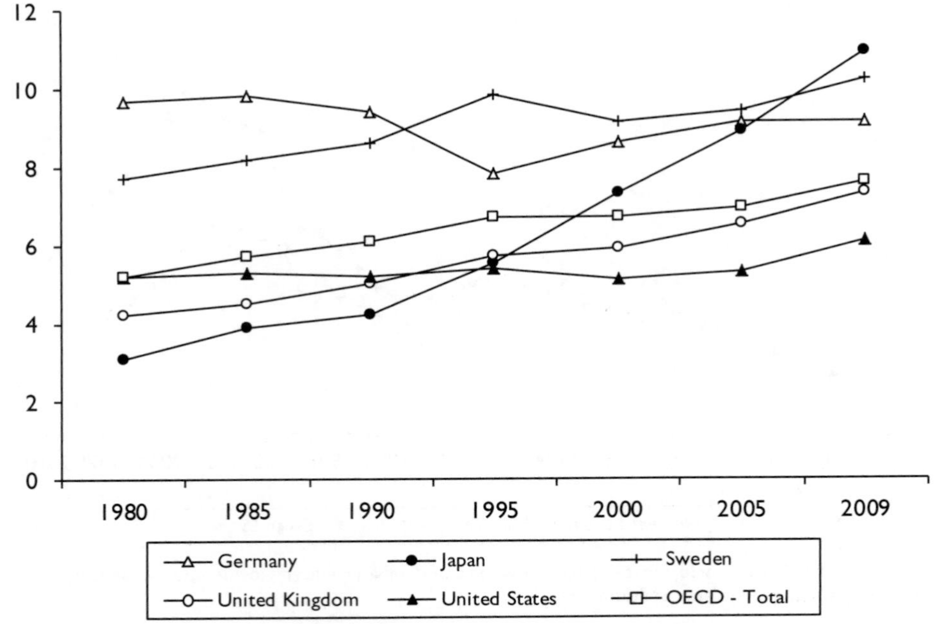

Source: OECD social expenditure database (www.oecd.org/els/familiesandchildren/
socialexpendituredatabasesocx.htm)

aged 65 and over. In 2005, the prior rule of 80 per cent reduction of pension benefits in the case of a retiree aged 60-64 receiving any wages was abolished. In 2004, there was an amendment to the Law Concerning the Stabilisation of Employment of the Aged. Taking effect from 2006, this amendment mandated employers either: (1) to raise the mandatory retirement age to 65; or (2) to introduce a re-employment system for employees between ages 60 and 65; or (3) to abolish mandatory retirement.

Keidanren, the Japan Business Federation (and the nation's largest business lobby), agreed to this as part of a set of reforms designed to restructure internal labour markets by making unions more flexible, modifying the *nenko* rules and agreeing to let 'management experiment with forced transfers of workers to other companies, especially to sub-contractors' (Mosk, 2008, p 313). However, failure to adopt a measure required by the amendment may result only in administrative advice, guidance or recommendation by the government. Nonetheless, around 93 per cent of employers implemented one of the measures in 2007. According to the Ministry of Health, Labour and Welfare (2011), around 3 per cent of companies abolished the mandatory retirement age, while 82 per cent introduced a re-employment system. In August 2012, the lower house of Japan's Parliament approved legislation to increase the mandatory retirement age from 60 to 65 (*The Wall Street Journal*, 2 August 2012). Unlike the 2004 Amendment which allowed employers to decide whether to keep employees after retiring at 60, this gives employees the right to decide whether to stay on until 65. In an attempt to deal with increasing pension costs due to an ageing society, the passage of this received bi-partisan support from the ruling Democratic Party of Japan and the opposition Liberal Democratic Party. It was also in business lobby groups' interests to raise the percentage of those remaining in the workforce between the ages of 60 and 64. For example, Keidanren sought to secure funds to keep hiring elderly people by reviewing its pay scales (*The Japan Times*, 13 December 2012).

Conclusions

With the recognition of multiple variants that may determine retirement and fertility decisions, much that has been presented here highlights the centrality of employment practices and their impact on retirement and fertility trends. In Korea, a very successful population control policy has fundamentally changed the way people see 'birth', not in the sense that they do not want more children, but in the sense that having less is better for their children, thereby becoming a social norm. The previous contraception, birth control, education and campaign promoted the idea of modernity, development and prosperity in relation to one or two children in the family. Although the government has recently introduced a number of economic incentives to reverse the trend, they have not yet been able to address the ways in which having more children is perceived to be a disadvantage rather than an advantage. Any attempts to reverse the trend now not only require the reversal of population control policy, but also a shift in people's normative value systems, especially in employment practices. The fertility decline has now turned into a complex issue inviting solutions to alter people's preference over life choices. Unless there is a substantial increase in financial support, a change in discriminatory workplace culture and a reduction of gender inequality in the home, fertility decline is likely to continue.

In the absence of any statutory guarantee regarding lifetime employment, little has changed in the labour market and employment practices in Japan despite some fundamental shifts in industrial conditions (cf Moriguchi and Ono, 2006). In fact, it has been the workplace norm to maintain elderly workers after the mandatory retirement age, hence Japan has one of the highest rates of elderly labour force participation. Older workers themselves prefer to remain in the labour force (Ministry of Health, Labour and Welfare, 2005). And the institutional structure reinforces this as the earnings-related employees' pension insurance becomes available at age 60 while workers become eligible for full benefit from the national pension plan at age 65. Also, the combined replacement rate of both pensions is around 60 per cent of pre-retirement income. Yet until the national pension plan kicks in, the replacement rate remains around 30 per cent, which provides a strong economic incentive to find a replacement job of some kind after their first retirement, at least until age 65 (Williamson and Higo, 2007, pp 2-3). For this reason, it has been the norm that most Japanese companies re-employ their first-time retirees using short-term contracts, albeit often with some selectivity criteria (Kajitani, 2006). For employers, re-employment systems are preferred to the extension of retirement as they are financially less demanding as the re-employed workers are often paid much less while they could still maintain labour market attachment. In short, the Japanese answer to the decline of the working-age population has been in line with the traditional practice of Japanese corporate culture that values seniority wages, lifetime employment and human capital.

The two cases examined in this contribution highlight that policy has been reversed to address exactly the opposite problem that the previous policy tried to solve. In Korea, the population control policy that was designed to reduce fertility rates became the source of one of the lowest fertility rates in the industrialised world. In the process of reversing this, however, the pro-natalist policy designed to improve work–life balance has been undermined by the lack of attention to changing labour market conditions and workplace culture. Policy reversal has led to an increasing expectation for women to engage in a dual role of working and caring. In Japan, the early mandatory retirement policy that was designed to control labour oversupply has become the source of undersupply of workers in the labour market.

In theoretical terms, the two cases presented here signal the need to reconfigure key theoretical claims associated with the explanation of policy change and reversal. Of the four variables that appear frequently in the literature (that is, the force of ideas, the primacy of interest, change in social habitat and policies themselves; for more detailed discussion, see Hood, 1994), policy reversal and change is often accounted for by the interface between the primacy of interest and the role of institutions. Here the extent to which policy change becomes possible is determined by the sort of interests and powerful influences that policy constituency generates. What needs to be added, however, is the conditioning effect of established norms and practices in the interface of these variables, for it is often this that limits the utility of social provision.

2.4

The demographic change theme emerges again in the following exploration by Pei-Yuen Tsai into changes in work–family balance policies in Taiwan. But here there is a particular emphasis on the factors that favour either stability or change. Once institutions or policies are initiated, they have significant and continuous influences on the subsequent development of policies (Hall, 1986; Skocpol, 1992; King, 1995; Pierson, 2004; Peters, 2005). Some of this work stresses the importance of 'path dependency', that if governments have chosen certain policies or institutional arrangements, this pattern of policies and institutions is very likely to persist, and the inertia of policies is difficult to overcome (Pierson, 1994, 2004).

However 'path dependency' theory has a tendency to explain policy stability rather than change. As Streeck and Thelen (2005) point out, the emphasis on path dependency is based on a punctuated equilibrium model which implies that significant policy changes are usually abrupt and discontinuous. However, policy changes are not always like this. Gradual, incremental and continuous changes can also lead to significant policy changes. Streeck and Thelen suggest five types of these changes: displacement, layering, drift, conversion and exhaustion. Through these mechanisms, incremental institutional changes may entail transformative effects on policy development. From this perspective, policies may transform and evolve without distinct and abrupt changes.

The development of new policies may show very different dynamics and patterns in different institutional situations and policy areas (Seeleib-Kaiser, 2008). However, Béland and Hacker (2004) point out that analysis from an institutional perspective tends to focus more on the prospects of policy change than on the specific forms policy changes take. Studies on how existing institutions affect specific ways of policy development are still relatively limited. This contribution therefore aims to go beyond the question of whether institutions contribute to policy stability or policy change. It examines the influences of institutions in more detail, and shows how the same institutions can lead to different directions of policy development at the same time.

This contribution explores the development of two policies that facilitate work–family balance in Taiwan, that is, parental leave policies and early childhood education and care (ECEC) policies, to demonstrate how existing policies can contribute to both policy stability and policy change.

Broadly speaking, work–family balance policies refer to all the policies that help families to reconcile work and family responsibilities. According to Lewis (2009), work–family balance policies involve three main policy areas: parental leave, childcare and flexible working time arrangements. The focus here is on the changes to parental leave and childcare in Taiwan. As both childcare and early childhood education policies are closely related to work–family balance and difficult to separate, this contribution examines the two policies together and adopts the term of 'early childhood education and care policies' to include both of these policies.

Stability with change: work–family balance policies in Taiwan

Pei-Yuen Tsai

Development of parental leave policies in Taiwan

During the 2000s, parental leave policies in Taiwan changed significantly, with a restructuring of childcare responsibilities between the state, the family and employers. With these changes, the regulation of parental leave policies in Taiwan was strengthened, with the government and employers taking more financial responsibility.

Although these policy changes were gradual and incremental, they dramatically transformed parental leave arrangements. Broadly speaking, the transformation of parental leave policy in Taiwan can be divided into two stages. Before 2002, there was no statutory parental leave for parents. In 2002, responding to the advocacy of women's groups for many years, the government enacted the Gender Equality in Employment Law (GEEL). This provided statutory parental leave for the first time, granting working parents the right to take parental leave for up to two years. However, this initial legislation did not include any provisions for paid leave.

In the policy-making process for the 2002 GEEL legislation, there was an important policy debate about the case for the provision of parental leave benefit. Women's groups argued strongly that the GEEL should include parental leave benefit along with the provision of parental leave. They argued that without the provision of a cash benefit, parental leave would be pointless because not many people would be able to endure the loss of income to take parental leave, and thus the take-up rate would be very low. Nevertheless, the government claimed that it did not have the financial capacity to provide the benefit in the face of its many fiscal pressures. Moreover, employer groups also refused to pay parental leave benefit. In Taiwan, employers generally have an obligation to provide maternity pay, and thus they argued that employers' financial responsibilities were already too heavy, and they were not willing to take on the costs of parental leave benefit as well. As a result, no financial resources were available to provide parental leave benefit and this impasse obstructed the passage of parental leave regulation (Tsai, 2012). In order to facilitate its passage, women's groups conceded, and the issue of parental leave benefit was put to one side. This concession was conditional, however – the women's groups requested the addition of an article in the 2002 GEEL that posed an obligation on Parliament to legislate parental leave benefit in the future. Nevertheless, this article did not clearly point out the time frame of the legislation and ways to formulate parental leave benefit, so in fact it had only declarative effects, and the legal effect on future Parliament members was negligible. With this concession, policy actors agreed to pass the parental leave regulation in 2002. Employers understood that without the payment there would not be many employees taking the leave, so this would not increase costs very much.

However, when concern about the low fertility rate arose in the mid-2000s, the provision of parental leave benefit was brought onto the policy agenda again. To some extent policy makers recognised the problem of a low fertility rate as a result of institutional weaknesses. There was growing recognition that modest state support for childcare increased parents' heavy burden of child-bearing which reduced people's incentives to have children (Ministry of the Interior, 2008; Secretariat of the Conference on Sustaining Taiwan's Economic Development, 2008). This recognition strengthened the imperative to solve work–family balance difficulties, and facilitated the development of a parental leave benefit policy (Tsai, 2012). At this time, the article gave policy actors who supported parental leave benefit an opportunity to break the status quo, and exerted pressure on the government to formulate a parental leave benefit policy.

Nevertheless, an important problem remained. How could the government find the financial resources to make the payment of parental leave benefit under such severe fiscal constraints? At this time, existing institutions provided an important foundation for the government to use to meet these new demands. In 2003, the government launched a new Employment Insurance scheme to address the unemployment problem. The implementation of unemployment benefit was very late in Taiwan. It was originally included as one of the contingencies in Labour Insurance in 1999, but in order to integrate it into the employment promotion system and to ensure its financial independence, unemployment benefit was singled out from Labour Insurance, and the government launched a new insurance scheme, Employment Insurance, to provide unemployment benefit from 2003 (Lin, 2006).

According to the Employment Insurance Act (2002), the main goals of the Employment Insurance scheme were to promote employment, raise workers' employment skills and to ensure the basic living standards of workers during vocational training and unemployment. It therefore provided several benefits to workers including unemployment benefit, early employment benefit, vocational training benefit and a National Health Insurance premium subsidy. However, unemployment benefit accounts for about 80 per cent of expenditure under this scheme (Council of Labor Affairs, 2009).

After the implementation of Employment Insurance in 2003, due to the relatively low unemployment rate in Taiwan, the benefit paid out was very little compared to the premiums received. According to statistical data from the Council of Labor Affairs (2009), there was about 10–13 billion TWD (new Taiwan dollars) surplus each year between 2003 and 2008. Hence, the Employment Insurance fund had accumulated about 72 billion TWD by the end of 2008. This surplus provided the financial resources that policy makers could manipulate to implement new policies against other social problems, such as the lack of parental leave benefit. Hence the Employment Insurance scheme, but not the labour insurance scheme, was adapted to provide parental leave benefit. The same change was also applied to the separate insurance schemes for civil servants, teachers, and military personnel. These occupational social insurance schemes were therefore all amended to include parental leave benefit.

Here, then, we see that the Taiwanese government finally used its existing institutions and resources to meet these new social demands. From 2009–10, Employment Insurance, Civil Servant and Teacher Insurance and Military Personnel Insurance were amended to provide a new parental leave benefit. These schemes provided about 60 per cent of an income replacement rate for six months for both parents – if both parents took the parental leave benefit, they could take leave for up to one year in total. With the provision of parental leave benefit through the social insurance schemes, a large part of the financial responsibility for parental leave was transferred from families to employers and the government. In Employment Insurance, employers generally have to pay 70 per cent of the premium, and the government has to pay 10 per cent, whereas employees (parents) only need to pay 20 per cent. In Civil Servant and Teacher Insurance, the government has to pay 65 per cent of the premium, whereas government employees (parents) need to pay 35 per cent. Therefore, parents can receive the full payment of parental leave benefit with a relatively low rate of contribution. The role of employers and the government in sharing childcare financial responsibilities has been strengthened (Tsai, 2012).

The adoption of existing institutions to meet new social demands entailed different influences on new policies. Some of these contributed to policy stability that followed previous policy logic, whereas some influences contributed to the conversion of existing policy routes. From the perspective of policy stability, the adoption of Employment Insurance to provide parental leave benefit continued the reliance on the social insurance principle to provide welfare. The adoption of Employment Insurance also strengthened the division between 'insiders' and 'outsiders' because this insurance excluded some vulnerable workers. It is important to recognise that the Employment Insurance scheme is a separate innovation in Taiwan, supplementing but not replacing the older Labour Insurance. The coverage of the insured in Labour Insurance is wider than in Employment Insurance. According to the Council of Labor Affairs (2009), about 8.8 million people were covered by Labour Insurance whereas only 5.4 million people were covered by Employment Insurance at the end of 2008. Workers who are self-employed or do not have constant employment can participate in the Labour Insurance scheme, but many are not covered by Employment Insurance. Thus, since the parental leave benefit is paid through Employment Insurance rather than Labour Insurance, there are many workers who are not able to receive parental leave benefit. However, as Labour Insurance is facing severe financial pressures due to an ageing population, the possibility of adapting Labour Insurance has been ruled out. While, according to the GEEL the parental leave policy is supposed to cover all workers, financial support is not available to the self-employed and workers in insecure employment, which dramatically reduces their ability to take parental leave.

In the meantime, the adoption of Employment Insurance also facilitates policy changes that deviate away from the original path of the Taiwanese welfare system. First, under the financial structure of Employment Insurance, in terms of the allocation of financial responsibilities in the care of young children, they have been largely transferred from families to employers and partly to the state, alleviating the responsibilities of families. From this perspective, the existing institutions provided an opportunity for a path-breaking policy development, from family responsibilities in childcare to the sharing of responsibilities between families, employers and the state. Second, because the financial mechanism of Employment Insurance is based on individuals rather than families, fathers and mothers can have the same level and duration of parental leave benefit and the parental leave benefits are not transferrable. This promotes the equal share of care responsibilities between fathers and mothers. It is also a path-breaking development that changes the assumptions of the previous welfare system built on the male breadwinner model. With this change, males are supposed to take more care responsibilities. However, the real impact of these policies may be less significant because the take-up rates of parental leave benefit are not very high for either men or women.

The development of a parental leave benefit policy in Taiwan provides an example of the way development of new policies is highly influenced by existing institutional settings. Nevertheless, that influence cannot be simplified to policy stability or policy change. In some areas, existing institutions may contribute to path dependency. At the same time the inherent logic in existing institutions may also facilitate policy evolution and the development of a new policy direction.

Development of early childhood education and care policies in Taiwan

The development of early childhood education and care (ECEC) policies in Taiwan in the last decade provides another example of the way existing policies promote both policy stability and policy changes in different policy dimensions. The existing policies affect the political structure of new policies and thus create the dynamics of 'increasing returns'. However, the 'increasing returns' do not just lead to the dynamics of path dependency; they also contribute to the possibility of policy changes.

Generally speaking, the intervention of the Taiwanese government in ECEC policies was weak before the 2000s. Childcare was generally regarded as individuals' or families' responsibilities rather than the state's. To some extent this policy orientation can be attributed to the prevalence of a familism ideology. Under the influences of this ideology, families were regarded as the first resort to meet the demands of childcare. The government only intervened when families were not capable of taking responsibility for their own childcare. Therefore, the government's role in childcare was purely auxiliary. Due to the lack of public provision, the demands for ECEC services were mainly met by families and private ECEC service providers. Moreover, among these private facilities, most were operated by for-profit rather than non-profit organisations (Fu, 1995; Lin, 1995; Wang and Lai, 1997; Wang and Sun, 2003).

The weak intervention of ECEC policies in previous decades entailed some significant social problems such as high fees for ECEC services, the unstable quality of these services and an unequal distribution of ECEC supply between urban and rural areas. These problems exacerbated parents' difficulties in reconciling work and childcare responsibilities (Feng, 1997; Wang and Lai, 1997; Wang and Sun, 2003; Lin, 2006; Wu, 2006). Moreover, the Taiwanese government came to believe that the insufficiency of ECEC policies to support parents was an important cause of the low fertility rate (Ministry of the Interior, 2008). In order to alleviate these problems, the government's attitude towards ECEC policies changed. It gradually recognised that the costs of ECEC services should not be carried just by families (or working women), but should be shared collectively by society (Ministry of the Interior, 2008).

In order to address these problems, in the last decade the government has implemented a series of policy changes in ECEC . Among these new policies, at least three types of policy instruments can be identified: provision of subsidies, raising the standards of ECEC facilities and an increase in public and non-profit ECEC facilities. (See the discussion of policy instrument theory in Part Four, particularly the contribution by Michael Prince, Chapter 4.2.)

In terms of the financing of ECEC services, in the past few decades the cost of ECEC services in Taiwan has fallen mostly on families. However, in response to the expensive fees for ECEC services, several ECEC subsidy policies were implemented to relieve parents' financial burdens during the 2000s. These subsidies targeted children in a variety of ways according to age and/or status. The development of ECEC subsidy policies involved incremental policy change through the accumulation of programmes split across several government departments. This expansion of subsidy policies can be understood in several ways. The provision of subsidy was very selective before 2000. However, there were more universal programmes after 2000, and the coverage of beneficiaries was gradually expanded. Second, the age of children entitled to the subsidies was gradually extended, from five-year-old children to younger children. Third, the level of the subsidy was improved. The government gradually took on higher percentages of ECEC costs with the development of subsidy policies. Through the expansion of these subsidy programmes, the state's role in financing was incrementally strengthened.

In the area of regulation, the Taiwanese government has gradually raised the standards of ECEC facilities while extending the provision of subsidies. ECEC subsidies are only provided to children enrolled in facilities that meet the standards set by the government; in this way the government has been able to set higher standards to layer onto the existing statutory minimum standards. Private service providers have to meet these higher standards so that their customers, that is, parents and children, are able to receive the subsidies. If these private service providers do not meet these standards, they may be disadvantaged in the market competition because their customers are not able to receive the subsidies and may choose other facilities. Through this mechanism, the government's role in regulation has been enhanced without changing statutory regulations.

In terms of the provision of ECEC services in Taiwan, development before the 2000s showed a trend of privatisation and marketisation, particularly after the mid-1980s. The highly privatised ECEC services were recognised by some policy makers as an important factor leading to expensive ECEC costs for parents (Wong and Huang, 1995; Wang and Sun, 2003; Lin, 2006). In order to tackle this problem, the government set up more public ECEC facilities; it also began to provide subsidies to encourage non-profit organisations to set up non-profit ECEC facilities with several programmes, such as the Community Day Care Centre Programme and Early Childhood Education and Childcare Friendly Experimental Programme (Ministry of the Interior, 2006; Ministry of Education, 2007). These policies are expected to provide universal and cheap ECEC services for parents. However, compared to subsidy policies and the rise in standards, the increase in public and non-profit facility supply has been relatively limited. Although there has been an increase in public facilities in disadvantaged areas, the overall provision of public and non-profit facilities did not change much between 2000 and 2010. The percentage of public facilities only slightly increased, from 24.9 per cent in 2000 to 26.0 per cent in 2010. Nevertheless, the number of children enrolled in public facilities decreased from 32.6 per cent in 2000 to 31.5 per cent in 2010 (Child Welfare Bureau, 2013; Ministry of Education, 2013). Moreover, the implementation of the Community Day Care Centre Programme and the Early Childhood Education and Childcare Friendly Experimental Programme only added eight non-profit facilities in total until 2009. Therefore, public and non-profit ECEC provision did not show much change during the 2000s.

Although the Taiwanese government used all three types of policy instruments to strengthen state intervention in ECEC policies, the pace and degree of policy changes in the three areas has not been all the same. First, subsidy policies were developed fastest. The government has increased its role in providing financial support, and several nationwide subsidy schemes have been launched to help parents relieve the financial pressures of ECEC costs. Second, the government also attempted to raise the standards of ECEC services to improve quality, but these policies progressed less smoothly than subsidy policies. The raising of standards was not only limited to statutory regulation; it was also implemented through the requirements attached to subsidies. However, many private service providers claimed that these requirements were too strict for them to achieve. Some of these requirements were therefore postponed due to the resistance and complaints of private service providers. Third, the government also tried to expand the supply in public ECEC facilities and non-profit ECEC facilities. Nevertheless, compared to the other two sets of policies, the development in provision was less impressive. Generally speaking, the government tended to rely on subsidies as the main measure. In contrast, the increase of public and non-profit ECEC supply was quite limited.

To understand how and why the government chose these policy instruments, it is crucial to pay attention to the influence of existing institutions and structure. As pointed out by many scholars, existing policies or regulations may shape the interests, goals, social identities and capacities of social groups (Hall, 1986; Skocpol, 1992; Pierson, 1994; Béland, 2010). Changes of policies alter the gains and losses that social groups experience. Hence, these social groups may take action to influence the policy-making process to promote or protect their interests.

In the case of ECEC policy development in Taiwan, the lack of state intervention in early years contributed to the privatisation of ECEC services. As a result, these private ECEC service providers gradually formed strongly organised interest groups to influence the development of new policies, and their preferences had significant influences on the change to ECEC policies. While the government gradually recognised the need to increase state intervention in ECEC services, the enhancement of the state's role could be through several dimensions and policy instruments. In the process of selecting policy instruments and deciding which dimensions to develop, private service providers played a pivotal role in influencing the direction of development. As the interests of these private service providers were more concentrated and they had relatively more financial resources compared to parents and non-profit organisations, they could have more influence on policy making. They took many actions to make the government choose the policy instruments that accorded with their preferences, such as lobbying Parliament members to affect government decisions, organising demonstrations and lobbying political parties.

Among the three sets of ECEC policies implemented during the 2000s, subsidy policies accorded with private service providers' interests most because they could stimulate parents' incentives to send their children to private facilities. Therefore, they gained support from private service providers. Compared to subsidies, the raising of standard requirements was less popular for these private service providers because that could increase their costs. So there was resistance in this policy dimension. With regard to the increase of public and non-profit facilities, there was severe opposition from private service providers because public and non-profit facilities could compete with private facilities and reduce the market for ECEC services.

The case of ECEC policy development in Taiwan also demonstrates that existing institutions provide opportunities for both path-dependent and path-breaking changes in different aspects and policy dimensions. We see path dependency inasmuch as subsidies reinforced and strengthened the market system. Nevertheless, with the provision of subsidies, the state gradually took more financial responsibilities for ECEC expenses. A large percentage of financial responsibilities has been transferred from families to the state. Hence, there has been a shift from family responsibilities to state responsibilities. In terms of the financing of ECEC services, the provision of subsidy may be regarded as a path-breaking development. To a large extent private service providers promoted the provision of subsidies as a result of previous institutional arrangements.

Conclusions

The influences of institutions on policy development are very complicated. With many different inherent logics of existing institutions, previous policies may limit policy change but may also provide opportunities for them. This contribution has drawn on the case of work–family balance policy development in Taiwan to show the different influences of previous policies on both policy stability and policy change. For instance, the adoption of Employment Insurance to provide parental leave benefit reinforced the tendency of the Taiwanese welfare system to rely on social insurance schemes to provide welfare. It also strengthened the division between 'insiders' and 'outsiders' in that core workers can receive more protection whereas precarious workers are excluded. However, from the viewpoint of state and family responsibilities, it shifted a large proportion of financial responsibilities in childcare from families to employers and the state.

The development of ECEC policies is another example. The provision of ECEC subsidies further entrenched the marketisation of ECEC services. From the viewpoint of service provision, it is a path-dependent development because it continues to follow the market approach rather than a public provision approach to address ECEC demands. However, in respect of financing, it shows a clear transfer of financial responsibilities from families to the state, and from this perspective this is a path-breaking development. As the influences of institutions also are multidimensional, existing institutions may lead to different development in different policy areas. The influences of institutions cannot be expressed simply in terms of just path stability or policy change. Existing institutions can contribute to path dependency in some aspects, but also to path breaking in others.

2.5

The last contribution in this section explores the relationship between policy stability and policy change, making use of the 'punctuated equilibrium' perspective developed by Baumgartner and Jones (1993) and the examination of advocacy coalition framework building by Sabatier and Weible (2007).

Daniel Nohrstedt examines the political context of nuclear energy policy making in Sweden from the early 1990s to 2010. This 20-year period was characterised by long-term stability interrupted by major policy change through a decision in 2009 to revoke a ban for new build as a means to allow for the replacement of existing reactors. In addition, in this period the Swedish nuclear energy subsystem experienced several shocks including multiple incidents in domestic reactors as well as the 2010 Fukushima disaster in Japan. These events presented potential triggers for policy change through heightened attention and temporary agenda change. This contribution explores these recent developments in Swedish nuclear energy policy to shed light on general explanations for policy change offered by policy process theory. To structure the analysis, the contribution focuses specifically on five general explanatory factors and developments: (i) external events; (ii) agenda setting; (iii) redistribution of political resources; (iv) venue access; and (v) incumbent policy beliefs and interests. Building from the empirical analysis, the concluding section discusses explanations for policy change in more general terms.

Understanding the political context of nuclear energy policy change in Sweden

Daniel Nohrstedt

Nuclear energy policy change in Sweden

In the public policy literature, the notion of policy change has multiple meanings. Prior research centres on different aspects of policy change including the level of change (minor versus major), pace (rapid or slow), content (goals and/or instruments) and longevity (temporary or lasting) (Durant and Diehl, 1989; Rose, 1991; Hall, 1993; Patashnik, 2006). Meanwhile, policy change research has suffered from significant dissensus over the theoretical and operational definition of policy change, which has been a major obstacle for cumulative knowledge (Howlett and Cashore, 2009). The objective of this contribution is to understand the dynamics leading up to major policy change, that is, instances where changes in policy programmes substantially deviate from the status quo. Following Sabatier and Jenkins-Smith (1999), the study defines policy change according to revisions in the normative and instrumental components of a policy programme. Specifically, it focuses on the overarching policy goal regarding the future position of nuclear power in Sweden's energy production system. Table 2.5.1 summarises key policy developments during 1996–2010.

Table 2.5.1: Government nuclear energy policy goals, 1996–2010

Policy action	Date made public	Main policy goal related to nuclear power
Bill 1996/97:176		Parliament decides to mandate the government to decide on the decommissioning of individual reactors by a date set by the government
Bill 2005/2006:76	20 April 2006	Parliament decides no reactors should be phased out in 2006–10; restrictions lifted on nuclear energy research
Government party agreement	5 February 2009	Alliance government parties publish new government policy allowing construction of new reactors on existing sites to replace existing units
Bill 2009/10:172	23 March 2010	Parliament decides to allow construction of new reactors on existing sites to replace existing units

These developments show that Swedish nuclear energy policies remained stable between 1996 and 2005. In 2006, the decision not to phase out any reactors in the period from 2006 to 2010 indicated a development towards a more pro–nuclear official policy. This trend continued in 2009 and 2010 following a decision by the four-party Alliance government (Conservatives, Liberals, Centre Party and Christian Democrats) to abolish a law to phase out nuclear power and to enable construction of a maximum of 10 new reactors on existing sites.

Prior studies have adopted different theoretical perspectives and empirical approaches to explain these policy changes. For example, Nilsson (2005) relies on the literature on policy learning to analyse patterns of knowledge acquisition, interpretation of knowledge and institutionalisation of knowledge in policy making. Focusing on nuclear energy policy developments in the late 1980s and the early 1990s, Nilsson (2005) concludes that policy changes have been driven primarily by conflicts between competing belief systems related, for example, to the relationship between nature and man, technology and modernity and the role of science in policy making. Since the 1970s these tensions fed politicisation, and nuclear power was elevated as an electoral issue. As nuclear power became subject to partisan politics, all major policy decisions were gradually subject to tight Cabinet control and negotiated in closed sessions at the highest political level rather than proceeding through traditional agency and committee work. High levels of politicisation in return fuelled distrust among key actors, and the task of attaining substantive policy goals was overshadowed by political considerations.

Turning to the 2009 decision to allow construction of new reactors to replace existing units, Nilsson (2011) attributes this to a combination of European Union (EU) influence, waning opposition and a broader change in national governance. According to this view, the fact that energy policy (nuclear power policy included) was aligned with the 2008 European climate and energy package gradually changed the framing of the nuclear power issue from party competition and ideological confrontation to a more technical issue about implementation. These developments were accompanied by changes in government appointment practices whereby new agency heads were more specialised and more educated in the engineering sciences, which in turn changed the terms of the political debate from a focus on ideology to technological solutions (Nilsson, 2011, p 1519).

In a longitudinal study of key nuclear energy policy changes in Sweden during 1945–2010, Holmberg and Hedberg (2011) found convergence over time between the direction of Sweden's official nuclear energy policy, public opinion trends and political party positioning on nuclear power. Thus, in their view, policy changes in this case are to be understood as being consistent with the basic principle of representative democracy: 'Swedish official nuclear power policy, party policies, and public opinion have to a remarkable extent followed each other over the last forty years' (Holmberg and Hedberg, 2011, p 22). Although they note that it is impossible to determine who leads whom in practice, they conclude that policy changes coincide with changes in party policies and public opinion trends.

These studies illustrate the breadth of theoretical perspectives adopted to explain changes in Swedish nuclear energy policy. The objective of this contribution is to shed light on nuclear energy policy developments in Sweden from the perspective of policy process research, which essentially has a broad focus involving 'change and development of policy and the related actors, events, and contexts' (Weible et al, 2012, p 3). The policy process literature is multifaceted and consists of multiple and partly overlapping theoretical frameworks and theories. For example, Capano (2009) identifies at least 20 different theories of social and political development seeking to explain policy change, and Sabatier (2007) introduces eight frameworks which all contribute to the understanding of policy change. These theoretical perspectives imply different theoretical emphases, that is, they posit different explanatory variables and different causal logics accounting for policy development over time. However, there is also substantial overlap, and many perspectives share similar assumptions regarding some general and interrelated factors, events and conditions that shape public policy making over time (Dudley et al, 2000; Cairney, 2007b; Capano, 2009; Nowlin, 2011). Among these common factors and developments are agenda setting, external shocks, the redistribution of political resources, venue access and belief system change. These factors and developments are detailed below.

- *Agenda setting:* in policy making, various events occasionally call new or renewed attention to policy problems. In return, the level of attention devoted to any given problem fluctuates over time, whereby periods of lack of public interest are followed by temporary spikes in attention (Downs, 1972). The interplay or interaction between different policy agendas is important to understand the role of agenda setting in policy making. In some cases, spikes in attention in the news media agenda will increase attention in governmental or legislative agendas, although this is not necessarily always the case. The effect of agenda setting on the policy process is mediated by a range of factors, such as image change, changes in public opinion and group mobilisation (Baumgartner and Jones, 1991).

- *External shocks:* most frameworks recognise that policy making is characterised by periods of equilibrium or near stasis over time, occasionally interrupted by periods of abrupt change. Since institutions and policy belief systems are generally stable, change must be triggered by some external force outside the control of actors involved in policy making. Whether or not shocks are likely to be followed by policy change depends in turn on a combination of agenda change, revision of policy images, redistribution of political resources, entry of new actors in the policy process and venue change (Baumgartner and Jones, 1991; Sabatier and Jenkins-Smith, 1999; Nohrstedt and Weible, 2010).

- *Redistribution of political resources:* policy change is partially conditioned by the amount of political resources available to different actors that seek to influence any given policy area. The ultimate resource involves veto-player capacity, that is, actors with a political mandate to make decisions about the direction of policy programmes and whose agreement is required for a change in policy (Tsebelis, 1995). Other important resources include public opinion, information, mobilisable supporters, financial resources and skilful leadership. Policy change depends on actors' access to and ability to exploit these resources and the distribution of resources between subsystem actors. Significant redistribution of resources between policy coalitions increases the likelihood of policy change (Sabatier and Weible, 2007).

- *Venue access:* participation of various actors in policy making is a key factor in policy process research. Policy venues – generally defined as decision settings where policy advocates can air alternative policy proposals (Pralle, 2003) – are important in two respects. First, changes in the exploitation or importance of one venue to another may be one underlying reason for policy change. Venues vary according to a number of characteristics (for example, rules for participation and decision making) and thus moving from one venue to another may change the terms for policy making. Second, entrance of new actors to key venues may bring in new problem representations and beliefs into the policy process, which in turn may pave the way for policy change.

- *Belief system change:* participants in the policy process espouse different beliefs about the nature and severity of problems and the viability of policy solutions. Since belief systems serve as filters, new information questioning certain beliefs is likely to be screened out. Beliefs are generally rigidly held and rarely change. Yet the gradual accumulation of knowledge or the occurrence of some external shock may result in belief change (Sabatier and Jenkins-Smith, 1999).

Existing policy process frameworks posit relationships between these (and other) processes and developments in terms of stability and change. For example, the advocacy coalition framework hypothesises that external shocks are a necessary but insufficient cause of policy change, and that the effect is mediated by redistribution of political resources or the opening and closing of venues (Sabatier and Jenkins-Smith, 1999; Sabatier and Weible, 2007). This contribution does not seek to validate any specific framework or theory in an effort to probe causal relationships or intervening variables. The objective is rather to describe the political context of nuclear energy policy development in more general terms, focusing on the role of external events and processes of agenda setting, the distribution of political resources and venue access.

The approach taken in this contribution adds to our thinking about the process of policy change in several ways. Empirically studying developments in agenda setting, the distribution of political resources and venue access helps in understanding how the political context shapes the policy-making process over time. 'Political context' is generally an elusive concept; it refers here to basic external conditions including specifically external events, attention, power relationships and participation in policy making. The analysis hereby challenges narrow perceptions of the policy process as being isolated from its external environment. Although policy subsystems tend to be dominated by specialised actors that regularly participate in policy making over time, they are susceptible to outside influence coming from a variety of sources. Furthermore, examining the relationship between exogenous forces and political action enables insight into the way specific political institutions enable and constrain policy change.

Analysis

Data for this analysis has been retrieved from multiple sources. First, to document trends in news media coverage of nuclear power multiple searches were conducted using the Presstext database. Four of Sweden's major newspapers (*Dagens Nyheter, Svenska Dagbladet, Aftonbladet* and *Expressen*) were included. Second, online records of the Swedish Parliament (www.riksdagen.se) were searched in order to trace parliamentary debates about nuclear power. These searches were conducted using multiple search terms (nuclear power, greenhouse effect, electricity pricing). Third, a selection of legislative documents was searched as a means of tracing policy-oriented beliefs guiding decision making. Fourth, secondary sources were consulted to collect complementary evidence on policy venues, public attention and partisan positioning on nuclear energy policy.

Agenda setting

Policy agenda-setting theorists generally assume that periods of low interest in any given issue are occasionally interrupted by a sudden and dramatic increase in attention by the general public and the news media, which spurs attention by political institutions (True et al, 2007, p 161). 'Attention at the individual and collective levels governs the shift from stasis to the positive feedback processes that define rapid change' (Jones and Baumgartner, 2005, p 329). Regarding public attention to nuclear energy in Sweden, Holmberg and Hedberg (2011, p 32) note that between 1992 and 2010, the level of importance attributed to nuclear power (as an electoral issue and as a societal problem) by the general public was rather low compared to the late 1970s and 1980s, when nuclear power gained much higher prominence among the general public. Between 1991 and 2010, only between 3 and 5 per cent of the Swedish population viewed nuclear power as an important electoral issue. In the same period, between 1 and 2 per cent of the population viewed nuclear power as an important societal problem. By contrast, as shown in Figure 2.5.1, the level of attention to nuclear power from the news media and Parliament has fluctuated over time. These agendas largely overlap over time with two peaks that coincide in 1997 and 2010 when attention by Parliament and the news media increased. However, Figure 2.5.1 also indicates some divergence; for example, the peak in parliamentary attention in 2000 was not accompanied by an increase in media attention, and in 2007 media attention increased while attention from Parliament decreased.

Figure 2.5.1: Newspaper articles and parliamentary debates per year

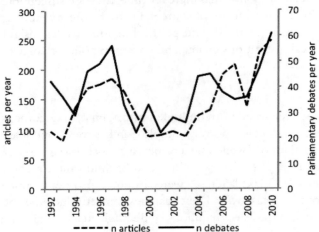

Waning agenda prominence appears to be one factor that helps explain the policy change in 2009. In the late 1970s and early 1980s, about one fourth of the Swedish population viewed nuclear power as an important electoral issue. But, as noted above, the public's interest in nuclear power declined significantly during the 1990s and 2000s. Furthermore, the level and intensity of news media attention devoted to nuclear energy policy making was fairly low in this period. Policy actions indicating change were followed by no increase or only short temporary spikes in news media attention (see Figure 2.5.2). One may speculate that the relatively low interest from the public and the media reduced the political costs associated with major policy changes on nuclear power. In this regard, the situation in the 2000s differed dramatically from the 1970s and 1980s, when political leaders made a strong connection between nuclear power policy making and electoral performance (Nohrstedt, 2010).

Figure 2.5.2: Monthly news media coverage of nuclear power (2006, 2009, 2010)

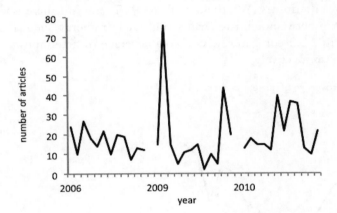

External shocks

On the role of external developments, the policy process literature is generally quite vague on what events are actually important as causal drivers in the policy process (Nohrstedt and Weible, 2010). For example, Sabatier and Weible (2007, pp 198, 204) define external shocks broadly as being 'outside the control of subsystem actors', which include 'changes in socioeconomic conditions, regime change, outputs from other subsystems, or disaster'. This study focuses on three categories of external events and developments: (i) incidents in Swedish nuclear reactors; (ii) climate change agenda setting; and (iii) agenda setting regarding electricity pricing.

Between 1992 and 2006, Sweden experienced seven INES (International Nuclear Event Scale) Level 2 incidents: July 1992 (Barsebäck plant), October 1994 (Ringhals 2), October 1995 (Studsvik), November 1996 (Oskarshamn 2), September 1997 (Ringhals 4), May 1999 (Barsebäck) and July 2006 (Forsmark). Events at each increasing level of the INES scale are 10 times more severe compared to the previous level. Level 2 events qualify as 'incidents' with no environmental impacts. Returning to Figure 2.5.1, the effects of these events on news media reporting and parliamentary attention are mixed. Several incidents

(1992, 1997 and 1999) did not seem to have any immediate effect on news media coverage and the parliamentary agenda, whereas events in 1994, 1995, 1996 and 2006 were followed by a relatively modest increase in attention by the news media or Parliament or both. In aggregate, these data suggest that incidents in domestic plants did not have an impact on policy making via major effects on agenda setting. Some events seem to have triggered temporary spikes in attention, but overall these incidents did not have any lasting effects on news media reporting or parliamentary agenda setting.

In relation to climate change, nuclear energy has been reframed as a viable low carbon energy option (Marshall, 2005; Bickerstaff et al, 2008). Meanwhile, other studies suggest that perceptions of global environmental problems are unrelated to nuclear power attitudes (Whitfield et al, 2009). To assess if there is a longitudinal relationship between climate change and nuclear energy agenda setting in Sweden, Figure 2.5.3 compares news media coverage of greenhouse effects and nuclear power respectively.

Figure 2.5.3: News media coverage of nuclear power

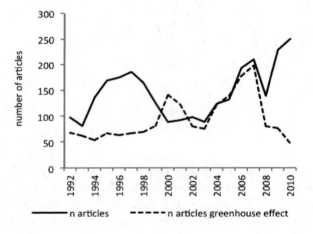

Two main trends can be noted. First, levels of attention devoted to nuclear power and the greenhouse effect largely converge in 2002–08, which is one indication that in this period the press was making a connection between nuclear energy policy and climate change. Second, following the decline in attention observed in 2008, the level of attention devoted to the greenhouse effect dropped further in 2009–10 while attention to nuclear power increased. The latter is likely explained by the 2009 decision to allow replacement of reactors on existing sites and the 2010 Fukushima disaster (see Figure 2.5.1). The convergence of agendas may be taken as tentative evidence of the gradual establishment of a policy image describing nuclear power as a viable energy source in response to global warming (cf Baumgartner and Jones, 1991). The establishment of this image coincided with preparatory work preceding the 2006 Bill, and may thus have influenced policy making. Climate change was furthermore one of the major justifications for the revised policy in 2009: 'Climate change is now in the spotlight and nuclear power will therefore in the foreseeable future remain an important part of Swedish electricity production' (Swedish Government, 2009, p 47).

Investments in nuclear power are sometimes justified against the backdrop of rising electricity tariffs. Figure 2.5.4 compares the level of news media attention devoted to electricity pricing and nuclear power respectively.

Figure 2.5.4: News media coverage of nuclear power and electricity pricing

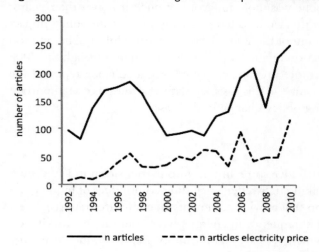

These data suggest that these agendas largely converge over time where high levels of news media attention to electricity pricing are accompanied by high levels of attention to nuclear power. One exception to this pattern is the period between 2006 and 2009 when these trends diverged. Electricity market developments may have been another external force that contributed to nuclear energy policy change, yet it may as well be the case that the convergence of agenda development is explained by uncertainty and public speculation regarding the future impact of nuclear power investments on electricity pricing. In fact, public inquiries (Ministry of the Environment, 2009, pp 302-3) as well as the 2009 decision (Swedish Government, 2009) emphasised the uncertain impact future investments in nuclear energy would have on electricity tariffs.

Political resources

Stakeholders may resort to a number of different resources to defeat opponents in the policy process. Public opinion is one such resource, which over time may sway the pendulum in favour of different policy preferences. Dramatic changes in public opinion may thus provide important stimuli for policy action and change (Erikson et al, 1994; Page and Shapiro, 1983; Sabatier and Weible, 2007). As mentioned above, prior research indicates covariation between public opinion on nuclear energy in Sweden and the direction of public policy making over time. However, public opinion data reported by Holmberg and Hedberg (2011) show that the 2009 decision to allow new reactors was not preceded by any sudden or major redistribution of public opinion. These data rather suggest that public opinion on nuclear power changed gradually from the early 1990s when opposition to nuclear energy started to decline and the support started to increase. The tipping point was between 2002 and 2003 when for the first time the relative majority of the general public was more in favour of nuclear power than against it. However, this shift does not seem to have had any immediate policy impact and cannot explain the timing of the 2009 decision. Meanwhile, public opinion indirectly affected the direction of energy policy development through the 2006 regime shift whereby the more pro-nuclear centre-right Alliance replaced the Social Democratic government. On this basis, legislative power was one important political resource explaining policy change in this case.

Venue access

Data reported by Uba (2010) give some insight into participation in key venues related to energy policy making in Sweden, including committees of inquiry and so-called *remiss* bodies (actors that provide comments on committee reports). These data document participation frequency in energy policy committees working on renewable energy issues, which yet have significant overlap with nuclear energy policy. Uba (2010) shows that the level of activity in these venues has fluctuated over time. Comparison between these two venues suggests that the relative openness (measured by the total number of actors appearing in each venue at any given point in time) of the committee venue gradually declined while the openness of the remiss venue increased over time. Next, among all committee members, parliamentarians constitute by far the largest category.

Participation frequency is a poor measure of the role of venues in explaining policy change, and other types of data would be required to study actual influence in these venues in greater depth. Specifically, other analytical approaches would be needed to assess the relationship between venue access and receptivity to new ideas in policy making. Yet a few observations can be made regarding venue participation and policy change in this case. First, the fact that parliamentarians have dominated the committee venue may provide additional support for the observation that the nuclear power issue remained politically sensitive throughout the 1990s and 2000s, and therefore that policy making was primarily subject to partisan negotiation. Meanwhile, the predominance of parliamentarians in committees is a more general trend that has also been observed across time and in other issues in Swedish policy making (Uba, 2010). Second, no major trends in venue access can be discerned that would account for the policy change in 2009. For example, there is no evidence to suggest that nuclear industry representation in key venues has increased over time, which would have been one potential explanation for the orientation towards more pro-nuclear policies. In summary, the data consulted for this analysis suggest that venue participation did not have any effect on policy change in this case.

Incumbent beliefs and interests

One straightforward explanation for policy change is the transformation of beliefs of incumbents into policy programmes. Such policy shifts may be enabled either by a regime shift – by which new actors with new policy beliefs enter office – or by the gradual shift in incumbents' belief systems over time (Cashore and Howlett, 2007). The latter is sometimes referred to as policy-oriented learning (Sabatier and Jenkins-Smith, 1999). In the case of Swedish nuclear energy policy, it can be noted that the trend towards more positive official policies started with the 2006 decision by the newly elected Alliance government not to phase out any reactors in 2006–10 and to lift restrictions on nuclear energy research. These shifts are consistent with the policy beliefs of the parties of the Alliance government, which gives some weight to the perception of policy change simply as the consequence of a regime shift.

Resorting to counter-factual reasoning, it can be noted that these policy changes would have been unlikely if the Social Democratic Party had remained in power after the 2006 election. In its election manifesto it stated that, 'We intend to phase out nuclear power step by step and in line with employment considerations and welfare and to the extent that it can be replaced with renewable energy and the efficient use of energy supplies' (2006, p 7). This statement was consistent with prior Social Democratic nuclear energy policy, and suggests that the 2006 regime shift was one necessary condition for the major policy change introduced in 2009.

Understanding the dynamics of policy change – particularly in highly politicised policy areas – also requires taking interests into account. Given high ideological conflict and issue salience, policy choice is likely to be driven by strategic political considerations and unpredictable bargaining processes (Jenkins-Smith, 1988). Such considerations include, for example, vote maximisation, office seeking, policy seeking, representation and party cohesion. Historically, political considerations have been critical to nuclear energy policy making in Sweden, particularly in relation to the 1979 Three Mile Island accident and the 1986 Chernobyl disaster, which were two events that challenged political decision makers regarding the future direction of Sweden's nuclear power programme. Since the level of politicisation was still high in this period, policy making was heavily influenced by partisan considerations including party cohesion, representation and vote maximisation (Nohrstedt, 2005, 2008). Political interests, particularly responsiveness to voter preferences, also appear to be one factor that accounts for the major policy change towards more positive nuclear energy policy in 2009. By the time of the decision, three out of the four Alliance government parties (Conservatives, Liberals and Christian Party) had relatively strong support for their pro-nuclear policies among their followers. Meanwhile, in order for the four-party Alliance government to ensure parliamentary majority for its new policy, the fourth Alliance party – the Centre Party – needed to give up its long-term resistance to nuclear power. Together with the Left Party and the Green Party, the Centre Party had been the most anti-nuclear party in Sweden for decades. Yet, in 2009 the party leadership unexpectedly committed to the revised nuclear energy policy. In Parliament, the new nuclear energy policy bill was approved by a tight majority (174 against 172), which in part was due to the fact that several Centre Party MPs voted against the party line and, thereby, against the government's official nuclear energy policy. Party leader Maud Olofsson explained the shift by arguing that 'the Centre Party has not changed its position on nuclear power, but we can live with nuclear power being part of Swedish electricity supply in a foreseeable future' (Svantesson, 2009, author's translation). The Centre Party decision to support the Alliance government policy may be partially explained by voter responsiveness. Through the 1970s and 1990s, Centre Party voters held strong anti-nuclear views. Yet between 2002 and 2009, the share of Centre Party voters supporting nuclear power more than doubled, from about 20 per cent in 2002 to over 40 per cent in 2009. This development was accompanied by a gradual shift of the official party policy towards more pro-nuclear beliefs in the 2000s (Holmberg and Hedberg, 2011).

Conclusions

Existing theoretical approaches to policy change seek to simplify the process by which external developments interact with institutions and motivational factors to influence policy making over time. This contribution seeks to clarify some of these elements and to demonstrate how they interact over time, using the case of Swedish nuclear energy policy during 1992–2010 as an empirical illustration. The scope of this analysis has been narrow, and the objective has been to grasp how external shocks, agenda setting, distribution of political resources, venue access, beliefs and interests interacted to influence policy making in this case. Several conclusions can be drawn from this analysis, which may inform comparative studies of policy change across policy areas and political systems.

One observation concerns the relative importance of broader sociopolitical forces vis-à-vis motivational factors as explanations for policy choice. To reiterate, policy process research seeks to grasp interactions between actors, events and contexts over time. One striking characteristic of Swedish nuclear energy policy is that the level of susceptibility of policy making to outside influence has changed over time. In the 1970s and 1980s, policy making was clearly susceptible to unanticipated events and developments (the most prominent example being the 1979 Three Mile Island accident, which paved the way for the Swedish nuclear power referendum), whereas the various incidents and shocks in the 2000s did not seem to have any long-term influence on nuclear energy debates and policies. It can be hypothesised that part of the explanation is a combination of public attention spans and the propensity to political risk taking. While the 2009 decision can be understood simply as the implementation of the more positive nuclear energy policies of the Alliance government, it can be noted that this decision coincided with relatively low public interest and modest opposition, which likely lowered the political risk associated with policy change. Once made public, the 2009 decision faced little opposition; some interest groups organised protests and demonstrations, which quickly faded. And so did the news media coverage (Figure 2.5.2). By the time of the decision, nuclear power was not seen as an important electoral issue or a prominent social problem, and in the last decade the majority of the Swedish population had become more supportive of nuclear energy. In return, the political risks of launching more pro-nuclear power policies were relatively low at the time of the decision.

Insights from this case inform theorising about general determinants of policy change and stability. According to Howlett and Cashore (2009), the understanding of major policy change depends on deeper theoretical analysis of the new orthodox-punctuated equilibrium model, which replaced incrementalism as the dominant approach to policy change analysis. Punctuated equilibrium theory has faced difficulties accounting for cases of major policy change in the absence of institutional change and also identifying causal mechanisms coupling institutions with policy outcomes (Robinson et al, 2007). The shift in official Swedish nuclear energy policy from a long-term emphasis on gradual phase out to replacement of existing plants shed some light on this interplay between institutions and policy making. Developments in this case cast some doubts over the assumption that the transformation of policy institutions is a necessary precondition for major policy change. The period studied here witnessed a gradual development towards more centralisation of policy making through tighter Cabinet control of nuclear energy policy making and a gradual decline in the importance of traditionally corporatist institutions (committees of inquiry). These developments are inconsistent with the punctuated equilibrium assumption that decision-making processes characterised by less 'friction' (that is, fewer participants and lower transaction and decision costs) are less likely to result in major policy change (Jones et al, 2003). Given the history of high political conflict over nuclear power in Sweden, the shift towards more centralisation of decision making is an insufficient explanation for policy change. What appears to have been more important was a combination of a gradual convergence between nuclear power policy and the climate change discourse and a gradual decline in public attention. Increasing attention to climate change may have changed the nuclear energy policy narrative from a focus on technological risks to the more profound challenge of climate change mitigation, whereas the drop in public attention lowered the political risks associated with policy change.

Part Three
Agenda setting

3.1
Introduction

There are close connections between the issues about stability and change examined in Part Two and the concerns about agenda setting here. Explaining the processes by which issues get onto the agenda is also obviously about explaining policy change. As Chloe Vlassopoulos argues in her contribution to Part Two (Chapter 2.2), the process by which social or public problems get onto the policy agenda is not straightforward. The contributions in this part, particularly that by Jennifer Curtin on gender equality policy (Chapter 3.5), reinforce this point .

On the one hand, the policy process is about problem solving, and policy actors will want their activity to appear purposive. But on the other hand, it is essential to frame analysis of public policy in the context of power in society. This means not just power to get things onto the agenda, but power to keep them off and power to influence policy formulation and implementation.

But the considerations about policy stability explored in Part Two are also relevant. Almost any policy we want to examine (1) has predecessors and (2) enters a crowded policy space. In that sense, while getting something onto the agenda may involve securing attention to fundamental policy change, it may be no more than securing a small shift of policy along a well-established pathway. Early in the history of policy process studies analyses of policy making that portrayed it as a relatively rational process of establishing goals and the best way to achieve them was challenged by a view that policy making is typically incremental in character (Lindblom, 1959).

Hence an approach to the examination of policy agenda setting is needed that is realistic about the power dimension and, in doing so, recognises the likelihood of resistance to shifts away from the existing status quo. Perhaps the most useful model is provided by John Kingdon (2010). He acknowledges the value of the incrementalist perspective, but argues that it is necessary to explain more discontinuous or sudden agenda change. In doing so he does not go back to the rational problem-solving model but rather sees policy processes as chaotic and hard to predict.

Kingdon describes three process streams flowing through the system:

- problems   • policies   • politics.

He argues that they are largely independent of one another, and each develops according to its own dynamics and rules. At some critical junctures the three streams are joined, and policy changes grow out of that.

Kingdon is of course not the only person who has tried to theorise agenda setting. Some further comments are necessary on his three 'stream' model, identifying the strengths and weaknesses of his approach and some of the alternative contributions on this topic.

It has already been argued that recognition of problems does not necessarily lead to policies. Taking issues about problems alone, there are matters to consider about their intensity. Birkland's (1998) notion of 'focusing events' is useful here, with its particular emphasis on environmental disasters. In her contribution to this part, Kristin O' Donovan's (Chapter 3.3) discussion of responses to floods in the USA develops this approach. So, in respect of rather different events, does Nao Kodate's (Chapter 3.4) examination of health and social care scandals. Consideration of problems in the context of power systems prompts the question: problems for whom? This takes the discussion on to Kingdon's other two streams.

Kingdon's arguments about his policies stream draws heavily on an extensive American literature on agenda building (see particularly Cobb and Elder, 1983). He explains the roles of what he calls 'policy entrepreneurs', likening them to – with his love of metaphors – surfers waiting for the big wave. Hence it is argued that there are many policies waiting to be adopted, and of course many are in competition with others.

There is an interesting comparative issue here. In the USA pressure groups are particularly evident in the policy process, making links with politics particularly through the teams of people serving members of Congress. While pressure groups are by no means absent elsewhere, the particular role of Congress in the legislative process makes this activity particularly salient there, and makes its competitive character particularly evident. In other countries either the unification of executive and legislature (as in the Westminster model of government) or corporatist consultative models may make policy building a less disaggregated process. Policy entrepreneurs may be more clearly integrated into the policy-making process, and indeed may even be within specific ministries. In this respect, as illustrated in Sonia Exley's contribution to Part Four (Chapter 4.5), their influence extends into policy formulation.

The 'big wave' (or 'window opening', another of Kingdon's metaphors) may come because of a crucial 'focusing event', but seems in Kingdon's analysis to be particularly associated with his third stream, a shift in political power. A related piece of theory that emphasises this is the notion of the 'issue-attention cycle' (Downs, 1972). In the most recent edition of Kingdon's book there is an appendix exploring US health policy reform in terms of his model. Here there is little dispute about the problem (although the question about 'whose problem' is relevant), and no lack of policy entrepreneurs with solutions (or part-solutions), but the third stream has been crucial: the election of a Democratic president.

But there are other issues about the politics stream. Weaver's notions of 'credit claiming' and 'blame avoidance' (1986) indicate ways in which political responses to problems and acceptance of policies may influence the agenda. In this respect a neglected element in Kingdon's analysis, the behaviour of the media, may be relevant. It is also important to see the politics stream as about more than the big electoral issues. The naming of many pieces of legislation in the USA after their congressional promoter pays tribute to something that may be more than simply political opportunism.

Again, therefore, comparative questions arise, one being whether significant shifts in political power are so important elsewhere. Several contributions in this book raise questions of this kind, notably Daniel Nohrstedt's (Chapter 2.5) discussion of nuclear power in Sweden and Jennifer Curtin's (Chapter 3.5) examination of gender equality policy in New Zealand. The other is whether the importance of mandates linking policies and politics make policy agenda-setting policies rather different elsewhere (see Hill, 2013, pp 174-6). In this respect, Gregory Marchildon's (Chapter 3.2) discussion of Canadian health reform is pertinent, together with another interesting institutional feature – a form of federalism in which a provincial government (in Saskatchewan) played a 'policy entrepreneur' role. What we have with these examples is in fact a lack of separation between Kingdon's policy and politics streams. Government departments may play roles as the promoters of policies to the extent that it may be relevant to talk of them as policy entrepreneurs or equally to stress the 'political' element in this activity. Jennifer Curtin's (Chapter 3.5) contribution highlights the role of a government agency as a promoter of policies.

These points about differences between countries in respect of both the policy and the politics stream point towards a more general issue about the way in which institutions (see the discussion of institutional theory in Part Two) affect the way in which the streams interact. Nao Kodate's (Chapter 3.4) comparative examination of responses to problems in Sweden and Japan particularly highlights this.

While this part has been labelled 'agenda setting', the reader may reasonably ask, where does agenda setting stop and policy formulation begin? There are many examples of issues getting onto the agenda but going no further. It is important not to forget the extent to which there is a 'symbolic' politics (Edelman, 1971, 1977, 1984) in which little effort is given to actually securing policy change. The discussion here has implied – most of the time – the use of the adjective 'successful' before agenda setting. It is important to recognise that the realisation of policy goals depends on a formulation process (that may be elaborate and extended) and an implementation process. These words get very often used in sometimes confusing ways in the policy process literature. For example, Marsh and Rhodes edited a volume called *Implementing Thatcherite policies* (1992b) that was rather more about the politics of the UK governments led by Margaret Thatcher in the 1980s and the ways in which aspirations were compromised 'early' in the policy-making process than about what most people call implementation.

Going back then to the arguments about incrementalism in the policy process, it is not surprising to find the agenda-setting process involving a sequence of compromises (as, for example, in the already mentioned health policy reforms in the USA) which then continue at least into the more detailed formulation process.

3.2

In the first contribution in this part Gregory Marchildon examines the development of the healthcare policy agenda in Canada. Events are explored, some of which are now fairly distant in time, but the value of this contribution is that it both highlights the value of Kingdon's analytical approach to the examination of agenda setting and also gives attention to institutional factors that need to influence the way Kingdon's model is applied. Hill (2013, chapter 9) has identified the need to take into account differences that apply when Kingdon's approach is used to analyse agenda setting within a Westminster-style of Cabinet government rather that in the context of the American-style congressional system of government. In the case of Canada, however, what is particularly interesting is also the interaction between provincial and federal governments highlighting the combination of Westminster-style government at the federal level, but a rather different kind of federalism with powerful federal units capable of playing agenda-setting roles.

The case study concerns how universal Medicare rose to the top of the policy agenda at the provincial and federal orders of government in Canada in the quarter century immediately following the Second World War, a position it would never again achieve in subsequent decades. After a brief description of agenda setting, the first phase of agenda setting for hospital coverage is reviewed, including the struggle over its design as either a targeted or a universal programme. This set the stage for the second phase, the emergence of universal medical care coverage, and the protracted struggle – including a 23-day doctors' strike in one province – aimed at defeating the policy. The contribution concludes with some potential reasons for the retreat of the policy of universal healthcare in terms of governmental agenda setting since the late 1960s.

Agenda setting in a parliamentary federation: universal Medicare in Canada

Gregory P. Marchildon

Introduction

Setting the policy agenda is one of the most basic yet overlooked components of the policy process. In his highly influential book, *Agendas, alternatives and public policies,* John Kingdon defined this *agenda* as 'the list of subjects or problems to which government officials, and people outside of government closely associated with those officials, are paying some serious attention at any given time' (2010, p 3). However, since policy agendas are invariably crowded with many worthy subjects and problems demanding redress, understanding how one policy subject or problem manages to take precedence over all others in a given time period is both interesting and instructive. Agenda setting describes the way in which key actors, working within a given institutional framework as well as historically contingent constraints and opportunities, are able to push one policy subject or problem to the front of a long line of other subjects and problems that a given government wants to address.

In this contribution, I apply Kingdon's concept of agenda setting to the policy case of universal Medicare in Canada. In the process, I investigate the extent to which Kingdon's findings, originally based on case studies of agenda setting and policy alternatives in the USA and its presidential-congressional check-and-balance system of divided authorities, are relevant to a Westminster parliamentary system, with its fused legislative and executive decision-making authority.

Like the USA, Canada is a federation in which policy responsibilities are divided between the central and substate governments. However, Canada is considerably more decentralised in terms of the policy responsibilities of its provinces compared to states in the USA or substates in most other federations (Marchildon, 2005). As a consequence, policy agenda setting often involves critical provincial actors, even in situations where the federal government subsequently plays a major role.

Case study of universal Medicare in Canada

The case study selected here is the introduction of universal Medicare, a major policy change that was phased in over two critical periods, each involving key actors in the provincial and federal governments. In the first phase, the provincial government of Saskatchewan first implemented universal hospital services coverage in 1947. A decade later, the federal government passed a law encouraging other provincial governments to initiate this same policy through shared-cost transfer payments. In the second phase, Saskatchewan again led the way by extending this coverage for all medically necessary physician services in 1962. Despite the significant opposition to this change, the federal government followed up a few years later with transfer funding that encouraged the adoption of the Saskatchewan model. Throughout this contribution, I identify the most important policy entrepreneurs in getting and keeping universal Medicare on the decision-making agenda. As will be seen, almost all of these individuals were key politicians in governing parties at the provincial and federal levels of government, a finding that is consistent with Kingdon's observation that politicians are more likely to be central in agenda setting. At the same time, these government leaders were assisted enormously by key bureaucrats in the specification of the policy, including the federal-provincial negotiations that produced the final model of Canadian Medicare.

Although the policy entrepreneurs never saw Canadian Medicare as static – they envisaged future additions to the basic package of coverage and contemplated eventual changes in the organisation of service delivery – their reform ambitions would not enjoy success, at least in terms of a national policy agenda, after the 1960s. The policy window for a more expansive universality at the national level had closed. Thereafter, policy development became more divided, with provincial governments acting on their own to improve health insurance coverage and the federal government attempting to protect what had already been achieved through the passage of the Canada Health Act in 1984. As a consequence, Medicare in Canada is historically defined in quite narrow terms, limited as it is to medically necessary hospital, diagnostic and physician services (Marchildon, 2012).

Before proceeding with this case study, I need to address a terminological challenge. The use of the word *universal* in healthcare policy is highly elastic. In one systematic review of 14 definitions of *universal health coverage*, the only common denominator was that the phrase meant people should get free or affordable medical and health services according to their needs (Bump, 2010). However, as pointed out by the World Health Organization (WHO, 2010b), an operational definition of universality should ideally address three essential dimensions of coverage: the population covered; the services covered; and the proportion of direct costs covered, even if priority has generally been given to the first of these factors. In the USA, for example, pro-reform advocates favouring the Patient Protection and Affordable Care Act of 2010 (that is, Obamacare) generally assumed that universality would be achieved if the vast majority of Americans had some form of health insurance (Kingdon, 2010; Starr, 2011). For the purposes of this contribution, universality is defined far more specifically as health coverage for the entire population on the same terms and conditions, and where none of the direct costs are borne by patients at the point of delivery. The former is known as single-tier coverage while the latter is called first-dollar coverage because it involves no user fees, co-payments or deductibles.

Phase I: universal hospital coverage

The story of universal Medicare begins with the provincial rejection of a federal proposal for national health insurance in the immediate aftermath of the Second World War. The key policy entrepreneur behind the federal offer was Dr John Joseph (J.J.) Heagerty, a senior bureaucrat in the federal Department of Pensions and National Health (MacDougall, 2012). Heagerty had been working on a national scheme of health insurance, one that would be administered by the provinces but developed in conjunction with the federal government under national standards in return for a significant federal contribution, throughout the 1930s. However, it was not until the 1940s that health insurance, as one dimension of the federal government's reconstruction efforts in the last years of the Second World War, became a viable possibility. There were four factors that most contributed to the opening of this new policy window: (1) rapidly growing federal revenues due to an improving economy after years of depression and a temporary wartime tax rental agreement with the provinces that contributed substantially to the federal treasury; (2) a shifting national mood that embraced a more expansive role for government in promoting individual security and equitable access to education and health; (3) the rise of a left-wing Social Democratic political party, the Co-operative Commonwealth Federation or CCF, which unambiguously supported a policy of universal health insurance and threatened the historic centre-left ground once occupied by the Liberal Party of Canada, which formed the government of Canada from 1935 until 1957; and (4) the space afforded to new welfare state policies in the Government of Canada's reconstruction agenda (Taylor, 1978; Finkel, 1993).

From the federal to the provincial policy agenda

Along with a number of major changes that included moving from means-tested public pensions to a single, universal pension scheme, universal health insurance formed a key part of the federal government's Green Book proposals that were tabled with provinces in August 1945, at the first of a series of Dominion-Provincial Reconstruction Conferences that would continue until their failure in 1946. The Government of Canada offered to support provincially administered schemes of hospital and medical insurance to the tune of 60 cents on the dollar. But, as part of the larger package of changes, the provinces had to agree to continue delegating their right to access personal, corporate and succession taxes to the federal government. This last condition proved impossible for a number of provinces to accept, especially for Ontario and Québec, the most populous and politically powerful provinces in the federation. Moreover, in the aftermath of the war and the decline of the threat of the CCF (at least at the federal level), Prime Minister Mackenzie King purposely engineered the failure of the negotiations (Finkel, 1993).

King was particularly hostile to the health proposals because he felt that the mechanism of federal transfers gave the provinces the politically enjoyable task of spending while saddling the federal government with the politically undesirable task of raising the revenues (Finkel, 1993). Instead, he wanted more policies with more voter appeal, and after the failure of the Conference in 1946, focused on a lower-cost federal programme of family allowances administered by central government. In King's view, Heagerty had overstepped his role as a civil servant by selling his health insurance plan to key stakeholders and provincial governments before and during the Reconstruction Conference (MacDougall, 2012).

Tommy Douglas and the CCF government of Saskatchewan

One of the premiers who had strongly supported the Heagerty Plan and the reformist impetus of the Blue Book proposals was the new Social Democratic premier of Saskatchewan. Elected with a strong majority in June 1944, Douglas was the head of the first CCF government in Canada, and what many at the time labelled the first 'Socialist' government in North America (Lipset, 1950). The CCF's platform included the principle that necessary health services were a fundamental human right that could be best achieved through universal coverage. Douglas' personal commitment to universal Medicare was so deep that he appointed himself Minister of Public Health, a position he would not relinquish until 1949 (Johnson, 2004). Immediately after the election, he established comprehensive hospital and medical care coverage for all social assistance recipients (Taylor, 1978; McLeod and McLeod, 2004).

At the same time, he invited Henry Sigerist, a medical historian at Johns Hopkins University, to visit Saskatchewan and to offer some recommendations as to how to proceed. The Sigerist report, which recommended a decentralised system of universal health coverage, helped Douglas set his position at the Dominion–Provincial Reconstruction Conference. When the federal offer was rejected by a majority of provinces in 1946, he decided that the province should proceed with universal hospital coverage on its own. Although his own officials were concerned about the lack of expertise and own-source funding needed to create and administer the plan, Douglas insisted on proceeding immediately, in part because of his fear that his government would be accused of not fulfilling a key component of its electoral platform in its first term of government (Johnson, 2004; McLeod and McLeod, 2004).

In the spring of 1946, Douglas introduced the Hospital Services Act in the provincial legislature, and set an implementation date of 1 January 1947. He then recruited Dr Fred Mott, Deputy Surgeon-General of the USA, who in turn hired fellow American Dr Len Rosenfeld, a senior health system specialist, to provide the expertise needed to implement an effective programme. Doing their best to put all the necessary pieces in place, Mott and Rosenfeld asked for an additional year to design and implement the programme. Douglas refused, insisting on his original date. Despite the early implementation, the programme turned out to be extremely well designed and managed, and every provincial government would eventually send their officials to the capital city of Regina to study the Saskatchewan scheme (Taylor, 1978).

Although Douglas had 'gone it alone', the Saskatchewan policy of universal hospital coverage would have national implications in terms of policy agenda setting. It had an immediate impact in other provinces. Attempting to emulate the Saskatchewan programme, the government of British Columbia (BC) introduced its own hospital insurance scheme in 1948. Although it shared the same objectives, the BC programme was not as well designed or managed and, years later, it would be fixed by a subsequent provincial administration in a manner that made it almost identical in design and operation to the Saskatchewan programme (Taylor, 1978; Marchildon and O'Byrne, 2012). In 1950, after concluding that the best defence was a good offense, an ideologically conservative government in Alberta introduced a non-universal alternative to the Saskatchewan plan in which private insurance carriers and user fees played a major role (Marchildon, 2012).

Impact of the Saskatchewan experiment on the Canadian federation

Saskatchewan's policy also had a demonstration impact within the federal government. This was something that Douglas always understood; he concluded after the failure of the Dominion-Provincial Reconstruction Conference that his province would first have to demonstrate the feasibility of universal coverage to get federal fiscal support in the future (Taylor, 1978). Although Mackenzie King, as well as his successor Louis St Laurent, were personally opposed to any major national health insurance initiative, they nonetheless had more left-wing ministers within their respective Cabinets who kept the idea alive. The individual most consistently supportive of a federally led health insurance initiative was Paul Martin Sr, Minister of National Health and Welfare from 1946 until 1957. He was able to support provincial initiatives and to keep the idea of federal involvement alive through a national health grants programme first introduced in 1948. Among the various provincial grants administered by Martin's department were hospital construction grants that allowed provinces such as Saskatchewan and BC to deal with the increase in acute care utilisation triggered by improved access, and health survey grants that allowed provinces to review their health systems with a view to introducing some form of public coverage.

In April 1955, Prime Minister St Laurent hosted the provincial premiers in a federal-provincial conference that would set the future working agenda for first ministers. Despite his best efforts to narrow the agenda down to fiscal relations and unemployment, a number of premiers insisted on returning to the unfinished business of national health insurance. Martin took advantage of the opportunity to convince St Laurent of the need to place health insurance on the agenda. On receiving a negative response, Martin threatened to resign unless St Laurent put health insurance on the agenda. Although St Laurent acceded, he insisted that the programme be restricted to hospital and diagnostic services, estimated to cost the federal treasury $22.60 (Canadian dollars) per capita, not including physician services estimated at a further $16.30 per capita (Taylor, 1978).

Martin's unlikely ally was Leslie Frost, the Progressive Conservative Premier of Ontario, who first laid the issue on the conference table. Frost made it clear that while the Ontario government was willing to proceed with universal hospital coverage, that it could not, and would not, proceed without federal cost-sharing. Frost had two reasons for forcing hospital insurance onto the federal-provincial agenda. The first was, by 1955, he had become convinced that despite the proclamations of the hospital associations, the doctors and the insurance industry, a policy of subsidising private health insurance on its own would not cover the whole population. Although Ontario was the most industrialised and wealthy province in the country, private health insurance still only covered two-thirds of Ontario residents. Moreover, due to special provisions that limited coverage for extremely expensive healthcare interventions as well as high co-payments, there was a serious problem of under-coverage. Access was blocked by high administrative costs, especially for individual policies, as well as cancellation clauses based on age or pre-existing conditions.

The issue of access loomed large in Frost's own mind as he had experience of losing his own private health insurance on reaching 60 years of age (Taylor, 1978). And despite the support of his party by business leaders and the insurance industry, he did not hesitate to criticise the private carriers in a meeting of the Standing Committee on Health that he had established himself to investigate the design of a provincial programme. As he put it, the carriers will 'insure you', but 'the minute there is some trouble, while they pay benefits for that particular illness, there is a rider attached to your policy, and that particular illness can never again be covered.... And then again, when you reach a certain age, you are cut off' (Frost, quoted in Taylor 1978, p 142).

The second reason Frost forced hospital insurance on a reluctant prime minister was that he faced an upcoming election in which two rival provincial parties – the Liberals and the CCF – were promoting universal health insurance. Added to this was his own belief that he could not introduce universal hospital coverage without running a large deficit. Frost's critical federal-provincial intervention was intended to take the political and fiscal monkey off his back and to put it onto the federal government so that criticism for any delay would be put on the prime minister and his federal Liberal government rather than his own provincial government. It was a position easily supported by a number of other provincial premiers who had even less fiscal room than Ontario.

Forced into a corner by the provinces and facing dissenters in his own Cabinet led by his Minister of Health and Welfare, St Laurent reluctantly agreed to put health insurance on the federal-provincial agenda. However, he stipulated conditions, which he privately hoped would delay if not defeat any ultimate agreement between his government and the provinces. The first was that coverage would be limited to acute care hospitals services and diagnostics, purposely excluding institutions (for example, mental hospitals and tuberculosis sanatoriums) and services (for example, physicians and home care that substituted for acute care) that the provinces hoped would be included. The second and most critical condition was that a minimum of six out of ten provinces with a majority of the population (thereby requiring the participation of either Ontario or Québec) had to agree before the federal government would proceed (Taylor, 1978).

On this basis, Paul Martin Sr began negotiating hospital insurance with the provinces on this basis, and was forced into the unenviable position of defending what became known as the six-province requirement. Even if there was considerable disagreement on the details of hospital insurance, all the key political actors, from the provinces and the federal government to the majority of provincial and federal opposition parties, appeared to favour the principle of universal hospital coverage (Boychuk, 1999).

When the Hospital Insurance and Diagnostic Services Act came before Parliament in 1957, John Diefenbaker and his Progressive-Conservative opposition argued for amendments, but nonetheless favoured the legislation and called for its early implementation. Diefenbaker was about to face the Liberals in an election and wanted to be clear he supported a policy that, according to opinion polls, was increasingly popular among Canadians. When the results were tallied in the general election of 10 June 1957, Diefenbaker's Conservatives won a minority government and the Liberals went to defeat after 27 uninterrupted years in power (Taylor, 1978). As a show of good faith to the provinces, Diefenbaker immediately announced his intention to remove the six-province requirement, and subsequently amended the law so that implementation could begin 1 July 1958. On that day, five provinces – BC, Alberta, Saskatchewan, Manitoba and Newfoundland – had eligible universal hospital coverage programmes in place. Ontario, New Brunswick and Nova Scotia would join six months later, Prince Edward Island on 1 October 1959 and Québec on 1 January 1961 (Taylor, 1978).

Phase 2: universal medical care insurance

When Saskatchewan received federal cost-sharing for its hospital programme, it freed up the fiscal resources to allow the provincial government to move to the next stage of Medicare – universal coverage for medical (that is, physician) services. The key actor in terms of agenda setting was again Tommy Douglas who would remain premier of the province until he left to become the federal leader of his party in October 1961. His successor, Woodrow Lloyd, in the face of an immense, organised opposition, was instrumental in keeping Medicare on the agenda and then implementing single-payer, universal medical care coverage in the months that followed (Johnson, 2004).

Douglas first announced his government's intention to introduce medical care insurance in a provincial by-election early in 1959. He then appointed an interdepartmental committee on Medicare made up of some of his government's most talented civil servants to work up the details of the programme and, after this, a public advisory body with committee members drawn from government, business, labour and the medical profession known as the Thompson Committee. In the provincial election of 1960, Douglas made medical care insurance the key plank in his platform. In response, the medical profession, with the support of the Canadian Medical Association, campaigned openly against Douglas and the CCF. Although the CCF would win the election, doctors continued to denounce the policy, threatening to leave the province if the government implemented its policy (Taylor, 1978; Naylor, 1986).

Trying to knock Medicare off the policy agenda

In October 1961, just days before his departure for federal politics, Douglas introduced the enabling law in the legislature. The original date set for implementation was 1 April 1962, but in response to the medical profession's demands for further discussion, Woodrow Lloyd moved the implementation date to 1 July 1962. Rather than appeasing organised medicine, the delay only fortified the growing sentiment in the anti–Medicare coalition that the government was backing down. This was further reinforced when the CCF government's former Minister of Health publicly resigned on the issue in April 1962. From this point forward, the conflict between the government and organised medicine intensified, finally culminating in a 23-day doctors' strike in July that was covered in detail not only by the national media in Canada but by major newspapers in the USA and the UK (Marchildon and Schrijvers, 2011).

Given the degree of opposition and the threatened doctors' strike before July 1962, the government could have found reasons first to delay implementation and later to abandon the policy. In fact, there are many examples of governments doing their utmost to place a policy at the top of its agenda only to abandon the policy in the face of virulent opposition, as occurred when the Clinton administration in the USA abandoned its proposed health system reform in the 1990s (Hacker, 1997; Starr, 2011). In contrast, Lloyd was determined to see the policy through to implementation, and although he conceded some ground in order to end the doctors' strike, the key features of single–tier universality were ultimately preserved (Marchildon and Schrijvers, 2011).

The immediate impact of the Saskatchewan initiative was again to force the agenda in some other provinces. Concluding that he had to fight the Saskatchewan model of universality with a viable non–universal alternative, Premier E.C. Manning of Alberta pushed the implementation of a targeted and voluntary approach that provided subsidies for those lacking the means to purchase private health insurance. Labelled 'Manningcare' by the media, the Alberta scheme actually resembled, in some key respects, the 'Obamacare' policy a half-century later (Marchildon, 2012). In response to public and CCF opposition pressure, Premier W.A.C. Bennett of BC introduced a similar programme based on subsidising private health insurance, although one with an attractive public option designed to boost enrolment (Marchildon and O'Byrne, 2012).

The Hall Commission and the national policy agenda

Although the birth of universal medical care coverage had been extremely perilous, the fragile infant grew into a robust child admired by many in the country. It proved so popular that it was preserved in Saskatchewan even after the CCF went down to electoral defeat in 1964. The popularity of universal Medicare was precisely what those opposed to the policy feared. In fact, in 1960, the anti-Medicare coalition attempted a pre-emptive strike by prevailing on Prime Minister Diefenbaker to establish a Royal Commission to examine health insurance so that non-universal alternatives could be set up to compete against the Saskatchewan model. Sensing an opportunity to buy some time, Diefenbaker asked a Saskatchewan jurist and fellow Progressive Conservative, Emmett Hall, to chair the Royal Commission on Health Services. Although he came from Saskatchewan, Hall seemed far from the ideology and objectives of the Douglas and Lloyd CCF governments, and therefore a safe choice from the perspective of the insurance lobby and organised medicine (Taylor, 1978; Naylor, 1986).

By the time the Hall Commission delivered its report in June 1964, Diefenbaker Conservatives were out of office, and the Liberals led by Prime Minister Lester B. Pearson were in. Although only leading a minority government, Pearson had been elected on a platform promising to modernise the welfare state in Canada, from improving access to post-secondary education and establishing a universal pension scheme, to working with the provinces to set up a national system of medical care insurance (Bryden, 1997, 2012). To almost everyone's surprise, the Royal Commission established by Diefenbaker and the Progressive Conservatives recommended that the federal government support, through shared-cost transfer funding, universal medical care coverage based on the Saskatchewan model. The Hall Commission rejected other models based on subsidies to private insurance carriers then being promoted by organised medicine and the business community, including Manningcare in Alberta, as incapable of achieving universality in terms of the percentage of population enrolled (Taylor, 1978; Naylor, 1986).

While the Hall Commission report made it easier for those within the Pearson government who were supportive of keeping universal Medicare high on the government's agenda, the fact remained that the environment in the 1960s was much less hospitable to the policy than that faced by the federal government in the 1950s. By the 1960s, the medical profession, led by a more radical anti-Medicare leadership, was much more adamant in its opposition to the principle of single-tier, first-dollar coverage (Naylor, 1986). Business leaders were more organised and eloquent on what they perceived as a dangerous and expensive expansion of the welfare state (Maioni, 1998). But what stood out most was the opposition of most provincial governments to universal Medicare. In particular, the premiers of British Columbia, Alberta and Ontario, were vocal in their opposition to the Hall Commission's recommendations and the Pearson government, set up subsidy-based models of Medicare, while successive premiers of Québec stated their opposition, on constitutional grounds, to federal involvement in shared-cost programmes (Taylor, 1978; Marchildon, 2012).

The struggle to keep Medicare on the national agenda

To make matters worse, Pearson's own Cabinet was sharply divided on the policy, with a left wing strongly in support and a right wing equally opposed. Led by Finance Minister Mitchell Sharp, Cabinet ministers in the right-wing clique did everything they could to push universal Medicare off the agenda, arguing that, in light of the government's decision to proceed with pension reform and funding transfers to the provinces to expand access for post-secondary education, there was no longer any fiscal room for universal Medicare. At a minimum, they reasoned, the government needed to delay implementation for a number of years. However, Pearson's most senior political staff member and top policy adviser, Tom Kent, supported by the left-wing group of ministers, continually pushed the prime minister to keep to his promise and timetable on universal Medicare. Kent was ably supported by A.W. Johnson, a senior finance official and federal-provincial negotiator, who had once worked for the CCF government in Saskatchewan (Kent, 1988; Bryden, 2012).

Initially, Pearson followed the left-wing script. In a federal-provincial meeting in July 1965, he made it clear to the premiers that federal funding would soon be available for medical care coverage, but on the condition that the provincial programmes be designed as universal and single-tier with first-dollar coverage. An enabling law – the Medical Care Act – was drafted with these conditions plus an implementation date of 1 July 1967. However, an early election in November 1965, urged on him by the left-wing group in the hope that he would get a more solid political mandate, produced no change, and diminished this group's influence in Cabinet. Months later, the federal government announced its intention to replace the original implementation date in the Medical Care Act with a later date of 1 July 1968, and it was this bill that was passed in Parliament in December 1966. Even then, Pearson continued to reconsider the implementation date as Sharp and his supporters pushed for an even longer delay. Only after a number of his left-wing ministers threatened to resign did Pearson agree to proceed on 1 July 1968. While only two provinces – BC and Saskatchewan – were immediately able or willing to meet the federal conditions, all provinces came into the scheme over the next three years, making universal Medicare for hospital, diagnostic and now physician services a reality for all Canadians.

Epilogue and conclusions

Since the 1960s there has been no sustained momentum by the federal government and provinces to expand universal Medicare. Instead, beginning in the 1970s, provincial governments focused on providing some subsidies and programmes for prescription pharmaceuticals, dental care and long-term care including home care. However, the vast majority of these initiatives have been targeted rather than universal policies, and none have operated under national conditions, including the principle that benefits are portable in all provinces. For its part, the federal government has limited itself to protecting the gains made in the 1950s and 1960s through the passage of the Canada Health Act in 1984.

At a deeper level, there has also been a sea change in the national mood, in particular the sustained attack on, and retreat from, the welfare state in general, and universality in social programming in particular. While there has been no shortage of major studies that have recommended the expansion of universal Medicare – the National Forum on Health in the 1990s and a Royal Commission in the early 2000s – these have had limited impact on the federal–provincial agenda (Marchildon, 2005). More importantly, the general intellectual climate has moved in the opposite direction, towards less state involvement in healthcare policy and a larger role for the private sector. In particular, federal and provincial governments have become more preoccupied with controlling programme costs and reducing individual and corporate tax burdens since the early 1990s, and since the late 1990s, in bringing down the rate in the growth of government health expenditure.

However, as Green-Pederson and Wilderson (2006) point out, the political dynamics of universal benefits, including the providers who benefit from public funding, can make it difficult for any government to reverse the original policy. This self-reinforcement has, over time, increased the cost of reversing course, and reverting to a model based on private health insurance (Pierson, 2004). In addition, the idea that access should be based on medical need rather than the ability to pay has become a part of the Canadian identity, one that right-of-centre governments have been careful to challenge.

In conclusion, despite the differences between the Canadian and American political systems, this case study bears out some of Kingdon's findings, especially the centrality of political rather than bureaucratic or interest group actors in the agenda-setting stage of the policy process. However, unlike the case in a divided congressional system, a more unitary parliamentary system, where the executive plays a critical role in setting the legislative agenda, changes in government and electoral mandates play a larger role in both agenda setting and, in parallel, the specification of the policy pursued by government. In the two decades the CCF government of Saskatchewan held office, for example, it was committed to its initial electoral promise of introducing universal Medicare, and a design of a government-administered, single-tier programme providing first-dollar coverage to all provincial residents. Even in the face of enormous opposition, as experienced from 1960 until the doctors' strike of 1962, universal Medicare could not be dislodged from that government's agenda.

Although Canada and the USA are both federations, Canadian provinces have much more policy authority and responsibility than US states. In this more highly decentralised environment, there is more latitude for key policy actors – policy entrepreneurs – at the provincial level. At the same time, there is an important interplay between policy actors at both levels of government. In this case, policy initiation was at the provincial level and that was eventually followed up at the federal level of government where the policy was locked in, achieved under a set of common, national operating principles.

The key policy entrepreneurs were largely at the political level, often the first ministers of these respective governments. Occasionally, a policy off-ramp was used, allowing for a policy entrepreneur outside government to exercise considerable influence. In parliamentary systems, the traditional policy off-ramp is a Royal Commission, and in this case Emmett Hall and his Royal Commission report helped ensure that universal Medicare would remain high on the federal government's agenda (Marchildon, 2007). Nonetheless, a majority of key policy entrepreneurs in this case study were provincial premiers such as Tommy Douglas, Leslie Frost, Woodrow Lloyd and Ernest Manning, or federal prime ministers such as John Diefenbaker or Lester Pearson.

3.3

The aspect of Kingdon's agenda-setting model that has probably been given most attention, and had the biggest impact on research, is the way in which problems influence policy. Birkland's exploration of 'focusing events' (1988) is particularly salient in this respect. The contribution here explores the respective relevance of focusing events and political dispositions in the development of flood mitigation policy in the USA.

The purpose of this contribution is to examine flood mitigation policy, specifically, land acquisition and relocation policy in the USA. It asks what are the important factors associated with state adoption of land acquisition and relocation policy in an intergovernmental system of government? It begins by introducing floods as a policy problem in the USA. Second, it presents the theoretical framework from diffusion of innovations theory and elements of agenda-setting theory, particularly focusing on events to identify the correlates of policy adoption . Third, it presents the important correlates associated with state adoption of land acquisition and relocation policy. Fourth, it discusses the results as they relate to flood mitigation policy and to theories of the policy process.

Flood mitigation policy in the United States

Kristin O'Donovan

Floods in the USA

Overall natural disasters play a unique role in the policy process. When cast as focusing events, natural disasters often draw sharp media attention, particularly to property damage and casualties. Images of disaster damage can be pervasive in the aftermath of a flood, and the symbolism stemming from a flood can have a powerful influence on the policy process. Floods are one of the most common natural hazards in the USA. They account for 80 per cent of all the disasters receiving a Presidential Disaster Declaration (Godschalk et al, 1999). In 2008, of the 75 major Disaster Declarations, 70 per cent were for flooding caused by severe storms (Department of Homeland Security, 2009, p 26).

In the Eastern USA and along the Gulf Coast hurricanes and tropical storms are the most common cause of floods. In the Western USA most floods are caused by snowmelt and rainstorms (USGS, 2006). Between 1964 and 2007, there were 1,500 Presidential Disaster Declarations, of which 605 were floods, accounting for 40 per cent of all the major Disaster Declarations during the 43-year period. Between 2000 and 2007 there were 377 Presidential Disaster Declarations, 62 Disaster Declarations were for floods, or 16 per cent of all the Declarations. Floods were second only to severe storms during that time, and represented 50 per cent of all the Presidential Disaster Declarations. In many instances, severe storms and flooding were both listed as the cause of the disaster. However, these figures tend to obscure the scope and magnitude of the flooding hazard in the USA. The increase of flood damage costs over time is more revealing. In terms of dollar value of flood damage, '... 1960s floods caused $41.69 million dollars of damage a year. By the 1990s, average annual property damage from flooding increased to $378.12 million dollars a year (in 1960 dollars)' (Brody et al, 2007, p 330).

The intergovernmental nature of disaster management means that local governments are initially responsible for the response to the disaster. If their resources and capabilities are overwhelmed, then they turn to state government for assistance. If the scope and magnitude is large enough to overwhelm the state government's resources and capabilities, then the governor requests assistance from the Federal Emergency Management Agency (FEMA) through the Presidential Disaster Declaration process. The majority of disasters that occur in the USA are not big enough to register federal attention, meaning that individuals, businesses and local and state governments bear the cost of recovery from disaster (Burby et al, 1998).

Floods in particular can be highly localised events. On average, the US Geological Survey (USGS) estimates that floods cost US$6 billion in damage and cause 14 deaths per year; major floods such as the 1993 Great Midwest Flood and the flooding that resulted from Hurricane Katrina caused US$20 billion and US$200 billion in damage respectively (USGS, 2006).

Flood mitigation policy In the USA

It is important to distinguish between the terms 'hazard', 'risk' and 'disaster'. I adopt the definitions employed by Haddow, Bullock and Coppola (2008, p 27) who adopt the National Governors' Association's definitions for 'hazard', 'risk' and 'disaster': *hazard* as 'a source of danger that may or may not lead to an emergency or disaster and is named after the emergency/disaster that could be so precipitated'; *risk* as 'susceptibility to death, injury, damage deconstruction, disruption, stoppage, and so forth'; and *disaster* as 'an event that demands substantial crisis response requiring the use of government powers and resources beyond the scope of one line agency or service.'

When a flood hazard and risk of flooding are both present, it suggests that there is a possibility that a community will be susceptible to injury, the loss of life, property or disruption in daily services and activities *as a result of* the flood hazard. However, it is possible for hazards to exist with no or very minimal risk to life and property. If a river routinely floods but there are no injuries, deaths, disruptions or property damage, it poses no real risk to human settlements. Managing hazards by minimising risk is the goal of mitigation. Gilbert White (1945) and others (Burby et al, 1998; Birkland et al, 2003) have long argued that land use practices and planning are usually more effective long-term mitigation techniques than building damns and levees to make flood-prone areas habitable. This idea is now central to modern hazard mitigation practices, but the extent and rate of adoption of these kinds of policies by the states is highly variable (May and Deyle, 1998; Godschalk et al, 1999).

In the most general sense, there are four key components of disaster management and policy: mitigation, preparation, response and recovery. These four components have been conceived in terms of pre-disaster activities in the mitigation and preparedness stages that are passive in nature and in the after-impact stages of the cycle that include response and recovery that are reactive in nature (Prater and Lindell, 2000). The idea that mitigation, preparation, response and recovery occur in an ordered, cyclical way is unrealistic. However, it is useful to consider these activities as interrelated and to some extent, mutually reinforcing.

Structural mitigation policy innovations include building dams, levees, floodwalls, floodgates and other constructed elements to control or divert the flow of floodwaters. The primary approach in structural mitigation has been to control the flow of water in flood-prone areas by using levees and other engineered systems. While this action has prevented significant losses in flood damage, it has also encouraged development in hazardous areas, with sometimes catastrophic effects on cities like New Orleans and broader environmental concerns associated with floodplain management (Birkland et al, 2003).

Non-structural mitigation policies include insurance requirements, comprehensive land use planning mandates, hazard mitigation planning requirements, hazard-sensitive building codes, land acquisition and relocation and wetland reclamation and protection. Rather than engineer structures to control floodwaters, states can adopt policies that work with the environment, minimise damage to naturally occurring flood control measures, and do not create a false sense of security about flood risks while making catastrophic disasters more likely. The most common non-structural hazard mitigation policy innovations adopted by states include: regulation of development in hazardous areas; requirements for local governments to enforce hazard-specific portions of the state building code; comprehensive planning mandates; policies supporting land acquisition in hazard-prone areas; and public infrastructure investment decisions (May and Deyle, 1998).

Land acquisition and relocation policy

Land acquisition and relocation policies are designed to physically move people and property out of flood-prone areas, including wetlands and floodplains that have usually been subjected to repetitive flooding. Acquisition and relocation policy emerged in the 1970s when the state of Florida adopted the Environmental and

Land and Water Management Act in 1972, and has been on the forefront of land acquisition and relocation policies (Godschalk et al, 1999). Land acquisition and relocation allows areas that are subject to severe flooding a permanent way to mitigate floods. Land acquisition tends to be compatible with other non-structural mitigation techniques such as floodplain conservation (Godschalk et al, 2003). However, land acquisition and relocation policies can be difficult to implement for two reasons: one, because of landowner resistance or reluctance to be relocated; and two, complex funding sources to purchase the land (Burby and Kaiser, 1986; Godschalk et al, 2003). In spite of these challenges, land acquisition and relocation policies have been found to be very effective, particularly for communities that already have high levels of development in a floodplain or for communities that have few alternative sites for development outside of a floodplain (Burby and French, 1985).

Until the mid-1990s, land acquisition and relocation policies had been the domain of state and local governments, but in 1995 Congress amended the Stafford Act (PL 100-707) to provide disaster mitigation assistance to states. This programme came to be known as the Hazard Mitigation Grant Program (HMGP) and it included, among other mitigation techniques, federal funding for states and communities to purchase flood-prone land to mitigate the effects of floods and to relocate people and property outside of the floodplains. The HMGP was created in response to the devastating 1993 Great Midwest Flood. The 1993 Great Midwest Flood affected nearly every state in the Midwest, resulting in US$15 billion in damage and 50 deaths, but Iowa, Kansas, Minnesota, Missouri and Nebraska bore the brunt of the flooding (Sylves, 2007). A significant shortcoming of the HMGP, however, is that it provided funding after a disaster for mitigation, not before a disaster when it might do the most good. Significant policy changes have occurred since the adoption of the Stafford Act, most notably the adoption of the Disaster Mitigation Act of 2000 (DMA). Under the DMA, the HMGP was continued and supplemented, and a new pre-disaster mitigation was also created. However, executive branch requests and congressional appropriations for these programmes have lagged far behind the demand for mitigation assistance, and less money and effort are being devoted to mitigation programmes now than were expended in the 1990s.

In 1995, 20 states had adopted land acquisition and relocation policies, 13 of the states set aside state funds specifically for the purpose of acquiring flood-prone land for mitigation, and the other states assisted local governments in securing federal HMGP funding for post-disaster mitigation (Godschalk et al, 1999). State-level adoption of land acquisition and relocation policies and federal policy priorities for mitigation, particularly land acquisition and relocation, suggest that there may be different underlying causes leading certain states to adopt their own acquisition and relocation policies, while others chose to rely solely on federal resources to acquire flood-prone land.

Diffusion of policy innovations

Policies represent ideas that are solutions to public problems (Stone, 1989; Kingdon, 2010). Policy ideas emerge and are introduced into the public debate, are considered, and are subsequently adopted or rejected. For a policy idea to be considered, it must possess some degree of acceptability with policy makers and the general public. For example, the best way to completely mitigate flood hazards is ideally to permanently remove people and property out of floodplains and away from shorelines. This would be unacceptable as a policy innovation for a number of reasons including the cost associated with complete mitigation, the political unpopularity of such a policy and the implications for private property rights (Prater and Lindell, 2000).

The broader policy environment influences the feasibility of adopting a policy idea, or innovation. This broader policy environment contains two sets of influences: those internal to a state and influences external to a state. Internal influences include political and institutional factors, economic conditions and sociodemographic conditions. External factors that influence adoption include the actions of neighbouring or regional states, the decisions of the federal government and flooding events.

In terms of political and institutional factors, classic diffusion studies have examined public opinion, specifically political ideology, and hypothesised that ideologically liberal states tend to adopt certain policy innovations that conservative states reject (Berry and Berry, 1992; Allen et al, 2004; Daley and Garand, 2005). For example, in the case of tax policy, Berry and Berry (1992) found that more liberal states would adopt new income taxes because ideologically liberal states would have more spending programmes, rendering new tax revenue necessary. Political institutions also play an important role in the diffusion process, and these institutions can create a favourable climate for adoption (Berry and Berry, 1992). Finally, diffusion studies have considered the influence of elections on the process of state policy adoption (Walker, 1969; Gray, 1974; Berry and Berry, 1992; Mintrom, 1997; Mintrom and Vergari, 1998). The proximity of elections has an effect on state policy adoption. '[S]tates with four-year gubernatorial election cycles are most likely to adopt a new tax in the year after an election, less likely to adopt a tax in the second and third years after an election, and least likely to adopt in an election year' (Berry and Berry, 1992, p 729). Diffusion was expanded to consider the legislative agenda and in off-years for legislative elections, a policy innovation is likely to be *considered* for the legislative agenda but the same innovation is less likely to be placed on the legislative agenda during an election year (Mintrom and Vergari, 1998).

State financial health is sometimes used as a proxy for economic stability and is positively associated with policy adoption. Often state financial health is assessed using state GDP (gross domestic product), a state's manufacturing outputs (Walker, 1969; Allen et al, 2004; Daley and Garand, 2005) or state budget performance

(Berry and Berry, 1992). The underlying rationale is that the better the financial health of a state, the more likely it will be to adopt a policy innovation. This contribution relies on state GDP as a proxy for financial health for two reasons. First, not all states have equivalent manufacturing bases and second, state budget shortfalls may conflate state government fiscal health with overall state fiscal health.

Finally, with respect to sociodemographic characteristics, high levels of personal wealth in a state have been positively associated with the diffusion of policy innovations (Walker, 1969; Gray, 1974; Berry and Berry, 1992; Mooney, 2001; Daley and Garand, 2005).

External influences include policy decisions by neighbouring states, policy decisions by the federal government and the disasters themselves. While flood mitigation policies are intergovernmental in nature, the transfer of policies and ideas are murky at best. Specifically, reasons for the transfer of flood mitigation policies from state to state, from state to federal government or from the federal government to state governments, remain unclear. The federal government has been an actor in flood mitigation policy under a patchwork of pre- and post-disaster mitigation legislation including the Robert T. Stafford Act, as amended by the 2000 DMA, the Post-Katrina Emergency Reform Act (PKEMRA) and the National Flood Insurance Act of 1968.

In the context of diffusion studies, we know that when states face a lack of leadership or clear information from the federal government, they will act independently to address a particular policy problem. In this instance, states are motivated to adopt by the desire to have a competitive edge over neighbouring states, to avoid being at a disadvantage to neighbouring states or in response to public opinion (Berry and Berry, 1999). But while states have indeed acted independently of the federal government to adopt policies to mitigate natural hazards, adoption has been uneven and the types of policies have varied from state to state (May and Deyle, 1998). This variation has been attributed to a state's commitment and capacity to mitigate hazards (Godschalk et al, 1999). Obviously, risks also vary state to state because of differences in geography and topography. While Godschalk's and May and Deyle's research has explained the reasons underlying the *unevenness* of state-level mitigation policy adoption, it has not fully examined the reasons why states choose to adopt one type of mitigation policy instead of another. In addition it has not considered how recent flooding disasters might affect state-level policy adoption. This is relevant to research on hazards and disasters because it opens an avenue of study that focuses on states as policy leaders in hazard mitigation rather than the federal government. States do not adopt mitigation policies in a vacuum, and this accounts for the federal government's tendency to play an influential, but not the *primary*, role in mitigation policies.

Data and analysis

This study relies on a dataset that measures the factors associated with policy adoption. The data has been assembled from a variety of publicly available data sources. The indicator measuring state adoption of an acquisition and relocation policy was collected from official legislative and governmental records and supplemented by additional data from the Association of State Floodplain Managers (ASFPM). Twenty-eight states adopted a land acquisition and relocation policy from 1968 and 2008. There are two major clusters of states adopting in the 1970s and the 1990s (see Table 3.3.1).

Table 3.3.1: States adopting a land acquisition and relocation policy

Year	States	Year	States
1969	Wisconsin	1993	Illinois
1972	Mississippi		Iowa
	Florida		North Dakota
1976	Maryland		Oklahoma
	Virginia		Indiana
1977	Arizona		South Carolina
	Georgia	1994	Maine
	Michigan	1995	Alaska
1978	Colorado		Missouri
	Massachusetts		Nebraska
	Rhode Island		New Jersey
1986	Tennessee	1997	Kentucky
1987	Minnesota		North Carolina
		1999	Alabama
		2004	Connecticut

Measures for internal characteristics of adoption were derived form the following sources: mass liberalism was used as a proxy for state ideology and was calculated by Berry, Fording, Ringquist, Hanson and Klarner (1998). In this context, mass liberalism refers to citizen preferences on the size and scope of the role of government, ranging from liberal to conservative along a continuum. The measure for unified government was calculated by the author using data from the *Book of States* (1968–2008); electoral competition, that is, proximity to an election, year, was also calculated by the author using election cycle data from the *Book of States* (1968–2008); the measure for legislative professionalism was based on Squire's (2005) calculation; and state fiscal health was measured using state GDP from the US Census Bureau.

Measures assessing external influences were developed as follows:

• regional influence was measured based on the number of neighbouring states that had adopted the land acquisition and relocation policy in the prior year of measurement;
• federal fiscal influence is a lagged measure based on federal mitigation spending per state, per year;
• federal agenda influence was measured based on lagged count data on the number of congressional hearings held on mitigation policy;

- finally, measures for focusing events, specifically the fatalities, injuries and property damage caused by floods in a given state/year, was collected from the spatial hazard events and losses database for the USA (1968–2008).

Analysis

The question posed at the outset of this contribution asked, what are the factors that are important for state adoption of a land acquisition and relocation policy? The question is one of association, not prediction. Accordingly, this study presents the results of a simple correlation analysis to determine the important factors that are associated with adoption. Correlation coefficients for Kendall's tau are reported because of the ordinal and interval nature of the data. Because the data includes the entire population and contains no random effects, all of the results are statistically significant. However, to conform to convention, significance is reported at $p>0.05$ level. The results of this study should be treated as limited because they are simply indicative of association and relative magnitude, not causal or directional findings (see Table 3.3.2).

Political ideology, specifically state mass liberalism, is not strongly associated with adoption of land acquisition and relocation policies. Political ideology is believed to generally shape the policy environment in diffusion theory (Karch, 2007). The

Table 3.3.2: Correlates with state adoption of an acquisition and relocation policy

Theoretical construct	Variable	Correlation coefficient	Sig
Internal[a]			
	Citizen liberalism	−0.01	0.632
	Politically unified government	−0.038	0.109
	Gubernatorial electoral competition	0.019	0.416
	Legislative electoral competition	−0.01	0.696
	State GDP	0.044a	0.038
	Per capita income	0.022	0.293
	Legislative professionalism	−0.009	0.723
External			
	Regional influence	−0.022	0.403
	Federal legislative adoption	0.047	0.071
	Congressional mitigation hearing	0.031	0.212
	Federal mitigation spending	−0.022	0.392
Focusing events			
	Property damage	0.051a	0.02
	Injuries	0.006	0.806
	Fatalities	0.032	0.192
	Time since flood	−0.014	0.586

Note: [a] Correlation is significant at the 0.05 level (2-tailed).

presence of a unified government was negatively but weakly associated with a state adoption of a land acquisition and relocation policy.

Gubernatorial electoral competition, that is, the proximity to a gubernatorial election, is weakly and positively associated with state adoption of a relocation and acquisition policy. Conversely, this study finds that legislative electoral competition, that is, proximity to a legislative election year, is negatively and weakly associated with state adoption. Fiscal health, as measured by state GDP, was moderately associated with adoption of a land acquisition and relocation policy, while per capita income was weakly associated with adoption. Professional legislatures are negatively and weakly associated with adoption.

Regional influence, as measured by neighbouring states adopting an acquisition and relocation policy, was negatively and moderately associated with adoption. Federal influence, as assessed by federal legislative adoption, was positively and moderately associated with state adoption. Presence on the federal agenda, as measured by congressional mitigation hearings, was positively and moderately associated with adoption. Finally, federal fiscal influence, as measured by spending on mitigation programmes, was negatively and moderately associated with adoption.

Variables for focusing events have mixed association with state adoption of a land acquisition and relocation policy. Property damage was strongly and positively associated with adoption. Injuries were weakly associated with adoption and fatalities were moderately associated with adoption. The time since a flood was weakly and negatively associated with adoption.

Discussion

This study used diffusion of innovations to select indicators associated with state adoption of land acquisition and relocation policies to mitigate floods. It then produced a correlation analysis to determine which indicators had an important statistical relationship with adoption. This section discusses the results of the study as framed by the theoretical constructions outlined under diffusion of innovations theory.

Internal

As noted earlier, classic diffusion theory indicates that the internal characteristics of a state, such as political ideology, state fiscal health, electoral competition, politically unified government and professional legislatures, are indicators of adoption. In the case of land acquisition and relocation policy diffusion, state fiscal health, as indicated by state GDP, is an important correlate of adoption. It is impossible to determine the direction of the relationship, that is, whether states that adopt have higher levels of GDP or whether states with higher rates of GDP are adopters. However, the importance of the relationship between state GDP and adoption is well supported in the diffusion literature. This means that diffusion theory indicates that high levels of personal wealth in a state have been positively associated with the diffusion of policy innovations (Walker, 1969; Gray, 1974; Berry and Berry, 1992; Mooney, 1991; Daley and Garand, 2005).

External

In the correlation analysis, the relationship of external influences on state policy adoption of land acquisition and relocation policies is weak and negative. Given what we know from empirical research on diffusion theory, the role of regional influence is mixed. Regional influence is characterised by the assumption that 'states are influenced primarily by those states that are geographically proximate' (Berry and Berry, 1999, p 175). However, the influence of neighbouring states adopting a policy may not be the same over time, and the extent to which the influence of neighbours adopting may be limited. Mooney (1991) suggests that regional influence may be important during the early stages of diffusion when policy innovations are new and little information is available to decision makers, but over time, as the policy innovations are implemented, the regional influence will lessen.

This seems particularly true of states that were among the first adopters of land acquisition and relocation policies, Mississippi and Florida's respective adoptions in 1972 appear to have triggered subsequent adoptions in neighbouring states like Georgia in 1977. However, this pattern of regional influence does not appear to be consistent over time. The 1993 Great Midwest Flood affected nearly every state in the Midwest, resulting in US$15 billion in damage and 50 deaths, but Iowa, Kansas, Minnesota, Missouri and Nebraska bore the brunt of the flooding (Sylves, 2007). Among these states, only Iowa adopted land acquisition and relocation following the flood.

With respect to national influence, In terms of policy diffusion theory, indicators of national intervention or influence that have been used in diffusion studies include financial incentives to adopt a policy (Allen et al, 2004), federal agency spending per state (Daley, 2007), national legislation regarding a policy (Karch, 2007) and presidential statements indicating policy preferences (Karch, 2007).

For natural hazard mitigation policy and flood mitigation policies specifically, the influence of the federal government has shifted overtime. Traditionally flood mitigation had been the purview of local and state governments, but gradually the federal government has taken on more of a policy leadership role. This shift is consistent with trends in intergovernmental relations in other policy areas. Beginning in the 1970s and 1980s coercive federalism replaced more cooperative practices as the federal government assumed an active position in policy leadership that superseded the authority of state and local governments through mandates or financial incentives (Kincaid, 1990).

Land acquisition and relocation policies had been adopted by states and were well established by the time the federal government passed the Stafford Act in 1988. This seeming lack of federal influence could be explained by the mixed role that it has played in mitigation overall. Subsequent funding, defunding, refunding, repealing and re-adoption of a land acquisition and relocation policy by the federal government in the 1990s and 2000s suggests that states took the initiative to innovate based on unclear signals from the federal government. This is consistent with diffusion literature that indicates that when the national government sends a mixed message to states about policy preferences, its influence on state policy adoption is weak (Allen et al, 2004).

Focusing events

A clear, albeit weak, thread emerges suggesting that flood severity is positively associated with state adoption of land acquisition and relocation policies. Furthermore, property damage is an important element associated with the spread of the land acquisition and relocation policy. Property damage, along with casualty indicators, are used as a proxy to assess the severity of flood.

Flood severity tells a story about the role of flood damage as a contributing factor creating a favourable environment for adoption of a mitigation policy. For diffusion theory, this suggests a rationale that indicators of adoption need not always be direct to contribute to a favourable environment for state policy adoption. This idea is consistent with the favourable 'background conditions' rationale adoption for classic diffusion indicators such as legislative professionalism (Karch, 2007) and political indicators (Allen et al, 2004; Daley and Garand, 2005).

For agenda-setting theory, these findings support the idea that harm revealed by an event is a key aspect of potential focusing events. It is not possible to determine the extent of fears about future harm revealed by a flood played in this study. However, this case invites further exploration of the role that focusing events plays in the diffusion process as a catalyst to spark diffusion.

The correlation analysis indicates that the frequency of a flood is negatively associated with adoption. Although it is a weak indicator, it suggests that chronic floods may be associated with non-adoption. This means that the idea that focusing events are powerful triggers for policy change warrants further testing.

Consequently, the influence of the focal nature of the event and the policy had different implications on acute and chronic flood hazards. To wit, this provides preliminary evidence, suggesting that when in the context of a diffusion of innovations study, focusing events can lead to different motivations for state policy innovation. Potential harm from a flood might be revealed by the experience of a recent flood. If enough time has elapsed since a flood, a state might be less likely to adopt because of the perception that floods do not pose a serious threat to life and property.

Conclusions

This contribution introduced the idea of floods as a policy problem in the USA, and provides an overview of floods and flood mitigation policy. This was followed by a theoretical framework from diffusion of innovations theory and aspects of focusing events to identify the important correlates of adoption. It concluded by discussing the results of the analysis and what they might mean for flood policy and theories of the policy process. It shows that the relationship between focusing events and responses to them is far from straightforward, with political and institutional contexts having a significant impact.

3.4

Focusing events are, as in the last contribution, a central concern of this one, by Nao Kodate. But while Kristin O'Donovan offered us quantitative comparison within a single federal system, Nao's exploration of agenda setting, in respect of health and social care regulation in Sweden and Japan, uses a qualitative approach to look at the ways in which institutional and political differences are important for the explanation of events.

This contribution examines some major malpractice incidents in the late 1990s through the early 2000s in Sweden and Japan, comparing how these incidents opened up pathways for a new type of regulation for health and social care services in each case. Applying John Kingdon's model of agenda setting and policy change, Nao Kodate argues that governance arrangements determine how an event may be translated into a political agenda item by throwing light on the problems within the public domain. In Sweden and Japan, major malpractice incidents in the late 1990s served as 'focusing events' (Birkland, 1998), opening up pathways for a new type of health and eldercare regulation in each case. However, due to different political institutions, formal governance arrangements and 'priority problems' in public discourses, the long-term effect of such adverse events differed greatly.

By means of analysing and comparing two different care systems (with controlled variables such as parliamentary regimes and universal access to care services) based on the three-stream model, this contribution illuminates the fact that a seemingly technical policy issue, such as patient safety regulation, can be influenced not only by the focusing event, but also by formal governance arrangements. The dynamics of policy change is also determined by how actors, including the media, constantly seek to scrutinise the system by proactively setting the agenda around 'priority problems'. A higher level of political accountability underpinned by publicly funded care provision in Sweden led to elected officials taking a greater role in promoting reforms than their Japanese counterparts.

Focusing events, priority problems and governance arrangements: regulatory reforms in the health and eldercare sector in Sweden and Japan

Naonori Kodate

Introduction

Among the major sources for policy change, incidents, disasters and scandals are often mentioned as catalysts for sudden change because these sharply highlight defects and failures in existing policies (Birkland, 1998, 2006; Lodge, 2002; Smith, 2002; Butler and Drakeford, 2003; Baumgartner and Jones, 2005; Dekker, 2007).

How an event is transformed into a scandal, and then becomes a watershed moment for a particular policy domain, is a political process in itself. The impact of an event does not depend solely on the scale of damage or the level of initial shock, but also on the existence or absence of institutional mechanisms that provide legitimacy to ideas that encapsulate solutions that will prevent the recurrence of such events (Béland, 2005, Kodate, 2012).

Applying Kingdon's notion of 'multiple streams' of agenda setting (2010), this section explains how similarly significant emblematic events, in the form of malpractice cases, led to policy reforms in two contrasting types of welfare regime: Sweden and Japan. In both countries, dramatic scandals called attention to systemic issues, including negligence and risks to patients, which confirmed existing 'problems'.

The two selected countries share some common features, both in their political (unitary/parliamentary) systems as well as universal health coverage. However, the two countries are in sharp contrast in terms of publicly perceived roles of the state in financing and providing social services (Kato and Rothstein, 2006). The Social Democratic Party (*Sveriges Socialdemokratiska Arbetareparti*, SDP) held power of office for the most part after the Second World War until 2002 in Sweden, while in Japan the Liberal Democratic Party (*Jiyu Minshu-tou*, LDP) ruled continuously, except for a brief period between 1993 and 1994, and from 2009 to 2012. As a result, differences can be found in their modes of health and social care delivery (that is, their respective public/private mixes of service provision), as well as in the levels of political commitment to the principle of universality (that is, equal service for everyone across the country). In terms of the regulatory issues, however, governments in both countries are held equally responsible for the health and social care sectors.

For this contribution, two 'critical' cases were chosen from each country, as they were widely recognised as 'watershed' moments and also confirmed as 'catalysts' for regulatory reforms by the policy makers and stakeholders in the two countries interviewed by the author between March 2005 and July 2007. Equally significant emblematic events are conducive to critical examination of the interaction between such events and governance arrangements.

In Sweden, it was the negligence case at a private nursing home called Polhemsgården that gained the greatest media coverage, and that resulted in legislation. On 13 October 1997, a nurse named Sarah Wägnert appeared on the television programme *STV2 Rapport* and revealed negligence of elderly patients at Polhemsgården in Solna, a suburb of Stockholm. In Japan, a serious medical malpractice case at Yokohama City University Hospital (YCUH) captured the news headlines on 11 January 1999. A patient who needed a heart operation was mistaken for another patient who required a lung operation. The two patients underwent the wrong operation, and both died within the year.

The brief timeline of each episode is described in Table 3.4.1.

The incidents in each country came to be widely known by the public at around the same time, in the late 1990s. This section makes use of two sets of data: the print media and policy documents. The period covered by this study primarily runs from 1 January 1997 to 31 December 2011.

In order to examine and compare the mechanisms of translating a focusing event into a policy change, this contribution applies John Kingdon's three-stream model of agenda setting. As explained in the introductory section to this part, an important aspect of Kingdon's model is the concept of 'critical junctures' where

Table 3.4.1: Chronology, 1997–2002

Sweden	
1997	13 October: Sarah Wägnert, a nurse at Polhemsgården, appears on a television programme to reveal negligence there
	14 October: Anders Lindblad, Chief Executive Officer of the company ISS Care, admits mismanagement and accepts inspection by the National Board of Health and Welfare (NBHW)
	9 December: the NBHW's report criticises municipalities for contracting a company that has staff shortages and lacks competency. The minister promises that national legislation will be introduced. Polhemsgården is handed over to the municipality from ISS Care
1998	16 January: another elderly care home (also in Stockholm) is found by the NHBW to have committed similar negligence
	12 March: the third case is found, also in Solna. The leader of the local council resigns a few days after the tabloids reveal he knew about the negligence
	15 March: the Prime Minister steps in, announcing an additional budget to be spent on elderly care
	16 March: the opposition Liberal Party leader criticises the government's sluggish reaction
	26 March: the government puts forward the bill, Lex Sarah, taken from the whistleblower's name
	26 May: a national *Action plan for elderly care policy* is submitted
	10 November: the NBHW claims that doctors had no time for patients
1999	19 February: another incident at Danderyd, Stockholm, is revealed by a newspaper
2001	14 April: further negligence is reported at Polhemsgården

Table 3.4.1 *cont*

Japan	
1999	January: medical accidents occur
	21 January: an internal committee is established
	19 February: the hospital director and faculty head resign
	23 March: a report is submitted
	28 May: a report is circulated through the Ministry of Health and Labour (MHL) to each prefecture
	3 June: 31 staff are penalised
	23 June: MHL recommends withdrawal of accreditation
	7 July: the case is brought to the public prosecutor's office
	14 October: a victim dies
2000	16 February: reapplication for accreditation
	10 March: reapplication turned down by MHW
	21 March: the deputy manager steps down
	2 May: 2.5 million JPY (£12,500) is paid as compensation (from the city to the victim)
	12 July: reapplication turned down, with some other incidents discovered
	27 July: a public trial is opened
	24 September: the minister alerts health providers on safety issues
	15 December: MHL announces its tighter regulation on special-functioning hospitals
	21 December: reapplication accepted
2001	7 November: 'Safety Awareness Week' is announced by the ministry

the three streams become joined together at critical moments in time, opening windows of opportunity for policy change.

The following two sections outline the basic health governance structures and mechanisms for dealing with malpractice errors in Sweden and Japan. Unless otherwise stated, translations of Japanese and Swedish quotes through the rest of the article are the author's own.

Governance arrangements in the two countries' health and eldercare sector

Sweden: decentralised political representation, with a central steering mechanism

Swedish healthcare is primarily financed through taxes, but collected locally rather than nationally. County councils and municipalities have the right to levy proportional income taxes on their populations to finance these services. Accordingly, political responsibility rests with the county council or municipality, not the Parliament (the Swedish *Riksdag*). National bodies such as the National Board of Health and Welfare (*Socialstyrelsen*, NBHW) are able to influence legislation put forward by the Ministry of Health and Social Affairs (*Socialdepartementet*, MHSA). Central players also have to collaborate closely with the Swedish Association of Local Authorities and Regions (*Sveriges Kommuner och Landsting*, SALAR). SALAR acts as an employer's organisation, negotiating for and promoting the interests of its members (290 municipalities and 20 country councils/regions).

With an emphasis on democratic accountability at the local level, central government and the *Riksdag* officially play only a guarantor role to ensure the whole population has equal access to good-quality health and social care. The locus for policy making is thus found at various levels of government and geared towards consensus making among medical professions, local politicians and central government agencies. Central government normally shares responsibility with the chief executive of the agency and local councillors holding the portfolio in the committee (Pollitt and Bouckaert, 2004). Larsson argues that 'a minister is not responsible to a great extent when things go wrong in the bureaucracy. The directors-general are first in danger of losing their jobs.(…) In most cases the minister comes across as the person who tries to sort things out' (Larsson, 1994, p 179).

Although the power reserved for central government is limited to setting overall goals and policies by legislation, there is some scope for central government to 'steer' local actors by various policy tools such as 'framework' law, economic incentives and monitoring (Johansson and Borell, 1999). As the Health Act stipulates that the government has the right to secure equal healthcare service for the entire country, it has every right to put ceilings in place, for example, on the maximum annual out-of-pocket payments of patients.

The case in point for Sweden is the long-term care system, which underwent a major change known as the Ädel reform in 1992. The responsibility for delivering all kinds of long-term care for the elderly (65 years and older) was shifted from county councils to municipalities. They had already been responsible for the housing and social welfare needs of the elderly, but the objective of the reform was to let the municipalities assume primary responsibility for the administration of nursing homes and home care (Johansson and Borell, 1999; Trydegård and Thorslund, 2010). The reform redrew the boundaries for the long-term care system in Sweden, which clearly heralded the beginning of the three-level politics between central government, county councils and municipalities.

Japan: weak political representation, fragmented bureaucratic structure

In contrast, the governance of health delivery in Japan can be characterised by weak political representation, combined with a centralised but fragmented bureaucratic structure. Healthcare in Japan is financed through compulsory social insurance schemes, through which patients have universal access to any facility (Tatara and Okamoto, 2009). Hospital care is provided either through regional (15 per cent in total bed provision) or national (4 per cent) public hospitals, or through private hospitals (53 per cent). The remainder is accounted for by other types of providers including teaching hospitals, which are under the jurisdiction of the Ministry of Education, Culture, Science and Technology. The responsibility for overseeing public hospitals (national and local) is also split between two ministries: the

Ministry of Health, Labour and Welfare (MHW until 2001, then *Kōsei Rōdōshō*, MHLW, after a merger with the Ministry of Labour), and the Ministry of Internal Affairs (Ministry of Health, Labour and Welfare, 2008). Under these complex, diffused apportionments of responsibilities, the healthcare system in Japan does not hold politicians in Parliament (the Japanese *Kokkai*) directly to account for delivery issues; instead semi-autonomous providers simultaneously have the discretion and carry liability in this respect. In terms of provision, central government has allowed each prefecture (that is, governors) to decide the number of hospital beds, respecting the discretion of private practitioners or university professors on many practical decisions. Technical decisions are often delegated to experts in the councils, which are commissioned by the MHLW. Given the quick turnover of ministers in Japan (for example, there were 39 health ministers between 1970 to 2006, in contrast to 15 in Sweden), policy formulation must rely heavily on civil servants in the relevant ministries. As a result, the influence of each minister over health policy has inevitably been limited, and blame has also been shifted easily to someone 'more in charge', in particular the medical professions or individual hospital managers (who are also doctors). The bargaining for remuneration remains at the national level, however. Ultimately, the government thus retains leverage against private providers (Campbell and Ikegami, 1998). The functions of political representation and bureaucratic structure in the health service domain thus display some important differences in the two countries. The next section briefly describes the mechanisms for dealing with malpractice errors in Sweden and Japan.

Mechanisms of reporting and tackling malpractice in Sweden and Japan

The Swedish case in point is not a clinical mistake, but negligence of care, where no such system had existed. However, it is worth emphasising here that the system to deal with medical malpractice has long been established in Sweden, with national agencies (the NBHW, and the Medical Responsibility Board, *hälso – och sjukvårdens ansvarsnämnd*, MRB) playing a central part. The reporting of medical errors is also strongly institutionalised through law. The mandatory reporting system, called Lex Maria, for serious injuries caused by medical treatment, dates back to 1937. It was put in place to ensure that an injury or even risk of injury would not be missed, by obliging healthcare staff to report the event to the NBHW. The subsequent inquiries might lead to criticism of an individual doctor or nurse, or call for procedural changes in treatment. As the NBHW is responsible for regulation and inspection to ensure quality and standards in national healthcare, it can also initiate an inspection as to whether or not there are concurrent incident reports. Therefore, the reporting of concerns about clinical malpractice has been highly institutionalised in the public domain.

On the other hand, in Japan, there has been no such system. Article 21 of the Medical Practitioner Law in Japan postulates that on discovery of any 'unnatural death', medical doctors are obliged to report it to the police. When clinical errors are reported, disciplinary measures are taken by the Medical Ethics Council (*Idou Shingikai*, MEC). The MEC sits within the MHLW, which also licenses and regulates physicians, and consists of 30 members including the presidents of the Japan Medical Association (JMA). The political arm of the JMA was a longstanding electoral supporter for the LDP (Kondo, 2005). Conventionally, the MEC previously waited for judicial verdicts for such cases before deciding to sanction doctors or demand closure of their clinics or hospitals. The independence of the MEC, as part of the ministry, has long been questioned, as has its power to regulate physicians. Although 'unnatural death' is a contested issue, direct police involvement in such cases in Japan caused great anxiety among the medical professions, and later became the focal point for reform.

The next section provides an account of how the malpractice events became catalysts for various reforms, coupling three streams – problems, policies and politics. In each country's case, the questions in Figure 3.4.1 are answered to highlight the interactive aspects between the streams, in particular patterns of policy making in the two countries.

Figure 3.4.1: Interactions between the three streams – template

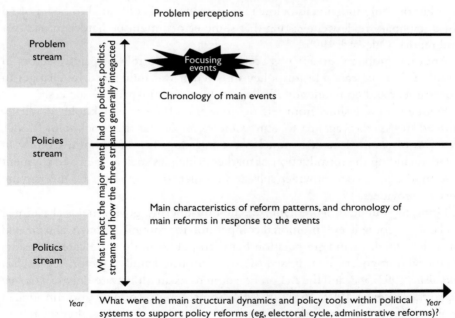

Problem stream: main policy agendas prior to the events

The 1992 Ädel reform in Sweden was mainly driven by the government's economic concerns created by the problem of 'bed-blockers' (hospital patients who were medically ready for discharge, but still in need of assistance and care), which was exacerbated by the financial crisis of the early 1990s. The reform shifted responsibility for financing and managing increasing demands on resources, particularly for home help services and residential care, from county councils to municipalities. Elderly people with extensive needs had previously been provided care within the health system, and after the reform, began taking a greater proportion of the municipal eldercare resources, in residential as well as in home-based care (Trydegård and Thorslund, 2010). The number of hospital beds and the length of stays in hospital were drastically reduced, and some viewed these changes critically as patients were sent home 'quicker and sicker' (Palme et al, 2002), slipping through the gaps between hospitals (county councils) and care homes (municipalities).

The 1992 reform had also some implications for reporting malpractice cases. Ödegård observed the increase in the number of reported Lex Maria cases between 1989 and 1993. According to his observation, the increase was caused by a new responsibility taken by nurses at the municipality level, which used to belong to clinical department heads in hospitals. This change was also certainly instigated by devolution of responsibility for eldercare from county councils to the municipalities. The report raised concerns about the difficulty in distinguishing malpractice committed by an individual from that caused by organisational failure. In addition, only individuals below management level continued to be reported for disciplinary review, suggesting that some errors might be harder to discover and report (Ödegård, 1999).

Another 'problem' stream was concerned with the role of private actors in health and social care. Health policy in Sweden was influenced by changes in government and consequently ideological (pro- or anti-market) stances.

Frequent power shifts from left to right after 1980 in Stockholm gradually pushed the 'market' agenda forward. One example was the Stockholm Model. A series of planned market models were introduced in Stockholm County in 1988, including the introduction of market principles such as the fixed payment system, the purchaser–provider split and an increase in choices by diversifying service providers.

Using the Public Procurement Act, the non-Socialist governments at national and county council level promoted competition for council contracts, and created provider pluralism and cooperation between public and private care provision. The coalition government passed the two bills (the Family Doctor Act, *Lag om husläkare*, 1993: 588, and the Act on Freedom to Establish Private Practice, *Lag om läkarvårdsersättning*, 1993: 1651) in 1994. Some county councils also introduced more private primary care institutions in the period. Nonetheless, after the return of the SDP-led government in 1995, these bills were withdrawn. Against this background, the Swedish case sparked a nationwide debate.

In October 1997, a nurse named Sarah Wägnert revealed, on a television programme, an incident (the negligence of elderly patients) at a private care home (Polhemsgården) in Solna, a suburb of Stockholm. She claimed that patients had been left alone for many hours without care or attendance, sometimes with cuts and bruises left as they were, or were given no baths for three weeks. The day following the report, the responsible municipal commissioner swiftly reacted and suspended the company ISS Care Service. ISS Care is one of the biggest private eldercare companies in Sweden, with headquarters in Denmark.

In the early 1990s, the perceived problem in Japan was a collegial, but often systematically corrupt, relationship among stakeholders in the formal policy-making process, of which the medical professions were only a part. The lack of accountability came to the fore when the then non-LDP Welfare Minister Naoto Kan officially apologised to the public regarding the involvement of the MLW in the HIV-tainted blood scandal. Through use of unheated blood products on haemophiliac patients, the HIV virus had been passed on for many years, while pharmaceutical companies and doctors were conscious of the risk. One clinician was found innocent, while a welfare officer was convicted in 2001. This was one of the memorable incidents in which a change of parties in government put patients' rights on the political scene and also highlighted the deficiencies of its policy-making process. Most government-led health reforms had previously concentrated on cost containment and reduction of hospital beds. In this context, the incident at YCUH came as a total shock to policy makers and the public. It broke out on 11 January 1999 when it was revealed that the wrong operations had been carried out on two patients whose identities had been mixed up (Yoshida, 2004). The hospital was a publicly run, well-reputed, regional hospital. As a result, medical errors abruptly began attracting intensive media scrutiny.

Despite several differences between them, these cases put the safety and quality of care services on the political agendas of both countries, generating a series of discussions, and resulting in policy responses from their respective governments. The next section examines how different trajectories appeared in Sweden and Japan in the process of the coupling of their individual policies–politics streams.

Policies–politics streams: similarities and differences

Blame game with varying degrees of central government involvement and transparency

In Sweden, the media first criticised the profit-driven private sector for eldercare, and then accused the municipality of its choice and decision to contract to those companies (*Aftonbladet*, 14 October 1997). The chief executive officer (CEO) of the company, ISS Care, Anders Lindblad, quickly admitted mismanagement, and accepted an inspection by NBHW and Stockholm County social services section. Some critical comments began to be heard against not only the company but also the local authority for this negligence (*Dagens Nyheter* (DN), 21 October 1997). From 24 October, the running of Polhemsgården was taken over by the Solna municipality.

At the end of November, the NBHW handed in the report to the MHSA. The report critically reviewed the municipalities for such deals with providers and the company for lack of staff and competency. Yet it turned into a blame-shifting game between the NBHW and the Ministry of Interior Affairs, which directs local authorities. The General Director of the NBHW, Claes Örtendahl, was criticised by Interior Minister Jörgen Andersson for accusing the municipalities instead of admitting their negligence. In reply, Mr Örtendahl claimed that the NBHW, as a supervisory authority, had a considerable amount of evidence to decide whose fault it was (*Expressen*, 8 December 1997; DN, 9 December 1997). He openly blamed the municipality for malpractice in the home.

Strikingly, in Japan, YCUH's hospital manager explained that their decision to just hold an internal inquiry was based on harmed patients' rights to privacy (*Asahi Shimbun* [AS], 14 January 1999; *Yomiuri Shimbun* [YS], 15 January 1999). The directly elected Mayor of Yokohama, Hidenobu Takahide, criticised the hospital manager's use of 'patient rights' as an excuse for not giving sufficient information to the public. In response to his intervention, the decision was reversed. The case inevitably sparked huge public concern and media reports, particularly because YCUH had been a government-authorised, special-functioning hospital. A 'special-functioning hospital' (*Tōkutei Kinou Byouin*) is a large hospital with 500 beds or more, intensive care units (ICUs) and more than 10 specialties, with advanced treatments on offer for patients as well as higher training for medical staff. Special-functioning hospitals were created by the second amendment to the Medical Service Act in 1992. Once accredited, a special fee schedule and tax cuts are granted to such institutions, and this incident revealed that the MHLW had no power to withdraw its status.

In both countries, a similar type of blame game was played between the provider and purchaser (the municipality), with varying degrees of involvement from central government. The difference was that in Sweden the incident had an immediate impact on policy surrounding the choice of public–private provider. In Gothenburg, use of the private sector in elderly home care was abandoned by the Social Democrats and Leftist coalition, although earlier in June they had agreed to call for bids in a more open market (*Aftonbladet*, 18 October 1997).

Focus on resource factors and policy issues

Similarities were also found in the way Sweden and Japan's respective structural and systematic issues were scrutinised. In March 1999, the Japan Association of Medical Labour Union submitted its appeal to the ministry to increase the number of nursing staff, underlining their view that a shortage of staff was the main factor responsible for the incident (AS, 25 March 1999). Several other articles critically reviewed the government's policy of cost-containment, pointing out the lack of resources badly affecting work conditions for medical staff (AS, 1 May and 26 May 1999).

In Sweden, the NBHW report also concluded that the problem had arisen primarily due to insufficient resources in the care homes. The then Social Minister for Eldercare, Margot Wallström, promised that national legislation would be introduced on this issue. However, this created another source of conflict of interest within the government, between the MHSA and the Interior Ministry that defended the self-governance of local government.

The government then proposed several measures to redress the structural problems. One was about the lack of monitoring and inspection. The government promised that the NBHW would appoint 15 care home inspectors. Yet this was met with disagreement from an opposition party. The leader of the Liberal Party, Lars Leijonborg, criticised the SDP government proposal as lukewarm, and proposed to designate the third party, the National Pensioners Association (*Pensionärernas riksorganisation*, PRO) for inspection (DN, 22 January 1998). Since the year 1998 coincided with the four-year electoral cycle in Sweden, the party competition aspect became even more prominent.

Restoring the coordinating functions of central government: vertical or horizontal?

In March 1998, when the scandal seemed to die down, another incident hit the same municipality, Solna. This time, the negligence case was found in a different care home, Lunda Elderly Centre. A dementia patient's health condition became worse after he was admitted to that care centre, and the patient was brought into an acute hospital with gastric catarrh. This event caused the resignation of the municipality commissioner and chair for the eldercare committee.

When this incident occurred, there was no disagreement in the Cabinet about the need for intervention. The then Prime Minister Göran Persson (SDP) announced the government decision to put an additional 16 billion SEK (roughly £1,200 million into municipalities to tackle the problem. The focus of the media reports had shifted by this time, from its original question 'who is to blame: private care providers or the municipality?' to the incompetence of politicians and the government in its monitoring of the long-term care system.

Under pressure, the government put forward the bill, to be known as Lex Sarah, after the whistleblower Sarah Wägnert. Lex Sarah (The Social Service Act, effective from 1 January 1999), obliges care home personnel to report a workforce shortage problem as a preventive measure for such cases. In addition, while the PRO took up the inspection function, the state and its agency the NBHW increased its power to intervene in conventionally municipal affairs. Yet the SDP lost its control of Solna at the municipal election.

In Japan, the YCUH scandal immediately prompted a review of the accreditation system by the MHW. However, in contrast to the Swedish example, the focus was on strengthening the power of the ministries rather than tightening the grip on local authorities, and the process took much longer. In October 1999, the MHW decided to amend the regulation itself, empowering itself to withdraw accredited status as needed. In November, the Medical Research Council (now part of the Social Security Council, under the MHLW) ruled that there would be an amendment to the ministerial ordinance, enacted in April 2000, which requires all special-functioning hospitals to have guidelines for accident prevention and an internal committee for risk management.

The diffused responsibility for the hospital sector in Japan across multiple ministries signifies that important initiatives derived from ministries other than the MHLW. Soon after the incident at YCUH in July 1999, the Board of National University Hospital Directors, jointly with the Ministry of Education, Culture, Science and Technology, established a working group for formulating measures to prevent medical errors. In 2002, the National University Hospitals' Patient Safety Assembly was set up under the Permanent Committee of the Board. The assembly consists of 42 national university hospitals nationwide, and meets twice a year to discuss patient safety issues.

Furthermore, within the MHLW, a Patient Safety Unit was also created in April 2001. In May 2001, the government set up a consultative body named the Council on Patient Safety Measures, with several subcommittees. The interim report recommended that every healthcare provider should establish a risk management system. In order to provide an official complaints resolution system, Medical Safety Support Centres were also established in every prefecture and major cities. However, the decisions regarding crucial and sensitive issues (for example, the setting up of a judicial body that had power to remedy a situation or penalise hospitals in the case of adverse incidents) were delegated to another set of subcommittees. In October 2002, the MHLW amended the ministerial ordinance, obliging accredited health providers to ensure safety measures by reporting medical errors (enacted in October 2004).

The series of events and further developments: recurring 'problems' and the search for solutions

In Sweden in April 2001, after two years of a relatively quiet period, another scandal hit the same care home, Polhemsgården. An 80-year-old patient was found to have been neglected (DN, 14 April 2001). This time, nurses were criticised for neglecting their duties to report. However, the scandal did not stop there. After the municipality decided in June to partially privatise the home, in July, the news of an 81-year-old lady, left unattended with infected scars, made the headlines once again (*Aftonbladet*, 3 July 2001). In 2002, a complete privatisation of Polhemsgården was decided on, and from October, a company called Carema Care began operating the home. The SDP-led central government emphasised that with Lex Sarah a better and more transparent system had now been put in place, and promised an additional 15,000 staff for eldercare. However, the overall increase in demand for entry to care homes was also highlighted in relation to future difficulties in balancing the budget and quality of care (DN, 19 August 2002). The NBHW published a report, *Lex Sarah – Four years later: Review on application of Lex Sarah* in 2002. This showed that there was a huge variety between regions and localities. Types of reports also varied across the country. In subsequent years, the search for standardising care quality across the country continued under the banner of quality improvement and patient safety. In 2011, the NBHW was mandated by government to assume greater responsibility for acting on reports via Lex Maria and Lex Sarah and for disciplining healthcare professionals. Since July 2011, Lex Sarah has been extended, also obliging auxiliary staff to report serious wrongdoing, potential abuse and maltreatment in all social services. However, a series of scandals erupted again among private sector providers, including Carema Care. The government set up a commission to investigate the quality difference between private and public providers in November 2011. All the structural problems have been repeatedly raised over many years.

In Japan, there was also one further major development. In April 2004, the Supreme Court convicted the CEO of Tokyo Metropolitan Hiroo Hospital for failing to notify police of an 'unnatural death' at the time of another medical incident in 1999. This verdict hit the professional community as a huge shock. The incident resulted in the publication of a report by the independent government advisory body, the Science Council of Japan, and the launch of a model project for the investigation and analysis of medical practice-associated deaths in four regions in the following year. In March 2006, a gynaecologist at Ōno Fukushima Prefectural Hospital was arrested again, although a reconciliation process with the victim and her family was under way. 'Unnatural deaths' became a focal point of ensuing discussions and criticisms, and the public protested against the arrest (Leflar, 2009). The lack of gynaecologists in Japan and the worsening environment for doctors prompted this public apprehension and led to another outcry, in favour of the professionals. In July 2006, the JMA set up a working group to discuss the possibility of establishing an alternative dispute resolution mechanism. The series of arrests and convictions for manslaughter led to another policy initiative, resulting in a compensation scheme for cerebral palsy, which began in April 2009 (Nagamatsu et al, 2009).

Summary

In Sweden, the prompt policy response by central government following the Polhemsgården case reveals that governance arrangements in the Swedish welfare system (for example, party-political competition and general consensus around the role of the state) were part of the drive for joining 'streams' leading up to reforms. The spillover effects from the hospital sector to the social care sector were also explicable by institutional designs that legitimise interventions by the public authority.

In Japan, among many structural problems exposed by the YCUH case, criminalisation of the professionals became the main issue for stakeholders. In the absence of policy devices for coupling streams, the subsequent reform process was driven by professional societies that feared that their surgical mistakes could become subject to scrutiny by the police as possible criminal acts of manslaughter. The increased number of prosecutions has accentuated the desperate need for government intervention to design a new process for mediating malpractice cases.

In both cases, policy decisions were 'nested' in governance arrangements in each country (Hill and Hupe, 2006; Kodate, 2012). By means of analysing and comparing two different care systems (with controlled variables such as parliamentary regimes and universal access to care services) based on the three-stream model, this contribution has illuminated the fact that the seemingly technical policy issue such as patient safety regulation can be influenced not only by the focusing event, but also by formal governance arrangements. The dynamics of policy change is also determined by how actors, including the media, constantly seek to scrutinise the system by proactively setting the agenda around 'priority problems'. A higher level of political accountability, underpinned by publicly funded care provision in Sweden, led to elected officials taking a greater role in promoting reforms than their Japanese counterparts. It is worth examining further the long-term effect of such focusing events from the perspective of institutions.

3.5

I t was observed in Part One of this book that, in an effort to cover the wide range of policy process theories and concepts in some kind of overall structure, the obvious approach to that structure – the 'stages model' – offers a potentially misleading framework. As this book moves on from the starting theme of stability and change and this second theme of agenda setting, there is a need to recognise ways in which the evolution of the policy process is comparatively shapeless and feedback between 'stages' is much in evidence. The final contribution in Part Three, by Jennifer Curtin, bridges between agenda setting and policy formulation with an examination of the evolution of a policy where movement between symbolism and concrete action is complex: a discussion of gender equality policy in New Zealand.

Looking at this contribution in terms of the Kingdon model:

* policy *problems* are self-evident but nevertheless complex;
* aspects of *politics*, in the party-political sense, are manifest in the highly competitive environment of New Zealand politics, but there is also an underlying 'gender politics' in the context of the important role women play in political life there;
* and of course there are *policies*, with, in this case, significant influences coming from a ministry set up to address gender equality issues.

However, the story then to be told is one of a slow and tortuous process of policy evolution that does not fit with expectations of simple 'rational policy expectations'. Indeed, in line with Cobb and Elder (1983, p 172), it is evident that the 'problem' of gender inequality has been constructed, defined and contested in a range of ways over time. Government and non-government actors have been critical in this process, with women's issues reaching the systemic agenda periodically, and a range of policy solutions formulated in response. However, the development of policies dedicated to achieving substantive change for women, and gender equality outcomes, has always been a process that is fraught and contested, in New Zealand (although surely that remark has wider applicability). Indeed, while public policy textbooks may have chapters dedicated to social, education, health or environment policy, gender equality policy chapters are virtually non-existent. In part this is because it is not always clear to either scholars or policy makers what 'gender equality' means or what it should mean, theoretically or in substantive terms. In a reflection of Stone's arguments about the importance of causal stories to problem definition and agenda setting (1989), there has been much debate dedicated to how gender equality is best defined. Is it (1) treating women the 'same' as men (leading to policies of equal opportunity); (2) affirming gender differences (leading to policies of affirmative action); or (3) a process dedicated to transforming existing norms and policy-making practices (leading to policies of gender mainstreaming) (Squires, 1999; Verloo, 2001)?

Thus, from the outset, it is evident that gender equality is a complex policy issue: what 'counts' as gender equality is neither static nor temporally, geographically or culturally fixed. This complexity highlights why it is important to explore the evolving definition and development of policies relating to women's equality and gender mainstreaming over time; why it is crucial to acknowledge that the process of defining gender equality as a policy 'problem' is often contested, meaning policy 'solutions' will shift with different parties in government – and may even disappear from the systemic agenda; and why there is no singular domain where policies relating to gender equality and women's 'issues' reside. Indeed, in some cases, policy problems directly related to women's lives can be defined as 'wicked', requiring complex cross-agency cooperation for both the development and implementation of desirable policy solutions, complicating the agenda-setting process (Chappell and Curtin, 2013). While Rittel and Webber (1973) first coined the term 'wicked' in reference to the intrinsic complexity of policy 'problems', Steven Ney has revised this definition, suggesting 'wicked' refers to policy solutions that prove difficult not only because of contests over what 'the facts' are, but also because of the controversial task of how best to interpret those 'facts' in policy making (Ney, 2009, p 28). In an effort to combat this 'wickedness', there have been attempts in New Zealand and elsewhere to introduce gender mainstreaming onto the systemic agenda of government, as a process reform aimed at ultimately producing gender equality across policy domains.

The evolution of gender equality policy in New Zealand

Jennifer Curtin

The New Zealand context

New Zealand is an interesting policy example for a number of reasons. First, in terms of women's political citizenship, New Zealand was a front-runner in giving women the right to vote (1893), and since the 1980s, women from both the major parties have taken up leading positions in political life, in Parliament, as ministers and as prime ministers. While these features may not account for the development of gender equality policy, in combination they suggest that New

Zealand society is open to the pursuit of women's rights. Second, in 1840 the Treaty of Waitangi was signed by representatives of the British Crown and 500 Māori (indigenous) Chiefs. While the policy implications of this document lay dormant during the 19th and most of the 20th century, increasing activism on the part of Māori resulted in the passage of the Treaty of Waitangi Act 1975 and the establishment the Waitangi Tribunal. The role of the Tribunal has been to consider claims by Māori that the Crown had breached Treaty principles. The Tribunal can also make recommendations to government that have implications for law and policy (Orange, 2012). Indeed, the New Zealand Cabinet manual notes that ministers must draw attention to any aspects of a bill that have implications for, or may be affected by, the principles of the Treaty of Waitangi, prior to it being submitted to Cabinet (Cabinet Office, 2008, p 95).

A third contextual feature relevant to gender equality policy development in New Zealand was the comprehensive adoption in the 1980s of neoliberal economic and new public management principles. These new policy settings led to significant state sector restructuring and radical shifts in the direction of regulatory, social and labour market policies. These 'institutional' reforms have had implications for the kinds of gender equality policy initiatives governments have pursued and the options available for feminist-oriented bureaucrats looking to secure positive outcomes for women. To set the scene, the next section offers a brief examination of the development of gender mainstreaming generally, and in New Zealand with the establishment of a Ministry of Women's Affairs (MWA). This is followed by a review of how the MWA has engaged in problem definition and agenda setting since its inception, and the mechanisms it has implemented to promote cross-departmental gender audits. The case study then concludes with a discussion of how the process of gender mainstreaming and the advancement of substantive gender equality outcomes are influenced by political commitment of the government in power, reflecting Kingdon's recognition of the importance of politics to agenda setting and policy prioritisation.

Institutional context

Historically in New Zealand, as in many countries, women's policy concerns were primarily defined in terms of maternal wellbeing, childcare, domestic and sexual violence and equal pay (Nolan, 2000). Policy outputs were most often dependent on women's groups in society lobbying their male representatives or required individual women members of parliament (MPs) to use their status as ministers with relevant portfolio responsibilities to act as policy entrepreneurs and agenda-setting agents (Curtin and Sawer, 1996; Curtin, 2008). However, in recent decades claims have been reframed as 'all issues are women's issues', and as such it is argued that gender inequalities would be best addressed by ensuring gender analysis occurs at all stages within the policy-making process (Daly, 2005). This procedural initiative, known internationally as gender mainstreaming, involves introducing a gender equality perspective to all policies at all levels of public administration and policy making. Mainstreaming gender analysis does not mean that targeted gender equality policies (such as equal pay or sex discrimination policies) should be dismantled. Rather, the goal is to complement these substantive policy initiatives by institutionalising a sustainable auditing procedure across the policy-making environment. Advocates hope that by mainstreaming gender analysis in this way the beliefs, norms and institutional practices underpinning inequalities based on gender would be continuously and holistically addressed during agenda setting, policy formation, implementation and evaluation, potentially transforming gender relations (Krizsán and Zentai, 2006; see also Walby, 2005).

The Fourth World Conference on Women in Beijing in 1995 is credited with being the driving force behind the global dissemination of gender mainstreaming as a 'policy solution'. There delegates from 189 countries signed the Beijing Declaration and the Beijing Global Platform for Action, committing national governments to the goal of mainstreaming 'a gender perspective in all policies and programmes so that before decisions are taken, an analysis is made of the effects on women and men, respectively' (UN, 1995). This Conference defined gender equality as a procedural problem for the state to address, and set the agenda for many of the country-level initiatives that followed. For example, in 1996, the European Union (EU) committed itself officially to gender mainstreaming (GM), with the appointment of GM officials to the European Commission (1997), a framework and methodology published by the Council of Europe (1998) and in 1999, the Treaty of Amsterdam established a binding legal basis for the GM strategy at EU level (Rees, 2005).

Much has been written on the adoption of GM cross-nationally, and the relative success of this as a gender equality initiative. However, few studies recognise that a form of GM had been institutionalised in Australia and New Zealand well in advance of the Beijing Conference in 1995. In 1973, a women's adviser to the Australian prime minister was appointed, and a federal Office of the Status of Women (OSW) was established the following year. OSW was located in the central policy coordinating Department of Prime Minister and Cabinet, enabling OSW to monitor Cabinet submissions from across government for their impact on women (Sawer, 1990). In New Zealand, a Women's Advisory Committee was also established in the early 1970s, although it was less strategically embedded than its Australian counterpart. Deemed too weak a mechanism by feminist activists within the Labour Party, a new bureaucratic initiative was designed, whereby gendered policy audits would become the brief of a separate, independent MWA (Curtin, 1992, p 34).

With the election of a Labour government in 1984, the establishment of the MWA became a reality. In New Zealand at this time, client-oriented ministries were not uncommon: the Department of Māori Affairs had been in existence since 1947 and a semi-autonomous Pacific Island Affairs Unit (located within the Department of Internal Affairs) was also created in 1984, and upgraded to a standalone ministry in 1990. Although these were never highly ranked departments, they were seen to be efficient and cost-effective. The MWA was designed to be a small and unique agency (its budget was only NZ$1 million, equivalent to €650,000 or US$840,000) which would undertake strategic and targeted monitoring of the gender implications of policy initiatives, as well as communicating with women in the community (McCallum, 1993). More specifically, its objectives did not include the development or delivery of policy programmes, meaning it did not require a significant operating budget. Nor did it serve as a source of significant government funding for community-based women's groups (often a target during conservative periods of government; see Teghtsoonian, 2005). Rather, its mandate was to provide gendered policy analysis and advice to the government through its minister, and to represent the interests of diverse groups of women, particularly Māori (indigenous) women, in policy work across government. In one sense, its brief was to act as an agenda–setting agent on behalf of women in the community.

There are three features of the ministry's original design that were critical in attending to the complexities associated with addressing gender inequalities in policy across the whole of government (for more details on these features, see Curtin and Teghtsoonian, 2010). First, the government organised consultation meetings with 12,000 women around New Zealand, in advance of the ministry's creation, to establish priorities for the ministry's policy agenda in line with the Labour government's broader policy framework on women. This built a form of public mandate for the direction of the ministry and its proposed attention to issues of childcare, income support, health, education, employment equality, community services and 'doubly disadvantaged' women (Curtin, 1992). In other words, women were involved in the process of problem definition. Second, the ministry's terms of reference included an explicit commitment to biculturalism and the needs of Māori women. A dedicated sub-unit within the MWA (the Māori Women's Secretariat, or *Te Ohu Whakatupu*) was established to ensure that the policy interests of Māori women were taken into account in all areas of the ministry's work and to provide Māori women with an avenue to engage with the policy process (Tahi, 1995). In 1985, this made the MWA one of the first government departments to seriously address the issue of biculturalism in policy making (O'Regan, 1991, p 165), and the bureaucratic initiative was endorsed by the high profile Māori Women's Welfare League in a submission to the State Services Commission (Curtin, 1992, p 36). Over the decade that followed, policy officials from the Secretariat also worked with bureaucrats in the Departments of Māori Affairs and Pacific Affairs in developing frameworks that would integrate the needs of Māori and Pacifica women across portfolios (Curtin and Teghtsoonian, 2010). From the outset, then, women's issues were defined and constructed by the MWA in ways that recognised women's multiple identities and interests, giving particular attention to indigeneity.

Finally, while initially the ministry acted as both agent to the minister and advocate for women's groups inside the policy process, and had a feminist–inspired organisational design, state sector restructuring in 1988 required a reorganisation of the ministry's operational model and shifted the emphasis of the ministry's work. Advocacy was replaced with streamlined consultation, and more focus was placed on policy advice and accountability to government (rather than to the community) through the minister. There was initially some resistance to this change, but ultimately the restructure contributed to the survival of the MWA beyond the life of the Labour government (1984–90), and in part explains its continued institutional presence for over 25 years (Curtin and Teghtsoonian, 2010, p 554).

The policy process and gender analysis

In its early years, the ministry's brief was to advise the minister on the impact of government policies, public sector plans and expenditure programmes on women; to monitor and initiate legislation to promote equality of opportunity for women; and to provide advice on any matter which had implications for or explicitly referred to women (MWA, 1986). In this sense, the MWA's brief was to have input into the formulation, implementation and evaluation of policy relating to women's equality, but it was also constrained by the overarching strategic direction of the government in office. In effect, the ministry undertook this work in a manner that mimicked the twin-track approach identified by Verloo (2001), that is, at a procedural level and through substantive policy change, although its capacity to act as an agenda-setting agent would fluctuate over time.

There are three aspects of the GM process that can be identified with respect to the New Zealand case: (1) creating tools for gender analysis; (2) creating mechanisms to ensure such analysis occurred; and (3) ministerial oversight and leadership on substantive policy change.

Tools for gender analysis

The MWA developed a system of gender analysis training workshops soon after the ministry was established in 1985. Each department was asked to appoint a senior liaison person to engage with MWA officials, and a policy 'checklist' was designed and distributed. The checklist provided guidelines on how to incorporate gender and racial analyses into all policy work, and was piloted in four government departments during the late 1980s (Washington, 1988). Over the coming years this 'tool' or framework for gender analysis was further developed and refined, culminating in 1996 with the release of *The full picture: Guidelines for gender analysis* (MWA, 1996). This substantial document outlined how and why gender analysis could become a routine part of policy work across government and at all stages of policy development. It provided a step-wise progression on how to practice gendered policy analysis (reflecting the 'policy cycle' heuristic), included clear directions on how to attend to the differences among women in policy analysis and featured a number of case studies to illustrate how gender analysis worked in practice. In order to encourage its use, additional training workshops were provided and consideration of gender issues was undertaken through the formal and informal cross-departmental networks within which MWA staff worked (Teghtsoonian, 2004).

Yet, as has been discussed in depth elsewhere by Katherine Teghtsoonian (2004), the voluntary nature of its use, and the haphazard implementation of the tool across government departments, meant the impact of the guidelines for gender analysis on policy formulation and development was variable at best. In addition, the broader economic agenda of both the fourth Labour government (1984–90) and the centre-right National government (1990–99) was neoliberal in orientation, with a strong focus on reducing regulation in the financial and labour markets, and decreasing state expenditure particularly in areas of welfare. It is unsurprising, then, that some have argued that the 'transformation of gender relations' is unlikely to be the outcome of GM. Rather, GM could be coopted as a neoliberal strategy to further undermine state involvement in the pursuit of substantive gender equality (Bacchi and Eveline, 2003; Teghtsoonian, 2004).

Nevertheless, the MWA persisted with a truncated version of the guidelines through the 2000s. A one-page hand-out authored by the MWA, titled *Key questions for gender analysis*, guides officials through the policy process and identifies clear questions that need to be asked at each stage to ensure gender inequalities and issues are addressed (MWA, 2002). The questions also direct policy officials to consider the needs of Māori and Pacific men and women at different stages in the policy process, while reminding bureaucrats of the requirement to consider the goals of the government of the day. The *Key questions* sheet remains available on the website of the Department of Prime Minister and Cabinet, although it is not included in the MWA's own list of resources and publications online and, as is evident below, there have been few, if any, 'punitive' repercussions for agencies that choose not to engage in gender analysis.

Enforcement mechanisms

It has been difficult for the ministry to require the implementation of GM, although some mechanisms were established in an attempt to promote departmental application of the gender analysis tool. For example, the MWA was included in a formal certification of consultation process instigated by the Department of Prime Minister and Cabinet. In 1991, Cabinet Form 100/91 stated that 'most issues referred to Cabinet or a Cabinet Committee have implications for one or more departments in addition to the initiating agency.' As such, all government departments were required to make themselves familiar with those other agencies that had overlapping interests or concerns with that particular policy issue under consideration. A schedule of relevant departments was attached to the Cabinet form, and included the MWA. As such, any department submission that related to the economic and social status of women, especially Māori women, had to have been through a consultation process with the ministry. Ideally, the MWA would have been involved earlier in the policy process, at the issue identification or policy formulation stage, but at least theoretically this mechanism ensured some consideration of women's issues (COM December 1991, in Curtin, 1992). Although discretion on consultation lay with the initiating department, feminist oversight by the Minister of Women's Affairs in Cabinet could potentially ensure that the diverse range of women's interests across the policy spectrum would be addressed.

The generic consultation process was reformed in the early 2000s, when the Labour-led government determined that a Gender Implication Statement (GIS) accompany all departmental advice given in cabinet submissions to the Cabinet Social Equity Committee. To support this requirement, the ministry continued to offer training and other forms of support to assist departments in undertaking in-house gender analysis. However, few departments attended to this requirement, and those that did often provided poor quality statements (Curtin and Teghtsoonian, 2010). Partly as a result, the Cabinet Office restated the government's requirement for each department to undertake its own GIS in 2002. The Office also noted that gender analysis had not been sufficiently applied at the 'problem definition state of policy development, thereby limiting the usefulness and quality of the analysis and reducing the probability of successful policy outcomes for all population groups' (Cabinet Office, 2008). This is despite the MWA being available and open to assist other agencies with the GIS process (CabGuide, 2008).

Moreover, because the GIS requirements are largely limited to social policy and the consultation requirements are framed in terms of population groups (for example, women, Māori and Pacifica peoples), this means that a wide range of policy initiatives are perceived by ministerial advisers and officials as gender-neutral, thereby ignoring claims that all policy issues may have gender implications or produce gender or racially specific outcomes. For example, in 2011 an amended transport policy framework introduced by the Ministry of Transport to the Cabinet Committee on Economic Growth and Infrastructure did not involve consultation with the MWA. The memo noted that the minister would review whether the policy was compliant with the Bill of Rights Act (1992) after the legislation was drafted, but no mention of gender implications appears in the draft. This example suggests that agencies have a narrowly defined view of how gender and policy intersect. It also appears relatively easy to avoid the recommendations of the Cabinet Office that possible gender impacts are considered at the problem definition stage with assistance from MWA officials.

The GIS process outlined above, and the supporting *Key questions for gender analysis* tool, have been supplemented with informal networking undertaken by staff at the MWA, usually at the 'issue identification' stage of the policy cycle. One ministry official noted that while the expectation was that the MWA would be consulted on all issues that would or might have implications for women, in reality, it was relatively easy for the MWA to agree with other agencies about the issues and work streams in which the MWA wanted involvement. Moreover, it was argued that involvement at the early stages of policy development was often a lot more influential, and beneficial to women, than merely commenting at the draft Cabinet paper stage, when most of the design and formulation work is complete (Personal communication, 2013). However, the MWA's involvement in policy formulation across agencies is also determined by the broader political agenda of the government in office. For example, an evaluation by the MWA of the quality of GIS attached to Cabinet papers was planned for the period 2004–07 yet no explicit mention is made of GIS or gender analysis in the *Briefing to the incoming government* in 2005. Although some reference is made to particular social and economic aspects of Māori and Pacific women's lives in this document, neither group of women is discussed in a dedicated section, as was the case with the 2002 *Briefing* (Curtin and Teghtsoonian, 2010). By 2008, the only mention made of GIS is an aside that suggests they are unlikely to make a difference. In the annual reports published by the MWA since 2008 (and the election of the centre-right National-led government), assisting other agencies with gender analysis and impact statements is no longer reported as a key MWA role. Rather, the generic goal of providing policy advice on issues that have an impact on women (with a specific focus on economic independence and women in leadership) is what is listed as the key performance measures (MWA, 2012). This would suggest that the political momentum for further embedding and institutionalising GM no longer exists in New Zealand.

Ministerial oversight and feminist leadership

One criticism aimed at GM as a strategy has been that it assumes the policy-making process to be intentional and rational and, as such, is likely to produce policies that are focused on procedural features rather than developing substantive policy outcomes aimed at addressing gender inequality (Meier and Celis, 2011). While this is a valid criticism, in the case of New Zealand, the creation of the MWA was initially intended to be in line with the 'twin-track' strategy identified by GM scholars in Europe (Verloo, 2001). That is, in addition to establishing procedures that would enable gender analysis to take place across all policy domains at all points in the policy cycle (thereby ensuring gender equality retained a permanent place on the systemic agenda), the MWA's original brief was to initiate legislation to redress gender inequality and as such, both procedural and substantive policy goals were part of the ministry's early policy agenda.

However, substantive policy change can only occur if it fits with the broad strategic agenda of the government of the day (reflecting Kingdon's argument that agenda setting focuses on the procedural and the political). In the New Zealand case, the establishment of the MWA occurred in part as a result of feminist activism in both the Labour Party caucus, in civil society and within the bureaucracy. The MWA was established as an independent ministry, with representation in Cabinet, meaning that the political leadership and influence of respective ministers over time has been critical to both procedural and substantive attention that has been given to gender equality (Curtin, 2008). For example, in the first term of the Labour government elected in 1984, rape law reform was completed, additional funding was provided to rape crisis centres and refuges, and work was undertaken in the areas of child protection and parental leave. The MWA was active in promoting these policies, but the process of policy formation and decision making required the involvement of more than one agency. This cross-agency work was facilitated by the Minister of Women's Affairs who held multiple portfolios including welfare and police and was a highly ranked minister in Cabinet. Feminist policy leadership across two portfolios was also evident during Margaret Shield's term as the second Minister of Women's Affairs (1987–90). As Associate Minister of Education (1989–90), Shields was an important advocate for the advancement of early childhood services. She used her Cabinet position to argue for early childhood funding increases, for improved regulations and training, and to support the growth of the Māori language pre-schools (otherwise known as language nests or *Kohanga Reo*; see Meade in McCallum, 1993, p 174). In addition, Shields headed the Department of Statistics, and her influence ensured that a pilot time-use survey of women's unpaid labour was undertaken in 1990 (Curtin and Teghtsoonian, 2010). And during her tenure as minister, the MWA participated in a campaign to prevent the Labour government abolishing Family Benefit, a small universal benefit paid to mothers. The local New Zealand *Women's Weekly* and the National Council of Women became the main champions of the campaign, but the ministry's involvement in canvassing (and possibly mobilising opposition) was an important feature of retaining this policy (Curtin and Sawer, 1996, p 164).

However, while policy changes aimed at progressing gender equality procedurally and substantively were attempted by feminist Ministers of Women's Affairs under a Labour government, the possibility of this continuing was diminished with the election of a centre-right National government that held office from 1990–99. For most of this period, the MWA continued to enjoy strong representation in Cabinet under Minister Jenny Shipley (who later became Prime Minister from 1997–99), who also held other portfolios with significant political clout and relevance to women (social welfare and health). Some attention was given to matrimonial property settlements, continuation of the time-use survey and combating family and domestic violence. Although work on mainstreaming gender analysis continued under the National government, the MWA had little impact on increasing gender equality outcomes in areas of women's economic and social wellbeing, and Shipley actually oversaw significant cuts in social services and welfare benefits during her time as Minister of Women's Affairs.

Nevertheless, the ministry retained its status, position and budget, and the process of ministerial oversight could be claimed as a procedural and possibly a substantive success. It has been suggested by some scholars that even in politically unpromising contexts, women's policy agencies can nevertheless work to achieve incremental gains for women often on issues such as women and small business or violence against women (Sawer, 1996, p 23; see also Chappell and Curtin, 2013). More generally, the institutional survival of the ministry through the 1990s ensured continued visibility for gender as a relevant consideration in policy making, and provided an organisational context within which gender and diversity-inclusive initiatives could be developed and revised over an extended period of time (Curtin and Teghtsoonian, 2010, pp 557-8).

The (fifth) Labour-led government elected in 1999 included a woman prime minister (Helen Clark) and 35 per cent women in the Cabinet. This raised the expectations of many in the women's movement that more policy progress would be made on gender equality. Yet the commitment of the government to the MWA was more muted than its Labour predecessor in 1984. In her first term as prime minister, Helen Clark allocated the portfolio to a junior coalition minister. While this meant the MWA had less influence in Cabinet, the junior minister concerned (Laila Harré) was able to advance legislation on paid parental leave (Curtin, 1999). Several years later, in 2004, the MWA under Labour launched the *Action plan for New Zealand women* (MWA, 2004). This focused on economic sustainability, work–life balance and women's wellbeing, and also included sections devoted to Māori and diversity. The *Action plan* guided the ministry's core business and its design and implementation was initiated by a Labour Minister of Women's Affairs, and some policy movement was made on the gender pay gap. Elsewhere it has been argued that the Clark government intentionally 'masked' its feminist leanings to avoid being targeted by the media as governing for 'special interests' (Curtin, 2008), but it is also evident that the MWA lost considerable political clout during the 2000s, not helped by several State Service Commission reports that were critical of its internal workings (Curtin and Teghtsoonian, 2010).

It is not surprising, then, that with the election of a centre-right National-led government in 2008 few further advances were made on the procedural or substantive goals of GM. The MWA remains the smallest public sector agency and runs on a relatively small budget (NZ$4.56 million or €2.8 million; MWA, 2011), and it has been without representation in Cabinet for several years. The current National-led government elected for a second term in 2011 has introduced regressive policy changes in the areas of benefits and work requirements for single mothers, reducing childcare subsidies, and has made protection orders more difficult to obtain despite the MWA's goal of increasing women's safety. The ministry continues to 'work collaboratively across government and with stakeholders in business and the community to achieve positive change in women's lives' (MWA, 2010). However, 'gender mainstreaming' and 'gender analysis' initiatives or strategies no longer feature as a core component of the MWA's policy brief in contrast with the continued initiatives being pursued by EU countries. As such, the 'problem' of gender inequality has been redefined and, some would argue, diluted, resulting in a less concrete presence on the government's systemic agenda.

Conclusions

Scholars have argued that the prerequisites for the success of GM as an agenda in itself include the existence of gender equality policy and instruments, a strong feminist movement within and outside the state and the presence of political will (Krizsán and Zentai. 2006). In reviewing the policy history of the MWA in New Zealand, it appears that the institutionalisation of GM is contingent on impetus from within the MWA itself, continued resources and expertise being made available by a gender equality-oriented government, the openness of other agencies to the implementation of GIS, and a desire to see gender equality included on the government's agenda by relevant ministers.

At present, few of these are features of New Zealand's policy-making environment. However, this contribution has indicated that there have been variations over time in this respect, depending on the ideological orientation of the government and its openness to seeing gender inequality as a 'problem' defined as being the state's responsibility. Alongside this, the institutional location of key actors able to work as agenda-setting agents around gender equality issues is clearly significant. Nevertheless, the establishment of an institutional arrangement such as the MWA to address these issues continues to leave the door open for further opportunities to advance a gender equality agenda.

Part Four
Policy formulation

4.1
Introduction

There is a tendency for studies of the policy process to give substantial attention to the beginning (agenda setting) and the end (implementation), and insufficient attention to the decisions to be made about how to translate a policy aspiration into action. It is difficult to identify the 'middle' (formulation) processes in the context of the likely absence of a clear-cut staged process. To some extent, as already suggested in the Introduction to Part Three, the analysis of agenda setting includes some examination of the establishment of policy detail. At the implementation end of the process (as explored further in Part Five), a leading perspective has seen much implementation involving extensive interactions between this and the formulation process.

However, the perspective adopted for this part takes its cue from Knoepfel and Weidner's identification of the importance of 'policy programming' (1982; see also Knoepfel et al, 2007, chapter 8), using a model that sees the detail of a policy as forming a series of layers around a policy core. These layers include:

- more precise definitions of policy objectives;
- operational elements, which include the 'instruments' to be used to make the policy effective;
- 'political–administrative arrangements', which involve the specification of the authorities whose duty it will be to implement the policy – the notion that such authorities need money and other resources to do that follows self-evidently from that point;
- procedural elements, namely, the rules to be used in the implementation of the policy.

This formulation or programming manifests itself in both the detail in the originating laws, in the material governments publish to explain and amplify those laws and in the briefings they provide for implementing agents. The actual form these things take obviously varies from country to country, however. Similarly, there is likely to be variation from country to country in respect of the origins of these aspects of policy.

It is appropriate to digress a little here to identify a problem about how 'policy' is conceptualised. Definitions range between very simple notions of a stance determining future decisions (Friend et al, 1974) and complex ones, seeing it as 'a set of interrelated decisions … concerning the selection of goals and the means of achieving them within a specified situation' (Jenkins, 1978, p 15). In exploring policy formulation this part is obviously concerned with policy in the latter sense. But the point may be made that of course some goals are simpler than others. Many policy issues in the modern world concern very complex goals, to the extent that some of these are described as 'wicked problems' (Rittel and Webber, 1973). Many of the cases explored in this book involve complex policy issues (Anna Zachrisson and Katarina Eckerberg's [Chapter 4.3] discussion of ecological restoration in this part provides a good illustration of this). It is in the context of complexity that formulation activities become particularly salient.

There will be variations in the extent to which policy characteristics are the product of executive and/or legislative bodies, and then related variations in the roles played in their production by politicians, civil servants and pressure groups. While studies of 'who' actually does 'what' in policy formulation are rare, recognition of more than politician involvement in these processes is implicit in theoretical approaches that give attention to policy networks and in particular policy communities (Jordan and Richardson, 1987; Marsh and Rhodes, 1992a ; Smith, 1993). Particularly relevant in this respect is Sabatier's advocacy coalition theory identifying 'actors from a variety of institutions who share a set of policy beliefs' (1999, p 9).

The issues about instrument choice may be very important. Howlett goes so far as to suggest that 'Instrument choice ... is public policymaking' (1991, p 2). He has given particular attention to this theme, and therefore his textbook with Ramesh and Perl (2009) is a particularly good source on this topic. The key issue about instruments is that in many cases efforts to attain policy goals can be made in a variety of ways. This is particularly evident when governments decide to try to change behaviour. Srinivasa Vittal Katikireddi and Katherine Smith's contribution on alcohol pricing in Part Six (Chapter 6.2) illustrates aspects of this theme. In respect of forms of consumption that are deemed to pose health threats, options range from advice giving through to banning, with a variety of devices in between that may curb the behaviour, such as taxing, controlling pricing, restricting sales, limiting who may consume or where consumption can occur and so on (as exemplified by the case of smoking). Michael Prince (Chapter 4.2) sets out a taxonomy of kinds of instruments in his contribution, much influenced by Howlett's work.

Christopher Hood provides a widely used simple classification of instruments, listing what he calls 'tools of government'. He (1986) classifies these in terms of:

* 'nodality', meaning the use of information;
* 'authority', meaning the legal power used;
* 'treasure', that is, the use of money;
* 'organisation', the use of formal organisational arrangements.

It is unfortunate that Hood's fondness for acronyms leads him to use this rather odd terminology (added together they make NATO), but his approach is helpful.

Linder and Peters (1991) argue that in practice, choice depends on:

- resource intensiveness;
- the extent to which precise targeting of policies is required;
- levels of political risk;
- constraints on state activity.

In the case of smoking mentioned above, it is interesting to note how interventions evolved from less to more coercive instruments (information and taxing to banning in public places). In this case producers found it increasingly difficult to mobilise support against controls as the incidence of the habit declined.

There are various dimensions to another of the topics identified by Knoepfel and Weidner: the determination of 'political–administrative arrangements'. There are connections here back to the institutional theory discussed in Part One inasmuch as the establishment of policies has to involve some consideration of the pre-existing legal and political framework. Crucial here is the fact that in many cases policy implementation will have to be through organisations external to, and with some measure of independence of, the originating body. Corinne Larrue and Marie Fournier's (Chapter 4.4) contribution on flood management in France gives an important twist to this theme, showing a situation in which local governments (in coalition with each other and with other actors) actually sought increased autonomy to elaborate policies to deal with local problems. These issues are often explored in terms of the salience in the modern world of collaborative policy making ('governance' rather than 'government', a topic explored further in Part Six). While much of the emphasis there is on this as a phenomenon external to the nation state, much of the literature on governance (Pierre, 2000; Pierre and Peters, 2000) has been concerned with the increasing importance of networks within nations. Here formulation of policy has to entail the setting up of arrangements to mandate actors, steer their activities and ensure collaboration between them (see particularly Koppenjan and Klijn, 2004, on the management of networks). But even in comparatively simple systems (where, for example, a central government establishes a policy that imposes duties on local governments) there are formulation issues to be considered about the specificity of rules about those duties, about funding and about the resolution of disputes between bodies or between implementing bodies and the public.

These considerations also imply problems about the feasibility of analysing the public policy process in terms of notions of stages (discussed in Part One of this book). This theme is particularly brought out in the contributions here, where experts are seen as essentially 'developing policy' in respect of nature preservation in Sweden (Chapter 4.3), local governments are significant policy innovators in French environment policy (Chapter 4.4) and unelected outsiders have been brought into key areas of education policy development in England (Chapter 4.5).

Public policy formulation involves society–state interactions between preferences and claims of community actors and the calculations and decisions of government officials. Within the diffuse and complex context in which governments design policy and select instruments of governing, the perceptions and recommendations of programme clients and other stakeholders is an important component. Therefore, an analytically useful and politically realistic way for understanding policy formulation is to examine the beliefs and aims of societal actors. How decision makers conceptualise policy instrument choices, and how they adopt particular instruments and adapt them over time, is in part shaped by how decision makers understand and respond to or ignore the claims of groups in a given policy community.

Michael Prince explores these issues in terms of their relevance for the analysis of Canadian disability policy. First, he provides an overview of the disability policy field and of the disability community in the Canadian context. Then he describes the instrument preferences of the disability movement in relation to eight basic types of policy instruments. In the third part, he examines a selection of recent disability policy choices by Canada's federal government. This allows an assessment of the fit between the disability movement's preferences and the government's decisions. Political and organisational reasons are also suggested to help explain the differences noted. Finally, in the conclusion he presents some observations on policy formulation, social movements and contemporary disability politics.

Canadian disability policy formulation: social movement preferences and federal government choices of instrument design

Michael J. Prince

Introduction

For tackling social needs and responding to public aspirations, policy options are formulated not only within government agencies but also in think tanks, university research centres and social movement organisations. As democratic problem solving, Howlett and Ramesh define public policy formulation as a 'process of defining, considering, and accepting or rejecting options' for addressing public problems, and describe it as 'a highly diffuse, and complex, process which varies by case' (1995, pp 122, 123). The substantive focus of this contribution is on disability policy formulation in contemporary Canada, looking at both the policy instrument preferences of this social movement and recent decisions by the federal government in this liberal welfare state. Following work by Linder and Peters on policy instruments, the contribution employs a phenomenological approach which pays attention to configurations of subjective experience in public policy making by focusing 'on how instruments are viewed by actors inside and outside governments who make choices about them' (1989, p 36). As Howlett and Ramesh express it, 'Perception is just as real as reality in itself in the policy process' (1995, p 124). This approach has three virtues. First, it acknowledges the potential agency of disabled people and their formal status as citizens; second, it recognises the legitimacy of lived experiences as valid knowledge in policy formulation; and third, it assists in understanding the social constructed realities of policy making and implementation.

Accordingly, questions examined here are: how do disability groups perceive the attributes of policy instruments, and what do they see as the significant design options? What beliefs do the disability movement in Canada hold about the appropriate mix of policy instruments to lower barriers, prevent discrimination and advance full citizenship? What do disability activists think they are getting when they advocate for a particular policy instrument or a specific design choice by government? What, in turn, have been major policy decisions and instrument choices by the Canadian government in recent years? Is there much convergence or overlap between the instrument preferences of the disability movement and the design choices of the federal government? In other words, do disability groups and government agencies favour similar policy instruments in responding to issues of impairment and disablement in Canadian society? If not, why not, and what are some implications for policy making and social reform? Admittedly, these are ambitious questions, and this contribution offers only an initial exploration of them.

A main theme underlying this contribution is that design choices about the tools of governing matter: disability advocates and state officials attribute certain sociopolitical meanings to various policy instruments. A related theme is that disability advocates and their organisations are political actors actively engaged in processes of policy formulation through such activities as assessing existing policies and programmes, considering alternative courses of action, developing new options for reform and campaigning for public awareness, political support and governmental adoption of their agenda. The major issues of disability are not merely problems of individual capacity or health condition, but rather questions of community commitment or neglect, in short, matters of power relations at many levels and segments of communities. Struggling for full citizenship is the paradigmatic form of political action by groups representing people with physical disabilities, intellectual disabilities and mental health conditions.

Canada's disability policy field and disability community

Traditionally, and still today, most public policy on disability focuses on a person's functional limitations due to disease, injury or chronic illness as the cause or major explanation for relatively low levels of formal educational attainment, employment and income (Prince, 2001a, 2004). An image of people with disabilities still common is of a person who suffers from an affliction, thus to be pitied or to be feared.

Disability as a field of public policies and programmes in Canada is long established in some respects, with several programmes predating the emergence of the modern welfare state. As a consequence, various services and policies still embody traditional models of care, coupled with paternalistic images of people with disabilities as tragic figures or the 'worthy poor' (Boyce et al, 2001; Rioux and Prince, 2002). Most income support for disabled people emerged in the 20th century over many decades in an incremental and fragmented fashion, often as part of larger income security policy initiatives (Rice and Prince, 2013). In the 1950s, the community living movement began in Canada by families, usually led by mothers as 'accidental activists' (Panitch, 2007), who wanted alternatives to large institutions for their children with developmental and intellectual disabilities. Because public education was generally inaccessible, early service solutions included specialised schools for children with learning disabilities and 'special needs'. As children aged into adulthood, few options existed for employment in the labour market, and affordable housing was also unavailable, so solutions in the 1960s and subsequent decades involved sheltered workshops and day programmes as employment options and group homes for somewhere to live.

That disability is more than a biomedical impairment or individual pathology has led to a shift in expectations of people concerned with disability and in the way in which disability issues are defined on public agendas and formulated in policy and programme terms. The perspective that disability is in large part the result of social, attitudinal, economic and architectural barriers that people confront is loaded with political and public policy implications (Charlton, 1998; Chivers, 2008). From this perspective, disability is seen as a social issue, not as a personal trouble or an individual's defect. Disability as a public issue requires individual and community responsibility, social change, policy reforms and cultural changes. Alongside historical tendencies of medical care, individual treatment and professional assistance, the emphasis is on inclusion and self-determination. The shift is towards systemic conditions that act as obstacles to access, participation and inclusion of people with disabilities in all spheres of Canadian life. The disability rights movement in Canada for people with mental and physical disabilities emerged in the 1970s and was given official recognition in the 1970s and 1980s in human rights legislation and, more fundamentally, with the entrenchment of the Charter of Rights and Freedoms in the Canadian Constitution, as holders and seekers of equality rights (Stienstra, 2012).

Under Section 15 of the Canadian Charter of Rights and Freedoms, people with disabilities are specifically included and guaranteed a set of equality rights. Section 15(1) states that 'Every individual is equal before and under the law and has the right to the equal protection and equal benefit of the law without discrimination and, in particular, without discrimination based on race, national or ethnic origin, religion, sex, age or mental and physical disability.' This applies to the administration and enforcement of law, the substance of legislation, together with the procedurally fair provision (and non-provision) of benefits, be they regulations, transfer payments or public services.

Another characteristic of disability issues is that, despite these developments and efforts, the lives of people with disabilities have a relatively low profile in Canadian political life. This is not to suggest that disability policy and practice lacks controversy or struggle. Court cases over autism treatments, heated debates over closing (and reopening) institutions for people with development disabilities or mental health challenges, issues over euthanasia, mercy killings and selective non-treatment, biomedical techniques of genetic testing for predisposition to impairments – all illustrate the intense and crucial issues of disability at stake in Canada. All too often, however, such issues are in the shadows of public awareness, on the margins of Canadian politics, and the periphery of policy making. And too often, people with disabilities are treated as dependents and personal tragedies in schools and the workplace, or left out altogether from cultural and media representations (Prince, 2009).

Canadians with disabilities, as compared to people without disabilities, experience significant cultural, material and political disadvantages. This is evident in higher rates of poverty and unemployment, and inaccessible built environments in towns, suburbs and cities (Prince, 2008; Stienstra, 2012). People with disabilities cope with public ambivalence, in the form of pride and prejudice, as to their needs for inclusive policy actions. They confront persistent barriers to participation in politics, education, the labour market and other realms of community living.

Policy instrument preferences of the disability movement

As a politically active and organisationally complex social movement, of which some elements have considerable history, the disability community in Canada has beliefs about the entire array of policy instruments available to governments for addressing human needs and social problems.

In principle, there are many policy instruments in a government's repertoire of responses to a problem, demand or crisis. For the analysis in this contribution, eight major types of public policy instruments can be identified. To affect the material and symbolic wellbeing of people and communities, and their democratic opportunities, and to ensure compliance with authoritative decisions, these eight policy instruments are listed in Table 4.2.1.

Table 4.2.1: Public policy instruments – types and applications

Type of policy instrument	Application
Voluntary action	Charities and foundations Family care Self-help groups
Moral suasion and information	Advisories Proclamations Social marketing
Procedural and organisational	Advisory councils Consultations Intergovernmental agreements
Direct expenditures	Benefits to individuals and households Transfer payments to other governments Grants and contributions to organisations
Service provision	Education Employment Health Housing Social services
Tax expenditures	Personal income tax credits Corporate income tax deductions Retail tax exemptions
Legislation and regulations	Civil rights Criminal code Human rights
Judicial action	Litigation Tribunal proceedings

Voluntary action

The disability movement views voluntary action and related acts of charity and family obligations with ambivalence. Within the disability community writ large, some disability organisations are themselves charities; others have close and long associations with particular charities and annual charitable campaigns; while still other organisations, in particular rights-based groups, are wary, and more openly critical, of the desirability of charitable responses to addressing the needs and claims of people with disabilities. In terms of family care as a public policy response, immediate and extended families in Canada provide a number of essential forms of help with activities for daily living for disabled people. If they did not, various household and personal care needs for people with disabilities would go unmet. In fact, many people do not have their everyday living requirements fulfilled (Stienstra, 2012). The heavy reliance on family members to provide this level of care, especially to individuals with complex needs, can have a negative effect on the health of both caregivers and care recipients as well as on the employment status of caregivers, and thus the overall household income.

For many activists and advocates in the disability movement, voluntary action and charity represent nostalgic, paternalistic and residualist notions of social policy (McCreath, 2011; Withers, 2012). The argument is made that such charity-based responses do not provide social justice or advance full citizenship. Indeed, these responses can normalise poverty and distract public attention from the responsibility of the state and other major institutions such as businesses and organised labour in dealing with fundamental needs. In short, reliance on this policy instrument is a limited and partial way to advance the public good. As one Canadian disability activist stated: 'We need to build strong communities that are inclusive of disabled people as equals, rather than as objects of pity or inspiration' (quoted in Withers, 2012, p 79).

Moral suasion and information

On the policy instrument of moral suasion and information, disability movement leaders and organisations recognise the importance of these soft tools of governing for improving public understanding about the persistent poverty and inequities facing many citizens with significant disabilities. This policy instrument is also seen as useful for challenging cultural attitudes and shifting social stereotypes concerning the assumed limited capacity of people living with impairments; for clarifying the belief held by some in the general public that disability is an illness or sickness or just physical handicaps, which it is not; and, for persuading people to adopt more positive language and images of children and adults with mental and physical disability. Such stigma and negative attitudes emphasise the ongoing cultural/symbolic exclusion of people with disabilities from Canadian society and the state. People with so-called invisible disabilities, for instance, certain mental health conditions, dwell in the shadows of prejudice and discrimination. There is cultural work to do in the teaching and learning curriculum for building awareness of disability issues, a process that involves groups working with teacher federations to raise their understanding on issues of inclusive education from the perspective of the disability community.

Interestingly among the Canadian public, according to survey research, the most common suggestion for improving the status of people with disabilities is by raising public awareness through education and information (Prince, 2009). In fact, a coalition of 50 disability organisations, led by the Council of Canadians with Disabilities (CCD) and the Canadian Association of Community Living (CACL), has employed findings from this kind of public opinion survey in their own documents to argue that, 'eight in ten [Canadians] ... agree with the statement that persons with even the most challenging disabilities should be supported by public funds to live in the community rather than institutional settings.... By a wide margin, Canadians believe governments have the primary role for supporting persons with disabilities when it comes to providing good health care, reliable transportation, specialized equipment, and good education' (CCD and CACL, 2005, p 1).

Procedural and organisational instruments

The disability movement holds strong views on procedural and organisational policy instruments aimed at managing societal–state interactions or coordinating government-to-government relations in the Canadian federation. Procedural policy instruments include consultation mechanisms, matters of organisation and intergovernmental agreements, and all tools of governance 'affecting the policy institutions and processes within which policy decisions are taken' (Howlett, 2000, p 419). In modern disability politics, citizenship is a leading term of discourse and a central target of policy reform. Claims making by the movement includes a politics of representation that encompasses traditional concerns of citizen participation and voting, and more recently, the practices of deliberative democracy and community dialogue. Ideas such as citizenship are linking actions, processes and structures across levels of society exemplified by the disability movement's watchword, 'Nothing about us without us' (Charlton, 1998). Thus, disability activists view organisational reform as a strategic governing resource; for example, the formation of disability issue offices with a policy analysis capacity within federal and provincial governments; the creation of advisory councils with statutory mandates concerned with matters of inclusion and disability; the establishment of special task forces on major policy issues such as employment or tax reform; the existence of robust parliamentary committees on human rights and the status of people with disabilities; and coordinating centres within governments for overseeing the implementation of the United Nations (UN) Convention on the Rights of Persons with Disabilities, to which Canada is a signatory and has ratified.

No mere cogs in the machinery of government, these sorts of organisational developments are seen by the disability movement as vital to gaining recognition of their identities and claims, to generating evidence and sharing information on disability issues and to monitoring and reporting on policy developments and programme execution of state commitments. The ideal is that such procedural reforms will enable direct and meaningful participation in public policy making on an equal basis with others in the political community.

Beyond these procedural tools are substantive policy instruments of direct expenditures and grants, the provision of goods and services, tax expenditure measures, judicial avenues and rules and regulations.

Direct expenditures

On direct expenditures, members of the disability movement generally view income security programmes as concrete expressions of social citizenship. For people with disabilities, financial benefits are especially critical for overcoming obstacles in alleviating poverty and recognising the additional costs of living with impairments. At the national level, three major income programmes relate expressly to disability: the Canada Pension Plan (CPP) disability benefit, veterans' disability benefits and the sickness benefit under the Employment Insurance (EI) programme (Prince, 2008). CPP and EI are social insurance programmes based on previous employment and contributions, and provide incentives for claimants to return to work, an objective that has received greater policy and administrative attention in recent years. Veterans' disability benefits have a distinctive purpose of offering societal recognition and financial reparations. Given these eligibility criteria, people with disabilities make applications as individuals with employment- or military-related claims, and all three programmes involve some form of medical assessment of the disability or sickness. Citizenship is not, therefore, the entrée to these income benefits, although the administration of the programmes does emphasise the rights and responsibilities of claimants, and includes mechanisms for the review and appeal of decisions.

To significantly tackle the persistent poverty of Canadians with disabilities, the movement calls for major changes to these existing income programmes, and for at least some disability groups, there are calls for the introduction of a national basic income plan for those with significant impairments (Mendelson et al, 2010).

Service provision

With respect to service provision as a policy instrument on disability issues, the aspirations today in the community living movement include children with intellectual disabilities attending local schools with other children from their neighbourhood; adults with disabilities entering the mainstream labour force, rather than sheltered workshops or other segregated enclaves of employment, doing 'real jobs for real pay'; and choosing homes and living within general communities. Moreover, the movement calls for 'service provision [that] recognizes and values the experiences the people with disabilities have' (Stienstra, 2012, p 11), and that enables people to exercise control over their lives and daily decision making.

In recent times, policy advocacy by the disability movement has focused on calls for action by the federal government to combat the poverty and exclusion of Canadians with disabilities by investing in disability-related supports, such as aids and devices, personal assistance and environmental accommodations. Canadian disability organisations emphasise that their priority has been, and remains, an investment in disability-related supports that assist people with disabilities to get an education, become employed, look after their families and enjoy the opportunities non-disabled Canadians expect as a right of citizenship (CCD and CACL, 2005). The vision is for a more comparable level of disability-related services available across the provinces. In addition, the desire is to move away from segregated and institutionalised systems and towards integrated and individualised service provision systems (Prince, 2011).

Tax expenditures

Tax assistance for people with disabilities has both advantages and disadvantages (Prince, 2001b). Tax relief is a relatively straightforward policy instrument for the federal government to select in regard to disability issues, although it is not necessarily the most needed or most beneficial reform for individuals and families. On the one hand, tax supports serve a welfare function of recognising human needs and influencing in a positive manner the income, goods and services available to people with disabilities and their families. Tax assistance is a way for government to respond visibly to group claims, and to connect directly with citizens with disabilities across the country. On the other hand, increasing use of the tax system for delivering disability benefits adds complexity, possible inequities and information challenges to clients in accessing the system. Consequently, for national disability groups, tax-related reforms are not always a high priority on their policy development agenda. Such measures place groups in an awkward position of deciding whether to loudly oppose, publicly support or just quietly accept these incremental reforms that tend to benefit only a segment of the disabled population and often those with modest to higher incomes.

Legislation and regulations

Legislation and regulations are rules of behaviour backed up by state sanctions. Such state authorised rules are variously expressed through laws, delegated legislation, guidelines, codes and standards, alongside judicial decisions and rulings by tribunals and courts. Thus regulation making occurs, and rules derive from, and are interpreted by, legislative, executive/administrative and judicial branches, as well as in the intergovernmental arena of Canadian federalism in the form of fiscal arrangements, policy accords and other agreements. Guidelines and codes, moreover, are often seen as realms of 'soft law' or rule making in the shadow of the law, that can be several steps removed from parliamentary or executive-level central agency scrutiny as well as scrutiny by other arenas of democracy.

The disability movement's agenda seeks to ensure that law making and the administration of justice account for the concerns of people with disabilities. For example, a change to the Criminal Code in 1994 added the matter of an aggravated offence when the crime was motivated by the vulnerability of the victim as a result of her or his disability. Amendments made to the Criminal Code and the Canada Evidence Act in 1998 improved the access of people with disabilities to criminal and civil proceedings and other justice matters under federal jurisdiction. After many years of lobbying by the disability community, the Canadian Human Rights Act was amended in 1998, adding a duty to accommodate to ensure that federal services and programmes are accessible to people with disabilities in a way that respects their dignity and provides them with equality of opportunity.

Overall, legislation and rule making and rule enforcement are recognised to be critical in eliminating barriers to full participation, protecting against abuse and exploitation of potentially vulnerable individuals and in ensuring the equal enjoyment of rights and freedoms by all citizens. The disability movement's preference is for governments and other public bodies to take proactive steps in removing systemic barriers and in anticipating possible exclusions and discriminatory effects, for instance, in building codes or employment standards legislation, and in regularly monitoring implementation and compliance.

Judicial action

From the perspective of a societal group such as the disability movement, judicial action is a public policy instrument that involves a series of activities: claiming rights before a court or tribunal, intervening as an interested party in major court cases, and filing a complaint to a human rights body, a public transportation agency or to the national telecommunications commission. Litigation is a strategic tool for seeking to advance the rights of citizenship of Canadians with disabilities. It can be a social movement's political activity, readily seen as the advocacy of interests through judicial means. Litigation can also be a constitutional reform process, aptly understood as affirming or altering fundamental legal norms of the country. Results in litigating for disability rights and against discrimination vary by type of disability and by area of law or public policy. There are a number of legal victories for individuals with disabilities or disability groups. In cases ranging from a local school board, the federal correctional services, to provincial healthcare services, the Supreme Court of Canada has held that employers have a duty to make reasonable accommodations to the needs of a person with a mental or physical disability. Accommodations, however, may not be as generic in programming as disability advocates or family members want, nor are legal victories promptly implemented throughout the institutions of government or the private sector. At times, these muted victories provoke calls for a national disability act, something that exists in the UK, USA and other democratic states, but not in Canada (Prince, 2010a).

Disability choices by the Canadian government

Recent policy decisions by Canada's federal government on disability issues reveal a series of choices on governing instruments and programme design: some reflect the wishes of the disability movement, while other policy decisions differ to some extent, and still other choices are at odds with, or even further, contradict the requests and perceived needs of this social movement. In other words, some government choices are more or less responsive to ideas of the disability movement, some choices differ from those preferred by the movement yet are judged to be basically acceptable in the current political context, and some choices are regarded as threats to the capacity and legitimacy of the Canadian movement and thus to the policy agenda of disability organisations.

A summary overview of the relation between the policy instrument preferences of the disability movement and the policy instrument inclinations and choices of the Canadian government are set out in Table 4.2.2.

Table 4.2.2: Overview of policy instrument preferences of the disability movement and the Canadian government

Public policy instrument type	Disability movement preferences	Canadian government choices	Nature of the relationship
Voluntary action	Ambivalent	Enthusiastic	Divergent
Moral suasion and information	Recognised as important to tackle stereotypes and challenge ableist language and attitudes	Appreciated as necessary to raise public understanding and the awareness of employers	Convergence
Procedural and organisational	Regular and open processes crucial to self-determination Collaborative federalism between governments	Periodical processes, some open, some closed 'Open federalism' with limited collaboration on many social issues	Widely divergent
Direct expenditures	Citizenship-based programmes	Selective and earned benefits	Convergence and divergence
Service provision	Major new federal investments in disability-related supports a high priority	Little interest in this agenda in recent years	Divergence
Tax expenditures	Not a high priority Call for refundable tax credits	A frequently used instrument Reliance on non-refundable tax credits	Convergence and divergence
Legislation and regulations	Human rights lens Strong standards Some calls for a national disability act	Programme lens Softer guidelines and voluntary codes No action on a national disability act	Divergent
Judicial action	Strategic and selective use	Cancellation of court programme	Conflicting

Disability policy decisions by the Canadian government that are supportive of claims by the disability movement fall, in part, under the governing instrument of moral suasion, information and social marketing, a coercively soft and relatively inexpensive tool of governance. Yet responses in this manner by governments to pressing issues can, over time, result in a feeling of *déjà vu discourse of disability*, a cycle of official declarations of promises and plans by public authorities, followed by relative inaction which, in turn, are highlighted by external reviews of the record, followed then by official responses with a reiteration of previously stated promises and plans for action, and so on (Prince, 2004). Another area where there is correspondence between community and government instrument choices is the ongoing funding of a labour market agreement between the federal and provincial governments for people with disabilities, although the level of funding has remained fairly static for some time.

A notable example of agreement between the preferences of the disability movement and recent policy formulation by the federal government concerns using the tax expenditure policy instrument, in particular, the establishment of the Registered Disability Savings Plan, a creative reform suggested by disability groups and, following consultations, adopted by the government to assist Canadian families with building lifetime savings trusts for their children with significant disabilities. In Canada's income tax system several major disability-related programmes deal with income support and tax relief, as well as promoting independent community living, education, employment, family support and care-giving (Prince, 2001b, 2010b). On the one hand, the tax system has been a frequent instrument used by government in disability policy making because of court decisions, sustained lobbying efforts by disability groups, the personal interests of finance ministers and the active support of parliamentary committees. On the other hand, disability groups have repeatedly called for the conversion of non-refundable tax credits to refundable tax credits so as to provide actual financial assistance to people with disabilities who have no earned or taxable income, yet to date little government action has taken place.

Gauging the fit between movement preferences and government choices

Differences exist over specific design elements in instrument choices favoured by government and the disability movement. On the role of voluntary and charitable action, the Canadian government actively promotes these for a number of reasons: to underscore the limits of the state in meeting needs; to pursue partnerships as a complement to, or as a substitute for, governmental initiatives; to promote informal care as family responsibility and resiliency; and to promote self-help groups and foundations as integral to social capital and community cohesion. At the same time that government extols these virtues of voluntary action, strict controls and even threats are directed at registered charities in Canada that engage in public advocacy and political activities (Rice and Prince, 2013).

On the regulatory instruments, for another example of differences, the movement tends to call for using legislative action and explicit standards to tackle discrimination and advance social or economic inclusion, while the government's inclination is to prefer the more flexible and less litigious devices of guidelines and voluntary codes. On funding for accessibility initiatives, the federal government has targeted physical and architectural aspects, while the movement would prefer investments in personal supports and services to enhance mobility. Government budgeting considerations and the constitutional division of powers are factors at play here. 'While the need for disability supports is great, the costs of a comprehensive program to meet these needs are very high. Governments have been reluctant to implement a programme with such significant costs, and, with the responsibility for disability supports at the provincial level, there remains a piecemeal group of programs across the country to provide disability supports' (Stienstra, 2012, p 86). On procedural tools such as stakeholder participation, opportunities still arise occasionally, but usually on issues and time frames of the government's choosing. Today, financial support for accommodations or capacity building that would allow disability groups to participate in departmental policy processes, tribunal hearings or in parliamentary committee meetings is less common than it was a decade ago. This clearly has a dampening effect on state–society interactions.

On various social issues, notable differences exist between preferences expressed by the disability movement and choices made by the Canadian government on policy instruments and programme design. Leaders and activists interpret such differences as threats to the viability of the movement itself. Examples include:

- the cancellation of the Court Challenges programme, a federal programme that provided funding for disability groups, among other equality-seeking social movements, to participate in leading constitutional cases to clarify the scope and nature of rights and obligations;
- funding cuts to national disability organisations and the elimination of funds for infrastructure and policy capacity;
- the lack of comprehensive action by the Canadian government on universal design across the entire federal public sector; and
- the absence of a designated coordinating mechanism for the federal government on monitoring and reporting on the UN Convention on the Rights of Persons with Disabilities.

Another significant difference that reflects the national institutional context in Canada of federalism is the practice of intergovernmental relations on issues of disability and social policy more generally. Divided sovereignty between federal and provincial orders of government is a central and dynamic characteristic of social policy development in Canada (Rice and Prince, 2013). Disability groups, certainly outside of Québec, frequently look to the federal government for leadership on such social policy issues as income security, affordable housing, accessible post-secondary education and funding for employment support services. These groups also look to the federal government to collaborate with provincial governments in developing national strategies, pan-Canadian initiatives on personal supports and services for people with disabilities.

Territorial politics have always figured in Canadian social policy and disability politics (Prince, 2001a). In current times a shift in orientation is playing out that emphasises social citizenship at the subnational level of provinces. The Conservative government of Prime Minister Stephen Harper, in power since 2006, espouses and largely practises a philosophy of intergovernmental relations that Harper calls 'open federalism'. This means respecting areas of provincial jurisdiction (which include most areas of health, housing, labour relations, education and social services) and keeping the federal government's spending power within bounds of traditional federal jurisdictions. Harper's action on what federal politics is about emphasises economic matters, foreign policy, arctic sovereignty and national defence, law and order, and public security, more the functions of the night watchman state than a modern welfare state (Prince, 2012b).

For social policy, Harper's most significant consequence is the shift in prevailing issues and terms of political talk, and in the underlying conception of Canadian federalism with Ottawa's place in the political community. The Harper government is by and large disinclined to undertake major new social programmes unilaterally or collaboratively with other governments. It is at the level of provincial governments and provincial political communities that much of the action on social policy and practice is taking place. Among other implications, this means that national social movement organisations need to focus on upwards of 10 provincial governments and three territorial governments for their political mobilisation and policy engagement.

Explaining the differences

In general terms, differences in perceptions and evaluations of policy instruments between community activists and government officials are to be expected due to dissimilarities in organisational mandates, roles, training and the status of actors inside and outside government (Linder and Peters, 1989). This can lead to differences in what problems are identified, how issues get framed, including their recognised causes, and inclinations towards one instrument design over another.

More specific to the Canadian disability context, Rioux and Valentine (2006) offer another explanation for differences in policy instrument preferences. They argue that a basic contradiction exists between the vision of inclusion as held by governments and the vision understood by disability groups; in other words, disagreement on what are the expected results or desired outcomes of public policy in this field. Canadian governments, Rioux and Valentine suggest, downplay a rights–based approach to inclusion and citizenship; instead, governments emphasise selective services, discretionary programmes and, through social insurance contributions, earned benefits. For some time now, governments have stressed spending limitations, viewing public programmes as expensive responses to social needs (Prince, 2005). Their preference is to promote social partnerships, which means other sectors of society are to play a significant role in tackling obstacles to participation. Most government activities and programming emphasise biomedical and functional approaches to disability.

Whereas governments interpret inclusion in terms of equality of opportunity, Rioux and Valentine argue that most Canadian disability groups emphasise equality of treatment and a human rights approach. Disability groups appreciate the importance of social partnerships, but look to governments to play a strong leadership role in tackling exclusions. Public expenditures in the form of general entitlements the disability movement regards as essential investments in advancing access and equality. The preferred approach to disability, by the community, is sociopolitical and environmental approaches. This difference between disability groups and governments in interpreting what inclusion means 'creates a circle of tension and confusion' (Rioux and Valentine, 2006, p 48), resulting in inconsistent messages, inadequate processes for dialogue and an incoherent policy context.

Conclusions

From this analysis observations may be offered on policy formulation, social movements and contemporary disability politics. This contribution has suggested that in regards to the tools of governing, the experiences and preferences of social movements are important features of public policy formulation. Certainly public policy formulation is both a state and societal affair. Alongside (or outside) the formal procedures and secretive practices of policy formulation within government bureaucracies and cabinets, there is a more publicly interactive and generally contingent side in civil society. In liberal democracies such as Canada, the search for and design of alternatives include debates on the mixture of policy instruments available, debates relevant to finding a consensus on an issue and building political support for a given response.

Disability movement organisations can and do play a role, both in the identification and definition of issues as well as in the articulation and presentation of alternatives for addressing social problems and advancing public objectives. By engaging in public policy development processes, disability organisations contribute to focusing on specific issues and even, at times, to a narrowing of the options under active consideration by state decision makers (Boyce et al, 2001; Rioux and Prince, 2002; Chivers, 2008).

The real world of policy formulation means dealing concurrently with several substantive issues, various procedural matters of governance, multiple groups and constituencies, numerous state structures at two orders of government, and diverse policy processes and instruments. For decision makers inside government, this world also means avoiding blame and claiming credit when undertaking new initiatives or reforming existing policies (Prince, 2010b).

In Canadian disability policy a broad selection of governing instruments operate, from soft tools of moral suasion and information, to procedural instruments of consultation, organisation and intergovernmental agreements, through substantive policy instruments of direct expenditures and grants, the provision of goods and services, tax expenditure measures, judicial avenues and rules and regulations. Moreover, a number of disparate paradigms of disability and thus models of favoured interventions and instrument preferences exist in this policy field, adding a certain tension both within the disability sector and between movement leaders and state actors. Value orientations and subjective perceptions of ordinary people on matters of social policy, disability, inclusion and citizenship do not often jive with the views of government administrators.

The main political outlook of the Canadian disability movement is a version of liberalism, a state-centred politics in large part, with faith in social change via legislative reform and other policy instrumentalities (Carroll and Ratner, 1996; Prince, 2012a). Without doubt, this perspective collides against the ever-present discourse of neoliberalism, generating ideological sparks in disability policy making. There is both cultural work and political advocacy required in getting the public to see disabilities and people with disabilities in more informed and positive ways than is currently the case. The Charter of Rights and Freedoms, in particular, bestows a highly significant constitutional status on people with disabilities, encouraging disability groups to express their interests in the language of equality rights and to seek clarification of rights through tribunals and the courts. The Canadian disability movement, while a diverse social institution, has forged an agenda of national priorities and achieved some progress in furthering community inclusion (Prince, 2004, 2009), although much of disability policy making continues to be a hit-and-miss affair of piecemeal actions and struggles. Disability as a public issue endures, often finding expression by policy makers, yet overshadowed by other issues, never attaining a high priority for transformative initiatives.

I n this next contribution Anna Zachrisson and Katarina Eckerberg explore
aspects of complexity in the policy formulation process, in an examination of
ecological restoration (ER) policy, using Sweden as an empirical illustration.
There is as yet no particular act directing ER in Sweden, but elements of it are
found in several acts and bills that are included in this analysis. Nevertheless, ER
activities are already taking place, often as projects within the context of a public
funding programme aiming at ecological sustainability or nature conservation
(in agriculture, water environments, forests and so on).

The analysis thus looks into the top-down element in policy formulation through
textual analyses of key policy documents, from the government and from the
relevant central authorities. Evidence is also drawn from a database that comprises
Swedish central government-funded ER projects since the 1980s. Specifically, it
analyses how the concept of ER is articulated and documented in government
policy from the late 1980s until recently, and how the policy has been translated
into implementation. This analysis comprises the policy objectives across levels,
sectors and actors, as well as which policy instruments are emphasised and how
they play out in a complex governance system on the ground.

A non-dogmatic perspective is adopted here that sees the policy stages as
interlinked rather than necessarily following a chronological order. With the
programmatic result of the policy as a contrast to the articulated policy goals,
the contribution is able to discuss the relationship between the formulation and
the implementation of ER policy in Sweden, and to draw conclusions that go
beyond the formulated policy as such.

Defining ecological restoration policy in Sweden

Anna Zachrisson and Katarina Eckerberg

Introduction

Ecological restoration (ER), understood as 'the process of assisting the recovery
of an ecosystem that has been degraded, damaged, or destroyed' (SER, 2004), has
moved to a new prominence on the public policy agenda. It is increasingly seen

as a means for solving many of today's environmental challenges such as climate change mitigation/adaptation and safeguarding ecosystem services, including biodiversity, food security improvement and flood protection. Several political actors, including states and international organisations such as the United Nations (UN) Environment Programme, have made a declaratory commitment to engage in ER (Nelleman and Corcoran, 2010). ER is thus stressed in declarations such as the Strategic Plan for Biodiversity 2011–20, the so-called Aichi Biodiversity Targets and in the EU Biodiversity Strategy. However, it can be argued that this concept still represents policy language in the stage of formulation at the same time as it is being implemented through a myriad of restoration projects of varying sizes and objectives (see, for instance, Light and Higgs, 1996; Bernhardt et al, 2005; Borgström et al, forthcoming).

Since ecosystems transgress administrative borders, ER policy operates across international, national, regional and local levels. This dynamic process is influenced by prior decisions and implemented through existing organisational structures and procedures. While ER policy is formally developed, notably by ministries of the environment, actions are required by a range of different sector agents, such as forestry, agriculture, energy, transport and water, which are, in turn, guided by a variety of other interests and governmental instructions. The science–policy interface is then particularly important, judging from the ER literature that suggests that ER practice is, to a large extent, driven by scientific experts (Bernhardt et al, 2005; Eden and Tunstall, 2006). It is, however, unclear to what degree experts are able to influence the definition of policy objectives and which policy instruments should be employed. Expert influence could be important for how different spatial and temporal scales are addressed, as emphasised both by environmental policy scholars and conservation ecologists. Further, the portfolio of policy instruments that is selected in consequence greatly influences the potential for implementation. Whether this relies on cross-sectoral collaboration and public–private partnerships, or mostly on authority, has implications for the involvement of actors and their motivations. Does ER policy differ accordingly between levels and sectors? In this contribution, ER is viewed through a policy formulation lens to cast light on (1) how different interests and conflicting values negotiate what elements in nature are restored and for what purpose, as well as (2) how such restoration is achieved and with what consequences for both ecological and social processes. In short, we ask how this policy phase serves as a means of 'negotiating nature' through processes and outcomes.

The formulation of ER policy is investigated at national level, using Sweden as an empirical illustration. There is as yet no particular act directing ER, but elements of it are found in several government policy documents that are included in this analysis. Nevertheless, ER activities are already taking place, often as projects within the context of a public funding programme aiming at ecological sustainability or nature conservation (in agriculture, water environments, forests and so on). Specifically, the analysis covers how the concept of ER is articulated and documented in government policy from the late 1980s until recently, and how the policy has been translated into implementation. What objectives and policy instruments have the government adopted? Where do they stem from? How do central authorities interpret ER? Are there differences between sectors? To what extent do the objectives correspond with implementation through programmes on the ground? A non-dogmatic perspective is adopted here that sees the policy stages as interlinked rather than necessarily following a chronological order. With the programmatic result of the policy as a contrast to the articulated policy goals, conclusions can be drawn as to the relationship between the formulation and implementation of ER policy in Sweden that go beyond the formulated policy as such.

Setting the scene: agenda setting and policy formulation

In the policy process literature, the 'policy formulation' phase is generally preceded by an 'agenda-setting' phase, before formal consideration of policy proposals. Our analysis does not focus on the agenda–setting phase, but since that is where public policy issues originate and become prioritised (or not), it is included to highlight the involved actors and their eventually conflicting objectives, as well as international drivers. In ER debates, ecology scientists tend to play a prominent role in identifying when certain species or ecosystems are under pressure or threat, often suggesting specific restoration solutions (Eden and Tunstall, 2006). Such interventions could play a key role in defining what the problem is and how it should be resolved, without recognising that different approaches to ER entail deep ideological disputes as to the purpose and value of restored nature. For instance, the definitions of 'naturalness' that can drive ER policy vary from aiming at historic fidelity through to absence of human modification in pristine nature (Hull and Robertson, 2000) onto human mastering of natural change and ecological function (Katz, 2000). Moreover, ER may involve a range of cultural and social values such as restoring cultural artefacts, improving visual landscape elements, urban renewal and recreational aspects that are likely to appeal to the broader community (Baker and Eckerberg, 2013). It is at the stage of agenda setting that disputes over the meaning and value of restoration can come sharply to the fore and the normative, as opposed to the merely technical, nature of ecological restoration may be revealed.

At the stage of policy formulation, decision makers take up the issue and formulate objectives and strategies to address the problem. In relation to ER, there is first the problem of scale. Conservation ecology has for a long time been aware of how ecological functioning is dependent on processes at several spatial and temporal scales as well as interactions across those scales (Levin, 2000; Gunderson and Holling, 2002). Social scientists are similarly concerned about how scale can have an impact on policy effectiveness through the territorial delimitation of political power, that is, the physical area over which one political structure holds sway (Meadowcroft, 2002, p 170). There is often a mismatch between territorial scale, understood in the political sense, and ecological scale, which can make it difficult to implement ER projects across the appropriate ecological scale. Spatial scales also interact with temporal ones in complex ways. Temporal scales relate to the ebb and flow of events and to regular cycles in political and bureaucratic life (Meadowcroft, 2002, p 170). ER requires a long-term perspective if it is to be guided by historical fidelity (Hull and Robertson, 2000), which is often lacking in politics. Reorienting the time horizon of the world of policy makers can be difficult given that 'a week is a long time in politics', as Harold Wilson so famously claimed when accused of inconsistency.

When policy makers explore policy options, they consider both the *what* and the *how*. They thus decide on a policy design, where they make a choice as to what policy instruments are to be used. 'Command and control' regulatory policy instruments have been clearly connected to government (Pierre, 2000, p 242), while it has been argued that so-called 'new' or 'softer' policy instruments have become much more widespread as a consequence of the development towards governance (Jordan et al, 2005, pp 478-9). The governance literature has shown a great interest in policy design choice (Hill and Lynn, 2005, p 179), and, Jordan et al (2005, 2013), for instance, have looked into this assumed relationship between modes of governance and policy instrument choice, showing that the differences are not that great. Still today, the question seems to be whether new modes of governance are actually adopted in the 'shadow of hierarchy'.

Quite a number of policy scholars consider types of organisation (such as corporations, courts or non-governmental organisations, NGOs) as policy instruments (Hood, 2007), for instance, Kronsell and Bäckstrand (2010). With this perspective, it is fair to say that the governance literature has mostly dealt with this type of policy instrument (the very quintessence of governance). The organisation instruments that are currently receiving the most attention are those based on collaboration between different sets of actors, such as partnerships or co-management (Emerson et al, 2011). The governance literature has also, to a limited extent, looked into informational instruments (Borraz, 2007) such as sustainability indicators that have become increasingly important (Hezri and Dovers, 2006; Mineur, 2007). The purpose of indicators is to be able to compare performance over time and/or space, and to improve behaviour through 'naming and shaming' (Rydin, 2007, p 612). Economic policy instruments have received considerable attention overall, but very little on the growth of temporary projects financed by public grants that the move towards governance has also brought (Andersson, 2009). This 'projectification' might well be one of the most important administrative changes that governance has brought about (Sjöblom, 2009).

The policy design will influence the potential for implementation, and also have bearings on subsequent monitoring and evaluation. The use, for example, of economic incentives such as grants or tax incentives may encourage public–private partnerships for project delivery or voluntarism. Both will open up opportunities for community or NGO involvement, which is likely to lead to demands for social or cultural criteria to be added to traditional ecological criteria for evaluation of ER project success (Baker and Eckerberg, 2013). Such project funding creates temporary organisations that are believed 'to mobilise the appropriate competencies on a just-in-time basis' (Sjöblom, 2009, p 166), thus synonymous with efficiency, innovation and adaptability. However, project funding also poses many challenges for the realisation and continuity of traditional administrative values (Sjöblom and Godenhjelm, 2009), such as the cornerstone uniformity of services (Pierre and Peters, 2000). Project-based management may cause considerable variation in financial support, procedures and outcomes at regional and local levels (Andersson, 2009; Sjöblom, 2009).

The 'what' and 'how' of policy formulation are thus interrelated – the choice of policy instruments influences what spatial and temporal scales are possible. A project-oriented organisation of governance favouring short-termism, and primarily the local level, risks neglecting long-term processes, larger-scale dynamics and cross-scale interactions. This scale mismatch has been suggested as an important reason for resource depletion and environmental degradation (Folke et al, 1998; Borgström et al, 2006; Cash et al, 2006; Cumming et al, 2006). Our empirical analysis is guided by Table 4.3.1, which summarises the issues and range of responses in the agenda-setting and policy formulation phases of ER.

Material and methods

The research reported here employs a qualitative content analysis of international and Swedish policy documents in order to study the agenda setting and policy formulation of ER. The policy documents encompass both those phases at different levels as well as two sectoral policies – water and forest. In total, the analysis comprises about 50 key policy documents over the period 1995 to 2012, from the international to the national level, including those from the Swedish government and relevant central authorities. In Sweden, issues are often first brought up and elaborated in *government commission reports*, which are prepared and written by experts and politicians. Most such reports are sent out widely for review by both other public organs and private associations/corporations. The government itself presents *bills* that are to be adopted by Parliament. The bills spell out the government policy which then, for example, results in funding programmes and directives to sector agencies, which, in their turn, might present policy reports, guidelines, manuals and the like. The government policy documents were identified through keyword searches in the official databases (both the government and Parliament ones). All documents were searched for terms used in relation to ER, that is, the Swedish equivalents to 'restore', 'reintroduce' and 'recreate'. The study searched for exactly how those terms were being used, including the issue to be addressed through ER, the context in which ER was used and for what type of response. There was a search for illustrative examples and emerging patterns, since the empirical material was very voluminous. For the two sectors, a contrast is made between the articulation of ER in policy documents and how it plays out in specific funded programmes and their implementation, when applicable, based on a previous study of ER projects in Sweden (Borgström et al, forthcoming).

Table 4.3.1: How agenda setting and policy formulation negotiate nature

Stage	Issue	Range of response
Agenda setting	Purpose of restoration	Biodiversity Ecological functioning Ethical Economic Cultural Visual, eg landscape Social, eg urban renewal Leisure
	Focus of restoration	Industrial/mining Urban Forests Rivers Agricultural land Marine Wetlands
	Actors	Experts Lay people (except fishermen) NGOs International organisations
Policy formulation	Spatial scale	Pragmatic Patch Landscape Ecosystem
	Temporal scale	Output-oriented, short-term Long-term Historical Ecological
	Policy instrument	Information Regulation Economic incentives Organisation
	Funding scale	Indifferent to spatial or temporal scale Adjusted for spatial and temporal scale
	Funding sources	Public Private Voluntary contributions Mixed

Source: Adapted from Baker and Eckerberg (2013)

Ecological restoration policy: internationally and in Sweden

United Nations and European Union level

At the international level, the Aichi Biodiversity Targets (under the Convention on Biological Diversity) state that at least 15 per cent of all degraded ecosystems should be restored. In the first and second Rio Declarations 'restore' is only mentioned once, in very general terms, while the recent Rio 2012 Declaration includes restoration both in its vision and in six of the thematic areas in its framework for action, in particular, in relation to oceans and seas and employment. It emphasises collaboration (to engage stakeholders and to realise capacity-building), green economy, finance, information/technology transfer and trade as means for implementation.

At the European Union (EU) level, ER is mentioned in several of its policies. The Water Framework Directive (WFD) (2000/60/EC) identifies restoration as part of the environmental objectives for both surface and ground waters. It is suggested in an annex that wetland ER may be pursued by the river basin districts. Similarly, the EU Marine Strategy Framework Directive (2008/56/EC) has an objective to restore the marine environment, where practicable. Its overall aim is to maintain biodiversity, but also to provide diverse and productive seas. In the EU Commission Biodiversity Strategy (EU, 2011) ER is stressed both in the vision for 2050 and in the 2020 headline target, and ER terms occur frequently. It also repeats the Aichi Biodiversity Targets (p 5). Regarding policy instruments, the strategies propose improved use of already existing funding to maximise co-benefits, fostering of market-based instruments and partnerships with non-state actors. Soft regulation is proposed in an annex, a strategic framework for restoration and a methodology to assess the impact of EU-funded projects. Fisheries is the only sector in which ER is explicitly mentioned in the Biodiversity Strategy, and some more 'hard' regulations are also proposed.

Central government policy

Since 1998, Swedish environmental policy has been guided by the Swedish National Quality Objectives (NEQOs), adopted in Parliament and implemented by the respective sector agencies (Prop 1997/98:145). In the wake of the Brundtland Report and the UN Conference on Environment and Development in Rio in 2002, sustainable development had a high salience on the policy agenda worldwide, not least in Sweden, which was seen as a forerunner state (Eckerberg, 2000; Lafferty and Meadowcroft, 2000). The creation of NEQOs, accompanied by milestones and plans for action, to guide all policies across sectors in Sweden, should be seen against this background (Prop 1997/98:145). More recently, in 2009/10, the entire environmental work towards the NEQOs was reviewed, and a new and supposedly 'more effective policy' formulated (Prop 2009/10:155). Monitoring and evaluation of the NEQOs, however, shows that progress has generally been piecemeal and very slow (SEPA, 2012).

ER is already mentioned in the first set of NEQOs with a specific focus on water environments and wetlands in relation to excessive nutrient loading or by hydropower dams. Particular threatened species are noted as a reason for restoring habitats. While ER is most frequently referred to in relation to biodiversity and ecological functioning, there is also some reference to social and economic issues such as sustainable fisheries and agriculture, and leisure qualities (Skr 2001/02:173). Interestingly, neither the government's *National strategy for sustainable development* from 2001/02 nor the National Climate Policy in Global Cooperation Bill mentions ER at all (Skr 2001/02:172; Prop 2005/06:172). However, the next NEQO Bill takes up ER frequently. The focus of ER remains largely on water environments, forest and agricultural landscapes, but is further widened to include even the ozone layer. Reference is made to historic 'sins' when lakes were drained and watercourses changed to facilitate timber floating in the 19th and 20th centuries (Prop 2004/05:150). ER is even more dominant in the last NEQO Bill in 2009, with all sorts of different environments in focus. A few new ideas as to why ER is important are introduced in the Bill: the need to 'restore ecosystems and develop important ecosystem services', and 'to build natural capital' (Prop 2009/10:155). The Sustainable Protection of Nature Areas Bill in 2008/09 mentions ER terms rather frequently. The focus of ER is on all types of natural environments, but there is neither any mentioning of urban nor industrial/mining environments (Prop 2008/09:214).

The policy documents on the NEQOs generally refer to multiple spatial and temporal scales in relation to ER, such as creating integrated elements of biological diversity in agricultural systems, preserving ecological functions in landscapes and restoring acidity in forest ecosystems and lakes to natural levels within four generations (until 2100 and 2050 respectively) (Prop 1997/98:145). Long-term perspectives are also visible in more recent updates of the NEQOs in which there is ample mentioning of landscape and ecosystem spatial scales and of historical as well as ecological temporal scales (Prop 2009/10:155).

In the Nature Areas Bill in 2008/09, it is emphasised that restoring ecosystem functions can be very costly, and that there is a need to introduce price mechanisms that visualise capital loss in ecosystem services that are being damaged or destroyed. Hence, a market perspective on the governance of ecosystems is increasingly advocated, in addition to the traditional regulatory and compensatory policy instruments of national parks, nature reserves and small-scale habitats on commercially managed lands (Prop 2008/09:214).

The government communication, *A coherent nature protection policy* 2001/02, signified an important change in devolving responsibility to local and regional actors to implement nature protection. At this time, the concepts of 'governance' and 'participation' were introduced as means for increased engagement, to facilitate access, increase local support, protect more nature in urban areas and to mobilise municipalities for nature protection (Skr 2001/02:173). With the governance perspective that penetrates this document, private landowners and industry (such as the energy and fisheries sectors) are being held responsible for restoring environments that were damaged or destroyed by economic activities. In the NEQO Bill of 2004/05, the need to involve a range of sectors in ER activities is reiterated (Prop 2004/05:150).

Sector policy responses

Water policy

The review of water policy shows that ER has grown considerably in importance over time. The objective of restoration in this area is to fulfil the NEQOs as well as the goals of the WFD. Stream restoration is the primary focus, clearly driven by a concern for fish conservation. Wetlands are also a prioritised area. Rural development is often stated as benefiting from stream restoration. The later bills and communications widen the scope to a more holistic view emphasising the restoration of natural (or natural-like) *landscapes*. This view is further developed in the *National strategy for stream restoration* that the two then involved authorities, the Swedish Environmental Protection Agency (SEPA) and the Swedish Agency of Fisheries (SAF) published in 2007, in which the restoration objective is not to bring the system back to an earlier 'original' or 'ideal' state, but rather to achieve good ecological water status in line with the WFD. Also the *National strategy for thriving wetlands* (SEPA, 2006) relies greatly on ER to protect species; to strengthen the ecological functions of wetlands; to protect the natural and cultural values of wetlands; and to improve the water status and reduce eutrophication.

The actors are not very visible either in the bills/communications or in the government commission reports, with reactions to the proposal only occasionally accounted for in the documents. These statements often refer to various county administrative boards (CABs) (where *Västra Götaland* is the only one mentioned in two different documents) that support different restoration measures. The fact that the Fisheries Secretariat, Gothenburg University and the National Aquaculture Association support fauna restoration is mentioned in one government communication (Skr 2005/06:171). A number of CABs, together with the Institute of Marine Environment and the World Wildlife Fund (WWF), stress that there is a need for national coordination of coastal restoration (Skr 2009/10:213). In the work on a water restoration manual led by SEPA and SAF (2008), a number of different actors participated: municipalities, other government agencies, researchers, businesses, NGOs and local actors.

Several of the government bills and communications have a multilevel perspective on the issue of geographical scale. For certain species there are international as well as national action plans (for example, eel and salmon), but most of the bills and communications do not include the international level. Instead they emphasise national coordination and regional plans, as well as local action. Two government communications mention the ecosystem approach in relation to ER. The *National strategy for stream restoration* (SEPA and SAF, 2007) states that national routines for restoration collaboration need to be developed by the CABs. The related manual (SEPA and SAF, 2008) stresses the landscape perspective and the need for collaboration between the regional and local levels. It also states that short-term and long-term measures must be combined. Although the issue of a temporal scale is otherwise difficult to trace, it can be supposed to follow the generation goal of the NEQOs. One of the milestones under the NEQO 'Flourishing lakes and rivers' was that 25 per cent of streams with high conservation values should be restored by 2010. This goal was not reached (Prop 2009/10:155, p 150), and has now been removed.

The most emphasised policy instrument is collaboration, for instance, the proposal to set up co-management pilot projects (Prop 2003/04:51; Skr 2009/10:213) and the watershed-based Water Councils (a consequence of the WFD) are mentioned as examples (Prop 2008/09:170). Almost all the bills and communications bring this up. An interesting tendency is that the latest bills and communications seem to prioritise business interests such as corporations, industries and unions (Prop 2008/09:170, pp 49-51) or 'users' (Skr 2009/10:213, pp 103-4). In a report from SAF (2006, p 36) users are defined as water right holders, licensed professional fishers, sport fishers, subsistence fishers and fish farmers. That rural development and creation of employment are important objectives is clearly spelled out, not only in these two bills but also in earlier ones. In the strategy and manual from SEPA and SAF (2007, 2008) collaboration is, however, much more broadly defined to include all concerned interests. The strategy also emphasises information in the form of the manual, courses, seminars and so on (SEPA, 2007). Both the strategy and the manual outline the legal framework for water restoration, which requires permission from either the Environmental Court or the CABs for any changes through 'water activities'. These are examples of regulatory policy instruments.

Finally, water restoration policy also includes economic instruments. The first bill that brings up the issue of funding (Prop 2003/04:51) discusses eventual fishing fees paid by fishers (a proposal that still, in 2013, has not been realised). What most other bills and communications bring up concerns the government fish conservation funding and different forms of EU funding. Most of these require at least 50 per cent co-funding. The EU Fisheries Fund (EFF) accepts that the other 50 per cent can be provided by other public means. According to the stream restoration manual, most restoration is funded by a mix of different funding from different sources (SEPA and SAF, 2008). In response to one of the bills, several stakeholders have stated that it is important that the fish conservation funding is distributed justly between regions (Skr 2005/06:171, p 57). There is also funding that is geographically restrained, such as hydropower fees that go to the affected area.

More than half of the Swedish ER funding is devoted to water environments, and over three-quarters of this goes to streams and wetlands (almost equal shares), whereas lakes get 9 per cent, coastal environments 3 per cent and watersheds only 2 per cent (but these figures do not include funding from the EFF). Most funding has come through the LIP (Local Investment Programme for ecological sustainability), a central government programme in place from 1998 to 2003, and from fish conservation and LIFE/LIFE+. The funding is very unevenly distributed geographically – two counties receive significantly more water ER funding than any other county. The county of Skåne (in the south) gets almost three times as much as the county in third place, Västerbotten (in the north). Multiple actors are involved in less than a third of the water ER funding. Municipalities are involved in more than half of the funding, while regional authorities are less involved (almost a fifth). Certain species are particularly prioritised in stream restoration funding as they get almost half the amount, while they only receive about 14 per cent of the wetland ER funding. Funding is also rather unevenly distributed over time, in particular for wetland ER that received a lot of money in 2000 and 2009 (related to two large LIFE/LIFE+ projects), but rather small sums or nothing at all in all other years (Borgström et al, forthcoming).

Forest policy

ER terminology first entered the forest policy agenda in the late 1990s, when a government commission report was instigated on *Protection of forests: Needs and costs* (SOU 1997:98). It included an expert report by forest ecologists on the restoration needs in Swedish forests (SOU 1997:98, Appendix 4). In 2005, the *National strategy for forest protection* (developed by SEPA and the Swedish Forestry Agency, SFA) emphasised that it was needed to 'restore to a desired previous state', meaning that historic fidelity should guide ER. The stated purpose of ER is to 'create ecological functionality'. So-called valuable core areas should be preserved in the forested landscapes to avoid the need for future restoration of those areas. The ultimate goal is to conserve certain species that depend on natural forests (SEPA and SFA, 2005). Forest ecosystems are also targeted by water environmental policy, and the *National strategy for wetlands* (SEPA, 2006) reviewed earlier thus also mentions wet forests, forest wetlands and forest waters. Forest bogs and mires should thus be specifically targeted by ER measures. However, the ER terminology in these strategies remains invisible in the current Forest Act of 2012 that explicitly mentions ER only in relation to restoring the water flow in streams from forest debris and deep tracks from forest machines after cuttings (as well as restoring cultural artefacts in forest sites). Nevertheless, the joint proposal between the Agricultural and Forestry Agencies to the new and simplified Rural Development Programme 2014–20 (RDP, as part of Sweden's EU membership) occasionally mentions forest ER. The stated ER goal is to increase public benefits in terms of reducing nutrient leakage and to increase biological diversity, but also to increase resilience and contribute to climate adaptation.

Forest interests representing forest owners, forest industry and state authorities (the SFA), along with environmental interest groups such as the WWF and the Swedish Society for Conservation of Nature (SNF), are engaged in ER forest policy debates. In the discussion about the NEQOs there is considerable disagreement between the different ER actors: the environmental organisations argue that Swedish forests are generally in great need of ER to restore natural values, but the forest industry emphasises that forest ecosystems are under continuous development, which implies that there is no 'natural state' to restore to (Prop 2009/10:155). The emergence of voluntary certification schemes in the late 1990s and onwards – the Forest Stewardship Council (FSC) and the Programme for the Endorsement of Forest Certification (PEFC) targeting small-scale forestry – has, however, resulted in ER being increasingly voiced as a forest policy goal. Hence, large forest companies have also become active in promoting ER measures such as the use of forest fire, set-aside of woodland key habitats and promotion of broad-leaved species as part of the requirements (and incentives) of certification.

The temporal scale is generally long term in forestry, and this is also reflected in relation to ER. The government commission report on forest protection (SOU 1997:98) was dominated by a landscape perspective rather than restoring specific elements, and there was a discussion of the possibilities and challenges of different policy instruments in relation to spatial scale. Investments to restore the multifunctional roles of forest ecosystems at different spatial scales are also discussed at length in more recent forest policy (SOU 2005:39; Prop 2007/08:108). National coordination and regional plans, as well as local action, are generally emphasised.

Swedish forest environmental policy has for a long time been dominated by informational and voluntary instruments to complement the legally protected forest areas. New policy instruments have been introduced, including compensation for protection of small woodland key habitats, green plans in commercial forestry and market-based certification schemes (Eckerberg, 1998). However, a government report in 1997 argued that voluntary set-aside by private forest owners, along with landscape planning by large forest companies, would not suffice, but that ER needs would require much stronger instruments, including an increased size of protected areas. In particular, the southern part of Sweden and its broad-leaved forests need large-scale ER since forest management is most intense there (SOU 1997:98, Appendix 4). As a result, the NEQO Bill in 1997 stated that 'forest practice must manage forests so that living environments for different species are protected, and if needed, restored and recreated' (Prop 1997/98:145, p 9).

In 2005, the status of the NEQO 'living forests' was investigated in a government commission report. Both environmentalists and the SFA had complained that public funding was insufficient to protect environmentally valuable forests, and the complex goal structure and sector responsibility was being questioned. Unclear division of competence over forest management in practice was considered part of the problem, as the NEQO was being handled largely by the forest sector itself, prioritising production goals and struggling with limited resources for environmental protection. In particular, the strategy to protect 'pragmatic' and 'patch' elements of forest areas, such as woodland key habitats and dead wood, and to avoid deep tracks, had largely failed (SOU 2005:39). The resulting government bill pointed at renewed need for county administrations and municipalities to protect valuable forests through reserves, and stated the need to follow up on voluntary instruments (Prop 2007/08:108). This led to renewed economic compensation to forest owners for voluntary set-aside of woodland key habitats starting in 2007, entitled the Support for Nature and Culture Values in Forests (NOKÅS) programme. Still, in a more recent follow-up on the NEQO, it is deemed difficult to reach the relevant NEQOs of 'recovery of threatened species and natural environments' as well as those of 'biological and cultural values in the agricultural landscape that emanate from long-term traditional management systems' (SEPA, 2012).

Organisational instruments in the form of collaboration are not often mentioned in forest ER. Only one forest policy bill emphasises local involvement and broad participation in nature protection policy (Prop 2007/08:108). However, as mentioned, the SFA generally works in close collaboration with the private forest owners and voluntary ER instruments dominate in commercial forestry.

In their joint proposal for the RDP 2014–20, the Agricultural and Forestry Agencies suggest that certain forest-related restoration measures should not receive financial support, since farmers and forest owners had not used the previous RDP funding possibilities for such measures to the extent that was deemed administratively and economically viable (SFA, 2012). The EU also funds forest ER through LIFE/LIFE+. Nationally, SEPA uses part of its biodiversity conservation funding for forest ER, and the SFA manages the NOKÅS programme through which forest owners can apply for forest ER funding (Borgström et al, forthcoming).

Even though about two-thirds of the land area in Sweden is covered by forest, forest-targeted ER projects receive only 9 per cent of the overall public ER funding (Borgström et al, forthcoming). The LIFE/LIFE+ and NOKÅS programmes contribute the most to forest ER, as well as SEPA grants for threatened species. The southern parts of Sweden obtain most ER support in line with some of the defined ER needs (Borgström et al, 2013: forthcoming). More than a third of forest ER funding targets specific organism groups, mostly birds. Private small-scale forest owners are involved in 26 per cent of the forest ER funding. National, regional and municipal authorities are involved in 25 per cent of the total forest ER funding, respectively. For only 3 per cent of the funding is there an indication of multiple actors. It is fair to say that implementation of forest ER remains largely contained, with limited participation of non-forestry actors. Statistics Sweden reports that in 2010, between 6 and 7 per cent of the forested area in Sweden was protected, and only 2 per cent of this land was located outside the mountain areas (SCB, 2011). According to the forest industry, another 5 per cent is voluntarily protected (SFI, 2013).

Discussion

ER policy has definitely gained prominence in the last decade, both internationally and in Sweden, although it remains a rather 'fluffy' concept that is mostly mentioned in general terms. Both at the UN and EU level, marine environments in particular have recently been given attention. Bits and pieces of ER conceptualisations are found in different sector policies, such as biodiversity, marine policy and species protection. It should be noted, however, that within forest environments, neither the UN nor the EU has succeeded in establishing legal instruments in support of ER, but leans on economic incentives and organisational policy instruments. This pattern is also clear in Swedish policy, where most priority in ER policy is given to water environments (although inland waters rather than oceans), and to some extent forests, together with the protection of endangered species. Agricultural (in particular pasture) landscapes are important in ER policy too. Biodiversity goals are also a main driver at the national level, but social and economic issues, such as employment and resource use, seem at least equally important. The prioritisation of water environments is also mirrored in the implementation at regional and local level. In this sense, there is high correspondence between levels. Economic perspectives are increasingly added towards the end of the period of study, mentioning the need to set a price on nature and to think about natural capital.

To some extent, in particular in the Swedish policy texts, more holistic thinking on ER is emerging over time, where ER progressively targets several different types of environments simultaneously and with increasing combinations of 'purposes', at least rhetorically. When looking at the forest sector, however, the approach is primarily to restore patches of 'valuable core areas' rather than landscapes or ecosystems as a whole. In general, urban environments and industries are seldom mentioned in Swedish ER policy formulation. Ethical arguments for ER are totally missing. When it comes to temporal scales, short-sighted ER policies cannot be discerned in the policy language as there is common mentioning of the need for long-term ecological perspectives. In forest policy, the policy emphasis is on restoring to the past rather than for the future, even if arguments about resilience and climate adaptation appear at the very end of this period. In contrast, in the water restoration manual it is explicitly stated that restoring for the past is not possible. The analysis of the policy instruments, however, shows that the most common one is funding, either to projects or to individuals. In both cases it can be assumed that a likely consequence is a lack of holism and landscape perspectives, and that rather short-sighted measures are prioritised, contrary to the recommendations from ecologists.

Both in water and forest policy formulation, sectoral interests at central level are involved as well as regional level CABs and nature conservation NGOs and scientists. Municipalities, other government agencies, businesses and local actors also participate in the practice. In stream restoration the agreement is quite high, as there is a win–win situation where the 'industry' (mainly sports fishing tourism and recreational fishing) benefits on a par with nature protection interests. The only CAB that is mentioned twice in the water policy material stands out as the county that receives second-most funding, which points to the way that action in policy formulation seeming to help generate funding for implementation. The non-state actors also stressed the need for national coordination, which means that they argued for a larger-scale perspective. Disagreement instead clearly characterises forest ER, where the new strategy on forest protection has been delayed for several years due to a conflict between non-managed protected areas (natural development) and restoration (Steinwall, forthcoming). This conflict concerns fundamental views on nature, and what is valuable in nature. It has surely influenced the availability of financial means for forest ER, where most investments are made in area protection. The more restrained focus of forest ER may be a result of forestry actors being very strong in Sweden and actively lobbying against all kinds of binding nature conservation measures (Boström, 2003). To begin with, the concern for forest ER was obviously driven by a specific research environment of forest ecologists who advocated proactive restoration across multiple territorial scales based on defined landscapes and ecological functions, and with long-time and ecological temporal scales. This perspective also influenced the setting of the forest NEQO 'living forests'.

The choice of policy instruments shows that the NEQOs provide the baseline or rationale for much of the ER policies, although both in water and forest policy it is questioned to what extent these are actually effective. Descriptively they show the trends, but the 'naming and shaming' approach to behaviour change does not seem to work as, for instance, the relevant NEQO milestones to be reached by 2010 were not fulfilled. The critique led the government to change the NEQO structure in 2012, where the old milestones were replaced by a new structure containing less detail from administration and more political negotiation. The primary means to achieve the NEQOs is that the central state provides funding, and lower levels of the state, together with non-state actors, provide the action. Underlying these emphasised actions are, however, regulations, as shown, for instance, in the water ER strategy and manual. Interestingly enough the higher-level government documents seldom mention any regulations, nor do they propose any changes to the regulative framework, even if this might date back quite a while and not be thought to be well functioning. An exception is the EU-driven legislation on *ecological compensation*, where restoration is required elsewhere to compensate for planned damages due to exploitation (which has not been included in this review).

Similarly, in forest policy the reliance on voluntary and compensatory instruments remains high, and current forest ER policy seems to be driven more by requirements within certification schemes than by public-funded forest ER projects or set-aside of forests in protected areas. The preferred policy instrument to achieve the NEQOs is to provide economic incentives through direct funding, often requiring, however, co-funding from participating parties. In the water sector, funding is to a very large extent project-based, with the implications that funding has to be applied for again and again, and that there is little money for follow-up. In the forest sector there is primarily funding that goes to landowners, thus it is individually targeted. A quantitative account of the results of the emphasis on funding was seen in the overview of Swedish ER funding, which showed that it was unevenly distributed, both geographically and over time, in both the water and the forest sector. To some extent the need for ER is more pronounced in the southern parts of Sweden due to a much higher degree of modification, and they also receive more funding, so in that sense it might be justified. Still, the funding is largely provided on a short-term basis, which contradicts the policy objectives of the need for long-term solutions. In practice, ER policy implementation in Sweden leans heavily on specific programmes that provide public finance to short-term measures. These findings support the concern that 'projectification' may lead to variation in financial support at the regional level, which has not been part of the policy objective.

It was initially hypothesised that implementation through projects could be a way to increase participation. In the beginning of the period of study, there was more emphasis on state politics and programmes, while trust in governance approaches (including partnerships and participation) has grown from 2001 and onwards. There is, however, no clear direction as to who should pay for ER and how the responsibilities should be shared in practice (except briefly in Prop 2008/09:214). Towards the very end of the period, business interests were emphasised more, as well as voluntary measures, such as voluntary protection of woodland key habitats. Judging from the project database, there is not that much collaboration in practice, representing one-third of water ER funding and only 3 per cent of forest ER funding. This appears inadequate in relation to the stressing of collaboration in policy texts, in particular in the water sector. But even though there is little collaboration, many individuals participate in implementing the policies. There are, however, few signs of spillover from such engagement into the policy formulation, since even the preparatory documents (such as the government commission reports) seldom mention the interests and actions of stakeholders.

Conclusions

ER is not yet a policy domain of its own, either internationally or in Sweden, but it is increasingly becoming part of environmental policy, in particular for restoring biodiversity and marine environments. ER has thus made its way to the international agenda, at the same time as it has been pushed for nationally in Sweden by scientists, slowly crawling onto the Swedish policy agenda. At the general, rhetorical level, ER is a rather holistic, long-term concept, but in practice it appears almost the contrary. Through an emphasis on soft policy instruments, first, the information-based NEQOs, second, the economically based funding schemes, and third, the organisational instrument of collaboration, the implementation result becomes rather piecemeal and short-sighted. This would speak against the recommendations from ecology. Moreover, it appears as if funding for many of the ER measures in Sweden has been available for a long time, although varying in extent (Borgström et al, forthcoming). This implies that before the ER concept/terminology entered into the debates, similar activities took place as part of environmental protection more generally. Hence, to some extent, implementation of certain ER measures has thus preceded both agenda setting and the more precise policy formulation.

It seems as though the shift from government to governance is taking place both in ER policy and practice, primarily implying an increased emphasis on soft (or 'new') policy instruments. However, both water and forest ER are restrained or fostered by regulations too, but these authority-based instruments do not show up much in the policy texts. In this study it has not been possible to explore the reason why this is excluded, so the interesting question as to whether 'new' policy instruments are in fact adopted in 'the shadow of hierarchy' cannot be answered here. However, the estimation that neither the water nor forest NEQOs will be reached by 2020 (www.miljomal.se) could be a signal that perhaps a renewed focus on 'hard' regulation will be brought forward in the future debate on how to achieve ER goals. More research on goal steering as well as the effectiveness of funding as policy instruments would then aid policy makers in making their choices.

4.4

This next contribution, by Corinne Larrue and Marie Fournier, explores issues about the relationship between policy formulation and implementation through the examination of significant changes in the distribution of roles between the various levels of government in France. It was noted in the Introduction to this part of the book that in many cases policy is developed through the formulation process, with roles given to organisations external to the originating body. Further to this, Corinne Larrue and Marie Fournier explore a situation in which local governments (in coalition with each other and with other actors) actually sought increased autonomy to elaborate policies to deal with local problems.

In France, the implementation of environmental policies was traditionally mainly oriented and supervised by central government, the origin of this being the important regulatory nature of these policies and a concentration of power in the hands of the executive body (in charge of numerous deconcentrated services, able to initiate and monitor the implementation of its policies). In the last 30 years, this situation has gradually been transformed: the decentralisation of powers begun in 1982 has left more room for territorial actors (communes, general and regional councils), and at the same time, the range of instruments of environmental policies has broadened. Local and territorial actors have increasingly become actors of a policy they have 'territorialised', that is, adapted to their specific geographic and political context. As a result, the processes involved in formulating environmental policies have become more complex, with the territorial level playing an ever more important 'design' role in the elaboration of public policy.

It is this process described here, with two examples – flood prevention and the natural restoration of water bodies – that show how the communal and especially intercommunal levels have asserted themselves in the implementation of environmental public policies, on the one hand, with regard to central government (in the case of flood prevention) and on the other, faced with private actors (the natural restoration of water bodies).

What is reported here is therefore a policy-making process where the use of the stages model is particularly misleading. Local actors dealing with local problems, and of course working within a context of national law, are in many respects agenda setters, formulators and implementers of policies. While what follows could be described as an analysis of implementation, the strong emphasis on formulation (or reformulation of policy) at the local level makes it an appropriate contribution to this part.

The role of local actors in water and flood management in France: between policy formulation and policy implementation

Corinne Larrue and Marie Fournier

Environmental problems dealt with via ad hoc territorial frameworks: a gradual increase in community involvement in the field of environment

We begin with a discussion of the institutional framework and involvement of local authorities in the elaboration and implementation of environmental policies in France, and how both have evolved.

Environmental policies have always focused mainly on natural environments, both for the purpose of protecting biodiversity and of preventing damage to those environments caused by pollution, consumption of natural resources, land planning and landscaping (Poujade, 1975; Lascoumes, 1994; Barraqué and Theys, 1998). These policies rested on a large and old corpus of rules (the first French law on dangerous installations dates from 1810, that on the protection of sites from 1930) whose implementation relied essentially on state services (in the case of air pollution, see Knoepfel and Larrue, 1985). In this framework, territorial levels remained to a great extent outside activities concerning implementation, except, in certain cases, to provide political legitimacy and financial resources (involvement of the *département* in carrying out water protection policies; see Larrue, 2000).

However, with their greater human and financial resources, urban communities soon brought two additional preoccupations to the environmental issue:

- that of hygiene: the environment was then mainly linked to questions of local pollution and especially to a technical approach, with the result that the environmental issue got lost in the technical services of municipalities;
- that of green spaces: the maintenance and management of these spaces weighed heavily on local budgets.

These two fields of intervention are linked to the health and hygiene movement at the origin of urbanism in the 19th century.

Depending on specific local issues, European laws and constraints (in particular the Water Law, Air Law, and so on), other matters appropriated by elected deputies and described by them as environmental policies have been added to these traditional approaches, such as:

- heritage issue: historical, cultural heritage and recently the added question of urban landscape;
- natural (flooding in particular) and technological risks issue;
- energy issue: with proactive and incentive policies on the part of entities such as ADEME (Agency for the Environment and Energy Agency, a state agency);

On the communal level, this resulted in the creation of environmental services, whose emergence has been analysed by Barraqué (1998).

The management of environmental issues by the municipal services relied on two groups of agents: one specialised in problems of air and noise pollution due to urban functioning, and the other a more transverse or at least not specifically technical group responsible mainly for everyday municipal management, but liable to appear in the context of operations such as urban planning – master plans, land use or sectoral plans such as the urban mobility plan. It is this second group that has increased in number the most, especially in the context of decentralisation initiated in 1982 and steadily reinforced afterwards.

The setting up of different forms of cooperation between communes has also led to greater involvement among local communities on issues concerning the environment.

A long French tradition of intercommunal cooperation

If we look at the traditional divisions of the French communal landscape (more than 36,000 communes, of which at least 32,000 have fewer than 1,000 inhabitants), we must also take into consideration the fact that early on, these small communes got into the habit of setting up different forms of cooperation among themselves.

The law of 22 March 1890 created intercommunal associations with a single purpose (*Syndicat intercommunal à vocation unique*, SIVU), that is, devoted to a specific field of community action for which intercommunal cooperation was an advantage. In 1959, these associations were able to involve several competences (*Syndicats à vocations multiples*, SIVOM). The decree law of 30 October 1935 also established mixed associations, stipulating in its first article the possibility for *départements*, communes, Chambers of Commerce and public institutions regrouping themselves in the form of associations to manage public services representing an interest for each of the legal entities in question by means of concessions.

In the following decades, the creation of many different forms of intercommunalities was proposed to the communes (urban districts for cities in 1959, urban communities in 1966). In these cases it was a matter of real transfers of competence from the commune to the intercommunal structure created. Later on, the law of 6 February 1992 created commune communities and city communities.

This proliferation of intercommunal cooperation structures made the intercommunal institutional landscape much more complex. Its interpretation was all the more complicated because, alongside these structures existed other forms or other intercommunal cooperation tools such as intercommunal ententes, agreements and meetings (law of 5 April 1884), city networks (Prime Minister's circulars, no 3678/SG of 17 April 1991 and 5 June 2000) or *pays* (groups of communes) (laws no 95–115 of 4 February 1995, no 99–533 of 25 June 1999).

The law of 12 July 1999 on the simplification and reinforcement of intercommunal cooperation was an effort to bring concrete solutions to this proliferation of divisions, by reducing the categories of existing intercommunal cooperation structures. The creation of agglomeration communities brought about the suppression of districts and communities of cities.

The result of these reforms is the coexistence of the following forms of cooperation between communes in France today:

- flexible forms of intercommunality: associations of communes, voluntary and/ or based on freely determined competences, with financing made up of the financial contributions of the member communes or communities (SIVU, SIVOM and mixed associations);
- forms known as 'integrated': associations of communes with an imposed framework (a regime defined according to the number of inhabitants, obligatory and optional competences to be transferred) and whose financing is ensured by local taxes levied directly by the intercommunal body instead of by the communes concerned) (community of communes, community of agglomerations and urban community).

In all cases concerning competences transferred to the intercommunal cooperation body (*Établissement public de cooperation intercommunale*, EPCI), the latter has decisional and executive power.

Intercommunal cooperation: a way for communes to view environmental issues from a wider angle

The setting up of intercommunal structures has allowed local authorities to deal with environmental issues that were previously difficult to address. Environmental questions are incompatible with administrative borders, be they national, regional or local. Furthermore, historically, intercommunalities have involved themselves mainly in the field of environmental public services (waste, water). Thus the intercommunal intervention framework should potentially favour greater harmonisation between problem area and solution area (Berdoulay and Soubeyran, 2000). In fact, studies on these questions show that intercommunality leads to the production of new action areas and a rethinking of environmental issues (Amalric et al, 2011).

In particular, the latter research points out the various motivations for intercommunal regroupings: political affinities, which remain a very constant factor, but management needs as well, or the opportunity for closer relations in view of a specific project. We are thus able to distinguish several configurations of intercommunalities: management communities (organised around the common management of a service for the population); relay communities (serving as intermediary actors, bringing together competences of different levels) and project communities (built around a project to be developed in common), mobilising different action rationales (normative, economic, cooperative or initiating).

Thus, setting up and strengthening intercommunalities made it possible to increase their competences as well as the funds needed for them. Beyond obligatory competences, bodies concerned with environmental issues are granted funds by intercommunal structures. Intercommunal construction can thus be considered a vector of improvement of services and a strengthening of the implementation of environmental policies. This supports the observations of Hervé, who notes that although intercommunalities were initially set up for the management of technical public services, an increasingly strong political dimension is now emerging with the evolution of intercommunal forms (1999).

Intercommunalities thus turn out to provide excellent support for strategies of local actions in the field of the environment, capable of working on themes adapted more or less to their area, of mobilising the various local and state actors, and, according to the field, of playing the role of manager or leader. In some cases, intercommunality also serves as a basis for consolidating real implementation processes coordinated with public policies. Such is the case in particular of the *syndicats mixtes* (mixed associations), which serve, for example, as a support for the management of regional natural parks. However, there is nothing automatic about these processes, and although we can identify a few factors that favour them, we cannot really generalise.

Finally, it should be pointed out that there has been much greater involvement in the field of environment on the *département* level (*conseil général*) and on the regional level (*conseil régional*). These two levels back up local and intercommunal authorities, both technically and financially. They aim to ensure certain coherence between policies led by local authorities, by compensating for the lesser means of rural communities. In addition, in certain sectors such as water and sanitation, and in certain geographical sectors, the department level has to take full responsibility – strategic, technical and financial – for the leading of policy (Barbier et al, 2011).

We now, by means of two examples, show how local authorities impose their ways of taking action in two fields: flood prevention on the one hand, and the natural restoration of a river on the other. On the basis of these examples, we try to show how local authorities, organised in intercommunal cooperation institutions, are able to formulate and put in place new public policy tools adapted to their contexts and almost entirely independent of central government action.

Flood risks in the mid-Loire: when the communes, through their intercommunalities, take over a field of action traditionally in the hands of state administration

After having situated the main policy issues, we present the means by which interactions occur between local actors on the one hand, and state representative services on the other.

Saint-Pierre-des-Corps, a commune under considerable stress due to the risk of flooding

Saint-Pierre-des-Corps (SPC) is located to the east of Tours and stretches between the Loire (to the north) and the Cher (to the south). The development of the city was linked to the installation of the rail marshalling yard, which thus became a city of railwaymen with a strong workers' tradition. Today, the city has approximately 16,000 inhabitants. This commune is a kind of basin, bordered by two large water bodies.

These particularities make the territory a very vulnerable area in case of a break or overflow of the dikes that protect it. The whole of the territory of SPC risks being flooded, and is classified as a medium or high-risk zone in the regulatory mapping of risks. Another particularity of the risk for SPC is the rarity with which it occurs – the last catastrophic flooding was in 1856. Thus, aside from a few inhabitants who might remember the floods of the 1940s or that of 1969, due to a deficiency in the network of storm drainage systems, the risk of flooding is not a reality that has been experienced by the inhabitants. However, a special communication effort on the part of the municipal authority expressing concerns about potential problems has been made since the 1970s, with articles published in the municipal bulletin *La Clarté* and distributed to each inhabitant.

An issue and a ruling imposed on local public actors

Beginning in the 1970s, the flood prevention policy relied to a great extent on equipping the dams upstream of the Loire, with the aim of making urban spaces more habitable and of urbanising the cities in the Loire valley. This equipment policy relied on the know-how of state civil engineers and on national and local political determination, expressed in significant funding.

However, in 1992, central government renewed its fight against floods policy: following a number of dramatic events in the south of France, which showed the weaknesses of a policy based mainly on defence against floods, the government determined to reduce urbanisation in the floodplains. The *Plans de prévention des risques d'inondation* (PPRI, Flood Risks Prevention Plan) were then issued, their major aims being to stop any new urbanisation in floodplains that were barely or not at all urbanised, to preserve flood storage areas, and to pursue and adapt urbanisation in already urbanised zones.

The many communes along the Loire river are very densely built up. The commune of SPC, as well as a number of other smaller communes, faced a total prohibition of any new form of urbanisation. This sort of constraint was a challenge to the commune's development projects and led to a real tug of war between the two main actors: the commune on the one hand, and central government, represented by the department prefect, on the other. During this tug of war the commune twice brought the public authorities to court, without success. The commune then created an Association for the Defence of the Communes Bordering on the Loire, supported by its senator/mayor and grouping together 30-odd communes of the Indre-et-Loire department affected by the project of prohibiting any new urbanisation in the floodplains.

What transpired from this conflict was that the commune of SPC became greatly involved in the action field of flood risk management. It increasingly sought to show itself capable of making a number of proposals and of going beyond the constraints imposed by central government. The conflict calmed down in 1997, thanks to a mediation process organised between the government and the SPC municipality, but also to the constitution on a wider scale (that of the Loire watershed) of a multidisciplinary team (central government, water agency, local authorities) in charge of detailed studies of the evaluation of risk in the mid-Loire and its potential socioeconomic consequences. Following this, a study was made by a bureau of engineering consultants to define the future risks to SPC and possible strategies to put in place. Since then, the commune has been very much involved in studies concerning the reduction of vulnerability on its territory.

The Association for the Defence of the Communes Bordering on the Loire then became the Association of the Communes Bordering on the Loire (*Association des communes riveraines de la Loire*, ACRL), which denotes a gradual transition from a 'defensive' approach to a more constructive one. Today, the commune has reached a state-of-the-art participation point as concerns involvement in various processes aimed at trying to conciliate the development of floodplains and risk management (*Démarche de planification concertée*, joint planning process) in a field where the state traditionally played the main role.

Intercommunalities increase their power in the field of environment

Thus the example of the commune of SPC and of other communes that are members of the ACRL shows a very real capacity on the part of local actors to involve themselves in a specific aspect of flood risk management that is not a high priority for the state: actions for the reduction of vulnerability. Although the central government's PPRI policy provided for the integration of measures for the reduction of vulnerability, a number of studies have shown that little progress was made in this field (cf Ledoux, 2005).

This action field has a very limited regulatory framework. In France, flood risk prevention initiatives crop up more or less on an autonomous, ad hoc basis, depending on the will of the actors (often local authorities or their groupings) ready to involve themselves in those actions. It is thus a more disparate and moving field of action, in constant evolution. Although little developed in the 2000s, the communes (and their groupings) now seem to have found in it an action space.

One should take into account that the two forms of intercommunality mentioned above are involved in these policies: on the one hand, the flexible forms of intercommunality represented by the ACRL, but beyond it, intercommunality represented by the EPLoire (a *syndicat mixte*). This territorial public establishment of the basin (recognised as an intercommunal water actor in the 2006 Water Law) groups together communes, *départements* and Loire regions that are members of the structure so as to better understand issues related to the planning and management of the river. A large number of the structure's tasks concern issues related to flood management. The EPLoire has strongly engaged itself in the field of vulnerability reduction, mobilising European (European Fund for Regional Development [EFRD], Operational Programme Loire) and national funding (*Plan Loire grandeur nature*) intended for an industrial process for the vulnerability reduction of enterprises.

The involvement of integrated intercommunalities can also be seen in this domain all along the Loire, for example, an initiative for a diagnostic project of habitats in a flood risk area carried out by the *Communauté d'agglomération d'Orléans*: 605 people asked for information and 555 properties benefited from a diagnosis of buildings at risk of flooding. Similar diagnostic processes were led by the Val d'Oise Community of Communes.

The case described here not only illustrates the modalities of conflict and cooperation between government services and territorial authorities, but also shows the latter's capacity for innovation in terms of the piloting and instrumentation of public policies. The above-mentioned local authorities and intercommunalities succeeded in participating in a field of public action by proposing a diversification of means of interventions, which even changed the aim of the policy, from one of restriction of urbanisation to one of adaptation of existing buildings.

Management of water bodies: when communes and their intercommunalities assert themselves in a field of action with a strong private sector component

The aim of the second example is to show in detail how environmental policies are put into practice, and to explore the interactions between local actors and the targeted groups and beneficiaries of these policies.

To introduce our subject: the Veyle is an affluent of the Saône river. It is at the interface between two natural regions: la Bresse and la Dombes. Its watershed is strongly affected by an artificial network of waterways gradually built up since the 12th century. It is a linear river that is privately owned: the owner of land bordering the river also owns the riverbed, from the bank to the middle of the bed. All public action therefore requires either purchase or the activation of complex legal mechanisms.

Changing issues for river management associations

The involvement of local authorities in this policy was organised as a result of the creation of a river contract procedure launched in 1998 by three hydraulic associations that already existed on the territory. The river contract is a mechanism initiated by government and aimed at coordinating interventions of the various operators of public action in the water domain. It is signed by the government representative, the prefect, by the participating communes and other partners such as the Water Agency, for example. It is an instrument of intervention on the level of watersheds. For the river concerned, it sets objectives in terms of water quality, valorisation of the aquatic environment and a well-balanced management of resources. It also provides for operational facilities for carrying out studies necessary to reach those objectives. Although it has no formal legal basis, it has the advantage of creating a place for consultation and discussion between the various stakeholders and signatories.

The implementation of this contract led in 2000 to the constitution of a specific intercommunality of the flexible type, the *Syndicat mixte pour l'aménagement et la mise en valeur du bassin versant de la Veyle et de ses affluents* (mixed association for the planning and valorisation of the Veyle watershed and its tributaries, *Syndicat mixte Veyle Vivante*).

This organisation was then able to take charge of coordinating actions and the management of projects. Launched in 2003, the projects can be divided into three subgroups:

- a project for the meandering of the Veyle bed at the locality Moulin de Geai, named *Détournement de la Veyle* (Diversion of the Veyle River);
- the creation of a new minor bed for the river, with a more sinuous path over a 1,800m section, whereas it had previously crossed a gravel layer;
- multiple projects for pike spawning grounds and numerous restorations all along the linear path of the watershed.

These different projects gave rise to numerous interactions between the intercommunal bodies and the users and owners affected by the projects.

A leading role in identifying local river issues

Putting these projects in place for the Veyle had to take place along an entirely privately owned river. For all the operations involved, negotiation times were a necessary prerequisite, as well as various forms of arrangements with the landowners. As agricultural activity is predominant locally, the places identified for carrying out works could also be the object of local leases or of more flexible forms of contract such as exchanges of plots of land between users. In that particular local context, the projects and their continuity could only be assured through partnerships established with the users: landowners, farmers and enterprises for the extraction of materials. The *Syndicat Veyle Vivante* thus played an essential role in leading these negotiations, and allowed the local authorities to carry out their projects successfully.

However, these projects could only come about through the involvement of the initial users of the sites, with whom the *syndicat mixte* established different forms of partnerships. In the context of the *Détournement de la Veyle*, the enterprise for the extraction of aggregates, for example, led all the operations involving negotiation and land purchase with the local landowners, instead of the *Syndicat Veyle Vivante*, which in fact lacked the same advantages as the enterprise as far as the local context was concerned (good knowledge of users, prices of plots and time available for negotiation).

In the same way, although the planning phase is the responsibility of management, maintaining economic activity is a necessity for which forms of agreements are signed as a guarantee for the upkeep of the works. In order to ensure the proper maintenance of sites following works, 'loans for use' are granted to farms already located on the site (and former owners) in order to enable them to continue to let their cattle graze in the meadows (Moulin de Geai). In the case of the *Détournement de la Veyle*, multiple agreements were made with the various users of the site: the extraction enterprise already located on the site but also the local fishing association, the riverside farmers and a local association for the protection of nature.

This example shows how an intercommunality organisation initiated and became leader of a water policy on a territory constituted specifically for that purpose. This role of political, technical and financial management played by communities is one of the guarantees of the success of the implementation of this kind of policy. Without strong local involvement, a simple regulatory order is not enough to produce the desired effect. However, this involvement also requires taking into account territorial issues that can substantially transform the character of a policy.

Conclusions

To conclude this presentation of the implementation of environmental policies in France, we can only once more emphasise the growing importance of local public actors: far from playing the passive role of accompanying governmental policies that was the case until the 1990s, territorial authorities/communities are now essential actors – in the full sense of the term – of the implementation processes of these policies. In order to play that role, they organise and regroup themselves, and innovate in the definition of instruments of intervention. They are at the heart of interactions between the state and the targeted and concerned groups. These strong involvements lead them to transform the policies, adapting them to specific territorial contexts.

In that sense, local actors are able to refashion for their specific territory the objectives of public policies, to elaborate new action instruments and to position themselves as essential actors in the mechanism even in the absence of – if not in place of – central government, and to organise coordination procedures with users or targeted groups in their territories. These various involvements show that in France the processes of formulation of framework environmental policies depend on complex mechanisms, combining a national regulatory framework and subsidiary territorial frameworks. These modes of construction of government environmental policy are not, however, centrally coordinated.

Indeed, such a deep change in implementation modes might have led central government to redesign the policies. Although there is an overall withdrawal of central government within the territory (mainly due to a determination to reduce public funding), this does not go along with a strategic reflection on the respective roles of the different hierarchical levels: on the part of central government, we can still see a will to organise the territory from on top, according to imposed and similar schemas whatever the contexts. It seems to us that thought should be given to the necessary solidarities between territories, based on existing or potential organisational forms, and that this should underlie the organisation of responsibilities, notably in the field of complex policies such as those concerning the environment.

Although equality in the treatment of inhabitants on the national level remains an important principle in the functioning of the French politico-administrative system, the actual inequality in local actors' capacities to take responsibility for their environmental problems needs to lead to a reconsideration of the modes of formulation and implementation of government policies. In that sense, we feel that instead of withdrawal, the central government should initiate a reflection on how to support the less fortunate and most vulnerable territories.

4.5

In the last contribution in this part, Sonia Exley's exploration of aspects of the government of education in England is obviously looking at a radically different policy area to the French environment policy issues explored in the last one. Nevertheless, it provides us with another study that illustrates the problematic nature of a clear-cut and straightforward 'stages' approach to public policy analysis, separating politics from administration.

In England the declining influence and marginalisation of traditional corporatist partners – local government and teacher trade unions – in the governing of education has both allowed for and been driven by: (1) an increasingly overt politicisation and faster-paced, more informal and experimental style of policy formulation within central government; and (2) what has often been termed 'polycentric governance' and a huge rise in policy network activity spanning the state, private and third sectors. Corporate philanthropists, private for-profit and not-for-profit education providers and 'knowledge actors' (Stone, 2000) involved heavily with think tanks act as 'policy entrepreneurs'. Such entrepreneurs play a growing role in the formulation of government initiatives, influencing policy not just via the promotion of particular discourses and a general feeding into the discursive construction of social problems, but also 'leading by example' in the experimental funding, piloting and promulgation of detailed innovations, technologies and policy models. Lines between *state policy formulation* and *non-state policy implementation* are also blurred. Education is an area in which policy is often described as being changed and further produced as it becomes enacted and negotiated by those tasked with its implementation (Ball et al, 2012). Outside actors and interest groups in the current world of education policy are increasingly invited and indeed formally contracted to *co-produce* policy. They are recognised as voices of authority, possessing as they do a new and coveted expert knowledge on 'what works' on the ground and in practice, as statecraft shifts inexorably towards 'governing at a distance'. Within shifts towards privatised policy networks, however, some ideas and actors can certainly be said to hold greater influence than others.

This raises questions about the extent to which power is distributed unequally within policy networks and also the interests ultimately represented by a non-neutral capitalist state. Themes discussed in this contribution can, in many senses, be considered to be UK-wide, although the focus of the contribution is on English policy given education is governed separately in devolved Scottish, Welsh and Northern Irish administrations.

Think tanks and policy networks in English education

Sonia Exley

Introduction

Studies of public policy making have often put forward the notion that policy is descriptively something that happens in a linear series of stages, starting out with early political agenda setting, through more detailed formulation by civil servants to a final stage of implementation, as actors engaged in frontline service delivery get to grips with imperatives 'from above'. One feature of such a 'stages approach' has also sometimes been the highly rationalist notion that early stages of agenda setting in the policy process are where 'politics happens', but that later stages of formulation are – and indeed should be – more impartial and non-political.

Over time, however, the notion that there exist clear-cut policy stages, in particular with distinct phases separating politics from administration, has come to be viewed as problematic. Policies can rarely be said to have a clear time point at which they were 'initiated', and policy is also rarely initiated purely by politicians then developed purely by civil servants. Although a 'middle' phase of complex formulation is often readily identifiable in the development of policy, specific models, instruments and technologies are designed, proposed and promoted by actors inside and outside of government involved at any or all stages of the policy process. In such a context, it can be argued that politics certainly does not end at the point of intentions being announced in Parliament. Permanent civil service staff are known to wield influence in their own right, but in the UK they are also increasingly 'complemented' in the work they do by appointed political advisers, in addition to a proliferation of further overlapping and influential private and third sector actors. Such actors, particularly those with strong financial backing and operating as part of complex and highly political policy networks, play roles not just in the contracted implementation of policy, but in its formulation, development and evaluation.

Breaking down of an old order

Within the governing of English education, an increasingly overt politicisation and privatisation of the formulation of policy over time has taken place in parallel with a progressive marginalisation of teacher trade unions and local government as traditional corporatist 'partners'. Trends can be traced back to the centralising 1980s, when Prime Minister Margaret Thatcher, who had previously served as Secretary of State for Education in England, held deep mistrust not only towards teacher unions and local government but also towards a civil service Department for Education and Science (DES) she deemed as being subversively 'left-wing' and excessively influenced by historically dominant 'producer interests'. Frustrated by and seeking to challenge the status quo, Thatcher granted increasing power and influence to quango organisations (quasi-autonomous non-governmental organisations) in the realm of education operating independently from DES such as the Manpower Services Commission (MSC) headed by (now Lord) David Young, who had previously been an adviser to Education Secretary Keith Joseph and also the Director of the Centre for Policy Studies (CPS), a right-wing think tank founded by Thatcher and Joseph in 1974. MSC was given the power to 'innovate', bypassing DES with funding from the Department of Employment for more radical policy experimentation in the field of youth employment and skills training.

At the same time, numbers of temporary political advisers within central government began to expand. Within their ranks were people from right-wing think tanks such as the Hillgate Group, the National Council for Educational Standards and the Institute for Economic Affairs (IEA), as well as CPS. Clear intentions could be seen on the part of Thatcher and Joseph, and then later Education Secretary Kenneth Baker, to 'shake up' the DES in particular, breaking the Whitehall model of consensus-seeking policy making and bringing policy formulation activity more into line with radical New Right ideology. Examples of famed political appointees inside DES during this time included Stuart Sexton, adviser to Keith Joseph and a member of the IEA, alleged to have viewed civil service approaches to policy formulation during the 1980s with derision (Greenwood and Wilson, 1990), and also Cyril Taylor, adviser to Kenneth Baker and a member of CPS and the Bow Group. In 1986 Cyril Taylor was tasked with setting up the City Technology Colleges Trust (later the Specialist Schools and Academies Trust), a charitable trust created in order to facilitate and support the development of city technology colleges (CTCs) in England. Over time the Trust wielded significant influence in what would become the details of CTC policy formulation and implementation.

Under successive Labour governments from 1997 to 2010, numbers of political advisers and also communications experts operating alongside permanent civil servants inside central government multiplied. Ministerial advisers in government overall doubled in number to 75 between 1997 and 2000, with a trebling of similar staff inside 10 Downing Street in particular over the same time period (Butler, 2000). Advisers during this time were described by one former Permanent Secretary of the Cabinet Office, Sir Robin Mountfield, as behaving like 'unaccountable junior ministers'. Rising informality in policy making has been documented (see Bevir and Rhodes, 2006), and arguably a growing preference for policy experimentation and policy 'on the hoof', with advisers on education in particular speaking candidly about the importance of avoiding 'long formal notes' or the 'formal hierarchies of the civil service', cutting through 'complicated loops' in order to preserve policy 'radicalism' so that ideas would 'move faster' in a context of urgent reform (Exley, 2012, p 236).

Numbers of political advisers across central government departments have remained broadly similar under the Coalition government rule since 2010 to those observed under Labour. Within education, there have been possible indications of a further overt politicising of activity within what is now the Department for Education (DfE). In February 2013, Education Secretary Michael Gove was accused of using the DfE as an 'ideological test-bed' after announcing plans to cut 1,000 permanent civil service jobs (Syal, 2013), part of a wider intention to create a slimmed-down and 'post-bureaucratic' department. At the same time, media attention has been paid to alleged partisan activities on the part of Michael Gove's political advisers, and to instances in which advisers are said to have bypassed civil service protocol regarding transparency in the formulation of policy (Vasagar, 2011; Helm, 2013).

Think tanks as 'do tanks'

One particularly notable feature regarding trends towards growing numbers of appointed political advisers within central government is the strength of professional connections that such advisers tend to have with a proliferation of think tanks and policy research organisations carrying out work in all areas of public services. Within the realm of education, under Labour, as Head of the Downing Street Policy Unit (DSPU) and advising on education among other areas, David Miliband had previously worked for the centre-left think tank Institute for Public Policy Research (IPPR). Special advisers to Education Secretary Ruth Kelly – Richard Darlington, Will Paxton, Dan Corry and Gavin Kelly – also all previously worked for IPPR (Slater, 2008), as did Nick Pearce (now Director of IPPR) who advised Education Secretary David Blunkett. Tom Bentley, also an adviser to Blunkett, later became Director of the think tank Demos, and Andrew Adonis, former journalist and adviser to Tony Blair on education, had written for Demos in his time before joining DSPU. Similar connections to think tanks can be seen under the Coalition government in the DfE. Henry de Zoete, adviser to Michael Gove, is a former campaigns manager for the think tank Reform. Sam Freedman, until recently an adviser at DfE, was formerly Head of Education at the centre-right think tank Policy Exchange. Gabriel Milland, Head of News at DfE, is a former Head of Press at Policy Exchange. James Frayne, until recently Communications Director at DfE, was formerly Campaigns Director at the Taxpayers' Alliance.

With Stephen Ball I have written elsewhere (Ball and Exley, 2010) about an extensive and growing national and international sprawl of think tank, research and 'knowledge actor' (Stone, 2000) sites of education policy activity. Such activity takes place in parallel and in the shadow of government reform, and it has supplanted a more traditional civil service reliance on academic policy expertise. New organisations are spawned in abundance out of old ones. Key actors slip between a politically ambiguous world of 'ideas' and the world of government then back again, taking discourses and colleagues with them as they go. Think tanks are important 'nodes' within education policy networks, connected in dense and complex forms to each other as well as to government. Key actors and ideas tend to be associated with multiple organisations and multiple individuals at any one time. There are initiatives created in partnership, co-authoring efforts, associate memberships, shared office spaces and mutual patterns of citation and referencing. Technology plays an important role in bringing together those who are like-minded. Virtual communities are created via the production of online sites, spaces, 'gateways' (see, for example, the blog ConservativeHome) and fora for discussion.

A clear overlapping of education policy actors between think tanks and government is relevant here, partly because it arguably lends support to the general notion that there is a more overt politicising over time of education policy formation inside government. Think tank experience on the part of policy makers is often described as being desirable because civil servants require 'help to think':

> Large organisations are generally poorly designed for original thought: indeed, modern bureaucracies are arguably much better designed for eliminating originality and dissent. Hence the need for specialised organisations that work with ideas, analyses and arguments.... The Civil Service will never again have a monopoly of policy advice for ministers. That world is now more open and competitive, and better for that. (Geoff Mulgan, co-founder of Demos and former Director of Policy at 10 Downing Street, 2006)

Classic depictions of think tank education 'policy work' and the role think tanks generally play in the education policy process are that this would be considered influential at a largely intangible, abstract and difficult-to-measure level of *ideas* – feeding into the flow and reinforcing of particular discourses or a 'mobilisation of bias' (Schattschneider, 1960), and contributing to the normative construction of agendas and social problems. Some evidence of such influence on the part of think tanks in recent English education policy can be considered clear. One report published by Policy Exchange in 2010 (a think tank co-founded by Michael Gove himself), entitled *Blocking the best*, is often considered to have been influential in the development of Conservative Party plans for the expansion of 'state-independent' academies and 'free schools', recommending as it does the broad removal of local government planning barriers to the market liberalising of English schooling supply. Work by the Centre for Social Justice is frequently cited as having played an important role in the development of Conservative Party rhetoric on education and social mobility. On the matter of 'slimming down' state bureaucracy in education, a 2009 report published by CPS (Burkard and Talbot Rice, 2009) recommended abolition of 11 'school quangos' in England, seven of which were subsequently abolished in 2012.

However, contemporary think tank activity and influence can also be viewed as complicating and challenging the basic notion that there exists a clear-cut distinction in policy-making stages (with different actors involved at different stages) between agenda setting/initiation and the subsequent more detailed formulation of initiatives. Although historically think tanks have been conceptualised as being there *in order to think*, exercising 'influence without responsibility' (Denham and Garnett, 1999) and less concerned with the details of making policy practicable, more recent writings on the role of think tanks have depicted these organisations as increasingly occupying a 'bridging' space between more abstract ideas and concrete policy or action (Mulgan, 2006). Education policy efforts on the part of think tanks in England might be argued to be focusing increasingly on the promotion of detailed policy models, policy choices and particular *instruments*. Innovations are produced and sold to government as practical and workable solutions to intractable problems. Think tanks have been rebranded as 'do tanks', turning ideas into concrete entrepreneurial action in a context where increasing policy informality within central government and a preference for policy by increment and by experiment has created a context ripe for the influencing not just of broad agendas, but of detailed policy formulation. In this context, as Lindblom (1959) has suggested, values may often not be chosen by government prior to thinking about what detailed policy options would fit with chosen values; rather, values and options may often be chosen all at once as part of governments 'muddling through', or at the very least values may easily become compromised by the politics of limited practical policy choices 'on offer'.

Experimental initiatives in education are financed and piloted by think tanks operating as 'do tanks', research organisations, charitable trusts and social enterprises, evaluated and then sold to government as 'tried and tested' packages, the detailed work of policy formulation happening outside the state, with initiatives already 'up and running' before governments decide to finance and expand them and thereby incorporate them into the 'formal' policy sphere. Charitable organisations such as The Sutton Trust in England headed by philanthropist Peter Lampl act strategically. Since 1998 The Sutton Trust has committed £30 million to the funding of 'a wide range of access projects in early years, school and university settings, with a focus on research, policy and innovative practical projects with a system-wide relevance' (The Sutton Trust, 2013). Seeking to 'break the link between educational opportunities and family background', The Sutton Trust has funded a number of detailed pilot projects which have sometimes acted as models influencing the subsequent government formulation of national education policies. In 2005, an experimental funding of Choice Advice by The Sutton Trust in Wandsworth, London, is known to have had an impact on the development of later government policy that mandated all local authorities in England to provide Choice Advice to disadvantaged families. Centre-right 'do tank' Civitas has established independent day schools 'roughly in line with the cost per pupil of state education' via an offshoot company called the New Model Schools Company Ltd. According to ConservativeHome, lessons learned in Civitas' New Model Schools have been 'an important influence on Michael Gove MP as he drafts a supply-side revolution for the whole ... schools system.'

A wider privatising of policy

An increasingly overt politicising of the formulation of policy and a concomitant growing influence for networks of think tanks and research organisations can be considered, however, to be merely the tip of a much bigger 'privatisation of policy' iceberg. Discussing a shift from hierarchical to heterarchical governance in education, Ball (2013, p 51) has stressed the importance of examining more broadly 'new educational alliances' which shake up education policy with practical and experimental innovations, existing 'in the borderland between the public, private and voluntary sectors', part of a 'move towards a more interactive, fragmented and multi-dimensional form of policy making'. In a classic 'stages' view of policy-making processes, contracted providers of educational services might be thought of as being involved in policy implementation, but that this, as a stage, would exist as distinct and independent from a prior stage of policy formulation. As suggested earlier, the boundaries between implementation and the formulation stages of policy making are becoming increasingly blurred. Here there is significant evidence of a growing political influence for large-scale 'edu-business' in the formulation of policy – both for-profit and not-for-profit suppliers of education.

In November 2009 Michael Gove announced in a speech to the CPS not just that *staff numbers* inside (what would become) the DfE would be cut as part of a move towards 'post-bureaucratic' government, but so too would 'the number of things they regulate, monitor and issue decrees on'. In England it can be asserted that alongside a gradual liberalising and exogenous privatising of educational service provision over time, there has also been a privatisation of policy making, with growing formal roles and influence for private and third sector agents as entrepreneurial voices of authority and expertise on 'what works' in practice. Civil servants are, by contrast, presented within dominant discourses as being increasingly ill equipped for the job of formulating policy details as the functions of the central state become gradually stripped away. Relations of trust are built between government and contractors – Newman (2001) has described this as being one core facet of 'joined-up government' – and non-state actors are in turn increasingly tasked with the 'ironing out' of policy details and problems as plans and initiatives evolve and develop (see also Mahony et al, 2004). Within English education, the management of entire local authority education departments – with all the policy formulation and decision making this involves – has been taken over in numerous instances (where they have been deemed by Ofsted, the Office for Standards in Education, to be 'failing') by private companies such as Capita and Serco. At the level of central government, private sector management consultancies such as PricewaterhouseCoopers, McKinsey and KPMG are ubiquitous as contractors in the carrying out of large amounts of education policy work on behalf of government – authoring documents, carrying out evaluations, developing guidelines and writing detailed recommendations (Ball, 2009). Recent plans for the 'slimming down' of the DfE have themselves involved Michael Gove contracting management consultancy Bain & Company to advise on where the biggest budget cuts ought to be made. Policy 'tsars' involved in the detailed formulation and implementation of policy have increased in number under Coalition rule since 2010, acting as 'bureaucratic entrepreneurs' (Smith, 2011). Although many are known to come from the worlds of public services and academia, four in ten are now from the world of business (Levitt and Solesbury, 2012).

During its time in opposition prior to 2010, the Conservative Party formed strong alliances with the 'anti-bureaucratic education charity', Teach First. Teach First is a particularly interesting example of policy entrepreneurialism and funded pilot activity taking place outside the state, and later being incorporated and expanded as part of formal government education reforms. Since 2002, Teach First in England, partnered with the US Teach for America scheme and set up by management consultant Brett Wigdortz on a six-month leave of absence from McKinsey, has provided flexibilised, employment-based initial teacher training as an alternative to traditional university-based schemes of initial teacher training. While in 2002 Teach First, sponsored in part by Citi and the Canary Wharf Group, trained just 183 graduates on an experimental basis, the organisation has grown over time to become the biggest single provider of new teachers in England, training over 1,000 university graduates per year. In a 2009 speech Michael Gove, as Shadow Education Secretary, praised Teach First as a valuable 'civil society programme' which had 'done more to make teaching an elite profession over the last decade than any action by any government minister or salaried bureaucrat'. In 2010 Teach First was formally named as being targeted for expansion through government funding in the Conservative Party manifesto:

> We will expand Teach First and introduce two new programmes – Teach Now, for people looking to change career, and Troops to Teachers, for ex-service personnel – to get experienced, high-quality people into the profession.

Since 2010, the Coalition government has dedicated £94.2 million in funding to the expansion of Teach First. Extra annual funding was announced for the charity in November 2012, with the aim that Teach First schemes would train 2,000 new teachers per year by 2015/16 (DfE, 2012). As with what was described above regarding think tanks as 'do tanks', this again constitutes policy by experiment, policy by increment and detailed policy formulation taking place very clearly outside the state. Former adviser at the DfE, Sam Freedman, has recently been appointed Director of Research, Evaluation and Impact at Teach First, responsible for 'challenging thinking internally and externally about what can be done to have the greatest impact on improving the outcomes of children from the least advantaged communities.'

In a similar vein, in 2010, a charitable organisation, the New Schools Network (NSN), headed by former adviser to Michael Gove, Rachel Wolf, was given an uncontested £500,000 grant to support and advise parents in the setting up of liberalised state-independent free schools:

> The New Schools Network will act as the first point of contact for all groups who wish to start schools and will provide them with information as they go through the process and prepare their proposals. (DfE, 2010)

The extent to which policy on free schools is shaped and determined by NSN staff rather than civil servants inside the DfE is difficult to establish, but here again the roles of policy implementation and policy formulation seem to merge, as NSN becomes responsible for the development of advice and guidance on the creation of free schools, when, as has been stated by one NSN representative: 'there are officials within the department [DfE] who would be well placed to liaise between parents and providers.' Former Secretary of State for Education Shirley Williams has commented that 'it is odd for a department of government to tell people they cannot answer inquiries directly in the first instance, but must instead refer them on to somebody else' (Clark, 2010). Rachel Wolf was a co-author of the Policy Exchange report *Blocking the best*, and is known to have contributed to the 2010 Conservative Party manifesto (ConservativeHome, 2010). A number of donors to NSN are anonymous, but trustees include Michael David George, a board director of the United Learning Trust (ULT), and Michael Clark, Director of UK Programmes for ARK Schools. ULT and ARK are two of the major private providers of chains of state-independent academies in England.

Outsourcing the devising of policy detail and policy solutions in English education is presented within networks as being partly a matter of expertise – those involved in the process of 'doing' are those who will know best which solutions are most viable. However, outsourcing is also presented as being a matter of urgency and of capacity. Greater policy informality focusing on experimentation and 'innovation' from outside is generally referred to in contrast with the more cautious and carefully considered process that is in-house policy formulation by permanent civil service staff. Responding to criticisms regarding £500,000 for NSN in 2011 in order to support the development of free schools, then Junior Minister for Schools Nick Gibb argued: 'Given the need for specialist skills and experience to be in place quickly, it was decided to award a time-limited grant to the New Schools Network' (quoted in *Hansard*, 2011). Another DfE response stressed that NSN 'has been active in this area for some time and was effectively the only organisation capable of providing the level of support needed by the number of interested parties quickly enough to enable the first free schools to open by September 2011' (Syal, 2010).

Power, interest groups and the capitalist state

An increasingly overt politicisation and privatisation of policy formulation in English education, blurring lines between formulation and agenda setting but also between policy formulation and policy implementation, might in some senses be viewed optimistically as one that is more democratic, granting influence to a 'big society' of actors compared with a system in which power is concentrated more clearly in the hands of central government departments. However, Frankham (2006) has cautioned against the characterising of networks as transformatory and utopian arrangements in which actors have equal power, working together as partners in a context of mutual learning. As the clear marginalisation of teacher trade unions and local government over time in England would suggest, clearly power is not distributed equally within policy networks. Increasingly it can be argued that ideas are tradable commodities within a global knowledge marketplace. Policy itself is being bought and sold, and power remains structured in the sense that ideas with the greatest financial backing are those gaining greatest legitimacy, travelling furthest, holding most 'sway'. Policy expertise mobilised within networks can be thought of as being politically ambiguous and transcending party political lines, but in no sense can it be considered 'non-political'. Academic methodology has become devalued in education policy networks. There is a 'false equivalency' in research credibility terms lent in news media to advocacy groups regardless of the extent to which such organisations 'emphasise policy and political advocacy over the professional norms of academic research' (Haas, 2007). Among advisers in government, often what matters is less that research knowledge is intellectually rigorous, and more that it is simple, dynamically presented and easy to understand. Attention must be paid to the privately funded political and economic agendas underpinning policy packages with the greatest success in influencing government. We might here consider what Barnett has termed 'corporate populism', where numbers of organisations outside the state and influencing policy may be growing in number to a greater degree than ever before, but they are also 'operating within increasingly limited intellectual boundaries' (1999, p 24).

Questions over how far shifts towards a 'neoliberal formulation of policy' described above might constitute a veering away from any distinct separation between politics and administration must also consider, however, the extent to which civil servants have ever themselves been 'neutral actors' rather than part of a community operating in line with and ultimately representing private sector capitalist interests. Authors writing about 'metagovernance' and the state have long posited the notion that state control over public services is not reducing as governments 'hollow out', but instead transforming (Jessop, 2002) towards 'steering at a distance'. Policy networks and the actors within them can be thought of as being 'managed' by government and their entrepreneurial agency can at times be overstated. Policy formulation, then, is perhaps political now, but just as it has always been, because states are designed by ruling elites as instruments for class domination, and perhaps it is also the case that power is more concentrated and less fragmented than much literature on networks might suggest. Dunleavy (1994), however, warns heavily against important risks inherent in a short-sighted incremental approach on the part of government leading towards a gradual 'privatisation of everything'. Core competencies become lost over time, and so too might scope for national decision making, the power to hold actors accountable and ultimately the ability to govern. Dunleavy draws on a dystopian vision of the future painted by author Marge Piercy in order to illustrate possibilities where 'radical outsourcing evangelism' has led to a 'withering away of the state' replaced by 'new forms of corporate feudalism':

> Urban megalopolies have slumped into ungovernability. Multiple fiercely competing transnational corporations dominate the economy, and maintain their own company enclaves … for professional elites. The collective life has shrunk into a worldwide computer network essential for economic exchange and information sharing…. It is easy to dismiss such fictional accounts. But … forty years ago it might have seemed almost as incredible that there could exist worldwide restaurant chains. Some unlikely extrapolations are worth taking seriously. (Dunleavy, 1994, p 61)

Part Five
Implementation

5.1
Introduction

While efforts to analyse implementation have many antecedents, much modern work takes as its starting point Pressman and Wildavsky's influential book *Implementation* (1973), where they offered us a simple definition of implementation as 'what happens between policy expectations and (perceived) policy results'. Then, of course, the study of implementation is about the explanation of 'what happens', with an inevitable emphasis on the situation in which expectations and results do not correspond. Pressman and Wildavsky, quite rightly, lead us to expect there may be a 'gap' here, and accordingly what they call an 'implementation deficit'. Simplistic explorations of this tend to focus on simple disobedience. But Pressman and Wildavsky give much attention, in their empirical study, to issues about the way policy is transmitted from its origins in the USA federal government to a town in a distant state (Oakland, California).

The problem is that what is implicit in their approach is an assumption that 'policy expectations' will be clear and undisputed, and that policy originators have a legitimate right to dictate what should be done. In the substantial literature that followed Pressman and Wildavsky's work we find, then, both efforts to operationalise the study of implementation that accepts, in various modified ways, the basic ideas of tracing 'what happens' without seeing too many problems about 'expectations', and approaches to the topic that see the whole notion of a traceable 'policy' to be problematical. These two approaches are often described as 'top-down' and 'bottom-up'. But at this point in history there has been much cross-fertilisation between the approaches, and it is a rather sterile exercise to try to takes sides on it. The only small point of warning appropriate here is to mention that the original debate was very much driven by views about what should happen: obedience to the 'top' or rights to determine action at the 'bottom'. This concern tends to get in the way of objective implementation studies.

Other parts of this book, particularly Part Four on formulation, have stressed policy complexity. So there is no need to labour here the view that this is likely to complicate implementation. An analysis that gets to the heart of this is provided by Matland (1995), who argues that there are two particular issues about policy that need to be taken into account in order to understand implementation: ambiguity and conflict. He goes on to set out a matrix exploring the interaction between the two. Low levels of both ambiguity and conflict are likely to make the management of implementation a relatively straightforward task. High levels of both will have the corresponding opposite effect. High ambiguity but low conflict will facilitate consensual problem-solving activity in the course of implementation, while in situations of high conflict and low ambiguity, implementation will depend on the feasibility of the resolution of political differences.

While a two-by-two matrix is a splendid teaching device, the reality is that both ambiguity and conflict need to be recognised as running along a continuum from low to high. Very low ambiguity is rare, and where it occurs, implementation is just a rather routine management issue (in which implementation scholars generally take little interest). An example from the UK would be the policy providing a cash grant in the winter to help older people with their fuel costs. The amount to be paid is a fixed figure – all those over a specified age qualify, and there is an official database (state pension records) to enable eligible people to be identified. So long as the activity is clearly specified to an adequately resourced team, implementation is straightforward.

Going away from that baseline, ambiguity comes in many forms. Matland writes of 'ambiguity of goals and ambiguity of means', and includes within the latter situations when:

> … there are uncertainties about what roles various organizations are to play in the implementation process, or when a complex environment makes it difficult to know which tools to use, how to use them, and what the effects of their use will be. (1995, p 158)

In this sense the concept of ambiguity may be extended to embrace complexity. With perhaps the exception of the Scottish alcohol pricing policy (Chapter 6.2), all the policies discussed in this book involve complexity and thus potential ambiguity.

Matland's conflict variable is perhaps more difficult to analyse since what is involved in this context is more than a dispute about a policy (even the fuel costs policy described above is the subject of dispute) but additionally disagreement that leads key actors essential for the implementation process to try to prevent its operationalisation. This suggests other considerations including the power to obstruct and strong feelings about the legitimacy of such action. Much will depend, then, on the ambiguity/complexity dimension, influencing the feasibility of enforcement in the face of resistance.

Van Meter and van Horn (1975) offer a useful model for mapping the implementation process in terms of the determinants of *performance*. Winter argues that researchers should 'look for behavioural *output* variables to characterize the *performance* of implementers' to explain variation in performance, thereby avoiding contestable questions about goal achievement (2006, p 158). There is an issue here about the distinction between outputs and outcomes. Winter suggests it is undesirable to work with the latter inasmuch as it involves a need to deal with influences on behaviour that are independent of the implementation process (2006, pp 161-3). However, there may be situations where there is a need to take into account policies where outcome goals are specified, leaving implementers to determine the means to achieve those goals, in which case attention to outputs may be beside the point. This topic is central to concerns about governance through networks (Koppenjan and Klijn, 2004) and to recognition that – particularly in respect of professional services – the mode of implementation may involve co-production with a management focus on outcomes (see Hill and Hupe, 2009, chapter 6). In that last sense the term 'performance' is particularly apposite, an analogy may be made with the efforts of a director to influence the acting or singing of others.

The contributions to this part involve complex system changes: in sociocultural organisations in the Netherlands (Chapter 5.2), healthcare delivery in England (Chapter 5.3) and higher education in Finland (Chapter 5.4). In each case, the policies whose implementation is being examined involve expectations about outcomes. Broadly speaking these involve concerns about the efficiency of policy delivery, but behind these may lie wider, and perhaps contestable, goals about, for example, consumer choice in the health case or national competitiveness in the higher education case. Here, then, the argument in favour of concentration on the examination of outputs lies in a concern to explain what happened in a way which is uncontaminated by controversy about goals. Nevertheless, inasmuch as positivist research designs require identifiable 'dependant' variables, these may be very hard to identify.

The influences on performance specified in the van Meter and van Horn model are *policy characteristics, interorganisational communication and enforcement activities, the characteristics of implementing agencies, economic and social conditions* and *the disposition of implementers.*

It might seem to be the case that policy characteristics could be seen as either defining the required performance or as a separable 'constant' in the process as a whole. However, as suggested in the discussion above, and in that on policy formulation, it is often complex and subject to change. There is likely to be feedback and negotiation during the implementation process that needs to be taken into account as an influence on performance. Indeed there may be variations between implementing agencies because these negotiations vary from place to place.

Most implementation processes involve vertical relationships of some kind; policy originators are rarely themselves implementers. The main exceptions are certain macro policy-making activities such as those involved in economic and foreign policy. However, Sonia Exley's contribution in Part Four (Chapter 4.5) provides an example of a situation in which some of the policy entrepreneurs who help to shape policy also implement it (as she notes, 'think tanks' become 'do tanks').

Even in more straightforward cases, implementation relationships may be more than simple bilateral ones. Moreover, they may be *inter*organisational rather than *intra*organisational. It was noted above that one of the main contributions to the study of implementation by Pressman and Wildavsky was the identification of change because of the chain between policy origination and policy output. However, the simple notion of a chain may be misleading for two reasons. One is the actors in any policy transmission chain are likely to be in a continuing relationship with each other, which will affect how they react to any new instruction (Bowen, 1982). The other is that these relationships may have institutional features (see the discussion in Part Two) defining elements of autonomy. The latter is particularly brought out in developments of Pressman and Wildavsky's work in the USA that stressed the significance of federalism (Goggin et al, 1990; Stoker, 1991). Corinne Larrue and Marie Fournier's contribution to Part Four (Chapter 4.3) illustrates the importance of issues about the roles of layers in the policy system and about interorganisational relationships.

Much policy implementation involves collaboration between organisations. Much implementation involves a search for ways to secure concerted action where more than one organisation is involved at the output level. This is often further complicated by vertical divisions, where two output-level organisations belong within different (vertical) hierarchies.

There are issues about collaboration within organisations that may be very similar to those between organisations. Probably the most important body of theoretical work on these issues is the literature on the roles of street-level bureaucrats (Lipsky, 1980, revised edn, 2010; Brodkin, 2012). Lipsky's original work on this stressed issues about the compliance of semi-professionals: 'the decisions of street-level bureaucrats, the routines they establish, and the devices they invent to cope with uncertainties and work pressures, effectively become the public policies they carry out' (1980, p xii). While Lipsky's perspective is widely summarised as just that, he goes on to explore the extent to which this non-compliance is a product of attempts to cope with pressures and to resolve difficulties in putting professional ideals into practice.

Propositions about street-level bureaucracy can be widened out to recognise discretion as an element in all implementation work, varying in terms of the extent to which precise inputs have been supplied hierarchically (Hill, 2013, pp 237-46). The exploration of this variation takes us back to Matland's identification of ambiguity as a source of variation in implementation. But his other variable 'conflict' may also be relevant where this poses difficulties for the specification of inputs.

5.2

Where there are multiple implementing agencies, implementation studies have been able to quantify some of the factors outlined above. René Torenvlied, the first of the contributors to this part, is making a significant contribution to this work (see, in particular, Torenvlied and Akkerman, 2004; Oosterwaal and Torenvlied, 2012). However, he has also given considerable attention to the less measurable aspects of the implementation process, and provides here a qualitative study. This illustrates aspects of the kind of complexity that has to be handled in qualitative studies.

René Torenvlied reports here on a case study into the effect of political conflict on the course and outcomes of the policy implementation process, which is an important object of study in the field of public administration (Wilson, 1887; Weber, 1925; Hill and Hupe, 2002; Riccucci et al, 2004; May and Winter, 2009). The case study used here is the reform of sociocultural work in a Dutch city. Intuitively, it sounds quite plausible that political conflict in a legislature affects the implementation of the policy decisions adopted. Suppose, for example, that local legislators strongly disagree about the necessity of urban development programmes in their community or city. The compromise policy decisions, ultimately reached by the different political parties, must be implemented by local agencies, such as housing corporations or community organisations. Given that the local agencies have their own preferences for urban development, they may use the political controversy to advance their own most preferred alternative for urban renewal. Hence, the actual renewal efforts, made by these local agencies, could diverge from the original compromise policy decision adopted by the local legislature. Instead of taking legislative output or the process of regulatory design as an exclusive framework for the analysis of policy implementation, the case study presented here takes into account the actions and preferences of multiple agencies to explain the policy divergence of agencies during implementation.

Agency preferences and political conflict: policy implementation in the Netherlands

René Torenvlied

Introduction

The public administration literature does not provide strong empirical support for the prediction that political conflict among legislators affects policy divergence by implementation agencies (Evans et al, 1985; Waterman and Meier, 1998; Meier and O'Toole 2006). In a series of theoretical-empirical studies, based on the implementation of social policy reforms in three Dutch municipalities in the 1990s, I have identified the core variables and mechanisms that drive the nexus between political conflict and policy implementation (see, for example, Torenvlied, 1996, 2000). From the general patterns in characteristics of political conflict and policy implementation it is inferred that political conflict reinforces the effect of agencies' preference incongruence with the policies set for their performance (Oosterwaal and Torenvlied, 2012).

The case presented in this contribution is the story of the implementation of reforms in the sociocultural sector of the city of Groningen, one of the three municipalities in the overall study. Sociocultural work aimed to solve all kinds of social problems at various levels in the city, such as unemployment or criminality. The political–administrative context of local government in the Netherlands is, foremost, defined by the primacy of the elected *city council*. In the city of Groningen seven parties held 38 seats, with the Green Left and the Labour Party holding 17 seats. The governing coalition consisted of the Labour Party, the Democratic Party and the Christian Democratic Party. Together with the mayor, who is appointed by the Crown, 'office holders' from these three parties formed the *city government*. City administration is organised in departments, for which the Education, Sport and Wellbeing (ESW) Department was the most important for the present case. Municipal civil servants in the departments prepare council decisions, and play an active role in coordinating their implementation.

In the domain of sociocultural work, *organisations for sociocultural work* are the most important policy implementers. In the city of Groningen, the social services organisation *Delta* was the largest (with 60 employees, 30 of whom were professionals working in the different neighbourhoods in the city of Groningen). Delta provided services to approximately 50 organisations in the field, receiving annually 20 million guilders from city government. Delta provided support services, and was formally the employer of professional social workers in 23 neighbourhood centres – key implementers of sociocultural work. Other implementers were: the Elderly People Wellbeing Organisation and the Bureau of Residents' Experts (BRE), which carried out technical tasks at the request of the residents and housing corporations. The Playground Centre provided support to the many playground associations in the city. In the field of sociocultural work we also observe various *societal implementers*. Social-cultural work was partly implemented by the target groups of social-cultural policy themselves: as many as 54 neighbourhood centres, residents' commissions, organisations for older people or minority ethnic groups, or volunteer associations (such as playground organisations) were active at the time of the case study.

The data collection was very intensive, and a full account is provided in Torenvlied (2000). Key informants, participative observation and document analysis were the main sources. References are made to a number of documents but these have not been cited in the bibliography since they are working papers in Dutch which readers are unlikely to want to follow up. Several stakeholders informally checked the case description. Many years have passed by since this implementation process took place, and much has changed since then in the city, as policy formation and implementation are inherently dynamic. Nevertheless, the case study is still valuable and suitable for discussion here. In the first place, it fits the current trend from 'government' to 'governance'. The more hierarchical government approach, which emphasises the primacy of elected officials and the loyalty of administration, is gradually being complemented by governance approaches that involve officials, professionals and citizens together in solving complex social problems (see, for example, Edelenbos and Klijn, 2006; Dekker et al, 2010; Mosley and Grogan, 2013). In the second place, the chain of events that occurs as the case unfolds is still revealing for scholars and practitioners. The fundamental dynamics of the implementation process are clearly visible: (1) the transposition of ideas into policy; (2) the adoption of decisions; (3) the introduction of the policy in administration and the public sector; and (4) its full implementation. In the third place, the story forms part of the critical underpinning (thick description) of the core variables used in large *n* studies that test various models of policy implementation. Without in-depth case descriptions, such models remain relatively empty structures. Although these models explain the scientific regularities we are interested in, they lack the proper description of how these regularities materialise in the real world we observe.

Changing perceptions about how to solve social problems

In 1984, the city government of Groningen, a medium-sized city in the north of the Netherlands, published a policy document entitled *Neighbourhood and club house work*. This laid the basis for social-cultural work activities in the future. Population groups, *systematically* deprived of the opportunity to participate in society (employment, income, housing and education) were identified among older people, minority ethnic groups, women, young people and the long-term unemployed. A broad range of social-cultural activities was offered for these groups:

club house activities; tenants' support; social work; activities for older people, women, minority ethnic groups and the long-term unemployed; childcare facilities; facilities for school children after school hours; playground work; and child and youth work. Such activities were viewed as instruments to fight unemployment and criminality.

The 1984 policy document assigned responsibility for social–cultural work to one central social services organisation, Delta. Emphasis was placed on the role of professionals – social workers who provided support to volunteers in order to reach a broader target group. Delta focused on *executive work* in neighbourhoods, working with contracts for social workers who provided activities for children, young people and minority ethnic groups. Delta also provided various forms of *support* to other organisations in the field of sociocultural work, for example, *management* support (formulating policy plans, applications for subsidies and personnel management), *financial-administrative* support, and the formal employment of all the city's social workers.

Policy perceptions about the role of social–cultural work changed over time. The new National Wellbeing Law, passed in 1987, delegated more power to the local governments and made large cut-backs in the budgets of national social services. A new policy perception on the role of social–cultural work developed at the end of the 1980s and the beginning of the 1990s. This perception focused on the prevention, rather than the solution, of social problems. The personal responsibility and involvement of citizens was more prominent. Conflicting opinions exist about the tasks of social–cultural work in modern societies. Some support the capability and obligation of citizens to take responsibility for their own future. Others emphasise the limited means that must be yielded to success. The Groningen approach to social–cultural work was *neighbourhood-oriented*. When government interventions take place closer to the citizen, societal problems can be prevented and solved more effectively. Social–cultural activities were redefined as those that stimulated: 'group formation and meetings of people with similar interests, problems, or sub-cultural values; the acquisition and exercise of certain capabilities directed toward expanding knowledge, the development of insights, and views or attitudes, and the development of skills; awareness of personal housing, employment or life situation, and the development of an active and critical involvement in the influencing this situation' (ESW Department, 1991a, p 11).

Transposition of neighbourhood approach: the 1991 council decision

On 13 June 1991, the city council Commission on Wellbeing ordered the city ESW Department to conduct research into the possibilities of a far-reaching reorganisation of social–cultural work. The aim was to abolish the Delta organisation and to save 750,000 guilders. Delta's abolition was thought to be possible by merging it with other social services organisations. A condition of the merger and cut-backs was that the quality of the executive work and support would be maintained.

The merger and financial cut-backs were motivated by three arguments. First, a central social services organisation such as Delta was thought to be incongruent with a neighbourhood-oriented approach. In bureaucratic language: 'The sectoral organization of professional support for residents (social work) and residents' experts (housing) does not accord with the present integral method of operation in the neighbourhoods' (Discussion document, RSNS, p 8). Second, many were not satisfied with the functioning of the central social services organisation, Delta. A number of problems that had been noted by the local council earlier had never been tackled. The problems listed in a previous evaluation were: too little resources to allow residents to participate; a suboptimal distribution of resources across the neighbourhoods; too little consultation of neighbourhood organisations and institutions concerning projects in their neighbourhoods; and a fragmentation in subsidies. Third, financial cut-backs were planned in relation to sociocultural work. A total of 2.2 million guilders of cut-backs were planned for the sport, wellbeing and recreation sector. The policy document *Perspective* stated that the budgets should not be cut incrementally, but that specific budgets should be identified – and cut. The ESW Department dutifully followed up on this assignment.

At the same time, the ESW Department wrote a discussion document, together with the Planning and Economic Affairs Department, on support for residents, which is part of social-cultural work. This document was published in September 1991, and was entitled *Residents support new style* (RSNS). It presented a structure for neighbourhood-oriented work by residents' organisations, proposing that neighbourhood organisations be established, and subsidised separately. Subsidies would first be bundled, and then allocated to the neighbourhood organisations. The Urban Residents' Platform (URP), representing residents' organisations, would become an umbrella organisation providing support to social-cultural work.

The residents' organisations themselves had proved to be a 'difficult' discussion partner for the city government: internally divided, opinionated, and with diverse levels of organisation and composition. The first reactions were, indeed, strongly divided: 'this document, like many others before it, [...] shows little understanding of local problems; the chosen design has an open end character; the residents' organizations believe that it is intended to solve the problems of ESW, rather than those of the residents' organizations'. The introduction of new neighbourhood organisations, and the allocation of resources and powers to these organisations, met with great resistance from the existing residents' organisations, which were often keen to operate independently. The city government was not sensitive to their criticisms. The main proposals in the RSNS document remained unchanged. However, in November 1991, the city government (mayor and office holders) proposed to the council that the new organisation structure be introduced one year later than originally intended.

The mayor and office holders were also prepared to give residents' organisations more involvement in the further development of a neighbourhood-oriented organisation structure. The governing body proposed to the council to 'give the city government the task of elaborating a new organization structure for professional support and the distribution of the neighbourhood budgets for professional support for residents in consultation with the residents' organizations, the Delta organization, and the Bureau Residents' Experts (BRE)'. The elaboration of this new organisational structure would be connected with the city council's plans for restructuring social-cultural work as a whole.

Meanwhile, a more broadly oriented policy document concerned with sociocultural work appeared that was commissioned by the council from the ESW Department. This document, entitled *Time for the neighbourhood*, provided a basis for the planned restructuring: (1) the abolition of Delta, coupled with the cut-backs and the merger of social services organisations: the Elderly People Wellbeing Organisation, the Playground Centre and the BRE; and (2) the introduction of neighbourhood platforms for the support of residents (as in the policy document RSNS). This introduced the third important issue involved in the restructuring of social-cultural work: *the establishment of neighbourhood platforms.* A sum of 200,000 guilders was reserved to implement the council's proposal. The council approved the policy document *Time for the neighbourhood* on 18 December, but specified, in an amendment, that *all* organisations should be involved in the implementation of the council's decision. This initiated large-scale political-administrative and societal conflict.

Political-administrative turmoil in the 'adjustment year' 1992

Optimistically, the city government of Groningen named 1992 as the 'adjustment year'. The social services organisations wrote proposals on the form of the restructuring, and all sorts of 'cooperation models' were proposed. In the document *Time for Delta*, Delta proposed a flexible form of cooperation in each neighbourhood. This proposal deviated considerably from that of the city government, which proposed Delta's abolition. Delta wanted to maintain full control, and expected that the other social services organisations would support that proposal.

The social services organisations did not want to reveal their preferences immediately. The Playground Centre was, broadly speaking, supportive of Delta's proposal, and wanted to cooperate voluntarily in a merger. The Elderly People Wellbeing Organisation did not go any further than a declaration of its intention to participate in a merger. The neighbourhood centres, which received professional support from Delta and were represented by the management consultation neighbourhood centres, could not reach a consensus with their own members. Three neighbourhood centres refused to cooperate: they supported a fully neighbourhood-oriented organisation, in which there would be no role for Delta.

The BRE, which performed all sorts of activities for the housing corporations and residents, was the final merger partner. The discussions with this organisation were very difficult. It had appealed for cooperation in the past, but had been turned down by Delta. The services provided by the BRE could also be offered in the free market. This made its continuation uncertain after a merger. The BRE requested that the restructuring be postponed. According to its proposal, its specialist knowledge would be protected within an urban 'federation', after which the BRE would change itself gradually into a more market-oriented organisation.

The neighbourhood-oriented reorganisation of the residents' organisations, represented by URP, was another point of discussion. URP feared a disintegration of its activities. It wanted to continue performing the function of a strong interest group (according to its own members) in the areas of planning and housing, particularly in relation to the housing corporations. The performance of this function was, according to URP, facilitated by having its own city-wide organisation. Together with the BRE, which was involved in the proposed merger, URP commissioned an independent research project. In a move that was characteristic of the 'adjustment year' 1992, Delta and the Elderly People Wellbeing Organisation refused to cooperate with this research. Nine residents' organisations brought out a separate policy document, *What residents want*, which was in broad agreement with URP's proposals. However, they were a small, unrepresentative group. The city government reacted fiercely: 'The URP still functions as an umbrella organization/discussion partner for the city government and the corporations, and it is highly questionable whether the residents' organizations support their interests. All things considered, we doubt whether the URP has been able to demonstrate that it is able to meet a need which justifies its existence during the past three years' (p 43). The tone of this reaction implies one option only: abolish that organisation!

A new organisation structure was proposed in which a single *new* social services organisation would be created, in which all organisations (including Delta) would be merged. This new organisation would be the employer of social workers, who would provide support to new neighbourhood platforms. The neighbourhood platforms would then receive the authority to commission contracts: they could determine the desired activities in the social-cultural area themselves. The city council did make two procedural concessions to the organisations and interest groups involved: (1) the start of the new social services organisation was postponed for one year; and (2) a management group was established 'to arrive at a more detailed plan for the implementation of the new model'. An additional sum of 150,000 guilders was reserved for this management group as a 'premium for cooperation'. It was almost the end of the 'adjustment year' 1992.

The council decision could then be implemented, but the 1991 decision turned out to be a political powder keg. The city government concluded dryly: 'The analysis of the proposals and the differences between them reveals that the main points of the council decision were apparently not clear or not (fully) supported'. Therefore, the ESW Department began to work on yet another council decision

– as a follow-up of the decision from 1991 – entitled *Time for the neighbourhood: Sequel*. The local council took a new decision on 2 December 1992. The council stood its ground – the earlier council decision (from December 1991) remained *substantively unchanged*.

Implementation of the council decision

At the end of January 1993, the city council Commission on Wellbeing, Assistance and Media Policy met in two sessions to discuss the further development of the 1992 policy document, *Time for the neighbourhood: Sequel*. It was decided to set up a broad management group that would be divided into two project groups: 'Organisation' and 'Neighbourhood Platforms'. A heated discussion took place regarding the participation of different organisations in these two project groups. The responsible office holder did not want to delay the process any longer and, although he favoured small project groups, he did not manage to obtain these.

The management group was installed by the city council on Wednesday, 17 February 1993. It consisted of an independent chair, a representative of each of the organisations that were to merge, representatives of the neighbourhood club houses and representatives of the residents' organisations from URP. It is important to note that each of the representatives had a mandate from their organisation. A city administrator was present as an observer. In addition, an independent adviser was brought in to manage the implementation. The management group received the task of working out the council decision before 1 January 1994.

Several events occurred which diverted the talks within the management group. Great unrest occurred when Delta sent its director (a member of its personnel), rather than the chair of its board, as its representative to the management group. Delta stated that it was entitled to do so, on the basis of its own responsibility and autonomy, and would not reconsider this decision. At the same time, URP announced in a letter to the mayor and office holders that some of the residents' organisations had blocked participation of URP in the management group. The two representatives of URP were therefore unable to make an agreement.

In April 1993, the external adviser was appointed and the two project groups were started. The adviser quickly got to work and drew up different models for the neighbourhood platforms and the new central organisation. The council decisions formed a firm basis for these proposals. Progress was, however, soon disturbed. Delta filed a complaint regarding the proposed financial cut-backs with the city council Commission on Appeal and Complaint. This complaint could delay the further implementation of the restructuring. Delta made an alternative proposal for restructuring. Its proposal was, however, unknown to the neighbourhood centres. BRE felt that its sheer existence was threatened by Delta's proposal. Thus, an acute crisis situation developed, and a great deal of political diplomacy was required on the part of the chair of the management group to ensure that the conflict did not escalate.

A period of reconciliation commenced. The different organisations began to cooperate with each other, which was inevitable given their common situation. They made such an extensive inventory of possibilities that they became convinced of their future success. They worked hard on a merger document, and this document contained the implementation agencies' elaboration of the council decisions from 1991 and 1992. It was agreed on in the management group on 7 February 1994. The demand for services in the sociocultural area would be formulated in neighbourhood platforms, and the supply would be provided by the new organisation. The city government gave the document its provisional approval. Only the Playground Centre remained recalcitrant. At the last minute, it claimed its own budget from the office holder, who was receptive to this influence attempt by the well-organised playground association. Despite the two council decisions, the office holder was prepared to continue to grant the Playground Centre its own separate budget. Consequently, it maintained strong independence – albeit within the new organisation.

The city council wanted to formally authorise the implementation of its council decisions. On 9 March, the ESW Department proposed that the governing body of the mayor and office holders approve the merger document. The document would then be laid before the city council. However, before this could be done, new local council elections were held, and a new office holder was appointed, this time a Labour Party member. On 15 March, he gave his approval to the ESW Department's proposal as a principle decision, but now concluded that additional consultations had to be conducted. Once again, the implementation of the two council proposals was delayed with the aim of creating broader support among the organisations and interest groups involved. Consultation evenings were held on 17 and 30 March. The organisations involved reacted to the governing body's proposals and, on the basis of the consultation report, made a proposal to the council. Their objections were concerned mainly with the specific design of the neighbourhood platforms. The council responded to these objections. The decision was approved by the council on 18 October, with the addition that the design of the neighbourhood platforms would not be dictated.

In the meantime, the new social services organisation was set up. It was called WING (Wellbeing in Groningen). The merger implied by the establishment of this new organisation was associated with much symbolism and feelings of attachment. Meetings were held for the neighbourhood platforms in January 1995, which were followed by discussions with residents' organisations in February. Those within the new WING organisation were able to cooperate with each other well. Many employees were shifted within the framework of this new organisation. Employees had to accept new roles, whereby former opponents of the new organisation were put in positions that compelled them to be supportive. It was intended that the BRE would grow into a market-oriented organisation within the new organisation, after which it could become independent. The situation was different in the neighbourhoods. The cooperation with the residents' organisations was not optimal, especially in the neighbourhoods where few professional social workers had been active in the past. The success depended largely on the extent to which these organisations were used to cooperating. Minority ethnic organisations were more prepared to become involved in the broader social-cultural work activities. The Playground Associations remained closed groups that did not seem to care about the implementation of the restructuring.

In retrospect: contested politics and compliant implementation

A full analysis of the case is beyond the scope of this present contribution. Nevertheless, the chain of events that developed in the mid-1990s in the city of Groningen, can be analysed from the perspective of the policy issues at stake: what were the ultimate policy issues, and what compliant behaviours were supposed to bring about success?

Merger of social services organisations

The first theme in the policy decision concerned the merger of the four social services organisations: Delta, the Elderly People Wellbeing Organisation, the BRE and the Playground Centre. Although there was a great deal of resistance to the merger, the local council remained determined. The council threatened the use of personnel measures if the merger failed. With this threat looming over them, the organisations cooperated successfully.

Size and allocation of cut-backs

The second theme in the restructuring of social-cultural work concerned expenditure cuts in the city's social services sector. Decisions were taken regarding the size of the cut-backs and the allocation of these across the diverse posts of social-cultural work. It was thought that large savings could be made by bundling the organisations' administrative, overheads and supportive activities – leaving the operational costs largely unaffected. Alternatives were proposed, ranging from 100 to 750,000 guilders. The city council eventually decided to impose a budget cut of 550,000 guilders. At the end of 1995, 480,000 guilders had been cut. As a result, the organisations creatively proposed to postpone the implementation of the remaining 70,000 guilders of cut-backs by budgeting them as future 'earning effects'. The city government viewed this as a time bomb that could wreck the merger: the factions within the new WING organisation apparently did not agree on the distribution of these 'earning effects'.

Introduction of neighbourhood platforms

The third theme in the restructuring concerned the introduction of neighbourhood platforms. These were territorially defined consultation structures that would assign contracts to the central social services organisation. They would set certain priorities regarding social-cultural work in their own areas. Concrete council decisions on the neighbourhood platforms were not taken until a later stage of the restructuring. These council decisions concerned four aspects of the functioning of the neighbourhood platforms: their structure, composition, their relationship with WING and their relationship with city government.

The *structure* of the neighbourhood platforms pertained to the level of decentralisation (number of platforms, the scope of their mission), and their level of standardisation. In some neighbourhoods, there was already cooperation between residents' organisations, social workers, volunteers and other actors. In other neighbourhoods, such cooperation did not exist. In both cases, there was little enthusiasm for a uniform 'imposed' cooperation structure. The *composition* of the neighbourhood platforms was a contested issue. Who should be allowed to participate? In October 1994, the council decided on a broad discussion platform, where residents could participate personally. There were many differences between the organisations in the field. For example, active residents were often also professionals in the field. The organisation of minority ethnic groups and older people supported the restriction in participation of professionals and volunteers. The Elderly People Wellbeing Organisation even stated that the proposed restructuring was utopian, and that the power would be held firmly by professional social workers.

The neighbourhood platforms' *relationship with WING*, the central organisation, was the subject of a number of other policy issues. They would be authorised to formulate the demand for services, and WING would have to supply these services. City government would authoritatively connect demand and supply. Neighbourhood work plans were developed, the feasibility of which would be tested by the city's social services department. The neighbourhood centres and residents' organisations fiercely attempted to contract out their demands to various organisations. In response, a controversial decision was adopted by the city council that basically forced the neighbourhood platforms to contract out exclusively to WING. Indeed, the social services organisations, merged in the central organisation WING, made forceful attempts to maintain their monopoly while at the same time displaying 'goodwill' towards the neighbourhood platforms. All the neighbourhood platforms had to accept the imposed monopoly of service provision by WING. The *relationship with city government* revolved around the flexibility in the allocation of budgets to the neighbourhood platforms. The city council decided on a small amount of flexibility. The residents' organisations, elderly people organisations and playground associations demanded much more protection regarding their future existence.

In retrospect, we conclude that the amount of political control which the city of Groningen exercised on this process was a key success factor, in the sense that despite all political conflict and the heterogeneous preferences of implementers, the reforms were seen as inevitable, and their implementation a success.

I n this next contribution, Anna Coleman, Kath Checkland and Stephen Harrison explore how implementation of a loosely specified policy, health service reorganisation in England, involved local choice influenced by the history of responses to earlier changes.

Central policies that are only loosely specified might be expected to result in local variations in interpretation and implementation, and practice-based commissioning (PBC) in the English National Health Service (NHS) is no exception. What is shown here is how local 'sensemaking' in relation to this policy has been influenced by local histories and by conceptual schemata derived from earlier reorganisations of the NHS. Changes to organisational formalities do not necessarily, therefore, result in reappraisals of sensemaking on the part of local actors. Some of the considerations explored in Part Two of this book in relation to policy stability arise again in looking at implementation processes.

Local histories and local sensemaking: a case of policy implementation in the English National Health Service

Anna Coleman, Kath Checkland and Stephen Harrison

Introduction

In a discussion of decentralisation and local decision making in the UK NHS, Exworthy and Frosini (2008) argue that, among other factors, local social networks and institutional relationships are important in determining how central policy is enacted on the ground. This contribution explores this issue in more detail, focusing on a previous NHS innovation known as 'practice-based commissioning' (PBC), a policy only loosely specified from the centre in a series of documents both aspirational in tone and relatively non-specific in detail (DH, 2004; Mannion, 2005). Our recent empirical study (Checkland et al, 2008) shows substantial local variation in enactment of the policy.

Analysis and explanation of this variation can be addressed with reference to Weick's (1995) concept of 'sensemaking'. Weick argues that managing consists of 'sensemaking', by which he means that organisational actors selectively 'extract cues' from the continual chaotic stream of events, actions and policies that surround any human endeavour. Perceptions about what constitutes a 'significant' cue are determined by underlying assumptions that themselves arise out of previous experiences. Action in response to a cue will also be influenced by these underlying assumptions, and will in turn affect future assumptions; moreover, cues and action in response to cues depend on beliefs about organisational identity. Weick emphasises that the process is ongoing and retrospective; it does not represent a rational consideration of facts and alternatives; rather, it is an instinctive response to 'puzzling' situations that arise, and will always be based on a plausible assessment of a given situation rather than objective accuracy.

The concept of 'sensemaking' has been widely used in the literature as an interpretive framework within which to study processes of organisational change. Of particular relevance to the present study is the work of Pope et al (2006), who studied NHS treatment centres, arguing that variations in the implementation of this centrally directed policy could in part be understood as a micro-level local enactment of reality by actors on the ground, 'making sense' of themselves and their enterprise in a particular context. However, commentators have criticised Weick's work (Anderson, 2006) arguing, among other things, that it fails to take account of either institutional effects (Weber and Glynn, 2006) or considerations of power (Mullen et al, 2006). Furthermore, much of the development of the theory of sensemaking has been derived from secondary analyses of data; Weick et al (2005) themselves note a paucity of original research seeking to further develop or clarify our understanding of how sensemaking operates or indeed how it can be of practical use. Weick et al also suggest topics for future research, including sensemaking and institutional theory, sensemaking within 'distributed' or diffuse organisations, sensemaking and power, and sensemaking and emotion. The relationship of sensemaking to institutional contexts was subsequently addressed by Weber and Glynn (2006). They argue that in addition to providing a cognitive constraint on sensemaking, institutions act more directly to influence the process of sensemaking. It should be noted that although Weber and Glynn do not explicitly define institutions, their approach implies the kind of definition employed by sociologists of organisation such as Scott (2008, p 48), that is 'regulative, normative and cultural-cognitive elements that, together with associated activities and resources, provide stability and meaning to social life.' First, institutions 'prime' sensemaking by providing frames and role expectations within which individuals both notice cues and act in response to those cues. Second, institutions 'edit' sensemaking by providing the social context within which groups of individuals negotiate shared sensemaking about the meaning of cues and actions by an ongoing process of interpretation and reinterpretation. Finally, institutions 'trigger' sensemaking by requiring a constant process of sensemaking in response to puzzles that arise as change occurs within institutions. Thus, as institutions adopt new working practices or reorganise their structures, sensemaking is required to reconcile old assumptions and identities with new realities.

This contribution develops Weber and Glynn's ideas on institutional impacts on sensemaking and uses Weick's ideas on sensemaking in relation to central policy within a 'distributed' organisation.

Practice-based commissioning

In the English NHS at the time of this study the bulk of NHS finance was allocated to primary care trusts (PCTs) that then paid providers for the services used by their local populations according to commissioning agreements. It should be noted that since the research, much of the NHS landscape has altered due to changes introduced as a result of the Health and Social Care Act 2012. By April 2013, the government hopes that approximately 211 clinical commissioning groups (CCGs) will be operational commissioning the bulk of NHS care and replacing PCTs and strategic health authorities (SHAs). NHS commissioners will be supported by a new body called the NHS Commissioning Board at a national level, and Commissioning Support Units more locally. (For further details refer to www.dh.gov.uk/health/2012/06/act-explained/.)

At the time of the research the shift to PBC aimed to involve general (family) medical practitioners directly in the commissioning of hospital and community services by delegating a proportion of the overall PCT budget to practices with which to commission services for their patients, for instance, by stimulating services that are more local and that use a greater variety of new providers (Marks and Hunter, 2005). These budgets were 'indicative' rather than real, with the PCT remaining responsible for any overspend. Coverage of these budgets varied by local negotiation, but could include attendances at accident and emergency departments, referrals to hospital for outpatient and inpatient treatments, community services, mental health services and prescription drugs. Any financial resources freed up by changes in services or referral practices could be reinvested in new services. Official guidance stated that PCTs were expected to facilitate PBC (by, for example, providing managerial support), and to ensure that PBC plans were integrated with both the priorities of the PCT and relevant national priorities (DH, 2005a, 2005b). Practice-based commissioners were accountable to their PCTs, who agreed the contracts with hospitals and other providers and remained legally responsible for the funds.

Official guidance on PBC was sketchy. Although there was an initial assumption by the Department of Health that general practices would implement PBC individually, the policy permitted them to join with other practices to form local PBC groups. The majority of practices opted to operate PBC by forming groups, termed consortia, localities or clusters ('consortia' hereafter) (Coleman et al, 2007). Consortia and their associated PCTs were able to choose for themselves how practices should organise to undertake PBC (forming loose federations, more tightly organised groups or even setting up more formal organisations such as social enterprises); which actors to include in the process of PBC (GPs, other primary care professionals, practice managers, PCT representatives); involvement of wider stakeholders (local government representatives, patients and the public); what aspects of the budget should be devolved from the PCT; which services to prioritise for change; and how to reinvest any savings. It is sensemaking in relation to these choices that forms the substantive topic of this contribution.

Methods

The data reported here are from a wider study investigating PBC in England (Checkland et al, 2008; see also Checkland et al, 2009a, 2009b; Coleman et al, 2010), and comprised detailed data collection in three 'early adopter' PCTs between January and November 2007. This sample was chosen purposively in order to include examples from a range of consortia types (size, ways of working, priorities for PBC) rather than as representatives of a population. The three sites described here were:

- one PCT with one consortium that covered the entire PCT area – this was straightforward (Site 1);
- two PCTs (Sites 2 and 3) with multiple consortia – agreement was eventually reached to study three of them in Site 2 and one in Site 3.

Hence this report deals with data from three sites (PCTs) and five consortia. Data collection included observation, interviews and analyses of available documentation.

Findings

Analysis of the variations in response across the five consortia led to the identification of two broad historical legacies, general practice (GP) fundholding (explained below) and past statutory organisation, that seemed to have shaped local sensemaking so as to produce these differences in PBC organisation, management and operation. For convenience, these legacies are summarised in Table 5.3.1, and explained in the following text.

Legacy of GP fundholding

The GP fundholding scheme of 1991–97 was broadly similar to PBC, although more limited in scope (Glennerster et al, 1994). Individual general practices were provided with an indicative budget with which to purchase only elective care for their patients, and the overall impact on service provision was probably small (Glennerster et al, 1994). Importantly, uptake of the scheme was voluntary, and in some areas created considerable ill feeling between GPs who wholeheartedly adopted the scheme (felt by others to have obtained financial advantages) and those who did not. Although fundholding was abruptly abolished by the incoming Labour government in 1997, these old rivalries remained strong in Site 1, and local GPs still tended to identify themselves as 'ex-fundholders' or 'ex-non-fundholders'.

Table 5.3.1: Summary of historical legacies in PBC arrangements

	General practice fundholding	Former organisation boundaries	Non-historical factors
Site 1	Former rivalries still evident; ex-fundholders dominant	Resentment towards former PCGs left GPs hostile to successor PCT and seeking as much independence as possible	Geographical homogeneity facilitates single consortium
Site 2	Consortium 1 dominated by ex-fundholders; Consortium 2 dominated by ex-fundholders; Consortium 3 dominated by former non-fundholders/reluctant fundholders	Recent PCT merger and earlier PCG boundaries define boundaries of PBC consortia	Physical features (rivers, motorways, new town) militate against single consortium
Site 3	PBC consortium consisted entirely of former non-fundholders, led by prominent anti-fundholder	PCT sought to re-impose pre-merger PCT localities on PBC – successfully resisted by GPs in order to define own PBC consortia	Geographical features include two separate major conurbations that militate against a single consortium

PBC was regarded by the former as an opportunity to recapture a perceived entrepreneurial past, and the initial moves to set up the single consortium were led by ex-fundholders.

Moreover, the ex-fundholders who dominated the Site 1 PBC board had had experience of providing services in their own practices under fundholding rules. They were keen to reproduce some of these perceived successes, bringing more services out into practices rather than providing them in secondary care:

> ... but in many cases there are things that could have been done at practice level because [for example] they have to refer on for [joint] injections in many cases ... which GPs should, could and should be doing the majority of. (ID 5, GP board member)

The leading individuals in Site 1 felt that increasing overall practice performance so that practices were capable of providing these extended services was key to the success of PBC. As a result, education and performance management formed a clear focus for the consortium:

> GP board member commented: 'We are very keen on not "dumbing down" general practice. We want to be doing more than other GPs might be doing. We want to see all skills brought up to that level.' (ID 8, field note)

In Site 2, the PCT allowed groups of GPs a free hand in deciding how to organise their consortia, and their previous experiences under fundholding partly shaped the decisions that were made, with like-minded GPs who shared previous experiences choosing to work together in groups. While the divisions were by no means absolute, the consortia that formed tended to be either dominated by ex-fundholders or by those who had eschewed that scheme. Consortium 2, like Site 1, was dominated by ex-fundholders who had worked closely together under fundholding, and who saw PBC as a welcome return to the dynamic days of the past. Their previously established social relationships and ongoing interactions formed a natural focus for the new PBC group:

> 'There is a long, there is a strong history of working together through fundholding days; there was a strong history of working together ... we almost had a PBC consortium nine years ago.... Except it fell apart at the last minute which was most disappointing because we would have been ... light years ahead of things.' (ID 40, GP board member)

Consortium 1 was a small consortium, formed by those who had declined to join a larger group in the area. It was also dominated by ex-fundholders, who felt that PBC offered an opportunity to regain some lost advantages and to develop new ones:

> '... we were fundholders originally so we were very keen to get back to ... purchasing arrangements ... we were happy to get back to anything that involved us back in the purchases of services for our patients.' (ID 34, practice manager, board member)

Members of Consortium 3, by contrast, had not been active fundholders, with most of them only being involved in the latter stages of that scheme, if at all. Whereas interviewees from other consortia frequently referred to PBC positively as a return to fundholding, members of Consortium 3 were less likely to mention fundholding when asked about their general attitude to PBC.

In Site 3, uptake of fundholding had been low. Many GPs remained ideologically opposed to a scheme they remembered as divisive, and their identity as 'ex-non-fundholders' was an important determinant of their sensemaking in the new situation. Thus, when PBC was announced, these GPs saw themselves as a natural grouping that could use the opportunity to demonstrate how collective action could work for the good of all GPs and patients. The Site 3 consortium chair was an individual who had been strongly anti-fundholding. When that scheme was abolished and replaced by primary care groups (PCGs, see below), he took a key role in the new organisations, and regarded the key aim of PBC to be to restore the mutual self-help among practices that they had enjoyed as a PCG.

As a consequence, less emphasis was placed on being entrepreneurial, and more on the idea of mutual help and support:

> 'We started off, obviously we're interested in working collectively, collaboratively and in partnership, and we wanted to engender the

values that we had in the PCG days, which were about facilitation, support, about recognising that we need to have a network, a sort of collegiate sort of atmosphere where everybody has the opportunities to develop. So really those were the drivers for us ... so at the moment we're a loosely based partnership.' (ID 58, GP board member)

Legacy of former organisational arrangements

In 1997, the newly elected Labour government abruptly abolished fundholding, replacing it with PCGs. The intention was also that PCGs would gradually assume greater responsibility over several years, until eventually becoming statutory PCTs, at which point health authorities (HAs) would be abolished. In the event, the process was much accelerated, and PCGs were rapidly merged to become PCTs (further mergers took place in 2006). We found that the particular local histories of such mergers and abolitions had substantial impacts on how many consortia were formed, and on which consortia individual practices decided to join. Some of the PCTs in our study sought initially to specify the configuration of PBC consortia, but soon found their plans disrupted by local histories, of which they were sometimes not fully aware:

'When we brought the clinicians together, from the [former PCT areas], the [previous PCT] GPs started to say, "Actually we've been put into these groups, to suit the old PCT; this is not clinically led, this is not necessarily how we would have wanted things to be." So there was a bit of a mini revolution really and they went away and reformed themselves into the arrangement they have now.' (ID 56, PCT employee, Site 3)

In Site 1, PCGs were never very successful, being dominated by antagonisms between fundholders and non-fundholders and by what was seen as hostility towards GPs from the then HA. Although an early move to a large PCT covering the entire district had alleviated some of the residual fundholding-related antagonisms between practices, two further legacies remained. First, one of the driving forces behind the development of PBC was a desire to be as independent of the PCT as possible:

Chair then said that they need a vision of where [consortium] might be in three years' time – his vision is that [consortium] will still exist, that it will be independent of the PCT and that it will have a significant infrastructure, including buildings and people.' (ID 2, field note)

'And the politics are for general practice survival ... and a recognition that [Site 1's] GPs are generally united and therefore difficult to separate or defeat.' (ID 3, GP board member, Site 1)

Second, when PCGs were formed, the HA at the time had done its best to break what it regarded as the monopoly of GPs on deciding local health policy, promoting nurse involvement instead. As a result, efforts were made to ensure that PCG boards (and subsequently the professional executive committee of the PCT) were not dominated by GPs, with some HA (and latterly PCT) managers being perceived as hostile to GPs. The official emphasis in the subsequent policy of PBC was on 'clinical engagement', and these historical resentments meant that this was interpreted in Site 1 as meaning 'GP engagement'. As a result, the PBC board at Site 1 was dominated by GPs, with no nurse representation. When asked about this, GPs reiterated the importance of GPs in determining overall practice behaviour with regard to referrals and other clinical decisions, and suggested that the PCG and PCT structures involving nurses and other professionals had 'failed'.

By contrast, as a clear geographical entity, covering a single local authority area, involvement of the local authority was seen by GPs in Site 1 as self-evidently important, and a representative was invited to sit on the PBC board.

In Site 2, there had been a recent merger between two PCTs, and formation of consortia followed both these boundaries and the old PCG boundaries. Those we interviewed often expressed strong feelings about the reconfigurations they had experienced, complaining about the disruptions to service delivery and to developing collaborations and partnerships.

For many of those who had not been enthusiastic about fundholding, PCGs were regarded as a high point, being small enough to allow successful teamwork:

> '... the whole lot was lost; the PCG was going for about three years, I think. And then we lost it, it was like starting from scratch. And we only started to get back to anywhere near where we were with the PCG after about a year. So that reorganisation wasted, none of the old, virtually none of the old stuff, virtually none of the old work that was done was carried forward; it was a completely new set up, policies everything.' (ID 52, grassroots GP)

Similarly, in Site 3 (in which two PCTs had also recently merged) consortia boundaries generally followed old PCG boundaries, with no cross-over between the two original PCT areas. As one informant pointed out, mergers did not necessarily abolish former practices and ways of thinking:

> '... because they were funded totally differently... operated in a totally different way and it amazes me, I mean this is PCT to PCT, so it amazes me how the same bodies can get the same sort of words down from on high, but interpret them in totally different ways and operate in totally different ways. So really although we are one PCT we [still] work as [several].' (ID 57, practice manager)

This PCT manager had been involved with all the various statutory bodies, and felt that the pace of change had had negative effects:

> A: 'I think that practice based commissioning can achieve much greater clinical engagement, that's my number one thing, and that was something that was there in the PCG days but got lost a bit in PCT days. That's what everybody says and that's what I've seen for myself as well. So I think clinical engagement's the number one thing.'
> Q: 'Do you think that happened through PCTs being bigger than PCGs?'
> A: [pause] 'No. Because in our area that wasn't the case. It is now, in that since October there's a single PCT, but the PCGs for [the area] were the same size as the PCTs, I think it was that the PCTs had so much more to do, and it happened very fast. So, you know, I worked in a PCG from 2000 and we were really finding our feet as a PCG when, and doing well with the clinical engagement stuff, when suddenly we were told, "Oh, by the way, health authorities are going, you've gotta take on all their roles as well." And I think that changed the relationship, so it was too much was given over to, when they became PCTs too quickly. I think that changed it.' (ID 66, PCT employee)

In addition to decisions about the configuration of PBC consortia, decisions about the constitution of the consortia boards in Sites 2 and 3 were also affected by experiences of the historical statutory arrangements. For example, the practices that made up Consortium 2 in Site 2 had had a long history of working closely together, initially under fundholding and then as a PCG. There was also a history of joint working with local social services. When the consortium was formed these factors influenced the decision to have a representative from *every* practice on the board rather than having elected representatives, and to appoint a representative from social services. In Site 3, the consortium board involved both GPs and practice managers, in part because there was a strong history of managerial involvement in PCGs, which were seen as the forerunners of PBC. Nurses, however, had never had significant involvement in decision-making bodies in the area, and so it was not regarded as a priority to involve them in PBC. There were also no local authority representatives on the Site 3 PBC board, and it is possible to trace some causal links between this and the initial conflicts about the configuration of PBC consortia in this area. In the early stages of PBC, the GPs had resisted pressure from the PCT to adopt a structure based on localities mirroring local authority boundaries, and as a result, an oppositional discourse had developed that played down the importance of collaboration, subsequently meaning that there was no question of asking the local authority to provide a representative on the board.

It is also important to note that decisions that *disrupted* local histories could affect PBC arrangements. In the two sites that had undergone PCT reorganisation in 2006, GPs felt that the new organisations were struggling to regain momentum after a period of introspection, and there was a sense that something important had been lost, as established relationships were disrupted:

> '... the merger has delayed things quite a lot, they've taken a long time at getting some people into post, which is just held things up really to be honest, and then I think it's all them finding their feet, sussing out their priorities, and things like that, and I think we've been sat on the side lines going, "Yoo-hoo, I'm here, come and talk to me".' (ID 61, GP board member)

However, it is also likely that the frequency of NHS organisational restructuring had the paradoxical result of allowing general practice to simply 'roll along':

> 'You see, by and large, you see, all these organisations and everything else, by and large, general practice just rolls along. If you actually don't want to change anything, it just rumbles on, dealing with the patients on a day-to-day basis, doing what they have always done, um, you know, oh well, they will be here one minute and gone the next sort of thing ... so we have seen it all before.' (ID 47, GP board member)

Discussion

We do not suggest that the above histories were the sole determinants of differences between the five PBC consortia in our three PCT sites. Site 1 is relatively compact and forms a single geographical entity, making a single consortium an obvious solution, while in Site 2, geographical features such as rivers and a new town were felt to be important. Moreover, PBC arrangements were partly shaped by influential individuals. However, it is important to note that a good deal of the ability of these individuals to influence matters itself derived from the histories that we have outlined. For instance, the consortium chair in Site 3 relied for influence on a track record of local medical politics and well-known opposition to fundholding, which fed local sensemaking about their appropriate position in the new climate.

Our analysis suggests that understanding the history of local health institutions is essential in understanding the way in which loosely-specified health policies are made sense of and therefore enacted, and we have identified specific features of history that were important in our study sites. Pope et al (2006) argue for an understanding that the process of policy implementation is dynamic, with feedback between local discourses and those at the 'meso level' responsible for translating government rhetoric into change. Policy makers, meso-level implementers and ground-level implementers all frame the policy in different ways, 'which opens up an opportunity for actors at the micro-level to construct something of their own' (Pope et al, 2006, p 77). We might add that the impact of local changes will influence the ongoing sensemaking process at all levels. This was evident in our study, as we observed local change over time, as new actors entered and left the arena in which PBC was operating, organisations were reorganised and other policies had an impact on the local context.

Our findings also go beyond those of Pope at al (2006) in that they contribute to a deeper understanding of the nature of local sensemaking. Our study offers an opportunity to confirm the contentions of Weber and Glynn (2006) about the impact of institutions on sensemaking. The impact of institutional 'priming' in shaping the local sensemaking was indeed visible; while the wider institutional context within PCTs is set by Department of Health directives and imperatives, local environments were surprisingly varied, with clear evidence of the impact of previous experiences. Thus, for example, in Site 1, the local GPs saw forming a large single entity to pursue PBC as the 'natural' thing to do in order to form a 'strong' grouping that would be able to counteract the power of the PCT, which had been regarded as excessive in the past. Weber and Glynn's institutional 'editing' of sensemaking was also visible in our study. Thus, for example, in Site 3, a newly formed PCT, acting in part on a central directive to try to align local health structures with those of the local government authority, attempted to impose 'locality' groupings on the local GPs, cutting across a series of local identities and rivalries that had long roots. Local actors who understood the histories at issue acted quickly to counter this. Institutional 'triggering' of sensemaking was also evident as the consortia and the managers designated to support them tried to reconcile their new roles with their ongoing responsibilities and established routines of behaviour. The result was that many actors reported ongoing confusion and conflict, requiring a constant iterative process of sensemaking and identity definition. Thus, the nature of the existing institutions in each of our study sites, including their histories, previously established norms and routines of behaviour and current responses to the 'cues' provided by the new policy of PBC acted to determine the sensemaking that occurred. Those PCTs that had recently reorganised were at a disadvantage, because they did not necessarily fully understand the local context. In one sense, this is unsurprising; Weick (1979) has noted the existence of 'schemata', standards derived from the past, against which subsequent organisational changes are framed.

Additionally, our study provides insights into what Weick calls 'distributed sensemaking' in large organisations made up of subsidiary units. Whilst there is a strong sense of loyalty to the NHS as a whole, individual employees are also members both of local organisations and of professional groups. The recent history of the NHS has been one of repeated reorganisation, with the formation of new organisations and the merger of existing ones a regular occurrence over the past 25 years. There is an implicit assumption with each reorganisation that the local organisations created will be 'new', and free of the problems associated with their predecessors. For example, a document issued by the NHS Executive describing the establishment of PCTs (DH, 1999, p 1), describes them as 'new, free-standing' organisations with 'new flexibilities and freedoms' that will deliver 'better health and better care'. Subsequent paragraphs describe in detail why the 'new' organisations will be free of the problems of the past. However, our study demonstrates that not only will local sensemaking already exist among those involved with the formation of the new organisation, but also that the dominant sensemaking is likely to exist at the level of the subsidiary organisation with the greatest longevity. Thus, in our study, the sensemaking that dominated during the development of PBC was that of the local GPs and their practices. This is in part the result of the relative job stability of the latter but also because, perhaps counter-intuitively, schemata at lower organisational levels can be resistant to change precisely because they are embedded in *practice* (Seely Brown and Duguid, 1991). Thus the fundholding/non-fundholding cleavage was effectively re-enacted on a weekly or monthly basis through the pattern of local social relations and routine contacts between GPs in our sites. Similarly, past administrative boundaries had served to structure a good deal of ongoing GP interaction with, for example, practices that had worked well together under PCGs maintaining social and practice-related contacts.

The implication of our findings is that, the more frequently reorganisations occur in a given locality, the more each new reorganisation will be shaped by schemata derived from earlier reorganisations. Thus, paradoxically, the more frequent the reorganisations (and there can be few institutions that have been reorganised as frequently as the NHS), the more likely is the local act of deciding how to organise to become a matter of practice, and thereby resistant to change. As noted earlier, PBC was a relatively loosely specified policy, and as such allowed significant local scope for interpretation and development. It is possible that more tightly specified policy might have acted to limit this local interpretation, a perspective from which our findings would not constitute a critical test of implementation. But loosely-specified policy is in fact relatively common, an observation that suggests that, rather than addressing the question of what accounts for differences between policy specification and its implementation, research should explore the main explanatory factors influencing local policy interpretation and implementation. The current NHS reorganisation (embodied in the Health and Social Care Act 2012) is an example of a policy that started off very loosely specified, but which policy makers have subsequently sought to constrain (Checkland et al, 2012). It remains to be seen how far such intentions can override the local schemata that are likely to have been adopted earlier in the implementation process.

Note

This contribution is based on an original article written by Anna Coleman, Kath Checkland, Stephen Harrison and Urara Hiroeh that first appeared in the journal *Policy & Politics* in 2010. The study was funded from the Department of Health core grant to the National Primary Care Research and Development Centre. We are grateful to all our participants for generously sharing their time with us and for making us welcome at their meetings and events.

I mplementation studies that try to use a simple output or outcome variable and examine the influences on it in quantitative terms tend to disregard policy complexity. While this may be possible in relation to some policy processes, in others policy change is essentially complex. This is particularly true, as this contribution by Turo Virtanen shows, in higher education and research. Key factors contributing to the complexity are the autonomy of higher education institutions (HEIs) and difficulties in measuring the output and outcome of education and research. On the one hand, implementation 'success' simply means that mergers occurred. On the other hand, the long-term goals of the mergers depend on many other influences and will be hard to assess.

In this contribution, the implementation of a structural development policy, a subpolicy of Finnish higher education and research policy, is addressed. The analysis has its focus on the mergers of HEIs. The author has been both an observer and a participant in the policy formulation of mergers.

Implementation of the structural development policy of Finnish higher education

Turo Virtanen

Implications of implementing structural development policy: using Winter's approach

In mapping the implementation process along the lines proposed by Winter (2006) (see p 194 above) we are not trying to measure the goal achievement of structural development policy as such, but focus our attention on the performance of the actors of that policy. When looking at the performance aspects of implementation, we need to ask, whose performance? When the implementation of the policy assumes new legislation, key actors are the entire government, the ministries in charge of the policy sector and their stakeholders and members of Parliament. Actually, if legislation is needed, you could say that it is Parliament that authoritatively decides the key content of the policy. In Finland, merging universities is only possible through new legislation – an amendment of the University Act – since all universities have to be mentioned in the Act.

New legislation for higher education can be understood as an output of policy implementation, but it can also be understood as a policy instrument (see the discussion of policy instruments in Part Four) to achieve the wider goals of institutional mergers, for example, better international competitiveness of higher education institutions (HEIs). It is not always clear how we conceptualise the policy design: what seemed to be a goal may turn out to be a means to an ends. The outputs relevant for achieving a wider goal of better competitiveness are complex and contestable. This also makes the output of the policy unclear. However, it is obvious that the achievement of this goal is more likely if extra funding is allocated to institutions. Economic incentives may turn out to be useful. As competitiveness is a complex concept, there is also a need for clarifications and operationalisation. Information as a policy instrument becomes important.

The relevant actors in implementing the wider goals of international competitiveness in education and research also include actors from the HEIs, since these institutions have their autonomy based on the principle of academic freedom.

In Winter's model, the actors are members of governmental organisations, in particular street-level bureaucrats, and target groups and their organisations in society. In this study, relevant organisational members in implementation are the leading bureaucrats of the Ministry of Education and Culture (MEC), the academic and administrative managers on different layers of HEIs, academic staff (teachers and researchers) and students. Staff and student unions are important stakeholders in the implementations phase. It is the organisational and interorganisational behaviour of these actors that affects how mergers of HEIs take place, and how successful the policy will be, although the specific criteria for success may be understood in various ways.

Finnish higher education system and its recent reforms

The Finnish higher education system is a dualistic system composed of universities and polytechnics. The first university in Finland, the University of Helsinki, was originally established in Turku in 1640 and moved to Helsinki in 1828 after Russia took over the eastern part of Swedish empire in 1809. Since that time, following the general trend of Western countries to enlarge higher education, new universities have been established, reaching 20 in 2009. Polytechnics were established by merging and upgrading relatively small vocational educational institutions, leading to the achievement of 29 institutions between 1996 and 2000. Today, most Finnish universities and polytechnics are public, and even the private ones get their basic funding from government. There are no tuition fees, but HEIs are dependent on external competitive funding, especially for their research activities.

In Finland, consecutive governments have had similar goals in modernising higher education (Höltä, 1988; Höltä and Rekilä, 2003; Virtanen and Temmes, 2008). In recent years, the government has been pursuing a policy aimed at strengthening the autonomy of universities, a reduction in the number of universities and polytechnics, clarification of their research and education profiles, a build-up of larger and more effective units, the creation of strategic alliances between universities and polytechnics (mostly on a regional basis), faster completion of academic degrees, and a higher level of internationalisation (MEC, 2008; Ministerial Committee on Education and Culture, 2010). The Evaluation of the Finnish National Innovation System (2009) and the OECD (Organisation for Economic Co-operation and Development) review of Finnish tertiary education (Davies et al, 2009) identified similar shortcomings in higher education, research and innovations. The lack of autonomy of universities has been remedied through the new University Act that has been in force since the beginning of 2010, but progress on many other areas has been relatively slow. However, by 2013, there were four mergers of universities (the total number of institutions being 14) and four mergers of polytechnics (25 institutions left), and there are ongoing negotiations about the new cooperative structures of 11 polytechnics.

The following section briefly describes the contents of a central subpolicy of Finnish higher education policy: structural development policy. This has been a reaction to the problem of the fragmentation of the higher education sector: too many institutions and little success in creating distinctive organisational profiles in education and research. The purpose of this discussion is to analyse the implementation of the structural development policy, focusing on the four institutional mergers of universities already accomplished.

Structural development policy within the higher education and research policy

For the purposes of implementation analysis, two questions arise: (1) where do we find the exact policy that should be or should have been implemented, and (2) when is it appropriate to start implementation analysis? There may be several descriptions of the policy. Outputs and outcomes of a policy may take years to emerge. The key document of Finnish higher education policy is the development plan of education and research decided by the government for five-year periods. What makes it the key document is that it is based on the programme of each government, it is the largest official description of the policy, and also a starting point for refinement of subpolicies, and its period roughly corresponds to the term of government (four years if no political crises emerge). As for the choice of the development plan as a reference point for implementation analysis, a pragmatic starting point would be that we look at the document for the period that has recently ended. So here we choose the policy document accepted for period 2007–12, and we also look briefly at its successor.

The development plan 2007–12 (Ministry of Education, 2007) sets objectives for several areas: level of education and knowledge; access to skilled labour; efficiency, retention rates and multiple education; *structural development*; steering and financing; research, development and innovation; internationalisation; immigrants and multiculturalism; connections between education and working life and the promotion of entrepreneurship; qualifications; quality and quality assurance; development of university and polytechnic education in research in technology; development of teaching; social coherence and active citizenship; student financial aid; supply of teachers; and support for evidence-based decision making.

As the scope of the policy in the plan is very broad, the focus of implementation analysis here is on one part of the most important subpolicy or policy line of Finnish higher education policy: structural development policy. This includes pre-primary, basic and general upper secondary education, vocational education and training, HEIs, and adult education and training, but here we focus on HEIs – and even more specifically – on universities.

According to the document, a policy of institutional network of HEIs will be formulated: 'overlapping supply will be pruned, administration and support services will be pooled and the infrastructure operation will be stepped up' (Ministry of Education, 2007, p 33). More specifically (p 34):

> The innovation university to be created through an alliance of the Helsinki University of Technology, the Helsinki School of Economics and the University of Art and Design Helsinki will be prepared so that the university will be operational on 1 August 2009. In this context, the possibilities for Swedish-speaking students to study in their own language will be secured at the current level. The joint consortium of the University of Turku and the Turku School of Economics will be launched in the autumn of 2008 and the new university will be operational in 2011. The University of Eastern Finland comprising the Universities of Kuopio and Joensuu will start operating by 2010. In addition, the structural development projects of other higher education institutions will be supported and encouraged.

The mergers with exact dates and names of institutions are very specific policy targets. The specificity can be explained by the fact that the mergers had already been prepared in ministerial working groups together with universities that had accepted the change (see below). In this way, universities had already taken part in policy formulation. The mergers were also part of the programme of the government when it took power. The development plan was decided by the government only after all this had taken place.

The successor of the aforementioned plan is the development plan 2011-16 (MEC, 2012). Its structure is different, but what is in our focus can be found in the area of 'higher education institutions and research'. There is a section on 'structural development to be expedited'. The institutional network is said to be 'too fragmented'. The policy paper says (MEC, 2012, p 43):

> The universities and polytechnics will be developed with emphasis on their specific characteristics and aims as differently, mutually supplementary forms of education with different degrees, degree

titles and missions. The financing models in higher education will be developed to give more incentive to cooperation and division of work.

In terms of the number of institutions, the policy paper sets no numerical target but a general principle (MEC, 2012, p 44):

> Every province has one or several higher education institutions. The different higher education structures in different parts of the country make for stronger university and polytechnic profiles and priorities to serve the development needs in the regions.[...] The mission of the universities will underscore academic research and education based on research and their national impact. The mission of the polytechnics will underscore links with business and industry and regional impact.

The emphasis of the new plan is on the structural reforms of the polytechnic sector. The operating licenses will be revised from 2014 onwards, giving an opportunity for mergers and other reforms. In the university sector, an additional merger is announced: starting in 2013, 'an art university will be created through a merger of the Sibelius Academy, the Academy of Fine Arts and the Theatre Academy' (MEC, 2012, p 43). This merger also has a long history in foregoing preparations. The reason for including the merger in this specific development plan was, in practice, that due to the preparation schedule the merger could not be taken into the programme of the previous government but into that of the next government after the elections in 2011. In this way, the new government was already committed to the merger. So far, there is no indication of further mergers of universities.

Implementation of structural development policy: mergers

The output of implementing a merger of universities can be defined in its simplest way as a formal decision that the universities to be merged stop existing as formal organisations, and a new formal organisation is established to include the former organisations. In terms of measuring the output, this definition is easy: either the merged university exists, or not. All the four mergers of altogether 10 Finnish universities took place between 2009 and 2012, and the new universities started in 2010 and 2013, as in the schedule envisaged by the governmental development plans. The Helsinki University of Technology, the Helsinki School of Economics and the University of Art and Design Helsinki now constitute Aalto University. Initially, during the policy formulation phase, this university was called an 'innovation university', which was changed to a 'top university' during the preparatory work to exclude the innovation aspect that was contested in the later phases of the work (the author was the secretary in chief of the governmental working group in question; see Virtanen, 2008). The governmental working group also proposed a governance structure making it a private foundation with substantial investment from the government. The proposition was later adopted by the new University Act. This was very radical at the time when all universities were regular public agencies and academic staff had the position of civil servants under public law.

The Turku School of Economics, initially a relatively small institution, is today one of the Faculties of the University of Turku. The University of Kuopio and the University of Joensuu now form the University of Eastern Finland. This merger was initially planned to be a federation university composed of two partly independent universities, but this objective was rejected later, as Aalto University paved the way for the more radical reforms of straightforward mergers.

All these three mergers were part of the new University Act. The Act itself was a culmination of a major university reform in 2009. It changed the legal status of all universities, gave each of them a legal personality under private law and economic autonomy (separate from the regular state budget) but kept them in the governmental steering and funding framework. The University of Art and Design was established by an amendment of the University Act in 2012, which merged the three small art universities into one.

The policy instrument used to create these new universities was a legal mandate: in Finland, this is the only way to establish a university, both for universities based on public foundation (12 out of 14 universities in 2013) or private foundation (two). Legally the difference is only related to some aspects of management system. This may be defined as an implementation success on the part of the ministry and Parliament, if we measure the success only with legal change.

In terms of larger policy design, the legal aspects of mergers were only technical policy instruments pursuing goals related to the missions, functions and societal effectiveness of the new universities. To understand these goals, we have to look at the policy formulation aspect of the mergers. Did the constituent parts of the new universities want to form a new entity? Who supported the idea and who fought back, and for what reasons? Where did the idea come from?

The governmental preparation of the three first mergers started with three ministerial working groups set up by the Minister of Education in 2006. The groups were very small. The group for the University of Turku was chaired by a former Permanent Secretary (the top civil servant) of the Ministry of Education, and the members were the 'rectors' (Finnish term for vice-chancellors) of the two constituent universities. The group of the University of Eastern Finland was chaired by the former Director-General of the Academy of Finland (a major funder of basic research), members being rectors and directors of administration of both universities, and the governor of the county where the universities existed. The group of Aalto University was chaired by the Permanent Secretary of the Ministry of Finance, and the members were the rectors of the three universities, a former scientific adviser of Nokia Corporation, and the chancellor of one of the universities to be merged, the University of Economics (that is, a business school), with responsibility for inviting an expert group of business leaders for consultation.

The merger of the small art universities was also prepared by a governmental task force, but it was not set up by the minister but by a top official of the ministry. The relatively large group submitted its proposal in 2010. The group was chaired by the Director-General of Finnish National Opera and the members were, among others, the rectors of the three universities and an opera singer.

The composition of the groups was instrumental to change. All members supported the idea of closer cooperation if not a merger straight away. There were no representatives from the staff and student core of the universities, from both of which there was some opposition to the mergers. In particular, students from the former University of Arts and Design protested loudly. Although staff and students were not members of the working groups, their opinions were heard both in the group meetings and by inviting statements from student and staff unions after the submission of the proposals at the same time as from many other stakeholders.

The main concerns of the opposition among the academic staff and students was the loss of autonomy as external members of the suggested governance structure would have been the majority in the university board (this was changed to a minority by Parliament); the fear of art students about the overwhelming business culture imposed by universities of economics and technology in the case of Aalto University; stronger dependence on private donations that would contribute only to technological and business sciences, not humanities and social sciences; and the reduction of participatory, collegial bodies (actually still possible by universities' own decision). The opposition was partly about the whole university reform, and partly about mergers, since both policies were interrelated. However, once the universities had accepted the proposals to merge, there were many working groups in all merging universities, also with representatives of staff and students, before the details of the legislation were finalised. So, although the policy formulation was more in the hands of the ministry and the top management of the universities, the policy implementation was clearly more participatory, and had the effect of making the opposition gradually weaker.

The official goals of the three first mergers are not mentioned in the bill to Parliament in 2009. The bill presented only the goals of the new University Act, actually the goals of the whole university reform. The governmental working groups provided their own goals for each new university, but the overall goals related to the institutional network of universities were specified in a discussion paper by the Ministry of Education (2008, p 8; author's translation):

> The goal of the structural reforms of the institutional network of higher education and the increase of efficiency in the functions of higher education institutions is to free up resources for teaching and strengthening the quality of research. This is done by creation of higher education units that have competitive capacity to act nationally and internationally in the changing field of higher education institutions and whose economic capacity is sustainable. The renewing structures of higher education institutions give better opportunities for cross-

and multi-disciplinarity, new innovations, and better services to the students. Strategic thinking and decision-making is supported by more serried structures of activities. The development of the internal structures of a higher education institution belongs primarily to the sphere of autonomy of higher education institutions.

To summarise, the goals were a reduction in the number of institutions and their units and making the units bigger, which would then lead to stronger economic capacity, better international competitiveness and more options of choice to students. Measuring performance in achieving these goals is much more difficult than measuring the emergence of institutional mergers. For example, the organisational measures of quality of research are, at best, indirect (for example, the share of publications in top journals), and there are more variables than mere mergers that can explain changes in publication practices. In the first three merged universities, organisational structures have been changed, new study programmes have been established, the principle of new encounters crossing the old organisational boundaries has been applied in various forms, and systems of tenure track and international recruitment have been adopted to replace the traditional Finnish open recruitment. The effects of these changes for the international competitiveness of the new universities are to be seen only in the future.

The goals related to the development of the institutional network are, of course, the same for the creation of the University of Art and Design. More specific goals are given in the bill proposing the merger by an amendment of the University Act in 2012, and they are too many to be described here in detail. The new university is expected to strengthen the status and autonomy of art in society and the entire art and cultural life of the country. The purpose is to strengthen the quality and effectiveness of education, research and artistic activity. The University of Art and Design is expected to act as a forerunner in 'artistic and other research'. It is expected to contribute in developing opportunities for researcher careers, new forms of cooperation in education and research, to improve the working life abilities of students and to improve the efficiency of the university administration and its capacity to provide a service. Measuring performance in achieving these goals is also very challenging, since many outputs only emerge after several years.

Apart from regulation, the central policy instrument of the government related to merger policy has been extra funding for the new, merged universities. For the University of Aalto, this funding has been substantial, from €80 to €90 million per year in 2010–13 (40-45 per cent of the initial total governmental funding of the three universities before the merger), for others much less. In addition to this, the government promised to give €500 million for the capital of the private foundation of Aalto University, provided there were private donations of up to €200 million first. As for Aalto University, the clearly larger financial support was grounded in the desire to create a top university of international relevance, and an institution to function as an engine of national competitiveness of Finnish technological industry. In respect to the other universities, with the governance structures of public foundations, as opposed to the special status of Aalto University, the government decided later on to invest to assist the foundations of all other universities as well, with the same 5:2 proportion, provided a university was able to collect private donations of at least €1 million.

In the end, most universities managed to get sufficient donations, and the government gave its shares to each university, but the scale of donation from the government was substantially smaller (the lowest was €5 million, the highest €98 million) than that for Aalto University (€492 million). What is noteworthy here is that the successful use of economic policy instrument depended on universities' ability to get private donators to comply. Extra funding can be considered as an economic incentive to merge. The purpose of the extra funding has been to support the renewal of organisational practices along the lines of the goals of the mergers. For example, the University of Aalto is using the revenue from the foundation capital for the rapid development extension of a tenure track system with a view to enhancing the recruitment of outstanding staff.

As for the organisational and interorganisational behaviour in implementing the mergers, one thing in common for all the four mergers is broad participation of academic staff and students as members of working groups. Groups were interorganisational in the sense that members represented all constituent institutions in each merger. The ministry supported financially the work of each merger project after the university boards had accepted their merger. Each university organised a campaign to collect donations.

Since universities have their organisational autonomy based on academic freedom, the implementation of the goals of the merger is, in the end, their own responsibility. The government and the ministry may offer economic incentives, for example, in the target and performance negotiations every four years between each university and the ministry, where the state subsidies to universities are discussed before the governmental decisions. The implementation within each university covers all members of the organisation. The 'street-level' bureaucrats may be understood as those in operational management responsible for recognising the connections of everyday activities to general objectives of the merger. However, in organisational practice, it is the strategy of the university and its implementation that needs to be the main reference point in the implementation analysis of the merger. This would require a separate discussion, which is not feasible here. However, the assumptions of rational policy making assume that both the ministry and the university actors pay attention to the original goals of the merger in the longer run. In practice, the links to the original goals may become fuzzy, since the strategy of each university is probably changing over the years both because of changes in higher education policy and other areas of the operational environment of HEIs.

The target groups of the mergers are the prospective and current academic staff and students who make the goals of the policy true in their everyday activities of research, teaching and studying. University administrators and support staff may be considered a secondary target group whose contribution is instrumental to the productivity and quality of academic staff and students and their activities. The activities of the target groups create, in the end, the outcome of the university mergers. For example, the international competitiveness of Finnish universities in terms of quality of research and international attractiveness for top researchers and students is, in many ways, dependent on what the current researchers, teachers and students do and how it is known in international scholarly communities, funding organisations and the international academic labour market and educational market. However, to achieve these types of goals also needs contributions from many other actors that can affect the infrastructure of universities, for example, governmental organisations responsible for research funding.

Conclusions

What explains the performance in merging universities? If we consider the emergence of merged universities by new legislation as an output, there are certain factors that contributed to the success. The behaviour of the top management of universities was crucial, since they committed to the idea of creating stronger cooperative structures despite internal opposition in their institutions. Without this commitment, the minister would not have been able to establish the governmental working groups for preparing the matter. Except for the merger of arts universities, governmental working groups were set at a high political level, and they did not have members from academic staff and students. The top management of universities expected to get additional funding, and especially in the case of Aalto University, a more managerial governance structure based on a private foundation.

The mergers were prepared at the same time as the whole university reform, and new legislation was needed for both. The general reform atmosphere of key governmental actors was favourable for major changes. Additional funding was clearly a strong incentive for universities. For the members of Parliament, the mergers were easy to decide, since the boards of the constituent institutions of the new universities had already approved of the mergers. Academic staff and students took part in numerous working groups in already implementing the mergers before the new legislation. The critics of the reform paid attention to this. One might say, however, that the autonomy of the universities and academic staff and students was respected by Parliament, as it just legally confirmed what was already going on in real life.

In terms of the impact of conflict and ambiguity on the implementation (Matland, 1995), the Finnish policy of mergers of universities can be characterised as low in ambiguity (as legal operations) and low to medium in conflict (depending on whose opposition is addressed). The political power was strong in the first phases of preparatory work (setting up the working groups and decision making by the university boards) and, formally, in parliamentary decision making, but actual implementation with the new additional resources was mostly administrative implementation.

In terms of larger policy design, where institutional mergers are a means for the pursuit of more general goals, such as better international competitiveness, implementation is carried out by the staff and students and stakeholders of the new universities. The ambiguity of both the goals and means is relatively strong, implying that results are uncertain. There is also space for conflict. The outputs and outcome will take years to emerge. At that time, the causal analysis of implementation will be very challenging, since many other issues than mergers will have affected the characteristics of the teaching, research and innovation activities of the merged institutions and their effects within the institutions and their environment.

Part 6
Governance and globalism

6.1

Introduction

The title of this part links together two concepts much used nowadays in discussions of the policy process. Both should be used with care, and have been criticised for their overuse. They bring out issues about complexity that may or may not help with the understanding of the process.

According to Richards and Smith:

> Governance is a descriptive label that is used to highlight the changing nature of the policy process in recent decades. In particular, it sensitizes us to the ever-increasing variety of terrains and actors involved in the making of public policy. (2002, p 2)

That seems relatively unproblematic. However, the term is used to encapsulate the development of networks, replacing government by governance. As Pierre and Peters put it:

> We believe that the role of the state is not decreasing ... but rather that its role is transforming, from a role based in constitutional powers towards a role based in coordination and fusion of public and private resources.... (Pierre and Peters, 2000, p 25)

But what does that so-called 'transformation' imply? Analysis is not helped by the number of writers who use the term but who acknowledge its ambiguity. Kooiman identifies 10 different meanings (1999), and Rhodes has argued that it has too many meanings to be useful (1997), yet both these statements are contained within writings with titles using the term. Davies offers a more forthright challenge to governance 'theory' for the way it involves the 'the proposition that network-like institutions ... transcend structures of power and domination' (2011, p 152).

Hence scepticism is appropriate about the extent to which the term 'governance' is used to imply a transformation in the overall relationship between state and society. On the other hand, it is less contentious to use it in the context of the description of complex interactions between many organisations, state and non-state (particularly in policy formulation and implementation) which make the policy-making process very much an interorganisational process. That has been the primary concern of much of the writing about networks (Kickert et al, 1997; Koppenjan and Klijn, 2004).

Much of this literature is particularly relevant to the formulation and implementation parts of this book, and some aspects of it were mentioned there (Parts Four and Five). The contributions earlier in the book, of Corinne Larrue and Marie Fournier (Chapter 4.4), Sonia Exley (Chapter 4.5) and Turo Virtanen (Chapter 5.5) are particularly pertinent.

What this part is particularly concerned with is the aspect of the shift towards 'governance' that involves changing relationships between the nation state and other states or indeed the rest of the world, which add to and perhaps make more complex the internal government process. However, before proceeding to discuss that, it is appropriate to warn that the notion of the 'nation state' is by no means unproblematic. States are still being divided and formed. Many are federal, with some powers devolved, and there are various types of federalism (see Lane and Ersson, 2000, chapter 4). One of the case studies in this part, by Srinivasa Vittal Katikireddi and Katherine Smith (Chapter 6.2), features some policy-making complexities in the emergent federalism in respect of the relationship between Scotland and the UK.

However, looking beyond the nation state, issues about governance are linked with another contested concept, that of 'globalism'. The problem about the extent to which a one-word concept is being used to theorise a trend is even stronger with globalism than with governance. Some forms of globalist theory see worldwide economic developments as of determining importance for contemporary policy making. This determinist thrust to the argument is reinforced by evidence on the development of international organisations and the emergence of global cultural flows. It is given particular relevance for the policy process by policy problems – pollution, conflicts over scarce resources, poorly regulated international trading, movements of people as economic migrants and refugees – that have global implications.

A particularly strong statement on this development, also linking it to the internal dimension of the shift towards governance, is provided by Hajer in an article called 'Policy without polity? Policy analysis and the institutional void' (2003). He argues:

> The weakening of the state goes hand in hand with the international growth of civil society, the emergence of citizen-actors and new forms of mobilization … *there are no clear rules and norms according to which politics is to be conducted and policy measures are to be agreed upon.…* (Hajer, 2003, p 175; original emphasis)

Hence Hajer writes of a 'dispersed' decision-making order and a 'new spatiality of policy making and politics'. Like Pierre, (2009), who is particularly concerned with analysing the internal aspects of the shift towards governance, he thus identifies a 'democratic deficit' requiring 'us fundamentally to rethink the basis of effective political intervention and thus of policy making' (Hajer, 2003, p 184).

But do we have here irresistible trends that render national governments impotent? Hay argues that while decision makers may believe that there is no alternative but to respond to perceived global economic forces, globalisation also 'may provide a most convenient alibi, allowing politicians to escape the responsibility they would otherwise bear for reforms which might otherwise be rather difficult to legitimate' (2002, p 259; see also Hay and Rosamond, 2002). An important structure/action problem is being highlighted here (see the discussion of this in Part Two).

To take this issue further requires an unbundling of the various ways in which the autonomy of nation state governments may be affected. This implies seeing globalism not as an irresistible structural trend but rather as a variety of developments, among which the following may be highlighted:

• The formation of 'regional' (in global terms) forms of government in which a measure of national autonomy is explicitly given up. The European Union (EU) is the clearest large example of this. Experts on EU affairs debate the extent to which this involves the gradual emergence of a new federal state. The alternative is to see it as an elaborate, largely economic, alliance in which nation states have measures of freedom to influence how policy initiatives are translated into national policies. Dorte Martinsen and Nikolay Vasev's (Chapter 6.5) contribution comparing the impact of EU healthcare policies in Denmark and Bulgaria identifies some of these issues here. National size and whether or not a country also belongs within the common currency group will affect this. Mairéad Considine and Fiona Dukelow's (Chapter 6.3) contribution on the Irish response to the economic crisis explores these issues.
• International agreements that limit national autonomy. Again, the issues about size and independence of the economy, highlighted in the first point above, are relevant here. The issues about climate change are worth paying attention to here, indicating both possibilities and limitations in respect of the strengths and weaknesses of such agreements. In this part Paul Burton's (Chapter 6.4) examination of response to concerns about climate change in Australia examines some aspects of this issue.
• More limited bilateral treaties, perhaps concerning trade or the regulation of a shared river or sea coast, which impose limitations on national action.
• More controversially, as already highlighted by the discussion of globalist theory, situations where private sector actors from outside a national state are able to impose policies. Again, the size and economic strength dimension is important, as some of the economic actors control more resources than many small nation states (as in evidence in the Irish case discussed in Chapter 6.3).
• Some similar points may be made, more cautiously, about situations in which influential international coalitions of social (as opposed to economic) actors can carry weight in the policy making of nation states.

There is a growing literature on policy transfer between countries. This is another phenomenon better described as a topic rather than a theory. It is easy to observe, indeed surely hardly a matter for comment, that policy ideas flow from country to country as nations encounter similar policy problems. On the other hand, there are things to be said about the influences on that flow, the extent to which there are international 'policy entrepreneurs' (see the discussion of policy entrepreneurs in Part Three) and interests that subsidise their activities. International organisations (the United Nations [UN] agencies, the OECD [Organisation for Economic Cooperation and Development], The World Bank) play a role in this respect (see Deacon, 2007). Holzinger and Knill (2005) offer a useful taxonomy of sources of policy convergence between nations, from 'imposition', 'international harmonisation' and 'regulatory competition', where the formal intergovernmental arrangements discussed above apply, through to 'transnational communication'. In the latter category they bracket 'lesson drawing', 'transnational problem solving', 'emulation' and 'international policy promotion'.

The cautious observations above, about both governance and globalism, suggest that there is no simple new theory here to transform how the policy process is analysed in the modern world. Rather, there is a need to recognise that processes within nation states may be influenced in a variety of ways by supranational actors.

6.2

The first contribution in this section, Srinivasa Vittal Katikireddi and Katherine Smith's exploration of the development of a policy on minimum unit pricing in Scotland, might have been included in the agenda-setting or policy formulation parts of the book. It is included here because it features issues about the interactions between policy making in Scotland and policy in the UK, raising interesting questions about governance complexity and about the partial 'federalism' of the UK.

This contribution illustrates the importance of considering complexity in policy-making processes and institutional structures when exploring the development of public policies. Traditional views of policy making often assume policies are made by single authorities with clear legitimacy to make decisions. However, this perspective is now widely discredited within the academic literature and often considered fundamentally inadequate for understanding the policy-making process (Rose and Miller, 1992; Shore, 2011).

This case study demonstrates the limitations of linear policy stages models, and highlights the need to study the potential interplay between different levels of governmental institutions and multiple policy actors. In particular, it suggests that in many cases central sources of authority are being replaced by multiple governmental and non-governmental actors that work in combination to shape policy development (see Shore, 2011). Multilevel governance theories are briefly introduced and applied to demonstrate that a consideration of these sources of complexity can be useful when seeking to understand the development of social policies. However, in contrast to claims that multilevel governance processes are 'hollowing out' the nation state (Rhodes, 1994, 1996), the contribution also argues that the development of minimum unit pricing represents a conscious attempt by the devolved Scottish Government to demonstrate its public health policy leadership.

Minimum unit pricing of alcohol in Scotland

Srinivasa Vittal Katikireddi and Katherine E. Smith

Introduction

Minimum unit pricing represents a novel and somewhat controversial social policy measure that is intended to reduce alcohol consumption by providing a base price below which alcohol cannot be sold, with the aim of reducing alcohol-related health harms (Katikireddi et al, forthcoming). While alcohol has been a cause of considerable health and social harms throughout the UK for many years, this contribution investigates why minimum unit pricing has been pursued as a policy by the devolved Scottish Government, which has resulted in its consideration elsewhere within the UK as well as internationally. It draws on qualitative interviews carried out with a broad range of policy stakeholders (including politicians, civil servants, health and other advocacy groups and industry representatives with an interest in alcohol) as well as analyses of relevant policy documents.

Multilevel governance and the complexity of policy making

Traditional views of government in modern democratic systems have tended to emphasise the ability and legitimacy of the state in constructing and implementing policies (through the use of force, if necessary) (Spruyt, 2002). The term 'governance' is often vaguely defined, and has been interpreted in multiple ways (Rose and Miller, 1992), but simply put, the literature on multilevel governance challenges traditional accounts of policy making, by suggesting that policy-making processes are increasingly complex, diffuse and contested.

Over the course of the last century, the complexity of government institutional structures has increased markedly (Hill, 2013). From a UK perspective, it has been traditional to view the British political system (at least in the 19th and 20th centuries) as characterised by a strong central government, with a hierarchical decision-making structure (Bache and Flinders, 2004). While the extent that the reality of British policy making has ever been reflected by this 'Westminster model' is debatable, there does appear to be a consensus that this model has become increasingly less accurate over the past 50 years or so (Bache and Flinders, 2004). The power of the UK government has been ceded to organisations operating both above the level of the nation state and within the traditional UK state. This includes the European Union (EU) (and its predecessor and affiliated institutions) which has gradually accumulated increasing influence across many areas (Bomberg et al, 2008). Within the UK, the ongoing devolution processes, notably in Scotland, Wales and Northern Ireland, but also within England, has led to some key policy responsibilities being delegated from Westminster to regional institutions (see, for example, House of Lords Select Committee on the Constitution, 2002).

A parallel process conveyed by the multilevel governance literature is the growing diffusion of power from government to broader institutions of governance: quasi-autonomous non-governmental organisations (quangos), arm's-length independent regulators and private sector actors, among others (Rhodes, 1994). However, it is not only those that are formally delegated responsibilities that enjoy influence in the complex world of 'governance'; the term also encompasses the diverse range of non-governmental interest groups attempting to influence policy making, such as businesses, charities, think tanks and lobbyists (Stoker, 1998).

A key claim in some of the multilevel governance literature is that, as traditional central and local government functions are ceded to other agencies, the nation state is being 'hollowed out' (Rhodes, 1994, 1996). Rather than resting with any one governmental authority, power is seen to be diffuse, residing at a variety of institutional levels and across a broad range of state and non-state actors. The multilevel governance literature therefore highlights the difficulty in identifying who has power to make decisions and also who has authority to do so (Bache and Flinders, 2004). In the absence of clear authority, Hajer has argued that those involved need to negotiate the *processes* through which policy is made, as well as its content (Hajer, 2003, 2005). In other words, policy actors may need to work to influence the 'rules of the game' by which policy is made, which may then influence the conduct of future policy-making negotiations, in addition to working to influence specific policy decisions.

Reflecting many of the claims in the multilevel governance literature, the case study of minimum unit pricing for alcohol in Scotland illustrates the necessity of examining the complexity arising from multiple and interacting tiers of government in a policy-making arena in which authority and the 'rules of the game' are contested. After briefly introducing alcohol as a public health policy issue, this contribution briefly outlines the key factors that seem to have made Scotland a receptive climate for the development of a minimum unit pricing policy for alcohol (for a more comprehensive account, see Katikireddi et al, forthcoming). It then concludes by reflecting on the extent to which the multilevel governance literature sufficiently explains Scotland's approach to minimum unit pricing, arguing that the commitment of the current Scottish Nationalist Party (SNP) government to Scottish independence suggests that while thinking about complexity adds explanatory power, some aspects of more simple policy-making models (such as consideration of clear political commitments) remain helpful.

Alcohol as a public health policy issue

The UK is one of many countries that has a longstanding and problematic relationship with alcohol (Rehm et al, 2009). The individual health harms directly arising from alcohol use are diverse, including liver cirrhosis and injury, and an increased risk of various cancers, heart conditions and mental health conditions (Room et al, 2005). The negative health effects of alcohol have long been known about. An expert report from the medical community presented to the UK's House of Commons in 1726, for example, stated:

> ... we have with concern, observed, for some years past, the fatal effects of the frequent use of several sorts of distilled Spirituous Liquors upon great numbers of both Sexes, rend(e)ring them diseased, not fit for business, poor, a burthen to themselves and neighbours and too often the cause of weak, feeble and distempered children, who must be, instead of an advantage and strength, a charge to their country. (cited in Royal College of Physicians, 1987, p 1)

As indicated in this quotation, alcohol-related harms extend well beyond individual drinkers, affecting the rest of the family and wider society (Babor, 2010). Much of the evidence suggests that the amount of consumption and the drinking pattern (for example, the consumption of a large amount of alcohol at one time – a 'binge') are the most important determinants of harms rather than, for example, the type of beverage (Bobak et al, 2004; Babor, 2010). Ultimately, these harms result in increased financial costs for many public services, including the health services, the police and justice system (York Health Economics Consortium, 2010). However, alcohol consumption has also played a central role in many Western cultures (Makela and Room, 2000), and the production of alcohol and its sales within the night-time economy and off-licensed premises (such as pubs and night clubs) contributes to the economy and job market (see, for example, Verso Economics, 2010). So the question is not 'when did policy makers discover alcohol was harmful?' but rather, 'at what points, and why, have policy makers decided that the harms caused by alcohol outweighed the benefits to an extent that policy intervention is required?'

Changing powers and political fortunes in Scotland

Historically, Scotland has been a separate state within the UK, but England and Scotland have had a shared Parliament in Westminster since the Acts of Union in 1707 (Cairney, 2011) so Scotland is often considered part of the UK in policy terms. However, there were important differences between Scotland and the rest of the UK even prior to political devolution in 1999, including a different legal framework, education system and, notably for this case study, a different licensing system for alcohol sales, although in broad terms alcohol policies did not substantially differ (Nicholls, 2012).

The political union between Scotland and England was, for the first half of the 20th century, supported by broadly similar electoral preferences (McCrone, 2006). However, the Conservative-led UK governments from 1979-97 lacked Scottish political support, creating a democratic deficit in Scotland (McCrone, 1991, 2006). This situation was exacerbated by widespread belief that the policies being pursued by the UK government during this period were having a particularly deleterious effect on Scotland (Collins and McCartney, 2011), a legacy which is evident in the subsequently poor performance of the Conservative Party in Scotland (for example, securing only one Scottish seat in the 2010 UK general election). Since this period, McCrone argues that a political discourse has emerged in which Scottishness 'is significantly linked to left-wing values' and a greater support for state intervention (McCrone, 2006, p 34).

Against this backdrop, the UK election of a Labour government (under Tony Blair) in 1997 promised a referendum concerning the introduction of a devolved Scottish Parliament. Having achieved the necessary political support, the first Scottish elections were held in 1999. Labour initially dominated, forming two consecutive coalition governments with the Liberal Democrats in 1999–2003 and 2003–07. Then from 2007 to 2011, the centre-left Scottish National Party (SNP) ran a minority government and, in 2011, the SNP (unexpectedly) achieved Scotland's first majority government. Under the Labour-Liberal Democrat coalitions, the administration in Scotland was referred to as the 'Scottish Executive', acknowledging its subordinate role to Westminster, but the SNP rebranded the administration 'the Scottish Government' in 2007. While significant policy divergence was not necessarily anticipated while Labour remained the dominant party at UK and Scottish levels, the SNP is a left-leaning, pro-independence party which might be expected to seek policy divergence from the rest of the UK to help highlight differences between Scottish and English interests, as well as its distinctiveness as a party and its ability to govern (Smith and Hellowell, 2012).

Policy innovation and public health in a devolved Scotland

The relationship between the Scottish and UK Parliaments is complicated by the fact that only some policy areas are 'devolved' to Scotland (Cairney, 2011). Health was one of the most important policy areas to be devolved to Scotland (alongside others such as education and social care), which means the Scottish administration has the responsibility of addressing alcohol-related health harms. However, as advertising and most trade and financial policy (including alcohol duties) remain reserved at Westminster, Scotland's ability to use these policy levers is significantly restricted, despite the fact that such policies are clearly important for alcohol consumption patterns and rates and, therefore, alcohol-related harms. In addition, both the Scottish and UK Westminster Parliaments are also subject to constraints imposed by supranational organisations and agreements (for example, EU policy and international trade agreements) (Katikireddi and McLean, 2012).

Despite these restrictions, devolution has already allowed Scotland to pursue high-profile divergent policies in some areas, including the abolition of tuition fees for Scottish students attending Scottish higher education sites and the provision of free personal care for elderly. people Perhaps most pertinently, Scotland was the first country within the UK to pass legislation to ban smoking in public places and it took an innovative route to doing so (Cairney, 2009). While the stated aim of the smoking ban in the Republic of Ireland, which occurred shortly before the Scottish ban, was to protect the health of employees in workplaces (including pubs, bars and restaurants), employment regulation remained a matter reserved to the Westminster Parliament (Cairney, 2007a). Therefore the Scottish ban on smoking in public places was introduced on public health, rather than employee health, grounds, demonstrating the potentially creative approach of policy making in a devolved context. England subsequently introduced its own ban two years later on the basis of protecting the health of those working in public places, but the early introduction of this legislation in Scotland has largely been perceived positively by public health policy actors. For example:

> Civil servant (Scotland): '... the smoking ban is widely recognised as being really successful – more so than anticipated. It demonstrated that the Scottish Government was in a position to take action that might be different from that in other parts of United Kingdom, with the powers that were available to it. They could take a legislative approach that was quite cheap and accepted by a surprisingly large proportion of the population, and the feedback from the evaluation showed it was highly effective with real health benefits. Some elements of government thought if we could do this then maybe we could tackle other similar problems using lessons from the smoking ban.'

Scotland's policy leadership on banning smoking in public places was consistently constructed by interviewees as a potential stimulus for taking action to reduce alcohol-related health harms in Scotland. For example:

> Civil servant (Scotland): 'I think you know the success of the smoking ban shows that such legislation can work. It was equally controversial pre-implementation but once it's been implemented, people just kind of accepted it. You would hope something similar would happen with minimum pricing. It's obviously been a controversial policy. Once implemented, hopefully people will see the benefits. So I think it's important you know, I think people in Scotland are beginning to realise, I would suggest, that our public health has not been the greatest for the last generation and something has to be done, so I think there's more support for minimum pricing than may have happened before the smoking ban.'

The above sections therefore suggest a number of aspects of Scotland's political climate potentially favouring the development of innovative policy proposals relating to alcohol. First, the increasing political distinctiveness in Scotland, reinforced by political devolution in 1999, involves a greater appetite for state intervention. Second, health was one of the most high-profile policy areas to be devolved to Scotland. Third, alcohol licensing within Scotland already operated independently of England. Fourth and finally, Scotland's leadership in terms of banning smoking in public places was generally well received and paved the way for Scottish leadership in other areas of public health.

Rise of alcohol policy in Scotland

Within the first three years of devolution, Scotland was already developing a distinct approach to alcohol policy. In 2002, a Labour–Liberal Democrat coalition introduced the first alcohol strategy for Scotland (Scottish Executive, 2002), two years before England developed an equivalent (Prime Minister's Strategy Unit, 2004). Both approaches focused on targeted specific subgroups of the population, seeking, for example, to 'reduce binge drinking and reduce harmful drinking by children and young people' (Scottish Executive, 2002, p 3). Two differences between the English and Scottish strategies are noteworthy. First, while the English strategy was heavily criticised for explicitly ruling out the use of price mechanisms entirely (Anderson, 2007), the Scottish plan did include a ban on irresponsible price promotions in on-sales premises (such as pubs and clubs). Second, a subsequent Licensing (Scotland) Act 2005 introduced the 'protection and improvement of public health' as one of five licensing objectives to be considered when making assessments on alcohol licensing applications (Nicholls, 2012), a measure absent from English licensing law. This can therefore be seen to represent an important change in the framing of alcohol policy, with a clearer public health framing of the issue in Scotland compared to England.

Following the first Scottish alcohol strategy, a growing epidemiological literature began quantifying the extent of alcohol-related harms within Scotland. This included international comparative work which found that liver cirrhosis deaths (a commonly used indicator of alcohol-related health harms) among Scottish men had more than doubled between 1987–91 and 1997–2001 (Leon and McCambridge, 2006), an increase that greatly exceeded the level observed in the rest of the UK and compared unfavourably to a general reduction across most of Western Europe. These findings appear to have made an impact on those in positions of influence, casting alcohol as a public health 'crisis' in Scotland, with one interviewee stating:

> Civil servant (Scotland): 'I was staggered by some of the graphs and some of the trends which you don't see in public health very often, you know, the Leon and McCambridge liver cirrhosis graph for example, the quadrupling of hospital admissions.[...] Kind of you know, while talking to ministers as well, I think the Cabinet Secretary was quite startled by some of the evidence we presented on the scale of the problem.'

Both the relatively small size of the Scottish policy-making community (compared to Westminster) and an active third sector facilitated the rapid dissemination of this kind of evidence, according to many respondents. For example:

> Politician (Scotland): 'I think it's just the way smaller nations with a relatively small government and a very active civic Scotland – third sector however you want to define it – how they operate – that if you've got a story to tell that is packed with a really strong persuasive evidence base, you get to speak to the most senior people in government very, very quickly in Scotland.'

In sum, this section highlights that the favourable political climate in Scotland did indeed appear to facilitate Scottish leadership on alcohol policy in the post-devolution context but, despite this, policy audiences were becoming aware of a growing body of evidence demonstrating that Scotland had a particularly acute alcohol problem.

From price to minimum unit pricing

Longstanding epidemiological evidence suggests there is a strong relationship between the price of alcohol, overall population consumption and the level of harms a population experiences (Booth et al, 2008; Babor, 2010). It has also been argued that a major contributing factor to the alarming increase in alcohol harms in the UK has been the increasing affordability of alcohol products (Gillan and Macnaughton, 2007). For example, it has been calculated that, largely as a result of increased living standards, alcohol was 62 per cent more affordable in 2005 than in 1980 (Gillan and Macnaughton, 2007). An important feature of the UK alcohol market has been the practice of aggressive cost-cutting of alcohol products, especially within supermarkets (Bennetts, 2008). This has resulted in alcohol sales on occasion being below the cost of duty alone (Record and Day, 2009; Black et al, 2011). Alongside the increased affordability within off-sales premises, a shift has occurred in sales from the licensed on-trade sector (pubs, etc) to off-licence retailers, suggesting more people are drinking at home (Holloway et al, 2008).

Changing the price of alcohol, along with controls on promotion and availability, have been identified as key methods for addressing alcohol-related health harms by the World Health Organization (2010a), and many governments have long used alcohol taxation as a mechanism to influence consumption levels, as well as to raise revenue (Griffith and Leicester, 2010). Epidemiological studies have also found that drinkers at the greatest risk of harm tend to consume the cheapest alcohol (Black et al, 2011). Within Scotland, increasing price was identified as a necessary component of actions to address alcohol-related harms by NHS Health Scotland in early 2007, an intermediary organisation responsible for providing advice on health-related issues to the Scottish Government (NHS Health Scotland, 2008). It was not until after the election of the SNP minority government later that year that action within this area was considered. As several civil servants noted, the change in government brought with it a 'window of opportunity' and appetite for a more radical approach to tackle alcohol-related harms:

> Civil servant (Scotland): 'Certainly, you know, the [new SNP] Deputy First Minister took a really close personal interest and saw this as a flagship policy area. So, you know, she was taking a really close interest. She had been ... she, when she was in opposition she had proposed a members bill on tobacco and so, you know, obviously that had then been delivered by the Labour/Lib Dem coalition and she saw this very much as, this was her tobacco bill, this was her kind of seminal moment to tackle a major public health problem ... if it hadn't been for Deputy First Minister's personal drive and commitment and seeing this as, no, we really need to address this, then, you know, we wouldn't have had such a radical policy as we have had.'

Despite the consensus on addressing price within the public health community and favourable political context, increasing alcohol duties remained reserved to the UK government and therefore not an option open to the devolved Scottish Government. Minimum unit pricing can therefore be seen to represent an alternative lever by which to influence alcohol pricing, which was within the Scottish Government's control. In 2007, a recently established advocacy group, Scottish Health Action on Alcohol Problems (SHAAP), created by the Scottish medical royal colleges and faculties in response to concerns about the increasing burden of alcohol harms, held an expert workshop to identify potential actions to address alcohol harms. SHAAP subsequently published the first public report outlining a minimum unit pricing proposal and calling for its adoption in Scotland. The impact of this report is reflected by interview data:

> Civil servant (Scotland): '... the Scottish Parliament doesn't have control over taxation so duty, VAT wasn't within our remit and to be honest, it's not as currently set-up, it's not a good mechanism or an equitable mechanism for addressing public health issues. I think, you know, SHAAP held a pricing workshop in 2007 with an influential report on the back of that. I think we just saw the minimum unit pricing as a straightforward, fair way of addressing pricing.'

An important aspect of SHAAP's report was the consideration it gave to the limited powers of Scottish institutions, to the extent that the authors obtained legal opinions about the potential for introducing minimum unit pricing with the wider UK and EU contexts:

> Fixing minimum drinks prices can achieve health goals that raising alcohol taxes alone cannot by preventing below-cost selling and the

deep discounting of alcohol that some retailers engage in. Fixing minimum drinks prices is possible under both UK and EU competition law, provided that minimum prices are imposed on licensees by law or at the sole instigation of a public authority. (Gillan and Macnaughton, 2007, p 15)

From an early stage, SHAAP worked to ensure that politicians and civil servants were closely engaged (as reflected by a civil servant representing the Scottish Government having attended the workshop as an observer). In line with multilevel governance theory, this demonstrates the potentially significant role that non-state actors can play in policy development.

Those in favour of minimum unit pricing proposals argue that it may be a better or complimentary mechanism for addressing alcohol-related health harms than alcohol taxation (House of Commons Health Committee, 2009; Health and Sport Committee, 2012). This is particularly true in the context of the fact that current legislation allows retailers to opt not to pass alcohol tax increases on to consumers (in the UK, large supermarkets have been particularly criticised for selling alcohol at a loss in order to increase footfall). Econometric modelling studies suggest that minimum unit pricing results in a greater reduction in health harms compared to an equivalent rise in taxation under the UK's current system of calculating alcohol duty (Purshouse et al, 2010). In addition, the setting of a floor price prevents drinkers from 'trading down' to cheaper drinks, given that cheap alcoholic drinks are no longer legally available. Advocates have also suggested that minimum unit pricing will incentivise the creation of lower-strength alcoholic products (increasing the potential health benefits) and may reduce the costs of supermarket products other than alcohol (as alcohol is no longer cross-subsidised by other products) (Record and Day, 2009).

In contrast, critics have expressed concern that lower-income households could be adversely affected, that rather than increasing Treasury revenues, price increases will instead enrich the alcohol industry, that minimum unit pricing constitutes an unnecessary intervention in the free market, and that it may be unlawful (Health and Sport Committee, 2012). The evidence for both sides of the debate to draw on is limited by the intervention's novelty, given that minimum unit pricing has not been pursued elsewhere (the nearest comparable intervention is the practice of reference pricing in some Canadian provinces [see Stockwell et al, 2006], but there are a number of important differences which make comparisons difficult).

A considerable diversity of opinion on minimum unit pricing (which has changed over time) has existed among the various policy stakeholders. While the SNP initially faced widespread opposition from the other political parties, two of the three major opposition parties eventually became supportive within Scotland (with the Scottish Labour Party abstaining in the parliamentary vote when minimum unit pricing passed into legislation in Scotland; see Katikireddi et al, forthcoming). Interview data suggests policy actors have also perceived a broad coalition of actors to be in favour of minimum unit pricing, from the health and voluntary sectors (for example, those working with young people, families and low-income communities) to the police. For example:

> Politician (Scotland): 'It hasn't just been those at the sharp end of dealing with the medical effects of alcohol – they're collecting data to say things are getting worse – but at the same time we've got, if you like, the Scottish kind of Civic Scotland, the voluntary sector, stepping forward and saying "we are seeing more people [affected by alcohol]."'

In contrast, there have been marked differences within industry positions (Holden et al, 2012). In general, many licensed trade representatives (who are expected to benefit as a result of a shift from home drinking to consumption within pubs and clubs) are supportive; various producers and off-trade retailers appear to have contrasting positions. For example, Tesco has been broadly supportive (presumably because, as the market leader in alcohol sales, it may benefit financially) while others such as Asda, which competes more strongly on price, have actively campaigned against minimum unit pricing (Health and Sport Committee, 2012). The existence of a broad and unified coalition in favour of minimum unit pricing, and the division among private sector actors, seems likely to have favoured the policy's adoption.

Scotland: a nation state in the making?

As noted earlier, institutional responsibilities within a devolved Scotland are complicated. The potential for overlapping responsibilities has allowed a devolved Scotland to redefine some public health policy issues to enable it to take action, as exemplified by the smoking ban in public places. By redefining alcohol pricing as a public health issue, this has helped the pro-independence SNP to pursue policy divergence from England and potentially demonstrate Scotland's position as an emerging nation state, playing a leading role in health policy (Smith and Hellowell, 2012). Interviewees certainly noted the benefits of Scotland pursuing a divergent public health policy from England and this divergence was seen, for various reasons, to help promote the idea of minimum unit pricing within the SNP government:

> Policy advocate: 'I think it's a lot to do with the Scottish National Party. [...] I suspect it's part of their Independence agenda, that it's about getting, they believe that getting hold of the revenue on alcohol – and I think this is seen as one route towards that objective – is a route towards greater independence and sovereignty.'

> Civil servant (Scotland): 'Being able to sort of say, we're being progressive, you know, is actually quite helpful. And, you know, lots

of rhetoric around, "we do hope that they'll [England will] follow us in doing this".'

The greater uncertainty about the 'rules of the game' arising as a consequence of multilevel governance may mean that political actors are not only negotiating the decision to be reached but also the processes by which future decisions are made (Hajer, 2003). In this case, bringing alcohol pricing within the remit of Scottish Government may have knock-on effects for Scotland's future decision-making competency.

The limitations of Scotland's current competence may still, however, serve as a barrier to the implementation of minimum unit pricing. The Scotch Whisky Association has queried the legitimacy of the Scottish Government in passing legislation on the area of alcohol price, arguing that this confers a trade policy, which remains reserved to the UK government. The legislation has also faced challenges at the European level (Cook, 2012), with several EU member states (Bulgaria, Spain, Italy, Portugal and France) arguing that minimum unit pricing may confer a barrier to the free movement of goods across European member states (STV News, 2012). While it is possible to create an exemption under public health grounds, in order to do so it must be shown that an alternative less trade-restrictive measure (such as raising alcohol duty) could not achieve the purpose just as well (Katikireddi and McLean, 2012) and, as the member state of European institutions is the UK, not Scotland, it is irrelevant to the European Commission's deliberation that the Scottish Government cannot itself implement such a measure.

Conclusions

The multilevel governance literature draws attention to the importance of considering the multiple levels of government that exist and the myriad governmental and non-governmental actors that may be involved in policy development. A focus on some of the distinct aspects of the Scottish institutional and political climate highlights a number of putative factors favouring the emergence of a distinct policy response to alcohol in Scotland. First, over the past three decades, a distinct political discourse has emerged in Scotland that is more amenable to state-level intervention than England. Second, partly stimulated by the increasing political differences between England and Scotland, political devolution occurred in 1999, and health was one of the most high-profile policy areas to be devolved to Scotland. Third, in relation to alcohol specifically, Scotland had already been operating a licensing system that was independent from England, reinforcing the possibility of divergence in this area. Fourth, Scotland's leadership in terms of banning smoking in public places had been viewed as an example of policy success and, according to interviewees, created an appetite for further public health policy leadership in Scotland. Fifth, and finally, the emergence of a wealth of epidemiological and other evidence outlining the extent of Scotland's alcohol-related problems, combined with the relatively small scale of the Scottish policy-making community, helped construct alcohol as a 'public health crisis' of particular relevance to Scotland.

Several factors then appear to have favoured the development of minimum unit pricing as a preferred policy intervention within Scotland. First, a consensus existed about the importance of price as a determinant of alcohol-related harms within the public health community, both internationally and within Scotland. Second, Scotland did not have (and seemed unlikely to quickly obtain) policy powers relating to alcohol duty favouring the development of an innovative, price-related policy response. Third, a change in the Scottish Government in 2007 resulted in a pro-independence SNP party seeking to distinguish Scotland from the rest of the UK (which, from 2011, has held an overall majority). If the Scottish Government is successful in implementing minimum unit pricing for alcohol, this may set a precedent that shapes future policy developments, as well as representing a high-profile example of policy divergence in itself. Fourth, a Scottish-led advocacy organisation facilitated an expert workshop to devise policy proposals to address alcohol harms (from which minimum unit pricing emerged) in the same year that the SNP's electoral success was creating a 'policy window' for more distinct, innovative Scottish policies. SHAAP worked hard to ensure the technical feasibility of this policy proposal and to promote it to multiple Scottish audiences. This ultimately paved the way for a broad coalition of support to be fostered in the absence of a unified opposition.

In many ways, this case study supports key claims made in the multilevel governance literature introduced at the start. It is certainly clear that the development of minimum unit pricing for alcohol in Scotland cannot be understood with reference to a traditional policy stages model. It is also clear, in line with multilevel governance theories, that multiple actors, including non-state actors, played an important role in the development of this policy, and that multiple institutional levels (European, UK, Scotland) are having an impact on the development of minimum unit pricing in Scotland (which may still be overturned by an EU decision). It is noteworthy that although institutional constraints help explain the policy's development, several actors argue minimum unit pricing is a better policy response than more traditional measures (such as alcohol duty) alone. However, application of a multilevel governance lens is not unproblematic in this case study. For one thing, the notion that the state is 'hollowing out' suggests a ceding of power from traditional government institutions. Yet minimum unit pricing appears to be part of the Scottish Government's efforts to 'act up' to attain the status of a nation state. Moreover, a focus on the different levels and range of actors potentially downplays other important explanatory factors. In particular, the public health framing of alcohol as a policy issue seems to have played an important role in facilitating the Scottish Government's decision to pursue minimum unit pricing. Ultimately, the multilevel governance literature provides a helpful, but partial, explanation for the development of minimum unit pricing. Acknowledging the historical and institutional context of moves towards Scottish independence, and the role of policy 'framing', supplements this interpretation, adding further layers of complexity to the case study.

6.3

airéad Considine and Fiona Dukelow's contribution on the Irish response to the economic crisis takes us to issues both about the European Union (EU) and about the impact of economic globalism on national policy making. Ireland is one of the states that has been profoundly affected by that economic crisis. The focus of analysis is on the interplay of national and international policy actors and influences, and their shifting power dynamics in the context of Ireland's crisis situation.

As a relatively small state within the EU and an open globalised economy, Ireland might be considered greatly subject to external influences and actors in its policy-making process, and even more so in the context of vulnerabilities an economic crisis creates. However, the concern here is to examine the interaction between external and internal factors, and how the Irish case, of a small open economy, demonstrates ways in which such countries continue to exert power and attempt to manoeuvre between economic opportunities and crisis constraints.

The contribution divides this analysis into three phases. The first examines Ireland's policy-making trajectory in the period prior to the emergence of the global financial crisis, and aims to show how Ireland's crisis was the product of what illusively appeared as a benign confluence of national and international policy influences and economic trends. The second focuses on policy responses to the crisis until the point of EU/International Monetary Fund (IMF) intervention, highlighting ways in which the state attempted to control the crisis during this period. The final part considers the most recent phase of the crisis by focusing on policy responses following EU/IMF financial assistance, noting how this marks a shift in the balance of policy-making forces and new tensions, but less of a deviation from existing nationally driven policy preferences.

The role of national and international policy actors and influences in crisis times: the case of Ireland

Mairéad Considine and Fiona Dukelow

Introduction

Ireland is one of the smaller states within the EU, contributing approximately 1 per cent of the Union's gross domestic product (GDP). It transformed from a poorly performing peripheral economy to achieving record growth levels by the mid-1990s, surpassing average EU living standards by the early 2000s. This earned Ireland the reputation of 'punching above its weight' in its ability to manoeuvre as a very open economy, capturing substantial international trade and investment flows. Its seemingly successful growth strategy became seen as worth emulating by other small economies, including some countries that joined the EU in 2004. Yet this attention hid not only economic weaknesses but also below-par welfare investment and social outcomes. The instabilities of this strategy were exposed by the global financial crisis when Ireland became one of the first countries to encounter severe economic problems, including a failing banking system and the bursting of related credit and property bubbles. Within the context of the ensuing Eurozone crisis, Ireland's standing as a peripheral economy returned as it came to be grouped together with other weaker Eurozone economies also in crisis. Ireland was the second country in the Eurozone to succumb to the direct financial assistance of the EU/IMF, whose intervention marks a new departure in the Irish policy-making landscape.

As a small, globalised economy, Ireland is highly vulnerable to outside events and influences. However, the tendency to characterise small states as states lacking in power and often viewing globalisation as a powerful homogenising force belies the diversity of impacts and interactions with local contexts that an event such as the financial crisis has had. In this regard, the impact of the crisis in Ireland requires an understanding of the policy trajectory preceding the crisis and subsequent policy responses as the product of the interplay of domestic and international influences and their changing dynamics with the various instabilities the crisis engendered. This interplay is examined over the course of three phases, from the late 1980s to the end of 2012. The starting point marks Ireland's emergence from an earlier economic crisis, a time when the international economic landscape and the design of the EU were also changing, both of which had significant implications. Our aim here is to highlight notable internal and external influences on Ireland's policy trajectory which set the context for subsequent changing dynamics as the crisis unfolded. We analyse policy making during the crisis period in terms of two phases distinguished by the point at which Ireland entered a programme of financial assistance with the EU/IMF in late 2010. While this event might signify loss of political and economic sovereignty, our focus centres on the evolving interplay of domestic and international influences on policy choices. This is especially important in small open state cases such as Ireland, where attention both before and after the crisis is often drawn to the dominance of external forces, thus overlooking the role that national factors and policy actors still play in policy making and policy priorities.

Pre-crisis policy making and the Irish growth model: between national and international influences

Ireland was beset by economic frailty, dependence and under-performance until its rapid transformation during the 1990s, while politics was historically shaped by post-independence party alignments to the detriment of attention to class or other social divisions. The result was a largely conservative party system dominated by middle-ground populist politics and powerful interests, with limited overt articulation of the ideological values that underpin economic and social policies. The foundations of Ireland's more open economy and its strategy of becoming a model site for inward foreign direct investment was strengthened during the 1960s, while the social infrastructure of the state was also being developed, albeit at a later point and in a more ad hoc way than many other European welfare states. Social investment has been in catch-up mode in the decades since, and the increased expenditure of the 1990s and early 2000s may be viewed as the coming of age of an expanded but dualist welfare state (Considine and Dukelow, 2009). This occurred in a period of unprecedented economic growth in which the shift to a more neoliberal approach to economic policy took root. This situation has been made sustainable, in part at least, by the maintenance of a culture of political avoidance of ideological debate around key concepts informing economic and social policy development. Mainstream political rhetoric tends to centre on nebulous ideas around the 'national interest', 'prosperity and fairness' and more recently 'restoring competitiveness' and 'protecting the most vulnerable'. Pragmatic expression of policy positions both obscured and limited the breadth of debate on the precise role of the state in economic and social relations, both national and global. In the view of Kitchin et al (2012, p 1306), this created a particular type of neoliberalism which 'was produced through a set of short-term (intermittently reformed) deals brokered by the state with various companies, individuals, and representative bodies, which cumulatively restructured Ireland in unsustainable and geographically "uneven" ways.'

At an institutional level, Ireland displays some commonality with small island states with public administrative bureaucracies characterised by informality, personalism, multifunctionality and a lack of capacity and resources (Connaughton, 2010). While the latter was a source of attention in the aftermath of the economic collapse (Report of the Independent Review Panel [Ireland], 2010) there were also many influential policy actors who did not acknowledge the risks Ireland's economic model exposed the state to. Moreover, political culture has been dominated by a form of clientelism that remains central to Irish electoral success. In the economic sphere, the vulnerability of smaller states to the risk of exposure to external shocks is evident in compounding the Irish crisis experience. However, as Moses (2012, p 2) finds, 'size, in itself, is not a significant explanatory factor for how states were affected by, or responded to, the economic crisis'; most crucial has been the growth strategies pursued in the pre-crisis phase. Key weaknesses in the Irish model include its over-reliance on US foreign direct investment, a poor link between economic growth and investment in social services, and the state's role in maximising competitiveness and profitability over developing social infrastructure and social rights (Kirby, 2010). And, as Kirby (2010, p 47) points out, 'these weaknesses are not accidental failures of the model that could be corrected, but are essential features of a growth model highly dependent on foreign investment and on a low-tax environment.' The highly centralised system of decision making has been a longstanding feature of Irish governance and the predominance of social partnership in economic and social policy making which developed in the late 1980s worked largely within the policy parameters of the emerging economic paradigm. In the move to '*shared* centralized government' (Adshead, 2005, p 175, original emphasis), the state remained central to its operation and continuity. The emphasis on a consensus-based approach, despite significant imbalances in the input of participants, ultimately implicated social partnership in the facilitation of an unstable growth model. McDonough and Dundon (2010, p 544) note that this 'quasi-corporatist regime obscured the extent of Ireland's integration with global neoliberal structures', the effect of which was a lack of sustained attention to the vulnerabilities facing the economy.

Internal features of the Irish political economy model need to be juxtaposed with the state's engagement with international economic developments and supranational political trends, particularly globalisation, financialisation and European integration. Although globalist literature emphasises the loss of control the globalisation of economic forces signifies for the state, as Yeates (2007, p 631) argues, 'a more nuanced view recognises that states have not been idle, passive, powerless actors in these processes. Indeed, different states have enthusiastically followed pro-globalization policies.' Ireland's pro-globalisation stance and the effectiveness of its policy steering to capture international investment rendered it the most foreign direct investment-intensive economy in the EU (Barry and Welsum, 2005). The largest source of inward investment to the EU is from the US, and over 2001-10 the share flowing to Ireland was 11.3 per cent (Quinlan, 2011). Historically, structurally adjusting the economy and embracing foreign economic participation has not been treated as a capitulation to outside forces. The state's opening up to financial globalisation in the late 1980s therefore marked a continuation with the previous pursuit of foreign direct investment by creating optimal taxation and operating conditions. Again, contrary to the globalist perspective, financial globalisation required active state engagement; as Lucarelli (2012, p 432) notes, it was specifically the policies of neoliberal states, including financial deregulation, that 'created the objective conditions by which the logic of financialization has gained the ascendancy'. Likewise, Thompson (2010, p 140) suggests that poor regulation was essentially a form of 'calculated weakness' for political and economic gain. In this context the centrepiece of the state's strategy during the late 1980s was the establishment of the International Financial Services Centre in Dublin, a state-led project designed to attract international financial service companies. It is estimated to comprise 5 per cent of all EU27 cross-border financial activity, ranking it seventh in this area in the EU27 (Accenture and Financial Services Ireland, 2010). Ireland's policy approach to financialisation demonstrated a particular openness, not only in its competitive tax terms but also in what a former governor of the Central Bank described as its 'supportive' regulatory environment (Neary, 2006, cited in *Irish Times*, 2010). The growing importance of financial services was met with a shift towards market-friendly forms of regulation and risk assessment, and a weakening of institutional oversight (Taylor, 2011). This played a significant part in the growing presence of an internationally attractive shadow banking system within Ireland which facilitated substantial financial flows outside the normal banking regulatory framework. In this regard, Stewart (2008, p 2) notes that 'it was not especially the low-tax regime that attracted funds to Dublin, but other features: Ireland ticks certain boxes for funds and the regulators in their home countries…. Perhaps most alluring of all, however, is its "light touch regulation"'.

Deeper economic integration and the liberalisation of European finance in the lead up to Economic and Monetary Union (EMU) meant that the European economy was adapting to and mirroring trends at a global level (Forster et al, 2011). The creation of a single currency enabled European banks to extend their lending activities in what became a more integrated banking and money market. However, economic balances across the Euro area masked imbalances within it, and economic surpluses in large economies such as Germany and France flowed from their banking systems to Ireland as well as to Greece, Spain and Italy (Forster et al, 2011). In Ireland mortgage lending to private customers grew by almost 400 per cent, but property-related business lending rose by near double that amount (O'Hearn, 2011). Credit tripled relative to gross national product (GNP), as bank lending grew from 60 per cent of GNP in 1997 to over 200 per cent by 2008, whereas normal levels of bank lending internationally stand at 80–100 per cent of GNP (Kelly, 2009). Consequently the Irish bank's net indebtedness to the rest of the world grew from 10 per cent of GDP in 2003 to over 60 per cent in 2008 (Honohan, 2009).

The Irish state's ability to manage the credit and property bubble was constrained by its inability to control interest rates, set centrally by the European Central Bank (ECB). Low interest rates over the 2000s suited the growth trends of the core European economies but were ill suited to the Irish boom. This in part attests to Ireland's position in the 'tacit hierarchy of states' in the EU (Anderson, 2007, cited in Coakley, 2012, p 203), but needs to be set against particular national characteristics that exacerbated the loss of monetary control the EMU introduced and the weak coordinating capacity embedded in its design. Member states retained primary responsibility for financial regulation and 'cyclically appropriate fiscal policy' (Lane, 2010, p 11). The constraints posed by centralised monetary policy must therefore be balanced by the policy choices made in the areas under domestic control. Through the light-touch regulatory system, governments paid insufficient attention to the risks incurred by the banks, while fiscal policy, which was pro-cyclical, reflected Ireland's low tax policy preference and was also used to further stimulate the housing market (Honohan, 2010). This latter policy choice reflected Ireland's long-term promotion of home ownership, and such factors warrant deeper consideration regarding the role national social policies played in credit market growth and its regulation over the course of the international property boom (Schelkle, 2012).

More broadly, the policy thrust of EMU, as Fitoussi and Saraceno (2012) observe, represented an internalisation of the principles of the Washington Consensus, creating a 'Berlin–Washington Consensus', emphasising macroeconomic stability via balanced budgets, price stability and competitiveness. These principles underpinned the deficit targets of the Stability and Growth Pact and the ECB's approach to interest rate setting. In this phase the only formal European censure of Irish fiscal policy occurred in 2000 when Ireland was found to be in breach of the terms of the Stability and Growth Pact (O'Leary, 2010). Besides this instance, the budgetary constraints of the Stability and Growth Pact were not of major policy concern during the boom; public debt levels were not an issue and remained low. Within Ireland, as O'Hearn (2011, p 4) points out, 'few commentators or economists considered that an unregulated private sector with excess wealth leveraging *private* debt could also cause severe crisis.' This was similarly overlooked by the ECB as Coakley (2012, p 174) observes, 'when it came to assessing what constituted inflation, the ECB did not include asset inflation in its calculations.' This absence of concern was more generally mirrored in other observations. The 2006 European Council Opinion on Ireland considered, for example, that, 'overall, the budgetary position is sound and the budgetary strategy provides a good example of fiscal policies in compliance with the Stability and Growth Pact' (Council of the European Union, 2006, p 21). Similarly the IMF (2006, p 5) concluded that 'the [Irish] financial system seems well placed to absorb the impact of a downturn in either house prices or growth more generally.' Against the backdrop of such benign external assessments, Coakley (2012, pp 174-5) notes how domestic regulatory authorities 'could use the imperator of the ECB and the IMF to justify their inaction in the face of the starkly evident credit and property bubbles.' In short, external fiscal surveillance mechanisms were also insufficiently robust to capture the severe risks emanating from the banking sector or the extent of the instability of the revenue base which underpinned the seemingly manageable imbalances and levels of indebtedness building in the Irish economy.

State-led policy responses to the economic collapse: from the bank guarantee to the sovereign debt crisis

By autumn 2008 the risks of Ireland's growth model materialised when it was the first country in the Eurozone to enter recession, and the economy contracted with a peak-to-trough decline of 12.4 per cent of GDP between 2007 and 2010. A key turning point early in the crisis was the state's decision to guarantee almost all liabilities in Ireland's domestic banks, in response to what was apparently interpreted as liquidity problems arising from the global credit crunch. From this point, until the state entered the Programme of Financial Support (EU and IMF, 2010), significant shifts in power relations took place in the Irish policy-making environment. Perhaps most significant about this period is the degree to which the state wielded power and attempted to take control of the crisis, and the manner in which it did this on a national basis, independent of other EU member states, exemplified by the bank rescue efforts and the early adoption of austerity policies.

The bank guarantee, announced on 30 September 2008 following an overnight crisis meeting between core members of government and the heads of the two main domestic banks, was a unilateral emergency decision by the Irish government taken initially without significant advice from, or recourse to, the EU and ECB. This early phase of the crisis was thus marked by decisive national policy action to avoid the possible collapse of the Irish banking system. However, the guarantee ultimately exposed the state to banking liabilities worth approximately 275 per cent of Ireland's GDP, and the initial government response unravelled during this critical phase as the scale of the banking debts were brought to bear on the Irish Exchequer. Other EU member states subsequently took action to safeguard their banking systems, although guarantees in these cases were more limited (Honohan, 2009). Such responses demonstrated the degree to which states were not rendered powerless by the global financial crisis exercising considerable power in their choices of market intervention, which, as Thompson (2010, p 130) argues, 'have pushed the state firmly back into the allocation of resources.' In addition to the guarantee, other bank rescue measures included bank recapitalisation, nationalisation, the asset purchase of non-performing loans via the establishment of a National Assets Management Agency and the provision of liquidity support. In a comparative study of banking crises assessing such policy responses in terms of fiscal costs, impact on public debt and the impact on GDP or output loss, Laeven and Valencia (2012, p 20) found the Irish instance to be 'the costliest banking crisis in advanced economies since at least the Great Depression.' Noting that fiscal costs in particular are driven by how large banking sectors become relative to the size of a country's economy (Laeven and Valencia, 2012), in the Irish case this was driven by the confluence of its weak regulatory regime and the unprecedented inward credit flow. The bank guarantee also raised questions concerning the transparency of how the decision was made, who was involved in making it and what advice was considered. A preliminary report by a government committee outlined several such unanswered questions, and noted that 'a major knowledge gap remains in relation to the events leading to the bank guarantee' (Houses of the Oireachtas Committee of Public Accounts, 2012, p 17). Subsequent policy measures adopted to respond to the banking crisis also warrant further examination; the guarantee's blanket scope, how what appeared to be a liquidity problem quickly became exposed as a serious solvency problem and the degree of corporate influence on political decision making, remain obscure. The guarantee quickly became a contentious issue across the political spectrum and in wider public debate; its scope in particular was and continues to be widely regarded as a major policy mistake.

What was less obscure was the breakdown of the social partnership in the crisis. Efforts at negotiating a new social partnership agreement in early 2009 broke down as the model fell out of favour with government and the public (Roche, 2011). The government subsequently acted independently by imposing expenditure cuts in the public sector for which it encountered relatively weak resistance. Subsequently, however, an agreement, known as the Croke Park agreement, was reached in mid-2010 with public sector unions to halt further pay cuts in return for alternative forms of cost–cutting until 2014. This occurred in the wider context of shifting debate that had moved from issues of financial contagion to focus on the role of domestic actors in the banking and economic crises. What was emerging more generally as a severe fiscal crisis was attributed to a public spending bubble on the part of successive governments and the budgetary preferences of the social partners. Trade union efforts at contesting Ireland's policy response, highlighting injustices of the allocation decisions of the state, and the contradictions of the fact that the '"state" so reviled by the neoliberals … [had] come to their rescue' (ICTU, 2009), found little broader resonance in debate. Similarly, the legacy of community and voluntary sector involvement in social partnership left such groups, Cox (2012, p 3) argues, with 'no concept of what to do when the state turned against them.' Their capacity to contest austerity was weakened by the fact that many were diminished by funding cuts and some found themselves having to deliver government austerity policies in Ireland's mixed economy of welfare (Crowley, 2013).

Ireland's early adoption of austerity policy in Europe contrasted with the 'emergency reconversion' (Hemerijck, 2012a, p 55) to Keynesianism evident in policy responses of many other states. While the economic pressure Ireland was under might have made such a response comparably more difficult, its rapid turn to self-imposed austerity marked it apart from other peripheral EU economies in trouble. Domestic political debate centred on the idea of no alternative to austerity and, in making the case, the notion of external pressures and constraints was frequently summoned by state actors. In this narrative both the response to the banking crisis and the turn to austerity were framed as part of the state's action to preserve its reputation for 'fiscal responsibility' from the perspective of globalised capital, in the form of market investors in sovereign debt, credit rating agencies and foreign direct investors. This further translated into policy decisions that aimed to minimise tax increases and to emphasise expenditure cuts, a policy mix justified with reference to best international evidence and advice, emanating from transnational policy actors such as the OECD and the IMF. Successive budgets have therefore been constructed around a norm of approximately one-third tax increases and two-thirds expenditure cuts.

Arguments relating to expenditure cuts also rested on the idea that expenditure was ramped up during the boom period. Two key components of the fiscal crisis, namely, the costs of the banking rescue and the dramatic decline in tax revenue that fell by 30 per cent between 2007 and 2010, were under-scrutinised in this narrative. In making the case for austerity, key actors were bolstered not only by the lack of influence of the political left but also by the manner in which public debate became dominated by a narrow range of economic perspectives which strongly advocated an austerity response. Faith in Ireland's underlying growth model remained largely unquestioned and framed as a matter of technical economic competence requiring a period of austerity and 'reining in' government expenditure to restore both state and economy to proper functioning. In this context, employer groups who advocated welfare retrenchment and measures to improve labour market competitiveness suffered few negative repercussions in the aftermath of social partnership in contrast to trade union actors. In part, therefore, the context in which austerity and the idea of 'no alternative' quickly took hold reflected the non-ideological expression of neoliberal politics in the Irish context. As such the promotion of neoliberal ideas as pragmatic, common sense and in the interests of all obscured the distributional consequences of the choices the state made and the interests served in the process. Such policy preferences and shifting power relations at national level were also underpinned by the wider institutional framework of the EMU that served to constrain policy options. Regan (2012) suggests that austerity is implicitly embedded in the design of EMU, meaning that retrenchment or internal devaluation is one of the few policy options available in the event of a fiscal crisis. In contrast with previous crises, and with Iceland in the present one, Ireland could not devalue its currency or impose temporary capital controls.

The state in crisis: the shift to external intervention and new policy-making contingencies

Outside of the costs of the bank rescue attempts, the fiscal crisis was extremely severe, but arguably manageable on its own. When compounded by escalating bank losses, the pressure began to overwhelm the state, as the banking crisis costs accounted for half the increase in government net debt, which rose from 11 per cent of GDP in 2007 to 95 per cent of GDP in 2011 (IMF, 2012a, 2012b). The precarious position of the Irish banks was reflected in their borrowing heavily from the ECB, unable to secure market funding. The scale of this ECB borrowing rose rapidly, from €36 billion in April 2010 to €74 billion in September of the same year (Whelan, 2011). The view of the money markets, whose power had grown with the increased mobility of private capital via economic globalisation

(Ravenhill, 2010), was increasingly negative; bond yields on Irish government debt rose sharply in autumn 2010. What characterises this phase of the crisis is the rapid diminution of the capacity of the state to act independently as it had previously done. Concern grew about the solvency of the state and with limited policy options at its disposal, the balance of power shifted to international actors and especially to the EU and ECB, given Ireland's seismic breach of the Stability and Growth Pact in the aftermath of its handling of the banking crisis. Membership of the Eurozone and the policy responsibilities therein meant that unprecedented decisions needed to be taken, but tensions between European and national economic interests were evident, and the response of the EU and ECB was in a sense to 'force' a solution in terms of financial assistance (Kirby and Thorhallsson, 2011).

The lead up to the announcement that Ireland was to enter its Programme of Financial Support (hereafter referred to as the Programme) was poorly handled domestically. There was widespread media speculation that talks with the EU/IMF were underway in November 2010, but this was denied. In the event it was the governor of the Irish Central Bank who confirmed to the public that such a programme was being negotiated. It had the appearance of a government in crisis, but it is likely that it was also a reflection of the accession to external pressures in which the state was no longer in a position to define the nature of the problem and generate its own policy responses. However, this is not to suggest that the conditions attached to the Programme were not shaped by existing national policy priorities. As talks with the EU/IMF/ECB were underway, the government launched its own strategy, *The national recovery plan 2011–2014* (Government of Ireland, 2010). It re-affirmed the necessity of continued fiscal consolidation, confirming a policy preference for spending cuts over revenue-raising measures and maintenance of the existing corporation tax rate as 'a cornerstone of our pro-enterprise, outward-looking industrial policy' (Government of Ireland, 2010, p 8). The re-assertion of policies consistent with the existing economic policy paradigm was to the fore as the Plan also sought to 'dispel uncertainty and reinforce the confidence of consumers, businesses and of the international community' (Government of Ireland, 2010, p 5). In fact, much political energy has been divested in restoring Ireland's reputation and negative international commentary remains a particular cause of concern. Pointing primarily to the positive endorsements of Ireland's response to the crisis (and its adherence to the terms of the Programme), by other heads of state, relevant international agencies and European monitoring bodies, the idea of Ireland as 'the role model' for other countries facing similar difficulties became increasingly prominent.

The general election held in February 2011 resulted in unprecedented defeat for the governing parties, and, on the face of it, significant change seemed afoot. A number of left-leaning candidates were elected, and the Labour Party had its best ever results, but the real winner of this election was the conservative centre-right party, Fine Gael. They entered coalition with Labour, together holding a comfortable government majority. Pre-election rhetoric, while mostly careful not to promise any decisive break from austerity policies, pledged renewed vigour in addressing Ireland's crisis and re-negotiating with the EU/IMF in this regard. Aspects of the Programme were revisited (such as the reversal of the minimum wage cut) although ultimately, the objectives surrounding the broad policy of fiscal consolidation remain. The current government strategy adheres to the repayment of the debt associated with the bank bailout, but on eased terms, with pursuit of this through diplomatic efforts and European political and official negotiation. This would seem from the outside to be a painfully slow process, the results of which remain to be seen. In the meantime, adherence to the broader policy trajectory of austerity has been unwavering, with the dominant political narrative centring on the need for conformity with the Programme as a pre-condition of economic recovery.

The Programme sets out the conditions attaching to Ireland's €85 billion loan agreement with the EU/IMF. Quarterly targets are set in areas of fiscal consolidation, financial sector reforms and structural reforms, oversight of which takes place on a quarterly basis with separate monitoring reports issued by the EU and IMF. Revised Programme updates have not altered the parameters of the agreement, apart from the extension from 2014 to 2015 to reach the 3 per cent of GDP deficit target. Working towards this target involved an adjustment of almost €29 billion (17 per cent of 2013 GDP) by 2013. The question is whether the scale of the austerity endured will ultimately deliver as concern remains about the massive overhang of banking turned sovereign debt, with the general government debt to GDP ratio expected to peak at 121 per cent in 2013. Against this economic backdrop and with social partnership now in abeyance, many lobby groups and civil society actors seek meetings with the representatives from the EU/IMF to advance their policy cases, providing further insight into the level of influence widely perceived to be held by the funders of Ireland's Programme. However the president of the Services Industrial Professional and Technical Union (SIPTU), Ireland's largest trade union, recently called for an end to these meetings stating that they 'serve no useful purpose whatsoever. Indeed, their only motivation is quite clearly to provide some veneer of consultation' (SIPTU, 2012). Separately, however, a European Community representative has pointed out that 'conditionality is negotiated with the government' and that 'there is no democratic deficit here' (Szekely, quoted in Slattery, 2012). These tensions have broader resonance in terms of capturing the changed dynamics of Irish policy making for both the social partners and the new negotiating role of government with the Programme funders. Pointing to particular circumstances that may exist in crisis situations, Bonoli (2012) notes how simultaneous political engagement with blame sharing and credit claiming may occur. In the current Irish case, conditionality underpinning the Programme restricts the choices of government while also facilitating blame sharing. At the same time, the scale of the crisis facilitates credit claiming around significant reforms, where doing nothing 'may become more unpopular, or politically dangerous, than retrenchment' (Bonoli, 2012, p 106). The balancing of retrenchment and reform agendas and the manner of their implementation has not, to date, generated the extent of public resistance that might have been anticipated. Substantial long-term reform in areas such as the raising of the state pension age were introduced with relative political ease, while the most effective resistance to welfare cuts has been demonstrated by the mobilisation of particular social groups rather than by mass opposition to austerity or any broader defence of the welfare state.

Implementation of the fiscal and structural reform elements of the Programme has significant implications for the Irish welfare state. While substantial retrenchment is being undertaken (Considine and Dukelow, 2012), in some respects social protection and activation reform also represent a 'catch-up' with more extensive reforms implemented in other European welfare states since the 1990s, albeit in very different policy-making circumstances (Hemerijck, 2012b). Unemployment, for example, has risen sharply; the rate trebled from 4.7 per cent in 2007 to 13.8 per cent by 2010, and is one of the most serious issues emanating from the crisis. Unemployment has remained at over 14 per cent since 2011 (CSO, 2013) and as yet, shows little sign of improvement. New activation measures have been introduced but are unlikely to be sufficiently widespread to tackle the scale of the problem, which is particularly acute for young people, 34.5 per cent of whom were without work in 2012 (OECD, 2012b). As for Ireland's policy trajectory and its relation to wider European debate about whether social policy reforms signify a shift to a social investment state (Morel et al, 2012), it would appear that the longer-term prospects of developing this model are restricted, not least by Ireland's overall recovery strategy. A key element of this is the aforementioned balance between expenditure cuts and revenue-raising measures, and specifically the fact that tax reform aims to broaden the tax base but ultimately maintain a comparatively low tax regime with a view to restoring Ireland's competitive positioning as a fiscally attractive, open and globalised economy in which to invest.

Conclusions

Our main aim has been to understand the dynamics between national policy-making conditions and international economic and political influences in the case of Ireland's economic crisis. We have shown that the overall strategic response to the Irish crisis has been marked by a very strong national effort, defined from the outset by an attempt to safeguard the banking system and a policy commitment to self-imposed austerity, notwithstanding wider policy constraints posed by financial globalisation and European integration. Moreover, Ireland's nationally driven policy preferences deviated little from the conditions imposed by external funders and the related transnational policy paradigm. Long-term recovery of the Irish economy appears largely contingent on outside forces, because of Ireland's small state status and the prevailing national economic paradigm that remains dependent on foreign direct investment. The return of global economic growth, or at least growth in Ireland's main exporting destinations, and the precise nature of the resolution of the wider European debt crisis, will be critical. The prospects for the Irish welfare state equally hinge on the nature of the economic recovery and the post-crisis policy-making landscape. While existing welfare state policy preferences remain largely intact, current retrenchment and reform policies represent an unfinished project. Elements of reform may indicate a catching up with aspects of the social investment policy paradigm (for example, activation), yet existing liberal welfare regime preferences continue to bear considerable influence in its national adaptation. When these considerations are situated in the wider EU context of the Fiscal Stability Treaty, which imply less room for national fiscal policy manoeuvre, the likelihood is that Irish welfare policy may become increasingly 'fiscalised'. Conditions emerging from such recent European policy developments would therefore appear to pose an augmented set of policy constraints in the national context in the phase that will emerge once Ireland has regained greater control of its policy-making choices post-EU/IMF intervention.

6.4

This next contribution examines the response of one nation to what is perhaps the quintessential global issue. The development and implementation of policy in response to climate change presents challenges for all levels of government, from the global to the local. It requires thoughtful engagement with a burgeoning and complex body of scientific evidence; it provokes intense debate about competing policy priorities, especially the pursuit of growth in all its forms; and it crystallises current disagreements about principles of intergenerational equity.

All these problems are present in Australian policy debate, examined here by Paul Burton, where a leader of the Federal Opposition (now Prime Minister) described the science of climate change as 'crap', mining-led growth remains a commitment of both major political parties and relatively certain needs of present generations dominate the relatively uncertain needs of future generations. But they are compounded further by disagreements about contributions and obligations, for while Australia's total contribution to global emissions of greenhouse gases is relatively small, its per capita emissions are comparatively high. Moreover, to the extent that Australia has avoided many of the impacts of the current global economic crisis, it has a buoyant resources sector which has been successfully exporting coal and hence emissions to the rapidly growing economies of India and China.

All of these factors and more help frame contemporary political debate about climate change policy in Australia, and in particular about the appropriate balance between local costs and global impacts. The development of climate change policy over the last decade offers, therefore, a rich case study of many aspects of policy making, from framing and issue definition, through the application of contested scientific evidence to the construction of complex multiscalar implementation networks.

Here these debates and challenges are explored through three separate but related themes: contestation, complexity and uncertainty. Each is used to illustrate a particular aspect of the development and implementation of climate change policy in Australia over the last two decades. Contestation is applied to the problem of reconciling global and local perspectives and to the arguments about obligation and contribution mentioned above. Complexity is applied to the challenge of incorporating complex science into more participatory approaches to policy development. Uncertainty applies to the continued framing of climate policy in Australia within a rationalist paradigm that struggles to deal with scientific reliability and uncertainty.

Policy responses to climate change in Australia: contestation, complexity and uncertainty

Paul Burton

The impact of climate change in Australia

What are the impacts of climate change in Australia? Australia is recognised by the Intergovernmental Panel on Climate Change (IPCC) as a country especially vulnerable to the anticipated impacts of climate change, being the driest inhabited continent as well as one of the most urbanised. Around 80 per cent of the population live in cities, mostly located along the eastern seaboard which is vulnerable to the effects of sea level rise; indeed, the federal Department of Climate Change (2009) estimates that it would cost approximately AUD$63 billion to replace existing residential buildings at risk from inundation due to a 1.1 metre rise in sea level. In a country used to long periods of drought punctuated by periods of heavy rain, these extremes are likely to increase in frequency and severity, leaving most regions exposed to greater risks of bushfires during hot and dry periods and to overland floods at other times. Furthermore, more prolonged periods of very hot days and nights (over 35 degrees Celsius) will have significant effects on public health, including a greater number of heat-related deaths, to the extent that the Australian Climate Commission claims, '... heat is the silent killer and is the leading cause of weather-related deaths in Australia' (Steffen, 2013). This combination of increasingly severe drought and flood is also having profound effects on Australia's ecosystems, threatening both individual species and larger systems such as the Great Barrier Reef, and on the viability of farming and food production in many parts of the country.

Climate change policy in Australia

The development of climate change policy in Australia has unfolded over a series of distinctive periods, commencing with a decade of 'naive altruism' from the mid-1980s (Christoff, 2005). This saw the emergence of 'global warming' as a policy challenge and the Hawke Labour government proposing a set of ambitious emission reduction targets which were manifestly not achieved by the time the first conservative government of Prime Minister Howard was formed in 1996. A period of 'fossil fuel pragmatism' followed in which a more sceptical position emerged within a government that set great store by 'no regrets policies' which imposed minimal costs on business and through voluntary emission reduction schemes for industry. The early years of the new millennium saw a short period of policy equivocation in which Australia joined the USA in refusing to sign the Kyoto Protocol, but some business organisations began to call for a more positive and certain stance on climate change. For the rest of the third and fourth terms of the Howard government scepticism remained entrenched, although in its last year the new Minister for the Environment, Malcolm Turnbull, helped introduce proposals for a Carbon Trading Scheme as well as a series of adaptation initiatives, including the establishment of a National Climate Change Adaptation Research Facility (NCCARF) to support practical research into adaptation measures.

The federal election of November 2007 saw both major parties promise carbon trading schemes, and when the Rudd Labour government was formed in December, a carbon pollution reduction scheme (CPRS) was developed as part of a review led by the economist Professor Ross Garnaut. A White Paper detailing the CPRS was published in December 2008 and attracted criticism from a variety of perspectives, ranging from those who saw its targets as far too low to achieve the necessary reduction in emissions to industry representatives who complained of its unfair burdens on business. While negotiations between Prime Minister Rudd and then Leader of the Opposition Malcolm Turnbull appeared at one stage to have paved the way for the successful passage of the bill that introduced the CPRS, it failed to obtain the support of the Senate, and in April 2010 the Prime Minister announced that the introduction of the scheme would be delayed. In June 2010 Rudd was replaced as leader of the Australian Labour Party and as Prime Minister by Julia Gillard, in part because of this policy delay, and in August the second Gillard Labour government was formed following an election campaign in which the Prime Minister promised not to introduce a carbon tax. In November 2011 the government succeeded in introducing its Clean Energy Legislative Package that enabled the introduction in July 2012 of a carbon price as the mainstay of a series of climate change measures. The question of whether the introduction of this set of measures constitutes a significant broken promise has remained at the heart of much political debate about climate change policy ever since. The coalition opposition stated that it would immediately repeal the carbon price legislation if it won power and introduce its own Direct Action Plan which comprises a package of fiscal incentives to businesses, a soil carbon sequestration scheme and reformed system of subsidies for domestic solar power generation (see the tailpiece to this chapter).

Mitigation and adaptation

While most political debate about climate change policy in Australia has been concerned with national measures to reduce emissions through carbon taxes and carbon cap and trade schemes and through other general programmes to reduce emissions by individuals, households, institutions and companies, a series of other adaptation measures has also been proposed. To some extent the distinction between mitigation policies which aim to reduce emissions and hence the causes of anthropogenic global warming and adaptation measures which accept the inevitability of some degree of climate change is unhelpful and unproductive. In the early years of climate policy development in Australia (as elsewhere) there was sometimes a tendency to see adaptation policy as an admission of the failure or futility of mitigation measures, and hence to avoid giving it serious attention. As the periodisation described above also suggests, the early years of policy development were characterised by a degree of naivety, certainly about the possibility of achieving a global political consensus around emission reduction targets. Moreover, from a more conceptual perspective, it can be difficult to distinguish and categorise particular practices as either mitigation or adaptation actions. For example, insulating homes so that they are better able to deal with hot or cold days is an adaptation to likely increases in temperature variability, but will at the same time help reduce heating and cooling requirements, and hence the demand for energy, the production of which is by far the largest source of emissions in Australia.

In recent years the case for adaptation has become more widely accepted, in part because of the success of so-called 'no regrets' arguments. Although these can take different forms, they typically claim that an action or policy can be justified on the basis of one set of cost-benefit calculations while generating an additional set of benefits that come, as it were, for free or with no regrets. For example, if houses were designed and oriented to reduce their energy requirements and new residential neighbourhoods laid out to reduce the need for car travel, then not only would aggregate energy demand and production requirements be reduced, but households would benefit from a cheaper means of achieving thermal comfort in their home and from a better quality of life in a less car-dependent neighbourhood.

Of course not all local adaptation measures take the form of no regrets actions or have minimal cost consequences. Indeed, some that take the form of restrictions on development rights in areas at risk of flooding, for example, impose clear short-term costs on individuals even though the long-term social costs may be reduced. Adaptation policy in Australia exists at all three levels of government – commonwealth, state and local – and within this federal system there is inevitably a degree of interdependency. As they are constitutionally the creation of state governments, local governments are subject to state requirements to prepare climate change adaptation plans, whereas the Commonwealth government is less able to impose its will on state and territory governments but relies instead on cooperative mechanisms developed through institutions such as the Council of Australian Governments (COAG), the peak intergovernmental forum.

COAG established a Select Council on Climate Change in February 2011 to oversee the development of a national response to climate change and to help coordinate the efforts of other tiers of government. The Select Council has specific responsibility for a number of initiatives, including overseeing the National Partnership Agreement on Energy Efficiency (which includes the National Strategy on Energy Efficiency and the National Framework on Energy Efficiency), providing a forum for the Australian government to engage state, territory and Australian Local Government Association COAG members on the implementation of the Clean Energy Future Plan.

Most states and territories have some form of climate change strategy, although recent changes of government in most states and territories have seen significant changes in their approach to planning for the effects of climate change. In Queensland, for example, the new conservative government, under the premiership of Campbell Newman, came to office in March 2012 with a clear commitment to promote economic growth, not least by reducing what it saw as unnecessary burdens on business including regulations developed as part of the previous Labour government's climate change strategy. Indeed, the Queensland Office of Climate Change was quickly abolished on the grounds that the Commonwealth's climate change measures, and in particular, the carbon pricing mechanism described above, rendered state measures redundant. The election in 2012 of a new set of conservative local governments throughout Queensland means there is now a high degree of political alignment between local and state governments, and a new period in which one of the primary concerns in developing climate adaptation policy is to minimise the burdens on business and to rely more on incentives for what might be termed 'good adaptation behaviour' within a market-based framework for action. While this particular pattern of political alignment is not apparent in all state and territories, there has been a pronounced shift in favour of conservatism at all three levels of government throughout Australia, and this is likely to continue in the near future.

Key themes in policy development and implementation

We now need to consider these processes of policy development, and to a lesser extent, of implementation, in the light of the three themes of contestation, complexity and uncertainty described in the Introduction to this chapter.

Contestation in reconciling global and local perspectives

Most of those concerned with climate tend to agree that dynamic processes of change occur at the global and atmospheric level, even if their causes and impacts are closer to the ground. They do not, of course, all agree about the extent or magnitude of these processes. It is this dual aspect of global and local significance that presents a particular problem for climate change policy. This lies in the fact that some elements of climate change policy require global action, while others require a much more focused set of local activities (Wilson, 2006).

For example, debate over the most appropriate target for stabilising greenhouse gas *concentrations* (not emissions) relates to a global figure: Stern (2007) in the UK proposed 550 parts per million, the EU has proposed 450 parts per million while Australian bodies such as the Australian Conservation Foundation and the Climate Institute call for 400 parts per million. These different proposals for a global target are often bolstered by presenting the local consequences of each. In Australia there is a tendency to illustrate the impact of different CO_2 concentrations and attendant mean temperature profiles on the sanctity of iconic landscapes and marine features such as Kakadu National Park and the Great Barrier Reef. The point is that it makes no sense for greenhouse gas concentration targets to be anything but global – a target for Australia that differed from a target for China would make no sense. This is not to say that Australia and China will readily agree on that common target, simply that they (and others) are struggling to adopt a target that must apply to them both.

However, the causes and drivers of climate change occur at a local scale, although again they contribute to global processes. In short, it is the sum total of individual behaviour that is causing the current acceleration of climate change at a global scale, which then comes back down to earth, as it were, to affect us in different ways depending on where we live. We contribute individually to a collective or global phenomenon that affects us differently as global phenomena interact with local circumstances to produce more localised effects. Policies to reduce the causes of climate change in line with these global targets as well as policies for adaptation to already occurring changes must relate to local circumstances and be the product of local processes. This is not to say that experience cannot be shared with other localities; simply that the specific causes of excessive emissions will vary from place to place and will require local solutions. In Cairo it may require the replacement of wood-burning ovens, in Mumbai the use of less polluting public transport vehicles, while in the Hunter Valley of New South Wales local responses may see less electricity generated from high-emitting coal-fired power stations.

Not only are the impacts of these global processes different in different places, the apparent capacity and the inclination of individuals and societies to respond also varies from place to place. Broadly speaking, wealthier people and places have more options to choose among when it comes to adaptation measures, although they might also have the most to give up when it comes to patterns of consumption and lifestyle. The commitment to act also varies, partly because of differences in wealth, but also because of local variations in more deep-rooted cultures and traditions of economic development, of conservation and exploitation of natural resources and belief in science.

The capacity and inclination to act also depends on the extent to which policy-making institutions see themselves as part of a global community and on the way in which global and local factors are to be reconciled. For many years the slogan 'Think global, act local' has served as a useful expression of the concept that what we do as individuals in particular localities is connected, both negatively and positively, with global phenomena. It has served to convince many people that their local actions can have detrimental as well as beneficial or remedial impacts at the global scale, and that everyone has a stake in the atmospheric health of the world as a whole (as well as its economic health, social security and political stability).

Targets relating to atmospheric CO_2 concentrations and to greenhouse gas emissions are the product of international processes of debate and policy development, and while we might not yet be able to speak of a truly global policy, there is movement in this direction. But as we know, meaningful policies require some capacity to act in pursuit of implementation (Sabatier and Mazmanian, 1980; Hill and Hupe, 2009). The more the capacity to act lies beyond the policy-making body, the harder it is to secure implementation and the more vulnerable the policy becomes to charges of symbolism. The principle of 'Think global, act local' is now being stretched to its limits by the global geopolitical dimensions of accelerating climate change. The historic contribution of different regions to this problem and the projected contribution of different regions to the solution or to the exacerbation of the problem are creating major political tensions in international processes of policy development. Of course these tensions do not go unnoticed at the local level and add to the difficulty of persuading local communities to accept dramatic changes to their lifestyles as part of an equitable global response.

In Australia there has been considerable debate about the relationship between the global and the local in terms of contributions and obligations. In short, while Australia was ranked only 15th among the top 20 CO_2 emitters globally, with a total 437 million metric tons emitted in 2008, it had the highest per capita rate of emissions at 20.8 metric tons. However, Australia's contribution to total global emissions was only 1.34 per cent. This illustrates the mix of empirical, moral and symbolic arguments deployed: being in the same frame as the leading global emitters places an obligation on Australia to contribute to emission reduction programmes, but the global impact of these is likely to be small; as a country likely to be significantly affected by climate change Australia should not only take steps to reduce the global drivers of change but demonstrate what can be achieved through adaptation measures; with one of the highest per capita emission profiles Australia should take steps to change this profile and can demonstrate how this can be carried out effectively. The counter-arguments point to the minimal global impact of changes in consumption patterns that would have enormous local impacts, although there is also intense debate over the positive and negative aspects of these changes.

In summary, while political debate about particular adaptation policy measures is intense in Australia, this debate takes place within a broader context which is best described as 'business as usual'. Neither of the major political parties is proposing a radical transformation of the national economy or to patterns and processes of consumption. From both political parties there is a belief in the power of technological developments to reduce emissions, for example, through 'clean coal' and carbon-farming initiatives while at the same time, and perhaps more significantly, both show a continued commitment to economic growth through support for mining and the export of resources such as coal, iron ore and other minerals. Apart from some worthy but relatively minor measures to promote domestic energy efficiency, such as home insulation schemes, solar power rebates and water-saving measures, there are no proposals to reduce domestic consumption as a means of reducing significantly Australia's national energy requirement, and hence emissions. Indeed, a major plank of macroeconomic policy during the global financial crisis was the stimulation of domestic consumption through one-off cash payments to the majority of Australian households. Such compensatory payments continue to be an important element of the introduction of carbon pricing and the transition to an Australian Emissions Trading Scheme in 2015, and are designed to cushion low and middle-income households from anticipated short-term increases in power and fuel prices.

Overall, the Australian government continues to struggle in reconciling local and global concerns and obligations, and its policy position could at best be described as one of 'naive optimism' in which ambitious targets are set while the means to achieve them are manifestly inadequate, or as the epitome of symbolic policy.

Complexity in participatory policy making

In many policy fields there has, for some time, been a powerful assumption that policy making should be more rather than less participatory. In democracies one of the most important opportunities to participate comes with the periodic opportunity to vote in elections that contribute to the formation of governments at all levels. While these participatory moments can help set the style and direction of government and establish a set of broad programmatic commitments, they do not allow for participation in more focused and detailed policy debates. These forms of participation, including citizen juries and focused public debate, have their historical roots in the direct democracy practised in ancient Athens and as representative forms of democracy have since come to dominate, so calls for greater participation in policy making between elections has grown. Greater participation in public policy making is believed to offer a number of benefits, from the increases in civic pride and self-esteem associated with participation to the checks and balances and diverse perspectives that come with more inclusive approaches to policy debate. While the rigorous testing of these beliefs remains undeveloped, they continue to underpin much policy rhetoric in Australia and elsewhere.

Adaptation policies developed by all levels of Australian government claim that participatory approaches are an important element in their formation and implementation, even if they do not explicitly claim all of the putative benefits described above. As in many countries, it is widely held that the local level is especially significant in developing adaptive responses, as it is here that most people experience directly climate change in the form of floods, bushfires, sea level rise, storms and hotter days. Local governments have an important role to play therefore, because of their closer connection to the everyday lives of most Australians and, in theory at least, their greater sensitivity to local concerns.

Local government in Australia is regulated primarily by state and territory governments, which determine the powers and responsibilities of local councils, their constitutions and forms of election and also how they go about their business. Local governments are elected every four years and vary considerably in the size of their electorate and of the land under their jurisdiction. Many are organised into electoral divisions and use a form of preferential voting for their divisional representatives and for the mayor who is usually elected at large.

In most of the capital cities, the metropolitan area is served by a number of local councils without any statutory overarching body. In Queensland the situation is somewhat different as the state capital of Brisbane has been governed by a single council since 1926 and is the largest local authority in the country, while the nearby city of the Gold Coast, which only came into existence in 1959, is now the second largest authority, serving a population of approximately half a million. At the other end of the spectrum, the Shire Councils of Burke and Croydon in the far north west of the state serve populations of 480 and 320 respectively, and cover a combined land area roughly equal to the state of Tasmania. This illustrates vividly the significantly different scale of local governments in Australia and hence their capacity to develop comprehensive climate adaptation policies.

In this context of variable scale and capacity at the local level, the policy guidance offered by state and territory governments and by the Commonwealth government is important, and all declare clearly the importance of public participation and community engagement in their climate strategies. In a recent review of climate adaptation policies at all levels of government we found a strong rhetorical commitment to public participation in the development of policy but much less detail on what this might mean in practice, and even less detail on how the public (in its many forms) might participate in implementation (Burton and Mustelin, 2013). We believe this demonstrates a relatively common lack of confidence among policy makers in the capacity of the public at large to participate effectively in complex policy debates and to deal with the volume, sophistication and uncertainty associated with much of the science of climate change and its impacts. Research on the effectiveness of more intensive and deliberative participatory techniques, such as citizens' juries, shows that, if properly supported and resourced, randomly selected members of the public can make valuable contributions to complex policy debates (Mooney and Blackwell, 2004). The need for sensitive management of participatory processes in the field of climate change is perhaps greater than in many others, but the evidence from our review suggests that many of the approaches used are relatively superficial and tend to occupy the bottom rungs of Arnstein's (1969) ladder of participation. While this is also the case in many other policy fields, in relation to climate policy the changes anticipated and proposed by many are of such importance and significance that the effective engagement of the public as a whole would seem to be paramount. The evidence from Australia suggests that participation in climate policy making is not yet being approached in such a way that its potential benefits are capable of being realised.

Uncertainty in the relationship between science and policy

The relationship between science and policy making has never been straightforward, and almost 40 years ago Martin Rein noted that the relationship between social science and policy was 'neither consensual, graceful, nor self-evident' (1976, p 12). The emergence in the middle of the 20th century of the nascent field of 'policy science' created a rationalist frame for understanding policy making that continues to this day to dominate the practice of policy making, despite continued and persistent criticism of the frame from many academic quarters. Within this rationalist frame the project of modernisation, embraced with some enthusiasm in many countries including the UK and Australia, has seen a preoccupation with the evidential base of policy and a belief that by strengthening this base, the policies built on it will be better. While there is some virtue in this conception of the policy-making process, it has created serious problems for policy makers in some fields where there has developed a preoccupation with evidence at the expense of other aspects of the process, including the resolution of political conflicts over policy goals. Climate change policy is one such area where widespread but often poorly-informed debate about the reliability of scientific models of climate systems and the robustness of models of climate change has had the effect of putting a brake on policy development and implementation. While conservatism may be welcome in some fields and at some times, it is particularly significant in the field of climate change where the need to act quickly to avoid rapidly increasing costs of action in the future is also a prominent feature of the wider policy debate.

A number of commentators (see, for example, Habermas, 1970; Rein, 1976; Sarewitz, 1996) have described the 'scientisation of policy' whereby perfectly respectable political disagreements over the ends and means of policy are superseded by ostensibly scientific debates about facts and evidence that are assumed to 'suggest' particular policy positions. At the same time there are related processes leading to the 'politicisation of science' in which the political motives of scientists are called into question, research agendas are driven primarily by political concerns and 'unhelpful' research findings systematically excluded from the public arena. While these have long been challenges faced, with carrying degrees of success, by researchers, there is a more pernicious manifestation in the treatment of scientific reliability and uncertainty. While constructivist philosophies of science tend to underplay notions of certainty and reliability, positivist and post-positivist conceptions of science recognise that while we may strive for certainty, scientific knowledge is always provisional and subject to change in the face of theoretical and empirical challenge. As Hulme notes, 'Climate change [is] a battleground between different philosophies and practice of science, between different ways of knowing' (2009, p xxvii).

However, in the climate change policy field perhaps more than in any other, public perceptions of scientific certainty and uncertainty are being mobilised in policy debate to both promote and to limit action. The well-established precautionary principle that would suggest taking action now to avoid harm in the future has been challenged by a new interpretation that says costly action should not be taken now in anticipation of an imprecise threat of future harm. The point is not so much whether one or another position is correct or sensible, but that the use of uncertainty to justify inaction runs counter to much contemporary professional practice in other fields, ranging from medicine to civil engineering. If the inaction/uncertainty principle currently advocated for climate change policy was applied in other fields, then great swathes of public action would cease.

The principle that we should avoid putting in place any policies that impose economic or social costs in the present until we are much more certain of the long-term benefits is one widely seen in Australian climate change policy debates. One of the best examples is in coastal management and planning in the face of predicted sea level rise. Most local councils are reluctant to publish detailed maps of coastal flood risks because of the detrimental effect they would have on property values, and there is even greater reluctance to implement policies that restrict development rights in these places. Of course, when coastal areas are affected by storm surges and erosion, there is often condemnation of the planning systems that allowed development in such flood or erosion-prone areas. In this way uncertainty is used to limit regulation and policy intervention in the present, but will, in all likelihood, be used to in the future to criticise policy inaction and a different set of consequential costs.

Conclusions

Policies made in response to climate change, whether they are designed to mitigate or reduce the factors causing change or to help us adapt to changes that are already locked into the global climate system, are subject to a number of problems over and above the substantive problem of climate change. They must deal with problems of scientific complexity and uncertainty, they must address issues of intergenerational and international equity and they must reconcile tensions between global and local perspectives. To some this makes climate change a prominent case of what Rittel and Weber (1973) called a 'wicked issue', what the economist of climate policy Ross Garnaut called a 'diabolical problem' (Garnaut, 2008) and what former Australian Prime Minister Kevin Rudd (2007) called the 'greatest moral, social and economic challenge of our time'.

It is not easy to make and to implement climate change policy in any country, and it is certainly not easy to develop global programmes and frameworks, but in Australia it seems to be especially difficult. In some respects this is perplexing as it possesses a number of advantages not enjoyed by others: there is an abundance of natural resources that could, in theory, be used in the transition to a low-carbon economy; it enjoys a relatively high degree of political autonomy, certainly in comparison with the complexities of operating within the EU; and it is a stable democracy with a comparatively robust economy and a high standard of living for most of its people. Some of these same factors make it more difficult to make climate change policy: because of its high level of exposure to the impacts of climate change, profound changes will be required, especially in terms of adaptation measures; much of the county's economic success is associated with its trading relationship with China and with the export of resources such as coal, gas, iron ore and uranium that will be curtailed if global programmes of emissions reductions are effective; and its symbolic position on the world stage of climate policy development is greater than its material impact.

In her poem, *My country*, Dorothea Mackellar wrote,

> I love a sunburnt country,
> A land of sweeping plains,
> Of ragged mountain ranges,
> Of droughts and flooding rains.

Australians accept that they live in a sunburnt country where droughts and flooding rains are commonplace, and it can be difficult to convince many that changes to these patterns are profound and anything more than 'climate as usual'. In this context the very need for policy is questioned and there is substantial scepticism about any argument for policy that would require significant changes to the Australian way of life. This way of life for most is now one of detached suburban living with very high levels of car dependency, and this is what underlies one of the highest per capita CO_2 emissions in the world. Few Australians are convinced that profound changes to this lifestyle are necessary, or that if achieved would make a significant contribution to limit global warming. However, a growing number of surveys of public opinion and attitude show that individuals, households and businesses want to see action on climate change and are willing in principle to make some contribution themselves (Ong et al, 2010; Fielding et al, 2012). Whether politicians and policy makers are able to harness this enthusiasm in the development and implementation of effective climate change policies remains to be seen, and until then it will remain a 'wicked' and 'diabolical' issue as well as one of the greatest policy challenges of our time.

Tailpiece

On 26 June 2013 Kevin Rudd replaced Julia Gillard as Leader of the Australian Labour Party and was subsequently reinstated as Prime Minister. He quickly announced his intention to move from a fixed price for carbon to a market-based trading system by mid–2014 rather than mid–2015. He also announced that the impending federal election would be held on 7 September, one week ahead of the date previously nominated by his predecessor. The election resulted in victory for the Coalition of Liberal and National Parties and the installation of Tony Abbott as Prime Minister. He has consistently claimed that the election constituted a referendum on climate policy and has claimed a clear mandate to repeal Labour's climate policy measures, including the abolition of a number of important policy institutions such as the Climate Commission, a body established to provide an independent source of information about the science of climate change; the Climate Change Authority which provides expert advice on carbon pricing and other mitigation policies measures; and the Clean Energy Finance Corporation, established to mobilise capital investment in renewable energy and low-emission technologies. On the other hand, the prospective Minister for Environment, Greg Hunt, announced just before the election that the new government would provide ongoing financial support of AUD$3 million for three years for the NCCARF from 2014. Finally, the Prime Minister has stated that the funds allocated to his Direct Action emissions reduction programme will not be increased, even if the target of a 5 per cent reduction in emissions by 2020 is not achieved. Australian policy in response to climate change is therefore entering yet another period of turbulence for both policy development and implementation.

F inally, Dorte Martinsen and Nikolay Vasev contribute to the extensive literature on European Union (EU)/nation state interactions. This features an aspect of governance not explored earlier, about the role of courts in policy determination, and goes on to show how an EU policy can run into difficulties in the face of pre-existing national policies and institutional arrangements.

This contribution examines increased EU regulation within the healthcare sector, exemplified by the Patient Rights Directive on cross-border healthcare. This provides an example of the various complexities arising from the operationalisation of an EU policy within nation states' health systems. The contribution first analyses the judicial and political process through which patient rights in cross-border healthcare became part of the EU regulatory competences, resulting in the adoption of the directive. The principles and content of this directive are found to be the most important regulatory piece of healthcare regulation within the EU to date. It then examines the different set of challenges that EU healthcare governance introduces to the different healthcare systems of the European Community. Third, it analyses these challenges in two selected member states: the universalist and national healthcare system of Denmark, and the insurance-based healthcare system of Bulgaria. The two cases have been selected because they vary in respect of healthcare models as well as healthcare packages, spending, degree of centralisation and administrative capacity, among other factors.

Cross-border healthcare in the European Union: EU governance and national responses in healthcare

Dorte Sindbjerg Martinsen and Nikolay Vasev

Introduction

Healthcare as a public policy has traditionally been governed exclusively by the nation state. As a policy area it belongs to the core of the welfare state. How to organise healthcare, which healthcare coverage to provide, how to prioritise and so forth – these are key themes in national elections, and an essential link in the social contract between the state and its citizens. Healthcare has developed in relative isolation as a result of domestic politics and actors (Greer, 2009, p 1). Its national isolation has, however, been increasingly disturbed by the integration dynamics of the EU. The meeting between national health policy and EU law marks tensions and contradictions:

> Health care policy in the European Union has, at its centre, a fundamental contradiction. On the one hand, recent Treaties, which are the definitive statements on the scope of European law, state explicitly that health care is a responsibility for Member States. On the other hand, as health systems involve interaction with people (staff and patients), goods (pharmaceuticals and devices) and services (health care funders and providers), all of whose freedom to move across borders is guaranteed by the same Treaty, it is increasingly apparent that many of their activities are subject to European law. (Mossialos et al, 2001, p 11)

For a long time the right to cross-border healthcare was governed by Community regulation 1408/71.[1] This granted Community workers and later European citizens the right to acute healthcare treatment in another member state as well as more limited access to planned healthcare treatment, where the costs of care would be paid by the home member state (Martinsen, 2009, pp 794-5; Palm and Glinos, 2010, pp 514-15). Access to planned treatment in another member state was, however, firmly controlled nationally, through the governing principle of 'prior authorisation'. According to this principle, a patient would have to have prior authorisation by a competent national institution in order to have planned treatment in another member state. In reality, therefore, few patients planned cross-border treatment as prior authorisation was seldom issued (Martinsen, 2007, p 14).

Since the European Court of Justice in 1998 laid down that healthcare was not an *îlot impermeable a l'influence du droit communautaire*,[2] judicial interpretation of internal market principles and the subsequent political process have fundamentally challenged the national ability to control cross-border care.

This EU development and its potential impact on national healthcare systems is examined below. For this purpose, this contribution first presents the judicial process where the European Court of Justice applied internal market principles to the healthcare sector, then sets out the political negotiations leading to the Patient Rights Directive. The subsequent sections examine the content and overall implications of this directive, how EU governance challenges the national healthcare systems in two selected member states – Denmark and Bulgaria – and how these two member states have initiated the transposition of the directive.

With the European Court towards EU healthcare regulation

In 1998, the European Court of Justice came out with two controversial rulings, laying down that healthcare was a service within the meaning of the Treaties thus, in principle, to be circulated freely.[3] Health ministers were upset, arguing that the rulings must be overturned by a Treaty amendment.[4] Such an amendment was, however, never adopted. In the end, member states did not prioritise the matter sufficiently when negotiating the Treaty of Nice, and a Treaty clarification exempting healthcare from the internal market was not inserted (Martinsen and Falkner, 2011).

This initial outburst was then later met by significant silence and a long period in which there was no EU initiative. The member states were evidently waiting for the Commission to come up with a proposal, which took a long time to prepare. In the meantime, the European Court of Justice went further in its interpretations on patients' rights and cross-border healthcare. Its reasoning in a number of cases implied that for the wide scope of non-hospital care, a patient could go to another member state without authorisation from his/her home state, pay for the cost of treatment up front, and subsequently have the costs reimbursed back home – up to what a similar treatment would have cost in their home member state.

Initially this was assumed only to applied to social insurance systems. National health service systems continued to argue that the rationale and reasoning of the European Court cases did not apply to their systems as they were genuinely different, with limited elements of private pay and healthcare provided as benefit in kind. However, in the 2006 *Watts* case,[5] for the first time the Court considered the implications for national health services, and concluded that the internal market principle applies to all healthcare systems, irrespective of how they are financed or how they provide healthcare. The Court also stated that patients have a right to cross-border treatment if the waiting time for a similar treatment in their own member state exceeded what is acceptable.

In the 2007 case of *Stamatelakis*,[6] the Court ruled that a member state could not exclude reimbursing treatment in another member state on the grounds that it was provided in a private hospital. In this case, the Greek government submitted that the balance of the system was at risk if citizens could travel to private hospitals in EU countries without Greece having established agreements with those hospitals. However, these concerns were over-ruled by the Court, which instead clarified that the Greek ban on reimbursement for private healthcare abroad was against Community law.

With this line of case law it took the European Court of Justice less than 10 years to apply internal market principles to national healthcare systems, disregarding how they were organised, financed or provided healthcare. Judicial decision making thus made a rapid intervention in a public policy domain once governed exclusively by national politics and protected by national borders.

Political negotiations on patient rights in cross-border healthcare

The first attempt to respond to the Court's rulings came when the Commission, rather unsuccessfully, attempted to integrate the healthcare area in the Bolkestein Directive on services in the internal market, inserted in the Commission's proposal as Article 23.[7] The health ministers, however, were alarmed to have their policy area regulated as part of a general directive on services, placed under the responsibility of the Directorate-General of the Internal Market. Article 23, and thus the healthcare area, was taken out of the directive.

Consequently it appeared clear that European healthcare could not be regulated from an overall internal market perspective, but the case law of the European Court still called for a political response. The case law had disturbed the traditional national demarcation of healthcare policies, and there was a need to re-establish legal certainty. After considerable preparatory steps, expert considerations and a failed attempt to present a proposal back in December 2007, the Commission finally proposed its directive on 2 July 2008 on patient rights in cross-border healthcare.[8]

The subsequent negotiation process became tense, ripe with conflicts on different dimensions of the proposal, and the Council of Ministers had great difficulty in establishing a common position between the member states. Only two to three member states were in favour when the proposal was first presented by the Commission (A. Vassillou, 2980th meeting, Press conference, 1 December 2009). A significant number of ministers expressed concerns about national sovereignty, and wished to tighten national control in cross-border care by means of prior authorisation. Southern European nations in particular expressed concerns, and in December 2009 Spain led a blocking minority against the Swedish presidency compromise text, and the Council thus failed to reach an agreement. However, during 2010 disagreements eased. In the second reading, a qualified majority was established in the Council, but Austria, Poland, Portugal and Romania voted no, and Slovakia abstained. The European Parliament also had difficulty in establishing a majority position. The Christian Democrats (EPP) and the Liberals (ALDE) were generally in favour of the Commission's proposal, but the Alliance of Socialists and Democrats (S&D) was divided internally on various issues, especially on the fundamental question of the correct legal base for the directive and the issue of prior authorisation. However, a compromise was gradually established, and by March 2011 the directive was adopted by both institutions. The adopted text differs from the original proposal by the Commission on several aspects. A dual legal basis has been reached. The internal market legal base, Article 114 of the Treaty on the Functioning of the EU, constitutes the main legal basis, but Article 168 (on public health) has also been inserted. Another significant compromise is that prior authorisation is accepted as the means of national control, but only allowed for care subject to planning, that is, hospitalisation or healthcare which are highly specialised or which involve cost-intensive medical infrastructure or equipment.

The process that finally reached a compromise on patient rights in cross-border care substantiates that it took the representatives of the welfare states in the Council and a considerable number of European parliamentarians quite some time to accept that healthcare fell under the rules of the internal market. The politicians managed to negotiate some exemptions to the general rule of free movement, but the process also substantiated that despite such political reservations, it was now a European binding norm that healthcare constituted a service within the meaning of the Treaties, with all its implications. The principles and content of the directive are substantial, with an impact for all member states, albeit depending on the national health system in place.

Content and overall implications of the Patient Rights Directive

Among the 22 articles of the directive, at least seven appear to challenge the established status quo of national healthcare provision across the EU, albeit to different degrees, and to a varying extent across the member states.

Article 4 establishes that where member states may be providing treatment, they are obliged to ensure that *national contact points* provide patients with the relevant information on the standards of national healthcare (Article 4.2.a). Member states are also responsible for ensuring that *healthcare provid*ers provide the relevant information for patients to make an informed choice on treatment options, availability, quality and safety, and that the providers have clear invoices and clear information on prices, among other aspects (Article 4.2.b).

Article 5 obliges the home member state (that is, the member state where the patient is insured) to ensure that there are mechanisms in place to inform patients about their rights and entitlements in relation to cross-border healthcare, conditions for reimbursement of costs as well as information on appeal and redress. Article 6 lays down that member states shall establish one or more national contact points. National contact points shall facilitate the exchange of relevant information regarding health services (Article 6.2).

Article 7 establishes the principles of reimbursement of the costs of cross-border care. Member states are obliged to 'to have a transparent mechanism for calculation of costs of cross-border healthcare that are to be reimbursed to the insured person by the Member State of affiliation. This mechanism shall be based on objective, non-discriminatory criteria known in advance' (Article 7.6).

Article 8 deals with the issue of prior authorisation, one of the most controversial issues in the case law and during the negotiations on the directive. De facto it lays down a distinction between three types of healthcare service: *hospital care, highly specialised and cost-intensive care* and *non-hospital care*. For hospital care as well as highly specialised and cost-intensive care, prior authorisation may be justified whereas it is not for non-hospital care. Prior authorisation may not be refused if the requested healthcare cannot be provided in the member state of affiliation 'within a time limit which is medically justifiable, based on an objective medical assessment of the patient's medical condition, the history and probable course of the patient's illness, the degree of the patient's pain and/or the nature of the patient's disability at the time when the request for authorization was made or renewed' (Article 8.5). The member state of affiliation shall make publicly available which healthcare is subject to prior authorisation (Article 8.7).

Article 9 obliges the member states of affiliation to ensure accessible administrative procedures, based on objective, non-discriminatory criteria that are necessary and proportionate to the objective (Article 9.1.). Member states shall also ensure that individual decisions are properly reasoned and capable of being judicially challenged (Article 9.4). Finally, Article 11 lays down mutual recognition of prescriptions, issued in another member state.

These seven articles are likely to have considerable consequences for national healthcare governance, depending on national healthcare schemes and how member state authorities understand and comply with their responsibilities. They oblige member states to develop and make accessible information on key components of healthcare provision: standards, quality, pricing, administrative procedures and exit rights. Accessible and transparent information becomes a public responsibility, and member states will have to intervene in relation to healthcare providers, be they public or private, to make such available. This calls for a certain degree of centralisation, where the national governance level ensures that the obligations are complied with.

The implications of these seven articles are manifold. Below we examine how the principles and content of the directive challenge two different healthcare systems represented by the Danish and Bulgarian member states, first, from an overall institutional perspective, then, by presenting in brief the first phase of transposition in these two rather different member states.

National healthcare systems and European governance

Albeit there are no two identical healthcare systems, European health polities can roughly be divided in two distinct families. On the one side is the universalistic, tax-financed Beveridge model, also known as National Health System (NHS); and on the other, the corporatist, social insurance contributions-based Bismarckian system, or Health Insurance System (HIS) (Neergaard, 2011, p 20). These two families differ on key characteristics that are of crucial importance for the successful implementation of the directive. Of specific importance to its implementation are: (1) the level of centralisation of the health system, that is, which institution or governance level is responsible for the supply of healthcare; (2) the financing principles and the importance of out-of-pocket payments (OPPs); (3) the presence of a defined benefits package and clear pricing of medical services as well as (4) governance principles in relation to the effectiveness and quality of the healthcare sector. The two cases selected for this study differ on all of these criteria, and this is the reason they were selected.

One of the most striking distinctions between the Danish and the Bulgarian cases is the level of centralisation found in the two systems. While the Bulgarian system is under the unconditional monopoly of the National Health Insurance Fund (NHIF), a semi-public, non-profit organisation charged with the payment of services procured by Bulgarian insurance carriers from healthcare providers (Dimova et al, 2012, p 55), the Danish system is considerably more decentralised.

Healthcare in Denmark is a shared responsibility between the state, the five regions and the 98 municipalities. Within this power equation the state is mainly responsible for legislation, the regions for organising and delivering services, whereas the municipalities have responsibility for a number of prevention and rehabilitation services (Martinsen and Vrangbaek, 2008, p 173). The decentralisation of the Danish system means that there is a political environment in which the implementation of the directive is in the hands of significantly more actors than in the Bulgarian system. This is likely to lead to complications and impediments.

Second, the Danish and Bulgarian systems differ in the ways in which healthcare services are financed and supplied. The Danish healthcare scheme is tax-financed, providing a universal public health service for all residents. The Bulgarian compulsory social insurance scheme is financed by contributions from Bulgarian citizens and from residents in Bulgaria and a scheme funded by taxes providing benefits in kind, other than those provided by the contribution-funded scheme.

In addition, the amount of OPP differs greatly between Denmark and Bulgaria. Here it must be underlined that these come under various forms, from complementary payment for services that are not fully covered, through user fees and ultimately to 'under the table payments'. Our data does not give us a direct insight into the individual forms of OPP, but they are clearly a lot lower in Denmark than in Bulgaria. In Denmark their figure stands at 14 per cent of the total current health expenditure for 2008 (latest available data), whereas in Bulgaria it is as high as 42 per cent (Eurostat, 2013). The data from Eurostat is based on national statistical and administrative sources, reflecting the national characteristics of the health system, which means that they may not be completely comparable. Nevertheless, what is certain is that the Danish NHS system operates at much lower levels of OPP in the financing of healthcare, whereas OPPs are a highly important financing source in Bulgaria. Ultimately the OPPs 'reflect a scarcity of resources in the health care system' (Balabanova and McKee, 2002, p 269). Informal payments in particular have severe consequences on the effectiveness of the system, because the flow of resources into the system in part depends on the willingness and need of patients to make informal payments. Budgetary transparency, capacity planning and equity are difficult to uphold in a system that in part relies on informal payments. In addition, the issue of widespread OPPs in Bulgaria could prove prohibitive to foreign patients who are unaware of more informal practices. The informal procedures of the Bulgarian system are likely to be challenged by the directive's Article 9, laying down that the member state of affiliation shall have accessible and transparent administrative procedures, which are accessible to judicial redress. This highlights the importance of functioning complaints procedures, as these will be particularly important for safeguarding patients' rights and, by extension, for the successful implementation of the directive.

A third distinction between the two systems stemming from their basic characteristics as NHS or HIS is the existence of specified benefits packages. HISs must provide a clear list of services that will be covered so health providers within the system operate with a pre-defined benefits package, whereas their

NHS counterparts are freer to choose the services they can offer. In Denmark, the lack of clear benefits packages is also a result of the decentralisation of the system and the lack of a clear division of responsibilities. The Health Act 2007, which delegated responsibility for the medical care of each patient to the regions, and the preventive services aimed at the general population and for rehabilitation and home care for patients to the municipalities, puts no one actor in charge of preparing the benefits package (Olejaz et al, 2012, p 62). When it comes to the presence of clearly defined prices, the two countries operate with different systems. Determined prices are a direct consequence of the precise benefit package in Bulgaria. In the Danish system, prices are calculated on the basis of DRG (diagnosis–related groups) prices, set between the regions and the national healthcare providers.

Finally, the governance principles in relation to the effectiveness and quality of the healthcare sector differ. In Denmark, the 'family doctor', that is, the general practitioner (GP), serves as an important gatekeeper for healthcare treatment, and has been regarded as important for the quality of care, bridging patients' demands and system supply. The GP thus has a most important control function in the Danish system, including access to pharmaceuticals by means of prescriptions, referring patients to specialist treatment and hospital care, ensuring continuity of care, providing information on care among other factors. In carrying out these tasks, the GP has an equally important function for the system, controlling healthcare expenditures. The GP refers all patients registered with him or her to specialised care and all patients to hospital care. Hence patients will not be able to access specialised care, hospital care or prescribed medicine without the GP's consent. A patient, once referred by the GP, has an extended free choice of hospital care if s/he cannot be treated within one month in his/her own region. In that case the patient can chose healthcare at a public hospital in another region or at a private or foreign healthcare provider with which the Danish regions have established an agreement beforehand. The waiting time for hospital care is set to be low by means of this extended free choice. The Danish NHS system thus currently operates relatively effectively, and the GP is regarded as an important gatekeeper for the quality of care. In Bulgaria the role of the GP is comparable to their Danish counterpart, serving as an access point for incoming patients, assessing their overall health condition and evaluating the needs of patients for further medical treatment. In this sense, the function of 'gatekeeper' is also to be found in the Bulgarian GP system, with one important addition. In order to receive specialised care (that is, laboratory tests, inpatient care, specialist examination, and so on), patients need to receive a medical referral from their GP. The medical referral keeps the cost of specialised care under control, effectively eliminates long waiting times for patients, but it also aggressively restricts access to potentially life-saving treatments. This is due to the fact that the number of referrals is limited to the GPs, causing patients to wait because GP referrals are rationed. Referrals are rationed every month, meaning that a Bulgarian patient might have to wait more than a month to receive a referral from their GP. Without a referral the patient has to pay extra to receive the treatment, unless they also have voluntary health insurance[9] (which only covers a marginal portion of the population). The only specialised medical treatment for which no referral is required is dental care. In a situation where medical referrals become unavailable to the patients for a prolonged period of time, this could lead to a situation where the Bulgarian state as the member state of affiliation under the provisions of the directive must provide prior authorisation because it cannot provide medical treatment within a medically justified time period, that is, without 'undue delay'. In this situation, the directive would effectively extend the coverage of Bulgarian patients, simultaneously crippling the control the GPs provide.

The complex situation of Bulgarian GPs means that they will be practically inaccessible to foreign patients. GPs are very unlikely to give out referrals to foreigners as they need to keep their 'personal' patients supplied. This would almost completely eliminate the option of seeking specialised inpatient treatment in Bulgaria unless foreign patients are prepared to pay the full price of the treatment, in which case they still have to consider the potential reduced standards of quality under which it will be delivered.

Ultimately the cases of Denmark and Bulgaria represent maximum variations of the possible developments of healthcare systems within Europe. In the subsequent paragraphs we examine how these variations are likely to influence the implementation of the Patient Rights Directive.

Transposing the Patient Rights Directive

At the time of writing this contribution in early 2013, member states are still in full process of transposition, for which reason it is only possible to draw out some overall challenges.

In Denmark, the Ministry of Health is responsible for the transposition of the directive. The regions will, however, be responsible for the practical implementation of the directive, when Danish patients request cross-border care or foreign patients Danish care. The regions express their increasing frustration of not being closely involved in the transposition process that is said to be carried out in a rather secluded manner by a few civil servants in the Ministry of Health (interviews, November 2012). The role of the contact points in particular is found to be crucial but unclear. Contact points with a high level of services are likely to lead to an enhanced inflow of foreign patients, whereas poor information is likely to limit de facto patient inflow, simultaneously increasing uncertainty. Key questions are still unanswered. How many contact points will have to be set up? Will they have to provide information in foreign languages? What will be the extent and standard of information?

In Bulgaria for the overall monitoring of the actual implementation the competent institution is the Ministry of Labour and Social Policy. It follows the legislation prepared by the Ministry of Health in close partnership with the NHIF. The NHIF prepares concrete suggestions for the reform of functioning national legislation and after these suggestions are accepted by the Ministry of Health, the process of transposition can begin in the National Assembly. On the issue of national contact points the Ministry of Health and the NHIF pass responsibility between each other as to who would have to take over the establishment of these bodies. Since staffing the contact points requires people with language skills, knowledge of the normative statute and the intricacies of the national and international health systems, neither the ministry nor the NHIF is willing to spare any of their staff to take on this new task (interviews, November, 2012). Concerning contact points, we already see how the resource unavailability of the Bulgarian system will start influencing the implementation in its early stages and is likely to lead to understaffing of the contact points and result in their inability to handle the workload.

Concerning the financing principles of the healthcare system, the limited OPP and no 'under the table payment' in Denmark limit the private economic motivation for patients to seek cross-border healthcare.

As an NHS system, Danish public healthcare has not traditionally operated with clear patient rights and defined healthcare packages. The Patient Rights Directive operates with a fundamentally different logic establishing a focus on patient rights, judicial redress and clear information on quality, standards and pricing. In this way, the governing principle of the EU directive is to enable the patient to carry out an informed choice and to eventually exit from the national supply if not satisfied. The national authorities become responsible for proving the information and processes to facilitate both exits and inflow. In addition, 'clear pricing' is not straightforward for the Danish model. So far the Ministry of Health point to DRG prices as the natural level of price setting, turning to existing solutions (interviews, August and November 2012). But representatives from the regions have pointed out that the DRG is a rather abstract means of price setting, not disaggregating the different components of a healthcare service, nor specifying when a healthcare treatment begins and ends (interviews, August and November 2012). DRG prices might function in a national setting, where between regions and national healthcare providers have learned to trust this price mechanism, but in an internal market they hardly constitute transparent or full prices (interviews, August and November 2012).

Prices of the medical services in Bulgaria are listed in the national framework contract, a record of all medical services offered in the Bulgarian system and covered by the NHIF. The framework contract, however, suffers from a central flaw – medical treatment prices in Bulgaria are drastically and inherently undervalued (interviews, November 2012). This has to do with the fact that the entire system is underfinanced because of extremely low social insurance contributions. Although they represent 8 per cent of the official income of employed people, the overall low level of payment in Bulgaria, the undocumented labour and other factors contributing to the 'shadow economy' leave the healthcare system necessitous and cash-strapped. A direct consequence is the aforementioned ubiquitous OPPs, where patients need to 'co-finance' their treatments. However, the low prices of medical services in Bulgaria are unlikely to lead to increased medical tourism after the implementation of the directive. All accounts point out that medical tourism in Bulgaria is underdeveloped, and a major impediment for it is the low quality of services (interviews, November 2012). In addition, the low pricing of services is sure to have a prohibitive influence on the cross-border mobility of Bulgarian patients since the services they might acquire abroad will only be reimbursed to a very low level, due to the undervalued Bulgarian pricing.

Finally, the governance principles concerning effectiveness and ensuring quality of care are seriously disturbed by EU governance. At the moment, waiting times are generally relatively low in Denmark. Thus the directive's principle that patients have a right to hospital, specialised and cost-intensive care if care cannot be provided without undue delay is no immediate challenge to Denmark concerning Danish patients seeking cross-border care. However, it may spur a considerable inflow of foreign patients. Some healthcare providers in Denmark may be highly attractive to patients in other member states due to effectiveness and quality of care. This will imply both challenges and new opportunities to a healthcare model, traditionally planning capacity strictly according to national demands. Furthermore, the Danish model of ensuring quality of care with the assigned 'family doctor', the GP, as gatekeeper is challenged. With the directive, a patient may ask a GP in another member state for his/her opinion and advice, and thus bypass the governance function that the GP has traditionally occupied. Also pharmaceuticals in other member states will be accessible by means of mutual recognition of prescriptions. The issue of pharmaceutical prescriptions is also expected to be problematic in Bulgaria as the country is the only one in the EU to use the Cyrillic script, effectively making its prescriptions a difficult read in the rest of the EU. The GP control function in the Danish model is thus in question and enhances de facto cross-border care. Also, doctors as a profession will be met by increased demands of Europeanisation to which they will have to adapt. This includes linguistic challenges, the demand and expectation of foreign medical practices and high mobility patients who can question doctors' assessments abroad.

Conclusions

The structural differences between the two systems presented here result in different conditions in which the directive must be implemented. These conditions effectively build two different environments in which the identical text of the directive is sure to have differing implications.

In the Danish case the lack of clear pricing and benefits packages will make the practical implication of the directive particularly difficult for the Danish authorities. The directive is also likely to challenge the control that the GP ensures over the system, as patients will have access to European GPs. These issues will introduce challenges to the planning and execution of the Danish system, depending on the extent of mobility. If patient mobility maintains its character of a marginal phenomenon, largely limited to the border regions (Baeten, 2012, p 26), its effects in Denmark are likely to be negligible. At first sight, high quality of care and relative efficient treatment, that is, low waiting lists, are likely to cause an inflow of foreign patients to the Danish system. However, if waiting times extend and limited quality is highlighted by European comparisons, the Danish system could face more Danish patients opting for treatment abroad. Both patient inflow and outflow could lead to pressure on the delivery of care, as capacity planning would become more difficult. Danish taxpayers would have to carry the additional administrative costs of foreign patients' entry into the Danish system as well as reimbursing procedures executed on Danish patients abroad.

In Bulgaria the overall low level of income is likely to cripple any of the benefits that the directive could provide. Since the directive covers expenses only to the point of coverage in the state of affiliation, medical treatment abroad under the directive's provisions will be near impossible for the majority of the Bulgarian population. Since medical services in Bulgaria are generally undervalued, this makes their pricing drastically lower in Bulgaria, and it means that the difference between the price covered by the NHIF and the price charged abroad would have to be paid by the patient. The directive is furthermore dwarfed in its influence by the functioning of Regulation 883/2004 that stipulates complete coverage of any medical treatment as long as it is offered by the state of affiliation and prior authorisation has been issued. Thus for the Bulgarian patient, the regulation is certainly the more attractive alternative.

The differing degree of centralisation in both health polities is likely to be an advantage in the Bulgarian case as it operates with a reduced number of veto players and concentrates the transposition and implementation tasks within very few central institutions. We have seen the issue of national contact points cause friction between two of these institutions, but the close communication between them is likely to facilitate a compromise on this issue. In the Danish case, the attempt to concentrate the implementation procedures within the Ministry of Health has caused some frustration to the regions responsible for the practical implementation of the directive.

The distinction drawn here between Denmark and Bulgaria, highlighting the main organisational features of the systems, accentuates the difficulties the national executive and policy makers face in the course of implementation of the directive on cross-border patients' rights. Although all of the member states are implementing the same legislative text, the domestic resources and institutional particularities of healthcare systems will lead to distinctive impediments and specific member state challenges. This means that further implementation analysis will need to pay closer attention to the existing national institutional environment, the actors within and around these, and the challenges that it is predisposed to cause in the course of implementation.

Notes

[1] Regulation (EEC) No 1408/71 of the Council of 14 June 1971 pertains to the application of social security schemes to employed people, to self-employed people and to members

of their families moving within the Community. The regulation was substantially reformed with the adoption of Regulation 883/2004, adopted on 29 April 2004.

[2] As formulated by the Advocate General Tesauro in the 1998 cases of *Decker* and *Kohll*.

[3] In the cases C-120/95 *Decker* [1998] ECR I-01831 and C-158/96 *Kohll* [1998] ECR I-01931.

[4] See, for example, the reaction of the former German Health Minister Seehofer (*Der Spiegel*, 1998 17/98; *Fokus*, May 1998).

[5] Case C-372/04, *Watts*, 16 May 2006.

[6] Case C-444/05, *Stamatelaki* [2007] ECR I-3185.

[7] Proposal for a Directive of the European Parliament and of the Council on services in the internal market, COM (2004) 2.

[8] Proposal for a Directive of the European Parliament and of the Council on the application of patients' rights in cross-border healthcare, COM (2008) 414.

[9] Usually the voluntary health insurance only covers a portion of the medical cost. This depends entirely on the kind of premium owned by the patient. Unlike the statutory health insurance, voluntary insurance does not cover dependants (that is, spouses and children).

References

Accenture and Financial Services Ireland (2010) *The IFSC: The International Financial Services Sector in Ireland*, Dublin: Financial Services Ireland.

Adshead, M. (2005) 'Europeanization and changing patterns of governance in Ireland', *Public Administration*, vol 83, no 1, pp 159-78.

Allen, M.D., Pettus, C. and Haider-Markel, D.P. (2004) 'Making the national local: Specifying the conditions for national government influence on state policymaking', *State Politics and Policy Quarterly*, vol 4, no 3, pp 318-44.

Amalric, M., Bertrand, F., Bonnefond, M., Debray A., Fournier, M., Larrue, C., Manson, C., Mozol, P., Richard, E. and Rocher, L. (2011) *Les politiques environnementales à l'épreuve de l'intercommunalité: vers de nouveaux territoires d'action?*, Report for PUCA, October.

Anderson, M.H. (2006) 'How can we know what we think until we see what we said? A citation and citation context analysis of Karl Weick's *The social psychology of organizing*', *Organization Studies*, vol 27, no 11, pp 1675-92.

Anderson, P. (2007) 'A safe, sensible and social AHRSE: New Labour and alcohol policy', *Addiction*, vol 102, no 10, pp 1515-21.

Anderson, T.M. and Kohler, H.-P. (2012) *Education fever and the East Asian fertility puzzle: A case study of low fertility in South Korea*, Population Studies Center Working Paper 12-07, Philadelphia, PA: University of Pennsylvania.

Andersson, K. (2009) 'Orchestrating regional development through projects: The "innovation" paradox in rural Finland', *Journal of Environmental Policy & Planning*, vol 11, no 3, pp 187-201.

Arnstein, S. (1969) 'A ladder of citizen participation', *Journal of the American Institute of Planners*, vol 35, no 4, pp 216-24.

Auer, P. and Fortunny, M. (2000) *Ageing of the labour force in OECD countries: Economic and social consequences*, Employment Paper 2000/2, Geneva: International Labour Organization.

Babor, T. (2010) *Alcohol: No ordinary commodity: Research and public policy*, Oxford: Oxford University Press.

Bacchi, C. and Eveline, J. (2003) 'Mainstreaming and neoliberalism: A contested relationship', *Policy & Society: Journal of Public, Foreign and Global Policy*, vol 22, no 2, pp 119-43.

Bache, I. and Flinders, M. (2004) 'Multi-level governance and the study of the British state', *Public Policy and Administration*, vol 19, no 1, pp 31-51.

Baeten, R. (2012) *Europeanization of national health systems. National impact and EU codification of the patient mobility case law*, OSE Paper Series, Brussels: European Social Observatory.

Baker, S. and Eckerberg, K. (2013) 'A policy analysis perspective on ecological restoration', *Ecology and Society*, vol 18, no 2, p 17.

Balabanova, D. and McKee, M. (2002) 'Understanding informal payments for health care: the example of Bulgaria', *Health Policy*, vol 62, no 3, p 243.

Ball, S.J. (2009) 'Privatising education, privatising education policy, privatising educational research: network governance and the "competition state"', *Journal of Education Policy*, vol 24, no 1, pp 83-99.

Ball, S.J. (2013) *The education debate* (2nd edn), Bristol: Policy Press.

Ball, S.J. and Exley, S. (2010) 'Making policy with "good ideas": policy networks and the "intellectuals" of New Labour', *Journal of Education Policy*, vol 25, no 2, pp 151-69.

Ball, S.J., Maguire, M. and Braun, A. (2012) *How schools do policy: Policy enactments in secondary schools*, London: Routledge.

Barbier, R. et al (2011) 'Le changement d'échelle dans l'action publique environnementale. Analyse comparée de régimes de gouvernance départementale de l'eau destinée à la consommation humaine', in Actes du Colloque 'Territoire et environnement: des représentations à l'action', Tours, 8–9 December 2011, pp 81-91.

Barnett, A. (1999) 'Corporate control', *Prospect*, February, pp 24-9.

Barraqué, B. (1998) 'Les collectivités locales et l'environnement', in B. Barraqué and J. Theys (eds) *Les politiques d'environnement: Evaluation de la première génération*, Paris: Editions Recherches, pp 347-72.

Barraqué, B. and Theys, J. (eds) (1998) *Les politiques d'environnement: Evaluation de la première génération: 1971–1995*, Paris: Editions Recherches, CNRS.

Barry, F. and Welsum, D. (2005) 'Services FDI and offshoring into Ireland', Paper prepared for the OECD Directorate for Science, Technology and Industry Panel Session on Offshoring, 9-10 June, Paris: Organisation for Economic Co-operation and Development.

Baumgartner, F.R. and Jones, B.D. (1991) 'Agenda dynamics and policy subsystems', *Journal of Politics*, vol 53, no 4, pp 1044-74.

Baumgartner, F.R. and Jones, B.D. (1993) *Agendas and instability in American politics*, Chicago, IL: University of Chicago Press.

Baumgartner, F.R. and Jones, B.D. (2005) *The politics of attention: How government prioritizes problems*, Chicago, IL: University of Chicago Press.

Baumgartner, F.R., Green-Pedersen, C. and Jones, B.D. (2006) 'Comparative studies of policy agendas', *Journal of European Public Policy*, vol 13, no 7, pp 961-3.

Béland, D. (2005) 'Ideas and social policy: an institutionalist perspective', *Social Policy & Administration*, vol 39, no 1, pp 1-18.

Béland, D. (2010) 'Reconsidering policy feedback: How policies affect politics', *Administration & Society*, vol 42, no 5, pp 568-90.

Béland, D. and Hacker, J.S. (2004) 'Ideas, private institutions and American welfare state "exceptionalism": the case of health and old-age insurance, 1915-1965', *International Journal of Social Welfare*, vol 13, no 1, pp 42-54.

Bennetts, R. (2008) *Use of alcohol as a loss-leader*, IAS Briefing Paper, St Ives: Institute of Alcohol Studies.

Berdoulay, V. and Soubeyran, O. (2000) 'Les perspectives du développement durable', in V. Berdoulay and O. Soubeyran (eds) *Milieu, colonisation et développement durable. Perspectives géographiques sur l'aménagement*, Paris: L'Harmattan, pp 247-54.

Bernhardt, E., Palmer, M., Allan, J., Alexander, G., Barnas, K., Brooks, S. and Carr, J. (2005) 'Synthesizing US river restoration efforts', *Science*, vol 308, no 18, pp 2-3.

Berry, F. S., and Berry, W.D. (1992) 'Tax innovation in the states: Capitalizing on political opportunity', *American Political Science Review*, vol 36, pp 715-42.

Berry, F.S. and Berry, W.D. (1999) 'Innovation and diffusion models in policy research', in P.A. Sabatier (ed) *Theories of the policy process*, Boulder, CO: Westview Press, pp 169-200.

Berry, W.D., Fording, R.C., Ringquist, E.J., Hanson, R.L. and Klarner, C. (1998) 'Measuring citizen and government ideology in the American states, 1960–93', *American Journal of Political Science*, vol 42, no 1, pp 327-48.

Bevir, M. and Rhodes, R. (2006) 'Prime ministers, presidentialism and Westminster smokescreens', *Political Studies*, vol 54, no 4, pp 6-16.

Bickerstaff, K., Lorenzoni, I., Pidgeon, N.F., Poortinga, W. and Simmons, P. (2008) 'Reframing nuclear power in the UK energy debate: nuclear power, climate change mitigation and radioactive waste', *Public Understanding of Science*, vol 17, no 2, pp 145-69.

Birkland, T.A. (1998) 'Focusing events, mobilization, and agenda setting', *Journal of Public Policy*, vol 18, no 1, pp 53-74.

Birkland, T.A. (2006) *Lessons of disaster: Policy change after catastrophic events*, Washington, DC: Georgetown University Press.

Birkland, T.A., Burby, R.J., Conrad, D., Cortner, H. and Michner, W. (2003) 'River ecology and flood hazard mitigation', *Natural Hazards Review*, vol 4, no 1, pp 46-54.

Black, H. et al (2011) 'The price of a drink: levels of consumption and price paid per unit of alcohol by Edinburgh's ill drinkers with a comparison to wider alcohol sales in Scotland', *Addiction*, vol 106, no 4, pp 729-36.

Blyth, M. (2002) *Great transformations: Economic ideas and institutional change in the twentieth century*, Cambridge: Cambridge University Press.

Bobak, M. et al (2004) 'Contribution of drinking patterns to differences in rates of alcohol-related problems between three urban populations', *Journal of Epidemiology and Community Health*, vol 58, no 3, pp 238-42.

Bomberg, E. et al (2008) *The European Union: How does it work?*, Oxford: Oxford University Press.

Bonoli, G. (2012) 'Blame avoidance and credit claiming revisited', in G. Bonoli and D. Natali (eds) *The politics of the new welfare state*, Oxford: Oxford University Press, pp 93-110.

Bonoli, G. and Shinkawa, T. (eds) (2005) *Ageing and pension reform around the world*, Cheltenham: Elgar.

Booth, A. et al (2008) *Independent review of the effects of alcohol pricing and promotion – Part A: Systematic reviews*, Sheffield: School of Health and Related Research, University of Sheffield.

Borgström, S., Elmqvist, T., Angelstam, P. and Alfsen–Norodom, C. (2006) 'Scale mismatches in management of urban landscapes', *Ecology and Society*, vol 11, no 2, p 16.

Borgström, S., Zachrisson, A. and Eckerberg, K. (forthcoming) 'Ecological restoration in policy practice – Short-termism and regional biases', *Journal of Environmental Management*.

Borraz, O. (2007) 'Governing standards: the rise of standardization processes in France and in the EU', *Governance,* vol 20, no 1, pp 57-84.

Bosso, C.J. (1994) 'The contextual bases of problem definition', in D.A. Rochefort and R.W. Cobb (eds) *The politics of problem definition: Shaping the policy agenda*, Lawrence, KS: University Press of Kansas, pp 182-205.

Boström, M. (2003) 'How state-dependent is a non-state-driven rulemaking project? The case of forest certification in Sweden', *Journal of Environmental Policy and Planning*, vol 5, no 2, pp 165-80.

Boudon, R. (1991) *La place du désordre*, Paris: Quadrige PUF.

Bovens, M. and 't Hart, P. (1996) *Understanding policy fiascos*, Brunswick, NJ: Transaction Publishers.

Bowen, E.R. (1982) 'The Pressman–Wildavsky paradox', *Journal of Public Policy*, vol 2, no 1, pp 1-21.

Boyce, W., Tremblay, M., McColl, M.A., Bickenbach, J., Crichton, A., Andrews, S., Gerein, N. and D'Aubin, A. (2001) *A seat at the table: Persons with disabilities and policy making*, Montreal and Kingston: McGill-Queen's University Press.

Boychuk, T. (1999) *The making and meaning of hospital policy in the United States and Canada*, Ann Arbor, MI: University of Michigan Press.

Brodkin, E.Z. (2012) 'Reflections on street-level bureaucracy: Past, present, and future', *Public Administration Review*, vol 72, pp 940-9.

Brody, S.D., Zahran, S., Maghelal, P., Grover, H. and Highfield, W.E. (2007) 'The rising costs of floods: examining the impact of planning and development decisions on property damage in Florida', *Journal of the American Planning Association*, vol 73, no 3, p 330.

Bryden, P.E. (1997) *Planners and politicians: Liberal politics and social policy, 1957-1968*, Montreal and Kingston: McGill-Queen's University Press.

Bryden, P.E. (2012) 'The Liberal Party and the achievement of national Medicare', in G.P. Marchildon (ed) *Making Medicare: New perspectives on the history of Medicare in Canada*, Toronto: University of Toronto Press, pp 71-88.

Bump, J.B. (2010) *The long road to universal health coverage: A century of lessons for development strategy*, Seattle: PATH and the Rockefeller Foundation.

Burby, R.J. (2006) 'Hurricane Katrina and the paradoxes of government disaster policy: Bringing about wise governmental decisions for hazardous areas', *The Annals of the American Academy of Political and Social Science*, vol 604, no 1, pp 171-91.

Burby, R.J. and French, S.P. (1985) *Floodplain land use management: A national assessment*, Boulder, CO: Westview.

Burby, R.J. and French, S.P. (1985) 'Coping with floods: the land use management paradox', *Journal of the American Planning Association*, vol 47, no 3, pp 289-300.

Burby, R.J. and Kaiser, E.J. (1987) *An assessment of urban floodplain management in the United States: The case for land acquisition in comprehensive floodplain management*, Technical report prepared for Association of State Flood Plain Managers, Inc. Madison, Wisconsin.

Burby, R.J., French, S.P. and Nelson, A.C. (1998) 'Plans, code enforcement, and damage reduction: Evidence from the Northridge earthquake', *Earthquake Spectra*, vol 14, no 1, pp 59-74.

Burkard, T. and Talbot-Rice, S. (2009) *School quangos: A blueprint for abolition and reform*, London: Centre for Policy Studies.

Burton, P. and Mustelin, J. (2013) 'Planning for climate change: is greater public participation the key to success?', *Urban Policy and Research*, DOI: 10.1080/08111146.2013.778196.

Butler, A. (2000) 'The third way project in Britain, the role of the Prime Minister's policy unit', *Politics*, vol 20, no 3, pp 153-9.

Butler, I. and Drakeford, M. (2003) *Scandal, social policy and social welfare*, Bristol: Policy Press. CabGuide (2008) *CabGuide. Guide to Cabinet and Cabinet Committee processes*, Wellington: Cabinet Office (http://cabguide.cabinetoffice.govt.nz).

Cabinet Office (2008) *Cabinet manual*, Wellington: Cabinet Office (http://cabinetmanual.cabinetoffice.govt.nz).

Cairney, P. (2007a) 'Using devolution to set the agenda? Venue shift and the smoking ban in Scotland', *British Journal of Politics & International Relations*, vol 9, no 1, pp 73-89.

Cairney, P. (2007b) 'A "multiple lenses" approach to policy change: The case of tobacco policy in the UK', *British Politics*, vol 2, pp 45-68.

Cairney, P. (2009) 'The role of ideas in policy transfer: the case of UK smoking bans since devolution', *Journal of European Public Policy*, vol 16, no 3, pp 471-88.

Cairney, P. (2011) *The Scottish political system since devolution: From new politics to the new Scottish government*, Exeter: Imprint Academic.

Campbell, J. and Ikegami, N. (1998) *The art of balance in health policy: Maintaining Japan's low-cost egalitarian system*, Cambridge: Cambridge University Press.

Capano, G. (2009) 'Understanding policy change as an epistemological and theoretical problem', *Journal of Comparative Policy Analysis*, vol 11, no 1, pp 7-31.

Carroll, W.K. and Ratner, R.S. (1996) 'Master frames and counter-hegemony: Political sensibilities in contemporary social movements', *Canadian Review of Sociology and Anthropology*, vol 33, no 4, pp 407-35.

Casey, B. (1998) *Incentive and disincentives to early and late retirement*, Ageing Working Papers, 3.3, Paris: Organisation for Economic Co-operation and Development.

Cash, D.W., Adger, W.N., Berkes, F., Garden, P., Lebel, L. and Olsson, P. (2006) 'Scale and cross-scale dynamics: Governance and information in a multilevel world', *Ecology and Society*, vol 11, no 2, p 8.

Cashore, B. and Howlett, M. (2007) 'Punctuating which equilibrium? Understanding thermostatic policy dynamics in Pacific Northwest Forestry', *American Journal of Political Science*, vol 51, no 3, pp 532-51.

CCD (Council of Canadians with Disabilities) and CACL (Canadian Association for Community Living) (2005) 'A call to combat poverty and exclusion of Canadians with disabilities by investing in disability supports', Winnipeg (www.ccdonline.ca).

Chappell, L. and Curtin, J. (2013), 'Does federalism matter? Evaluating state architecture and family and domestic violence policy in Australia and New Zealand', *Publius*, vol 43, no 1, pp 24-43.

Charlton, J.I. (1998) *Nothing about us without us: Disability, oppression and empowerment*, Berkeley, CA: University of California Press.

Checkland, K., Harrison, S. and Coleman, A (2009a) '"Structural interests" in health care: Evidence from the contemporary National Health Service', *Journal of Social Policy*, vol 38, no 4, pp 607-25.

Checkland, K., Coleman, A., Harrison, S. and Hiroeh, U. (2008) *Practice-based commissioning in the National Health Service: Interim report of a qualitative study*, Manchester: National Primary Care Research and Development Centre, University of Manchester.

Checkland, K., Coleman, A., Harrison, S. and Hiroeh, U. (2009b) '"We can't get anything done because…": Making sense of "barriers" to practice-based commissioning', *Journal of Health Services Research and Policy*, vol 14, no 1, pp 20-6.

Checkland, K., Coleman, A., Segar, J., McDermott, I., Miller, R., Wallace, A., Petsoulas, C., Peckham, S. and Harrison, S. (2012) *Exploring the early workings and impact of emerging clinical commissioning groups: Final report*, Manchester: Policy Research Unit Communication, University of Manchester.

Chevallier, J. (1994) *Science Administrative*, Paris: PUF.

Child Welfare Bureau (2013) 'Childcare service statistics' (www.cbi.gov.tw/CBI_2/internet/main/index.aspx). [in Chinese]

Chivers, S. (2008) 'Barrier by barrier: The Canadian disability movement and the fight for equal rights', in M. Smith (ed) *Group politics and social movements in Canada*, Peterborough: Broadview Press, pp 307-28.

Christoff, P. (2005) 'Policy autism or double-edged dismissiveness? Australia's climate policy under the Howard government', *Global Challenge, Peace and Security*, vol 17, pp 29-44.

Clark, T. (2010) 'New schools network lacks transparency', *The Guardian*, 6 July.

Coakley, M. (2012) *Ireland in the world order: A history of uneven development*, London: Pluto Press.

Cobb, R.W. and Elder, C.D. (1983) *Participation in American politics: The dynamics of agenda-building*, Baltimore, MD: The Johns Hopkins University Press.

Cohen, M.D., March, J.G. and Olsen, J.P. (1972) 'A garbage can model of organizational choice', *Administrative Science Quarterly*, vol 17, pp 1-25.

Coleman, A., Checkland, K., Harrison, S. and Hiroeh, U. (2010) 'Local histories and local sensemaking: a case of policy implementation in the English National Health Service', *Policy & Politics*, vol 38, no 2, pp 289-306.

Coleman, A., Harrison, S., Checkland, K. and Hiroeh, U. (2007) *Practice-based commissioning: Report of a survey of primary care trusts*, Manchester: National Primary Care Research and Development Centre, University of Manchester.

Collins, C. and McCartney, G. (2011) 'The impact of neoliberal "political attack" on health: the case of the "Scottish effect"', *International Journal of Health Services*, vol 41, no 3, pp 501-23.

Connaughton, B. (2010) 'Symptom or remedy? Mediating characteristics of the Irish central bureaucracy and their influence on the strategic capacity of a "small" state', *Halduskultuur – Administrative Culture*, vol 11, no 1, pp 110-26.

ConservativeHome (2010) 'ConservativeIntelligence's guide to the Tory Manifesto is now available to buy' (http://conservativehome.blogs.com/conference/2010/01/conservativeintelligences-guide-to-the-tory-manifesto-is-now-available-to-buy.html).

Considine, M. and Dukelow, F. (2009) *Irish social policy: A critical introduction*, Dublin: Gill & Macmillan.

Considine, M. and Dukelow, F. (2012) 'From financial crisis to welfare retrenchment: assessing the challenges to the Irish welfare state', in M. Kilkey, G. Ramia and K. Farnsworth (eds) *Social Policy Review 24: Analysis and debate in social policy, 2012*, Bristol: Policy Press, pp 257-76.

Cook, J. (2012) 'Analysis: Legal challenge to Scotland's minimum alcohol price plan', 23 October, BBC News (www.bbc.co.uk/news/uk-scotland-20028728).

Council of Labor Affairs (2009) 'Labor statistics', *Monthly Bulletin* (www.cla.gov.tw/cgi-bin/SM_theme?page=432f8367).

Council of the European Union (2006) 'Council Opinion of 14 March 2006 on the updated stability programme of Ireland, 2005-2008', *Official Journal of the European Union C 82*, pp 19-22 (http://eur-lex.europa.eu/LexUriServ/LexUriServ.do?uri=OJ:C:2006:082:0019:0022:EN:PDF).

Cox, L. (2012) 'Challenging austerity in Ireland: community and movement responses', *Concept*, vol 3 no 2, pp 1-6 (http://concept.lib.ed.ac.uk/index.php/Concept/article/viewFile/158/144).

Crowley, N. (2013) 'Lost in austerity: Rethinking the community sector', *Community Development Journal*, vol 48, no 1, pp 151-7.

CSO (Central Statistics Office) (2013) 'Unemployment rate (SA), %', Cork: CSO (www.cso.ie/indicators/default.aspx?id=2LRM03).

Cumming, D.H.M., Cumming, C.L. and Redman, G.S. (2006) 'Scale mismatches in social-ecological systems: Causes, consequences, and solutions', *Ecology and Society*, vol 11, no 1, p 14.

Curtin, J. (1992) 'The Ministry of Women's Affairs. Where feminism and public policy meet', Unpublished Master's thesis, Hamilton: University of Waikato.

Curtin, J. (1999) 'New Zealand Initiatives to pay parents: Possibilities for the Antipodes?', *The Economic and Labour Relations Review*, vol 10, no 2, pp 188-202.

Curtin, J. (2008) 'Women, political leadership and substantive representation of women in New Zealand', *Parliamentary Affairs*, vol 61, no 3, pp 490-504.

Curtin, J. and Sawer, M. (1996) 'Gender equity and the shrinking state. Women and the great experiment', in F.G. Castles, R. Gerritsen and J. Vowles (eds) *The great experiment. Labour parties and public policy transformation in Australia and New Zealand*, Sydney: Allen & Unwin, pp 149-69.

Curtin, J. and Teghtsoonian, K. (2010) 'Analyzing institutional persistence: The case of the Ministry of Women's Affairs in Aotearoa/New Zealand', *Politics & Gender*, vol 6, no 4, pp 545-72.

d'Addio, A.C. and d'Ercole, M.M. (2005) *Trends and determinants of fertility rates in OECD countries: The role of policies*, OECD Social, Employment and Migration Working Papers No 27, Paris: Organisation for Economic Co-operation and Development.

Dagens Nyheter (DN): 21 October 1997; 8 December 1997; 9 December 1997; 22 January 1998; 17 March 1998; 14 April 2001; 19 August 2002.

Daley, D.M. (2007) 'Voluntary approaches to environmental problems: Exploring the rise of nontraditional public policy', *Policy Studies Journal*, vol 35, no 2, pp 165-79.

Daley, D.M. and Garand, J.C. (2005) 'Horizontal diffusion, vertical diffusion, and internal pressure in state environmental policymaking, 1989-1998', *American Politics Research,* vol 33, p 615.

Daly, M. (2005) 'Gender mainstreaming in theory and practice', *Social Politics*, vol 12, no 3, pp 433-50.

Davies, J.S. (2011) *Challenging governance theory: From networks to hegemony*, Bristol: Policy Press.

Davies, J., Weko, T., Kim, L. and Thulstrup, E. (2009) *OECD reviews of tertiary education. Finland*, Paris: Organisation for Economic Co-operation and Development.

Deacon, B. (2007) *Global social policy and governance*, London: Sage Publications.

Dekker, K.K., Völker, B., Lelieveldt, H. and Torenvlied, R. (2010) 'Civic engagement in urban neighborhoods: Does the network of civic organizations influence participation in neighborhood governance?', *Journal of Urban Affairs*, vol 32, no 5, pp 609-32.

Dekker, S. (2007) *Just culture: Balancing safety and accountability*, Aldershot: Ashgate.

Denham, A. and Garnett, M. (1999) 'Influence without responsibility? Think tanks in Britain', *Parliamentary Affairs*, pp 46-57.

Department of Climate Change (2009) *Climate change risks to Australia's coasts: A first pass national assessment*, Canberra: Department of Climate Change.

DfE (Department for Education) (2010) 'Michael Gove outlines process for setting up free schools' (www.education.gov.uk/inthenews/inthenews/a0061366/michael-gove-outlines-process-for-setting-up-free-schools).

DfE (2012) 'Teach First to recruit more top graduates' (www.education.gov.uk/inthenews/inthenews/a00217450/teach-first-to-recruit-more-top-graduate).

DH (Department of Health) (1999) *Primary care trusts: Establishing better services*, London: The Stationery Office.

DH (2004) *Practice-based commissioning: Engaging practices in commissioning*, London: DH.

DH (2005a) *Health reform in England: Update and commissioning framework*, Gateway ref 6865, London: DH.

DH (2005b) *Making practice-based commissioning a reality: Technical guidance*, Gateway ref 4356, London: DH.

Dimova, A., Rohova, M., Moutafova, E., Atanasova, E., Koeva, S., Panteli, D. and van Ginneken, E. (2012) 'Bulgaria: Health system review', *Health Systems in Transition*, vol 14, no 3, pp 1-186.

Downs, A. (1972) 'Up and down with ecology – the "issue-attention cycle"', *The Public Interest*, vol 28, pp 38-50.

Dudley, G. and Richardson, J. (1998) 'Arenas without rules and the policy change process: outsider groups and British roads policy', *Policy Studies*, vol XLVI, pp 727-47.

Dudley, G., Parsons, W., Radaelli, C. and Sabatier, P. (2000) 'Symposium: Theories of the policy process', *Journal of European Public Policy*, vol 7, no 1, pp 122-40.

Duell, N., Grubb, D., Singh, S. and Tergeist, P. (2010) *Activation policies in Japan*, OECD Social, Employment and Migration Working Papers, No 113, Paris: OECD Publishing.

Dunleavy, P. (1994) 'The globalization of public services provision: Can government be "best in world"?', *Public Policy and Administration*, vol 9, no 2, pp 36-64.

Dunleavy, P. (1995) 'Policy disasters: Explaining the UK's record', *Public Policy and Administration*, vol 10, no 2, pp 52-69.

Durant, R. and Diehl, P. (1989) 'Agendas, alternatives and public policy: Lessons from the US foreign policy arena', *Journal of Public Policy*, vol 9, no 2, pp 179-205.

Ebbinghaus, B. (2006) *Reforming early retirement in Europe, Japan and the USA*, Oxford: Oxford University Press.

Eckerberg, K. (1998) 'Managing uncommon grounds: Swedish forestry policy and environmental sustainability', in A. Sandberg and S. Sörlin (eds) *Sustainability – The challenge: People, power and the environment,* Montreal: Black Rose Books, pp 90-8.

Eckerberg, K. (2000) 'Sweden: Progression despite recession', in W.M. Lafferty and J. Meadowcroft (eds) *Implementing sustainable development: Strategies and initiatives in high consumption societies*, Oxford: Oxford University Press, pp 209-45.

Edelenbos, J. and Klijn, E.-H. (2006) 'Managing stakeholder involvement in decision making: A comparative analysis of six interactive processes in the Netherlands', *Journal of Public Administration Research and Theory*, vol 16, no 3, pp 417-46.

Edelman, M. (1971) *Politics as symbolic action*, Chicago, IL: Markham.

Edelman, M. (1977) *Political language: Words that succeed and policies that fail*, New York: Institute for the Study of Poverty.

Edelman, M. (1984) *The symbolic uses of politics*, Urbana, IL: University of Illinois Press.

Edelman, M. (1991) *Pièces et règles du jeu politique*, Paris: Seuil.

Eden, S. and Tunstall, S. (2006) 'Ecological versus social restoration? How urban river restoration challenges but also fails to challenge the science-policy nexus in the United Kingdom', *Environment and Planning C: Government Policy*, vol 24, pp 661-80.

Emerson, K., Nabatchi, T. and Balogh, S. (2011) 'An integrative framework for collaborative governance', *Journal of Public Administration Research*, vol 22, pp 1-29.

Erikson, R., Wright, G. and McIver, J. (1994) *Statehouse democracy: Public opinion and policy in the American states*, Cambridge: Cambridge University Press.

Esping-Andersen, G. (1985) *Politics against markets: The social democratic road to power*, Princeton, NJ: Princeton University Press.

Esping-Andersen, G. (1990) *The three worlds of welfare capitalism*, Cambridge: Polity Press.

EU (European Union) (2011) *Our life insurance, our natural capital: An EU biodiversity strategy to 2020*, Brussels: European Commission.

EU (European Union) and IMF (International Monetary Fund) (2010) *Programme of financial support for Ireland*, 16 December, Dublin: Department of Finance.

Evaluation of the Finnish National Innovation System (2009) *Evaluation of the Finnish National Innovation System: Full report*, Helsinki: Ministry of Education and Ministry of Employment and the Economy.

Evans, P.B., Rueschemeyer, D. and Skocpol, T. (1985) *Bringing the state back in*, Cambridge: Cambridge University Press.

Evans, R.J., Jr (1991) 'The puzzle of early retirement and permanent layoffs in Japanese labor markets', *Journal of Asian Economics*, vol 2, no 2, pp 301-7.

Evans, R.J. (1997) *In defence of history*, London: Granta.

Exley, S. (2012) 'The politics of educational policy making under New Labour: an illustration of shifts in public service governance', *Policy & Politics*, vol 40, no 2, pp 227-44.

Exworthy, M. and Frosini, F. (2008) 'Room for manoeuvre? Explaining local autonomy in the English National Health Service', *Health Policy*, vol 86, pp 204-12.

Feng, Y. (1997) *Childcare services: Analysis from the ecological perspective* (2nd edn), Taipei: Chuliu. [in Chinese]

Fielding, K., Head, B., Laffan, W., Western, M. and Hoegh-Guldberg, O. (2012) 'Australian politicians' beliefs about climate change: political partisanship and political ideology', *Environmental Politics*, vol 21, no 5, pp 712-33.

Finkel, A. (1993) 'Paradise postponed: a re-examination of the Green Book proposals of 1945', *Journal of the Canadian Historical Association*, vol 4, pp 120-42.

Fitoussi, J.P. and Saraceno, F. (2012) *European economic governance: The Berlin-Washington consensus*, Paris: Observatoire Française des Conjonctures Economiques.

Fleckenstein, T. and Lee, S.C. (2012) 'The politics of postindustrial social policy: Family policy reforms in Britain, Germany, South Korea, and Sweden', *Comparative Political Studies*, Online ISSN 0010-4140.

Folke, C. et al (1998) *The problem of fit between ecosystems and institutions*, IHDP working papers, International Human Dimensions Programme on Global Environmental Change 12:30, Bonn: International Human Dimension Programme (IHDP).

Forster, K., Vasardani, M. and Ca' Zorzi, M. (2011) *Euro area cross-border financial flows and the global financial crisis*, Occasional Paper Series, no 126, Frankfurt am Main: ECB.

Frankham, J. (2006) 'Network utopias and alternative entanglements for educational research and practice', *Journal of Education Policy*, vol 21, no 6, pp 661-77.

Frederickson, H.G. and Smith, K.B. (2003) *The public administration theory primer*, Boulder, CO: Westview Press.

Friend, J.K., Power, J.M. and Yewlett, C.J.L. (1974) *Public planning: The inter-corporate dimension*, London: Tavistock.

Fu, L.-Y. (1995) 'Constructing the welfare state of women', in Y.-H. Liu (ed) *White Paper on Taiwanese women's situation*, Taipei: *China Times*. [in Chinese]

Garnaut, R. (2008) 'The implications of the financial crisis for climate change mitigation', Comments made at the launch of the Garnaut Report, 16 October, Melbourne.

Gillan, E. and Macnaughton, P. (2007) *Alcohol: Price, policy and public health*, Edinburgh: Scottish Health Action on Alcohol Problems.

Glennerster, H., Matsaganis, M., Owens, P. and Hancock, S. (1994) *Implementing GP fundholding: Wild card or winning hand?*, Buckingham: Open University Press

Godschalk, D.R., Brody, S. and Burby, R. (2003) 'Public participation in natural hazard mitigation policy formation: challenges for comprehensive planning', *Journal of Environmental Planning and Management*, vol 46, no 5, pp 733-54.

Godschalk, D.R., Beatley, T., Berke, P., Brower, D.J. and Kaiser, E.J. (1999) *Natural hazard mitigation: Recasting disaster policy and planning*, Washington, DC: Island Press.

Goggin, M.L., Bowman, A.O'M., Lester, J.P. and O'Toole, L.J., Jr (1990) *Implementation theory and practice: Toward a third generation*, Glenview, IL: Scott Foresman/Little, Brown.

Gordon, A. (1985) *The evolution of labor relations in Japan: Heavy industry 1853-1955*, Cambridge, MA: Harvard University Press.

Government of Ireland (2010) *The national recovery plan 2011-2014*, Dublin: Stationery Office.

Gray, V. (1974) 'Innovation in the states: A diffusion study', *American Political Science Review*, vol 18, no 4, p 693.

Green-Pedersen, C. and Wilkerson, J. (2006) 'How agenda-setting attributes shapes politics: basic dilemmas, problem attention and health politics developments in Denmark and the US', *Journal of European Public Policy*, vol 36, no 7, pp 1039-52.

Greenwood, J. and Wilson, D. (1990) *Public administration in Britain today*, London: Unwin Hyman.

Greer, S.L. (2009) *The politics of European Union health policies*, Buckingham: Open University Press.

Grenda, Y. and Rebick, M.E. (2000) 'Japanese Labour in the 1990s: Stability and stagnation', *Oxford Review of Economic Policy*, vol 16, no 2, pp 85-102.

Griffith, R. and Leicester, A. (2010) *The impact of introducing a minimum price on alcohol in Britain*, London: Institute for Fiscal Studies.

Gunderson, L.H. and Holling, C.S. (2002) *Panarchy. Understanding transformations in human and natural systems*, Washington, DC: Island Press.

Gusfield, J.R. (1984) *The culture of public problems: Drinking-driving and the symbolic order*, Chicago, IL: University of Chicago Press

Haas, E. (2007) 'False equivalency: think tank references on education in the news media', *Peabody Journal of Education*, vol 81, no 1, pp 63-102.

Habermas, J. (1970) *A rational society: Student protest, science and politics*, Boston, MA: Beacon Books.

Hacker, J.S. (1997) *The road to nowhere: The genesis of President Clinton's plan for health security*, Princeton, NJ: Princeton University Press.

Haddow, G.D., Bullock, J.A. and Coppola, D.P. (2008) *Introduction to emergency management* (2nd edn), New York: Butterworth-Heinemann.

Hajer, M. (2003) 'Policy without polity? Policy analysis and the institutional void', *Policy Sciences*, vol 36, no 2, pp 175-95.

Hajer, M.A. (2005) 'Rebuilding Ground Zero. The politics of performance', *Planning Theory and Practice*, vol 6, no 4, pp 445-64.

Hall, P.A. (1986) *Governing the economy: The politics of state intervention in Britain and France*, Cambridge: Polity Press.

Hall, P.A. (1993) 'Policy paradigms, social learning and the state: The case of economic policymaking in Britain', *Comparative Politics*, vol 25, no 3, pp 275-96.

Hall, P.A. and Soskice, D. (2001) *Varieties of capitalism: The institutional foundations of comparative advantage*, Oxford: Oxford University Press.

Hartlapp, M. and Kemmerling, A. (2008) 'When a solution becomes the problem: the causes of policy reversal on early exit from the labour force', *Journal of European Social Policy*, vol 18, no 4, pp 366-79.

Harvey, D. (2011) *The enigma of capital and the crisis of capitalism*, London: Profile Books.

Hay, C. (2002) *Political analysis: A critical introduction*, Basingstoke: Palgrave.

Hay, C. and Rosamond, B. (2002) 'Globalization, European integration and the discursive construction of economic imperatives', *Journal of European Public Policy*, vol 9, no 2, pp 147-67.

Health and Sport Committee (2012) *2nd report, 2012 (Session 4): Stage 1: Report on the Alcohol (Minimum Pricing) (Scotland) Bill*, Edinburgh: Scottish Parliament.

Helm, T. (2013) 'Michael Gove's officials act to clean up abusive @toryeducation Twitter feed', *The Observer*, 16 February.

Hemerijck, A. (2012a) 'Two or three waves of welfare state transformation?', in N. Morel, B. Palier, and J. Palme (eds) *Towards a social investment welfare state?*, Bristol: Policy Press, pp 33-60.

Hemerijck, A. (2012b) 'Stress-testing the new welfare state', in G. Bonoli and D. Natali (eds) *The politics of the new welfare state*, Oxford: Oxford University Press, pp 68-90.

Hervé, M. (1999) *Intercommunalité et gouvernements locaux: l'exemple des départements de l'Ouest de la France*, Paris: L'Harmattan, coll. Logique politiques.

Hezri, A.A. and Dovers, S.R. (2006) 'Sustainability indicators, policy and governance: issues for ecological economics', *Ecological Economics*, vol 60, no 1, pp 86-99.

Hill, C.J. and Lynn, L.E. (2005) 'Is hierachical governance in decline? Evidence from empirical research', *Journal of Public Administration Research and Theory*, vol 15, pp 173-95.

Hill, M. (2013) *The public policy process* (6th edn), Harlow: Pearson.

Hill, M. and Hupe, P. (2006) 'Analysing policy processes as multiple governance: accountability in social policy', *Policy & Politics*, vol 34, no 3, pp 557-73.

Hill, M. and Hupe, P. (2009) *Implementing public policy* (2nd edn), London: Sage Publications.

Holden, C. et al (2012) 'Cleavages and co-operation in the UK alcohol industry: A qualitative study', *BMC Public Health*, vol 12, no 1, p 483.

Holloway, S.L. et al (2008) '"Sainsbury's is my local": English alcohol policy, domestic drinking practices and the meaning of home', *Transactions of the Institute of British Geographers*, vol 33, no 4, pp 532-47.

Holmberg, S. and Hedberg P. (2011) *The will of the people? Swedish nuclear power policy*, Report 2011:6, Swedish National Elections Studies Program, Gothenburg: Department of Political Science, University of Gothenburg (www.valforskning. pol.gu.se/digitalAssets/1359/1359177_the-will-of-the-people---2011-6-.pdf).

Höltta, S. (1988) 'Recent changes in the Finnish higher education system', *European Journal of Education*, vol 23, no 1/2, pp 91-103.

Höltta, S. and Rekilä, E. (2003) 'Ministerial steering and institutional responses: Recent developments of the Finnish higher education system', *Higher Education Management and Policy*, vol 15, no 1, pp 73-92.

Holzinger, K. and Knill, C. (2005) 'Causes and conditions of cross-national policy convergence', *Journal of European Public Policy*, vol 12, no 5, pp 775-96.

Honohan, P. (2009) 'Resolving Ireland's banking crisis', *The Economic and Social Review*, vol 40 no 2, pp 207-31.

Honohan, P. (2010) *The Irish banking crisis regulatory and financial stability policy, 2003-2008: A report to the Minister for Finance by the Governor of the Central Bank*, Dublin: Central Bank.

Hood, C. (1986) *The tools of government*, Chatham, NJ: Chatham House.

Hood, C. (1994) *Explaining economic policy reversals*, Buckingham: Open University Press.

Hood, C. (2007) 'Intellectual obsolescence and intellectual makeovers: Reflections on the tools of government after two decades', *Governance*, vol 20, no 1, pp 127-44.

House of Commons Health Committee (2009) *Alcohol: First report of session 2009-10, Volume 1*, London: House of Commons.

House of Lords Select Committee on the Constitution (2002) *Devolution: Inter-institutional relations in the United Kingdom – 15th report of session*, London: House of Lords.

Houses of the Oireachtas Committee of Public Accounts (2012) *Report on the crisis in the domestic banking sector: A preliminary analysis and a framework for a banking inquiry*, Dublin: Stationery Office.

Howlett, M. (1991) 'Policy instruments, policy styles and policy implementation: National approaches to theories of instrument choice', *Policy Studies Journal*, vol 19, no 2, pp 1–21.

Howlett, M. (2000) 'Managing the "hollow state": procedural policy instruments and modern governance', *Canadian Public Administration*, vol 43, no 4, pp 412-31.

Howlett, M. and Cashore, B. (2009) 'The dependent variable problem in the study of policy change: Understanding policy change as a methodological problem', *Journal of Comparative Policy Analysis*, vol 11, no 1, pp 33-46.

Howlett, M. and Ramesh M. (1995) *Studying public policy: Policy cycles and policy subsystems* (2nd edn), Toronto: Oxford University Press.

Howlett, M., Ramesh, M. and Perl, A. (2009) *Studying public policy* (3rd edn), Don Mills, ON: Oxford University Press.

Hudson, J. and Lowe, S. (2009) *Understanding the policy process*, Bristol: Policy Press.

Hull, R.B. and Robertson, D.P. (2000) 'The language of nature matters: We need a more public ecology', in P.H. Gobster and R.B. Hull (eds) *Restoring nature: Perspectives from the social sciences and humanities*, Washington, DC: Island Press, pp 97-118.

Hulme, M. (2009) *Why we disagree about climate change: Understanding controversy, inaction and opportunity*, Cambridge: Cambridge University Press.

ICTU (Irish Congress of Trade Unions) (2009) 'Read Paul Sweeney's response to the crisis', 31 January (www.ictu.ie/press/2009/01/31/read-paul-sweeneys-response-to-the-crisis).

IMF (International Monetary Foundation) (2006) *Ireland: Financial system stability assessment update*, IMF Country Report no 06/292, Washington: IMF.

IMF (2012a) *Ireland: Sixth review under the extended arrangement*, Washington: IMF.

IMF (2012b) *World economic outlook database*, April (www.imf.org/external/pubs/ft/weo/2012/01/weodata/index.aspx).

Jenkins, W.I. (1978) *Policy analysis*, London: Martin Robertson.

Jenkins-Smith, H.C. (1988) 'Analytical debates and policy learning: analysis and change in the federal bureaucracy', *Policy Sciences*, vol 21, pp 169-211.

Jessop, R.D. (2002) *The future of the capitalist state*, Cambridge: Polity Press.

Johansson, R. and Borell, K. (1999) 'Central steering and local networks: old-age care in Sweden', *Public Administration*, vol 77, no 3, pp 585–98.

John, P. (1998/2012) *Analysing public policy*, London: Routledge.

Johnson, A.W. (2004) *Dream no little dreams: A biography of the Douglas government of Saskatchewan, 1944-1961*, Toronto: University of Toronto Press.

Jones, B.D and Baumgartner, F.R. (2005) *The politics of attention: How government prioritizes problems*, Chicago, IL: University of Chicago Press.

Jones, B.D., Sulkin, T. and Larsen, H. (2003) 'Policy punctuations in US political institutions', *American Political Science Review*, vol 91, no 1, pp 151-69.

Jones, C.O. (1970) *An introduction to the study of public policy*, Belmont, CA: Wadsworth.

Jordan, A.G. and Richardson, J.J. (1987) *British politics and the policy process*, London: Unwin Hyman.

Jordan, A.G., Wurzel, R.K.W. and Zito, A. (2005) 'The rise of "new" policy instruments in comparative perspective: Has governance eclipsed government?', *Political Studies*, vol 53, no 3, pp 477-96.

Jordan, A.G., Wurzel, R.K.W. and Zito, A.R. (2013) 'Still the century of "new" environmental policy instruments? Exploring patterns of innovation and continuity', *Environmental Politics*, vol 22, no 1, pp 155-73.

Kajitani, S. (2006) 'Japan's reemployment system and work incentives for the elderly', *Osaka Economic Papers*, vol 56, no 3, pp 51-65.

Karch, A. (2007) *Democratic laboratories: Policy diffusion among the American states*, Ann Arbor, MI: The University of Michigan Press.

Katikireddi, S.V. and McLean, J.A. (2012) 'Introducing a minimum unit price for alcohol in Scotland: considerations under European Law and the implications for European public health', *European Journal of Public Health*, vol 22, no 4, pp 457-8.

Katikireddi, S.V., Hilton, S,. Bonell, C. and Bond, L. (forthcoming) *Understanding the development of minimum unit pricing of alcohol in Scotland: A qualitative study of the policy process*.

Kato, J. and Rothstein, B. (2006) 'Government partisanship and managing the economy: Japan and Sweden in comparative perspective', *Governance*, vol 19, no 1, pp 75-97.

Katz, E. (2000) 'Another look at restoration: Technology and artificial nature', in P.H. Gobster and R.B. Hull (eds) *Restoring nature: Perspectives from the social sciences and humanities*, Washington, DC: Island Press, pp 37-48.

Kelly, M. (2009) *The Irish credit bubble*, UCD Centre for Economic Research Working Paper Series WP09/32, Dublin: UCD Centre for Economic Research.

Kent, T. (1988) *A public purpose: An experience of Liberal opposition and Canadian government*, Montreal and Kingston: McGill-Queen's University Press.

Kickert, W.J.M., Klijn, E.H. and Koppenjan, J.F.M. (eds) (1997) *Managing complex networks: Strategies for the public sector*, London: Sage Publications.

Kim, S.-K. et al (2004) *The 2003 National Survey on Fertility, Family Health and Welfare in Korea*, Report No 2004-23, Seoul: Korea Institute of Health and Social Affairs.

Kim, S.-K. et al (2009) *The 2009 National Survey on Fertility, Family Health and Welfare in Korea*, Report No 2009-33, Seoul: Korea Institute of Health and Social Affairs.

Kim, S.-S. (2009) 'Low fertility and policy responses in Korea', *The Japanese Journal of Population*, vol 7, no 1, pp 57-70.

Kincaid, J. (1990) 'From cooperative to coercive federalism', *Annals of the American Academy of Political and Social Science*, vol 509, pp 139-52.

King, D.S. (1995) *Actively seeking work? The politics of unemployment and welfare policy in the United States and Great Britain*, Chicago, IL: University of Chicago Press.

Kingdon, J.W. (2010) *Agendas, alternatives and public policies* (3rd edn), New York: Addison, Wesley, Longman.

Kirby, P. (2010) 'Lessons from the Irish collapse: Taking an international political economy approach', *Irish Studies in International Affairs*, vol 21, pp 43-55.

Kirby, P. and Thorhallsson, B. (2011) *Financial crises in Iceland and Ireland: Does EU and Euro membership matter?*, Working Paper, Dublin/Reykjavik: TASC/Centre for Small State Studies at the University of Iceland.

Kitchin, R., O'Callaghan, M., Boyle, M., Gleeson, J. and Keaveney, K. (2012) 'Placing neoliberalism: the rise and fall of Ireland's Celtic tiger', *Environment and Planning A*, vol 44, pp 1302-26.

Knill, C. and Tosun, J. (2012) *Public policy: A new introduction*, Basingstoke: Palgrave Macmillan.

Knoepfel, P. and Larrue, C. (1985) 'Distribution spatiale et mise en oeuvre d'une politique publique: le cas de la pollution atmosphérique', *Politiques et management public*, vol 3, no 2, pp 43-69.

Knoepfel, P. and Weidner, H. (1982) 'Formulation and implementation of air quality control programmes. Patterns of interest consideration', *Policy & Politics*, vol 10, no 1, pp 85-109.

Knoepfel, P., Larrue, C., Varone, F. and Hill, M. (2007) *Public policy analysis*, Bristol: Policy Press.

KNSO (Korean National Statistical Office) (2005) *Social indicators in Korea – 2005*, Seoul: KNSO.

KNSO (2010) *Population projections for Korea: 2010-2060*, Seoul: KNSO.

Kodate, N. (2012) 'Events, politics and patterns of policy-making: Impact of major incidents on health sector regulatory reforms in the UK and Japan', *Social Policy & Administration*, vol 46, no 3, pp 280-301.

Kondo, J. (2005) 'The iron triangle of Japan's health care: The Japan Medical Association is losing its grip on healthcare policy', *British Medical Journal*, vol 330, pp 55-6.

Kooiman, J. (1999) 'Social-political governance: Overview, reflections and design', *Public Management*, vol 1, no 1, pp 67–92.

Koppenjan, J. and Klijn, E.-H. (2004) *Managing uncertainties in networks*, London: Routledge.

Krizsán, A. and Zentai, A. (2006) 'Gender equality policy or gender mainstreaming?', *Policy Studies*, vol 27, no 2, pp 135-51.

Kronsell, A. and Bäckstrand, K. (2010) 'Rationalities and forms of governance: a framework for analyzing the legitimacy of new modes of governance', in K. Bäckstrand (eds) *Environmental politics and deliberative democracy*, Cheltenham: Edward Elgar, pp 1-22.

Krugman, P. (2010) 'Japanese demography', *The New York Times*, 8 September (http://krugman.blogs.nytimes.com/2010/09/08/japanese-demography).

Kwon, T.-H. (2001) 'The National Family Planning Program and fertility transition in South Korea', in A. Mason (ed) *Population policies and programs in East Asia*, East-West Centre Occasional Papers, Population and Health Series, No 123, July, Honolulu: East-West Centre, pp 39-64.

Laeven, L. and Valencia, F. (2012) *Systemic banking crises database: An update*, IMF Working Paper WP/ 12/163, Washington: International Monetary Foundation.

Lafferty, W. and Meadowcroft, J. (2000) *Implementing sustainable development: Strategies and initiatives in high-consumption societies*, Oxford and New York: Oxford University Press.

Lane, J.-E. and Ersson, S.O. (2000) *The new institutional politics: Performance and outcomes*, London: Routledge.

Lane, P. (2010) *European monetary union and macroeconomic stabilisation policies in Ireland*, Dublin: National Economic & Social Council.

Larrue, C. (2000) *Analyser les politiques d'environnement*, Paris: L'Harmattan.

Larsson, T. (1994) 'Cabinet ministers and parliamentary governing in Sweden', in M. Laver and K.A. Shepsle (eds) *Cabinet ministers and parliamentary government*, Cambridge: Cambridge University Press, pp 169-86.

Lascoumes, P. (1994) *L'éco-pouvoir*, Paris: Edition La Découverte.

Ledoux B. (2005) *La gestion du risque inondation*, Paris: Lavoisier Tec & Doc.

Lee, G.-Y., Nam, J.-R., Park, H. and Kim, E. (2004) *The actual utilisation of the parental leave scheme and policy tasks*, Seoul: Korea Labour Institute. [in Korean]

Leflar, R.B. (2009) '"Unnatural death", criminal sanctions, and medical quality improvement in Japan', *Yale Journal of Health Policy Law and Ethics*, vol 1, pp 1-51.

Leon, D.A. and McCambridge, J. (2006) 'Liver cirrhosis mortality rates in Britain from 1950 to 2002: an analysis of routine data', *The Lancet*, vol 367, no 9504, pp 52-6.

Levin, S.A. (2000) 'Multiple scales and the maintenance of biodiversity', *Ecosystems*, vol 3, pp 498-506.

Levitt, R. and Solesbury, W. (2012) *Policy tsars: Here to stay but more transparency needed*, London: King's College London.

Lewis, J. (2009) 'Introduction', in J. Lewis (ed) *Work–family balance, gender and policy*, Cheltenham: Edward Elgar, pp 1-22.

Light, A. and Higgs, E.S. (1996) 'The politics of ecological restoration', *Environmental Ethics*, vol 18, no 3, pp 227-47.

Lijphart, A. (1999) *Patterns of democracy*, New Haven, CT: Yale University Press.

Lin, W.-I. (1995) 'The perspective of Kuomintang on social welfare', in W.-I. Lin (ed) *Social welfare in Taiwan: Perspective from the civil society*, Taipei: Wu-Nan. [in Chinese]

Lin, W.-I. (2006) *Social welfare in Taiwan: Historical experiences and institutional analysis*, Taipei: Wu-Nan. [in Chinese]

Lindblom, C.E. (1959) 'The science of "muddling through"', *Public Administration Review*, vol 19, pp 78-88.

Linder, S. and Peters, B.G. (1989) 'Instruments of government: Perceptions and contexts', *Journal of Public Policy*, vol 9, no 1, pp 35-58.

Linder, S.H. and Peters, B.G. (1991) 'The logic of public policy design: Linking policy actors and plausible instruments', *Knowledge in Society*, vol 4, pp 15-51.

Lipset, S.M. (1950) *Agrarian socialism*, Berkeley, CA: University of California Press.

Lipsky, M. (1980) *Street-level bureaucracy*, New York: Russell Sage.

Lodge, M. (2002) 'Regulatory failure and the railways in Britain and Germany', *Journal of Public Policy*, vol 22, pp 271-97.

Lowi, T.A. (1972) 'Four systems of policy, politics and choice', *Public Administration Review*, vol 32, pp 298-310.

Lucarelli, B. (2012) 'Financialization and global imbalances: prelude to crisis', *Review of Radical Political Economics*, vol 44, no 4, pp 429-47.

MacDougall, H. (2012) 'Into thin air: making national health policy, 1939-45', in G.P. Marchildon (ed) *Making Medicare: New perspectives on the history of Medicare in Canada*, Toronto: University of Toronto Press, pp 41-70.

McCallum, J. (1993) *Women in the house: Members of Parliament in New Zealand*, Picton: Cape Catley.

McCreath, G. (2011) *The politics of blindness: From charity to parity*, Vancouver: Granville Island Publishing.

McCrone, D. (1991) '"Excessive and unreasonable": the politics of the poll tax in Scotland', *International Journal of Urban and Regional Research*, vol 15, no 3, pp 443-52.

McCrone, D. (2006) 'Scotland and England: Diverging political discourses', in I.Z. Denes (ed) *Liberty and the search for identity: Liberal nationalisms and the legacy of empires*, Hungary: Central European University Press, pp 21-36.

McDonough, T. and Dundon, T. (2010) 'Thatcherism delayed? The Irish crisis and the paradox of social partnership', *Industrial Relations Journal*, vol 41, issue 6, pp 544-62.

McLeod, T. and McLeod, I. (2004) 'T.C. Douglas', in G. Barnhart (ed) *Saskatchewan premiers of the twentieth century*, Regina: Canadian Plains Research Center, pp 161-212.

Mahony, P., Menter, I. and Hextall, I. (2004) 'Building dams in Jordan, assessing teachers in England: A case study in edu-business', *Globalisation, Societies and Education*, vol 2, pp 277-96.

Maioni, A. (1998) *Parting at the crossroads: The emergence of health insurance in the United States and Canada*, Princeton, NJ: Princeton University Press.

Makela, K. and Room, R. (2000) 'Typologies of the cultural position of drinking', *Journal of Studies on Alcohol*, vol 61, p 475.

Mannion, R. (2005) *Practice-based commissioning: A summary of the evidence*, Health Policy Issue 11, York: University of York.

Marchildon, G.P. (2005) *Health systems in transition: Canada*, Copenhagen: WHO Regional Office for Europe on behalf of the European Observatory on Health Systems and Policies.

Marchildon, G.P. (2007) 'Royal commissions and the policy cycle in Canada: the case of health care', in H.J. Michelmann, D.C. Story and J.S. Steeves (eds) *Political leadership and representation in Canada: Essays in honour of John C. Courtney*, Toronto: University of Toronto Press, pp 110-32.

Marchildon, G.P. (2012) 'Canadian Medicare: why history matters', in G.P. Marchildon (ed) *Making Medicare: New perspectives on the history of Medicare in Canada*, Toronto: University of Toronto Press, pp 3-18.

Marchildon, G.P. and O'Byrne, N. (2012) 'From Bennettcare to Medicare: the morphing of medical care insurance in British Columbia', in G.P. Marchildon (ed) *Making Medicare: New perspectives on the history of Medicare in Canada*, Toronto: University of Toronto Press, pp 207-28.

Marchildon, G.P. and Scrijvers, K. (2011) 'Physician resistance and the forging of public health care: a comparative analysis of the doctors' strikes in Canada and Belgium in the 1960s', *Medical History*, vol 44, no 2, pp 203-22.

Marks, L. and Hunter, D.J. (2005) *Practice-based commissioning policy into practice*, Durham: Centre for Public Policy and Health, Durham University (www.dur.ac.uk/resources/public.health/publications/PBCFeedbackReport.pdf).

Marsh, D. and Rhodes, R.A.W. (1992a) *Policy networks in British government*, Oxford: Oxford University Press.

Marsh, D. and Rhodes, R.A.W. (eds) (1992b) *Implementing Thatcherite policies: Audit of an era*, Buckingham: Open University Press.

Marshall, E. (2005) 'Is the friendly atom poised for a comeback?', *Science*, vol 309, no 5738, pp 1168-9.

Martinsen, D.S. (2007) *EU for the patients. Developments, impacts, challenges*, SIEPS report, no 6 (www.sieps.se/sem/2007/sem_0615/sem_0615_en.html).

Martinsen, D.S. (2009) 'Conflict and conflict management in the cross-border provision of healthcare services', *West European Politics*, vol 32, no 4, pp 792-809.

Martinsen, D.S. and Falkner, G. (2011) 'Social policy: Problem solving gaps, partial exits and court-decision traps', in G. Falkner (ed) *The EU's decision traps. Comparing policies*, Oxford: Oxford University Press, pp 128-45.

Martinsen, D.S. and Vrangbaek, K. (2008) 'The Europeanization of health care governance: implementing the market imperatives of Europe', *Public Administration*, vol 86, no 1, pp 169-84.

Matland, R.E. (1995) 'Synthesizing the implementation literature: The ambiguity-conflict model of policy implementation', *Journal of Public Administration Research and Theory*, vol 5, no 2, pp 145-74.

Mavrogordatos, G.G. and Hatziiosif, C. (eds) (1992) *Venizelism and urban modernization* (2nd edn), Iraklion: University Press of Crete.

May, P.J. and Deyle, R.E. (1998) 'Governing land use in hazardous areas with a patchwork system', in R.J. Burby (ed) *Cooperating with nature: Confronting natural hazards with land-use planning for sustainable communities*, Washington, DC: Joseph Henry Press, pp 57-82.

May, P.J. and Winter, S.C. (2009) 'Politicians, managers, and street-level bureaucrats: Influences on policy implementation', *Journal of Public Administration Research and Theory*, vol 19, pp 453–76.

Meadowcroft, J. (2002) 'Politics and scale: Some implications for environmental governance', *Landscape and Urban* Planning, vol 61, no 2-4, pp 169–79.

MEC (Ministry of Education and Culture) (2012) *Education and research 2011-2016. Development plan*, Reports of the Ministry of Education and Culture 3, Helsinki.

Meier, K.J. and O'Toole, L.J. (2006) 'Political control versus bureaucratic values: Reframing the debate', *Public Administration Review*, vol 66, pp 177–92.

Meier, P. and Celis, K. (2011) 'Sowing the seeds of its own failure: Implementing the concept of gender mainstreaming', *Social Politics*, vol 18, no 4, pp 469–89.

Mendelson, M., Battle, K., Torjman, S. and Lightman, E. (2010) *A basic income plan for Canadians with severe disabilities*, Ottawa: Caledon Institute of Social Policy.

Michel, S. and Peng, I. (2012) 'All in the family? Migrants, nationhood, and care regimes in Asia and North America', *Journal of European Social Policy*, vol 22, no 4, pp 406–18.

Mineur, E. (2007) 'Towards sustainable development: Indicators as a tool of local governance', PhD dissertation, Department of Political Science, Umeå: Umeå University.

Ministerial Committee on Education and Culture (2010) *Strengthening the quality and effectiveness of higher education institutions – The statement of the Ministerial Committee on speeding up the structural development of higher education institutions.* [in Finnish]

Ministry of Education (Finland) (2007) *Education and research 2007-2012. Development plan*, Helsinki: Ministry of Education.

Ministry of Education (Finland) (2008) *The guidelines for structural development of higher education institutions for 2008-2011*, Helsinki: Ministry of Education. [in Finnish]

Ministry of Education (Taiwan) (2007) *Early childhood education and the childcare friendly experimental programme*, Taipei: Ministry of Education. [in Chinese]

Ministry of Education (Taiwan) (2013) *Statistics of school, teachers, staff, class, and graduates between 1950 and 2010* (www.edu.tw/statistics/content.aspx?site_content_sn=8869). [in Chinese]

Ministry of Health, Labour and Welfare (Japan) (2005) *Report on the future patient safety measures* (www.mhlw.go.jp/topics/bukyoku/isei/i-anzen/3/kongo/02.html). [in Japanese]

Ministry of Health, Labour and Welfare (Japan) (2005) *White Paper on ageing society*, Tokyo: Office of Government Public Relations.

Ministry of Health, Labour and Welfare (Japan) (2008) *Survey on medical institutions*, Tokyo: Kyoku.

Ministry of Health, Labour and Welfare (Japan) (2011) *Employment situation of older workers*, Tokyo: Office of Government Public Relations.

Ministry of the Environment (Sweden) (2009) *Nuclear power: New reactors and increased liability*, Public inquiry, SOU 2009:88. [in Swedish]

Ministry of the Interior (Taiwan) (2006) *The implementation programme of community day care centre subsidies*, Taipei: Ministry of the Interior. [in Chinese]

Ministry of the Interior (Taiwan) (2008) *Population policy White Paper: Strategies towards declining fertility, ageing population, and immigration problems*, Taipei: Ministry of the Interior. [in Chinese]

Mintrom, M. (1997) 'Policy entrepreneurs and the diffusion of innovation', *American Journal of Political Science*, vol 41, no 3, pp 738-70.

Mintrom, M. and Vergari, S. (1998) 'Policy networks and innovation diffusion: The case of state education reforms', *The Journal of Politics*, vol 60, no 1, pp 126-48.

Mooney, C.Z. (1991) 'Information sources in legislative decision making', *Legislative Studies Quarterly*, vol 16, no 3, pp 445-55.

Mooney, G. and Blackwell, S. (2004) 'Whose health service is it anyway? Community values in healthcare', *Medical Journal of Australia*, vol 180, no 2, pp 76-8.

Morel, N., Palier, B. and Palme, J. (eds) (2012) *Towards a social investment welfare state?*, Bristol: Policy Press.

Moriguchi, C. and Ono, H. (2006) 'Japanese lifetime employment: A century's perspective', in M. Blomstrom and S. La Croix (eds) *Institutional change in Japan*, New York: Routledge, pp 152-76.

Moses, J.W. (2012) 'Introduction: small states and the global economic crisis', *European Political Science* (www.svt.ntnu.no/iss/Jonathon.Moses/Personal/small%20states%20eps2012.pdf).

Mosk, C. (2008) *Japanese economic development: Markets, norms, structures*, New York: Routledge.

Mosley, J.E. and Grogan, C.M. (2013) 'Representation in nonelected participatory processes: How residents understand the role of nonprofit community-based organizations', *Journal of Public Administration Research and Theory*, vol 23, no 4, pp 839-63.

Mossialos, E., McKee, M., Palm, W., Beatrix, K. and Marhold, F. (2001) *The influence of EU law on the social character of health care systems in the European Union*, Report submitted to the Belgian Presidency of the European Union (Brussels), Brussels: European Union.

Mulgan, G. (2006) 'Thinking in tanks: The changing ecology of political ideas', *Political Quarterly*, vol 77, no 2, pp 147-55.

Mullen, J., Vladi, N. and Mills, A.J. (2006) 'Making sense of the Walkerton crisis', *Culture and Organization*, vol 12, no 3, p 207.

Muller, P. and Jobert, B. (1987) *L'État en action. Politiques publiques et corporatismes*, Paris: PUF.

MWA (Ministry of Women's Affairs) (New Zealand) (1986) *Report of the Ministry of Women's Affairs for the year ended 31 March 1986*, Wellington: MWA.

MWA (1996) *The full picture: Guidelines for gender analysis*, Wellington: MWA.

MWA (2002) *Key questions for gender analysis*, Wellington: MWA (www.dpmc.govt.nz/sites/all/files/circulars/coc_02_2.pdf).

MWA (2004) *Action plan for New Zealand women*, Wellington: MWA.

MWA (2010) *Briefing to the incoming Minister of Women's Affairs*, December 2010, Wellington: MWA (http://mwa.govt.nz/sites/mwa.govt.nz/files/bim-2010-pdf.pdf).

MWA (2011) *Ministry of Women's Affairs annual report. For the year ended 30 June 2011*, Wellington: MWA.

MWA (2012) *Ministry of Women's Affairs annual report. For the year ended 30 June 2012*, Wellington: MWA.

Nagamatsu, S., Kami, M. and Nakata, Y. (2009) 'Healthcare safety committee in Japan: mandatory accountability reporting system and punishment', *Current opinion in anaesthesiology*, vol 22, pp 199-206.

National Board of Health and Welfare (2002) *National action plan for care of the elderly: Final report*, Stockholm: Socialstyrelsen. [in Swedish]

Naylor, C.D. (1986) *Private practice, public payment: Canadian medicine and the politics of health insurance, 1911-1966*, Montreal and Kingston: McGill-Queen's University Press.

Neergaard, U. (2011) 'EU health care law in a constitutional light: Distribution of competences, notions of "solidarity", and "social Europe"', *Health Care and EU Law*, pp 19-58.

Nellemann, C. and Corcoran, E. (eds) (2010) *Dead planet, living planet – Biodiversity and ecosystem restoration for sustainable development. A rapid response assessment*, United Nations Environment Programme, GRID-Arendal (www.grida.no).

Newman, J. (2001) *Modernising governance: New Labour, policy and society*, London: Sage Publications.

Ney, S. (2009) *Resolving messy policy problems: Handling conflict in environmental, transport, health and ageing policy*, London/Sterling VA: Earthscan.

NHS Health Scotland (2008) *Alcohol: Logic Model 1 (Strategic level)* (www.healthscotland.com/OFHI/alcohol/logicmodels/lm_01.html).

Nicholls, J. (2012) 'Alcohol licensing in Scotland: a historical overview', *Addiction*, vol 107, no 8, pp 1397-403.

Nilsson, M. (2005) 'The role of assessments and institutions for policy learning: A study on Swedish climate and nuclear policy formation', *Policy Sciences,* vol 38, pp 225-49.

Nilsson, M. (2011) 'Changing the decision-space: European policy influences on energy policy and systems change in Sweden', *Public Administration*, vol 89, no 4, pp 1509-25.

Nohrstedt, D. (2005) 'External shocks and policy change: Three Mile Island and Swedish nuclear energy policy', *Journal of European Public Policy*, vol 12, no 6, pp 1041-59.

Nohrstedt, D. (2008) 'The politics of crisis policymaking: Chernobyl and Swedish nuclear energy policy', *Policy Studies Journal*, vol 36, no 2, pp 257-78.

Nohrstedt, D. (2010) 'Do advocacy coalitions matter? Crisis and change in Swedish nuclear energy policy', *Journal of Public Administration Research and Theory*, vol 20, no 2, pp 309-33.

Nohrstedt, D. and Weible, C. (2010) 'The logic of policy change after crisis: Proximity and subsystem interaction', *Risks, Hazards & Crisis in Public Policy*, vol 1, no 2, pp 1-32.

Nolan, M. (2000) *Breadwinning: New Zealand women and the state*, Christchurch: Canterbury University Press.

Nowlin, M. (2011) 'Theories of the policy process: State of the art and emerging trends', *Policy Studies Journal*, vol 39 (special issue), pp 41-60.

O'Hearn, D. (2011) 'What happened to the "Celtic tiger"?', *Translocations: Migration and Social Change*, vol 7, issue 1, pp 1-8 (www.translocations.ie/docs/v07i01/Vol%207%20Issue%201%20-%20Peer%20Review%20-%20Celtic%20Tiger,%20O'Hearn.pdf).

O'Leary, J. (2010) 'External surveillance of Irish fiscal policy during the boom', *Irish Economy Note*, no 11 (www.irisheconomy.ie/Notes/Notes.htm).

O'Regan, M. (1991) 'Radicalised by the system', in M. Cahill and C. Dann (eds) *Changing our lives: Women working in the Women's Liberation Movement*, Wellington: Bridget Williams Books, pp 161-8.

Ödegård, S. (1999) *Säkerhetsarbete i högrisksystem: Tänkbara tillämpningar för ökad patientsäkerhet* (*Safety and security in high risk systems: Potential applications for increased patient safety*), Institutet för personsäkerhet & olycksfallsforskning (IPSO) Factum 53, Stockholm

OECD (Organisation for Economic Co-operation and Development) (2007) *Babies and bosses – Reconciling work and family life: A synthesis of findings for OECD countries*, Paris: OECD.

OECD (2011) 'Household savings', in *OECD factbook 2011-2012: Economic, environmental and social statistics*, Paris: OECD Publishing (http://dx.doi.org/1787/factbook-2011-22-en).

OECD (2012a) *Education at a glance 2012: OECD indicators*, Paris: OECD Publishing (http://dx.doi.org/10.1787/eag-2012-en).

OECD (2012b) 'OECD harmonised unemployment rates', News Release, September (www.oecd.org/std/labour-stats/HUR_NR11e12.pdf).

OECD.StatExtracts (http://stats.oecd.org/Index.aspx?DatasetCode=ANHRS).

Olejaz, M., Juul, N.A., Rudkjøbing, A., Okkels, B.H., Krasnik, A. and Hernández-Quevedo, C. (2012) 'Denmark health system review', *Health Systems in Transition*, vol 14, no 2, p 62.

Ong, A., Zafiris, M. and Govan, C. (2010) *Community attitudes to climate change*, National Climate Change Adaptation Research Facility, Australian Climate Change Adaptation Research Network for Settlements and Infrastructure Report, Gold Coast, Australia.

Oosterwaal, A. and Torenvlied, R. (2012) 'Policy divergence in implementation: How conflict among decisive legislators reinforces the effect of agency preferences', *Journal of Public Administration Research and Theory*, vol 22, no 2, pp 195-217.

Orange, C. (2012) 'Story: Treaty of Waitangi', in *Te Ara Encyclopedia of New Zealand* (www.teara.govt.nz/en/treaty-of-waitangi).

Page, B. and Shapiro, R. (1983) 'The effects of public opinion on policy', *American Political Science Review*, vol 77, no 1, pp 175-90.

Palm, W. and Glinos, I.A. (2010) 'Enabling patient mobility in the EU: between free movement and coordination', in E. Mossialos, G. Permanand, R. Baeten and T. Hervey (eds) *Health systems governance in Europe: The role of EU law and policy*, Cambridge University Press, pp 509-60.

Palme, J., Bergmark, A., Bäckman, O., Estrada, F., Fritzell, J., Lundberg, O., Sjöberg, O., Sommestad, L., Szebehely, M., Swedish Welfare Commission (2003) 'A welfare balance sheet for the 1990s. Final report of the Swedish Welfare Commission', *Scandinavian Journal of Public Health Supplement*, no 60, pp 7-143.

Panitch, M. (2007) *Disability, mothers, and organization: Accidental activists,* London: Routledge.

Patashnik, E. (2006) *Reforms at risk: What happens after major policy changes are enacted*, Princeton, NJ: Princeton University Press.

Peng, I. (2011) 'The good, the bad, and the confused: Political economy of social care in South Korea', *Development and Change*, vol 42, no 4, pp 905-23.

Peters, B.G. (2005) *Institutional theory in political science: The 'new institutionalism'*, New York: Continuum.

Pierre, J. (ed) (2000) *Debating governance*, Oxford: Oxford University Press.

Pierre, J. (2009) 'Reinventing governance, reinventing democracy?', *Policy & Politics*, vol 37, no 4, pp 591-609.

Pierre, J. and Peters, B.G. (2000) *Governance, politics and the state*, Basingstoke: Macmillan.

Pierson, P. (1994) *Dismantling the welfare state? Reagan, Thatcher, and the politics of retrenchment*, Cambridge: Cambridge University Press.

Pierson, P. (2000) 'Increasing returns, path dependence and the study of politics', *American Political Science Review*, vol 92, no 4, pp 251-67.

Pierson, P. (2004) *Politics in time: History, institutions, and social analysis*, Princeton, NJ: Princeton University Press.

Pollitt, C. and Bouckaert, G. (2004) *Public management reform: A comparative analysis* (2nd edn), Oxford: Oxford University Press.

Pollitt, C. and Bouckaert, G. (2009) *Continuity and change in public policy and management*, Cheltenham: Edward Elgar.

Pollitt, C. and Bouckaert, G. (2000/2011) *Public management reform: A comparative analysis* (3rd edn), Oxford: Oxford University Press.

Pope, C., Robert, G., Bate, P., Le May, A. and Gabbay, J. (2006) 'Lost in translation: a multi-level case study of the metamorphosis of meanings and action in public sector organizational innovation', *Public Administration*, vol 84, no 1, pp 59-80.

Poujade, R. (1975) *Le ministère de l'impossible*, Paris: Calmann–Levy.

Pralle, S. (2003) 'Venue-shopping, political strategy, and policy change: The internationalization of Canadian forest advocacy', *Journal of Public Policy*, vol 23, no 3, pp 233-60.

Prater, C.S. and Lindell, M.K. (2000) 'Politics of hazard mitigation', *Natural Hazards Review*, vol 1, no 2, pp 73-82.

Pressman, J. and Wildavsky, A. (1979) *Implementation* (2nd edn), Berkeley, CA: University of California Press.

Prime Minister's Strategy Unit (2004) *Alcohol harm reduction strategy for England*, London: Cabinet Office.

Prince, M.J. (2001a) 'Federalism and disability policy making', *Canadian Journal of Political Science*, vol 34, no 4, pp 791-817.

Prince, M.J. (2001b) 'Tax policy as social policy: Canadian tax assistance for people with disabilities', *Canadian Public Policy*, vol 27, no 4, pp 487-501.

Prince, M.J. (2004) 'Canadian disability policy: Still a hit-and-miss affair', *Canadian Journal of Sociology*, vol 29, no 1, pp 59-82.

Prince, M.J. (2005) 'From welfare state to social union: Shifting choices of governing instruments, intervention rationales, and governance rules in Canadian social policy', in P. Eliadis, M.M. Hill and M. Howlett (eds) *Designing government: From instruments to governance*, Kingston & Montreal: McGill-Queen's University Press, pp 281-302.

Prince, M.J. (2008) *Canadians need a medium-term sickness/disability income benefit*, Ottawa: Caledon Institute of Social Policy.

Prince, M.J. (2009) *Absent citizens: Disability politics and policy in Canada*, Toronto: University of Toronto Press.

Prince, M.J. (2010a) 'What about a Disability Rights Act for Canada? Practices and lessons from America, Australia, and the United Kingdom', *Canadian Public Policy*, vol 36, no 2, pp 199-214.

Prince, M.J. (2010b) 'Avoiding blame, doing good, and claiming credit: Reforming Canadian income security', *Canadian Public Administration*, vol 53, no 3, pp 1-30.

Prince, M.J. (2011) 'Integrated and individualized service provision for people with disabilities: Promising practices in liberal welfare states', *Journal of Comparative Policy Analysis*, vol 13, no 5, pp 545-60.

Prince, M.J. (2012a) 'Canadian disability activism and political ideas: In and between neo-liberalism and social liberalism', *Canadian Journal of Disability Studies*, vol 1, no 1, pp 1-34.

Prince, M.J. (2012b) 'A Hobbesian prime minister and the night watchman state: Social policy under the Harper Conservatives', in G.B. Doern and C. Stoney (eds) *How Ottawa spends 2012-2013: The Harper majority, budget cuts, and the new opposition*, Kingston and Montreal: McGill-Queen's University Press, pp 53-70.

Prop 1997/98:145 *Swedish environmental goals*, Stockholm: Ministry of Environment. [in Swedish]

Prop 2003/04:51 *Coastal and lake fishing and aquaculture*, Stockholm: Ministry of Agriculture. [in Swedish]

Prop 2004/05:150 *Swedish environmental goals – A joint mission*, Stockholm: Ministry of Environment and Planning. [in Swedish]

Prop 2005/06:172 *National climate policy in global cooperation*, Stockholm: Ministry of Environment and Planning. [in Swedish]

Prop 2007/08:108 *Forest policy in pace with time*, Stockholm: Swedish Ministry for Rural Affairs. [in Swedish]

Prop 2008/09:170 *A coherent Swedish marine policy*, Stockholm: Ministry of Environment. [in Swedish]

Prop 2008/09:214 *Sustainable protection of nature areas*, Stockholm: Ministry of Environment. [in Swedish]

Prop 2009/10:155 *Swedish environmental goals – For more efficient environmental work*, Stockholm: Ministry of Environment. [in Swedish]

Purshouse, R.C. et al (2010) 'Estimated effect of alcohol pricing policies on health and health economic outcomes in England: an epidemiological model', *The Lancet*, vol 375, no 9723, pp 1355-64.

Quinlan, J. (2011) *Built to last: The Irish–US economic relationship*, Dublin: American Chamber of Commerce Ireland.

Ravenhill, J. (2010) 'Economic interdependence and the global economic crisis', in C. Hay (ed) *New directions in political science: Responding to the challenges of an interdependent world*, Basingstoke: Palgrave Macmillan, pp 148-66.

Record, C. and Day, C. (2009) 'Britain's alcohol market: how minimum alcohol prices could stop moderate drinkers subsidising those drinking at hazardous and harmful levels', *Clinical Medicine*, vol 9, no 5, pp 421-5.

Rees, T. (2005) 'Reflections on the uneven development of gender mainstreaming in Europe', *International Feminist Journal of Politics*, vol 7, no 4, pp 555-74.

Regan, A. (2012) 'The political economy of social pacts in the EMU: Irish liberal market corporatism in crisis', *New Political Economy*, vol 17, no 4, pp 465-91.

Rehm, J. et al (2009) 'Global burden of disease and injury and economic cost attributable to alcohol use and alcohol-use disorders', *The Lancet*, vol 373, no 9682, pp 2223-33.

Rein, M. (1976) *Social science and public policy*, London: Penguin Books.

Report of the Independent Review Panel (Ireland) (2010) *Strengthening the capacity of the Department of Finance* (www.finance.gov.ie/viewdoc.asp?DocID=6708).

Rhodes, R.A.W. (1994) 'The hollowing out of the state: The changing nature of the public service in Britain', *Political Quarterly*, vol 65, no 2, pp 138-51.

Rhodes, R.A.W. (1996) 'The new governance: Governing without government', *Political Studies*, vol 44, no 4, pp 652-67.

Rhodes, R.A.W. (1997) *Understanding governance: Policy networks, governance, reflexivity and accountability*, Buckingham: Open University Press.

Riccucci, N.M., Meyers, M.K., Lurie, I. and Han, J.S. (2004) 'The implementation of welfare reform policy: The role of public managers in front-line practices', *Public Administration Review*, vol 64, pp 438-48.

Rice, J.J. and Prince M.J. (2013) *Changing politics of Canadian social policy* (2nd edn), Toronto: University of Toronto Press.

Richards, D. and Smith, M.J. (2002) *Governance and public policy in the UK*, Oxford: Oxford University Press.

Rioux, M.H. and Prince, M.J. (2002) 'The Canadian political landscape of disability: Policy perspectives, social status, interest groups and the rights movement', in A. Puttee (ed) *Federalism, democracy and disability policy in Canada*, Kingston and Montreal: McGill–Queen's University Press, pp 11-28.

Rioux, M.H. and Valentine, F. (2006) 'Does theory matter? Exploring the nexus between disability, human rights, and public policy', in D. Pothier and R. Devlin (eds) *Critical disability theory: Essays in philosophy, politics, policy, and law*, Vancouver: University of British Columbia Press, pp 47-69.

Rittel, H. and Webber, M. (1973) 'Dilemmas in a general theory of planning', *Policy Sciences*, vol 4, pp 155-69.

Robinson, S., Caver, F., Meier K.J. and O'Toole, L.J. Jr (2007) 'Explaining policy punctuations: Bureaucratization and budget change', *American Journal of Political Science*, vol 51, no 1, pp 140-50.

Roche, B. (2011) 'The breakdown of social partnership', *Administration*, vol 59, no 1, pp 23-37.

Rochefort, D.A. and Cobb, R.W. (eds) (1994) *The politics of problem definition: Shaping the policy agenda*, Lawrence, KS: University Press of Kansas.

Room, R. et al (2005) 'Alcohol and public health', *The Lancet*, vol 365, no 9458, pp 519-30.

Rose, N. and Miller, P. (1992) 'Political power beyond the state: Problematics of government', *British Journal of Sociology*, vol 43, no 2, pp 173-205.

Rose, R. (1991) 'What is lesson-drawing?', *Journal of Public Policy*, vol 11, no 1, pp 3-30.

Rose, R. and Davies, P.L. (1994) *Inheritance in public policy: Change without choice in Britain*, New Haven, CT and London: Yale University Press.

Ross, J.A. and Finnigan, O. (1968) 'Within family planning: Korea', *Demography*, vol 5, no 2, pp 679-89.

Royal College of Physicians (1987) *A great and growing evil: The medical consequences of alcohol abuse*, London: The Chaucer Press.

Rudd, K. (2007) Address to the 13th session of the United Nations Framework Convention on Climate Change Conference, Bali, Indonesia.

Rydin, Y. (2007) 'Indicators as a governmental technology? The lessons of community-based sustainability indicator projects', *Environment and Planning D*, vol 25, no 4, pp 610-24.

Sabatier, P.A. (1988) 'An advocacy coalition framework of policy change and the role of policy oriented learning therein', *Policy Studies*, vol 21, pp 129-67.

Sabatier, P.A. (ed) (2007) *Theories of the policy process* (2nd edn), Boulder, CO: Westview Press.

Sabatier, P.A. and Brasher, A.M. (1993) 'From vague consensus to clearly differentiated coalitions: environmental policy at Lake Tahoe, 1964-1985', in P.A. Sabatier and H.C. Jenkins-Smith (eds) *Policy change and learning. An advocacy coalition approach*, Boulder, CO: Westview Press, pp 177-208.

Sabatier, P.A. and Jenkins-Smith, H. (1999) 'The advocacy coalition framework: An assessment', in P. Sabatier (ed) *Theories of the policy process*, Boulder, CO: Westview Press, pp 117-66.

Sabatier, P.A. and Mazmanian, D. (1980) 'The implementation of public policy: a framework for analysis', *Policy Studies*, vol 8, no 4, pp 538-60.

Sabatier, P.A. and Weible, C.S. (2007) 'The advocacy coalition framework: Innovations and clarifications', in P.A. Sabatier (ed) *Theories of the policy process* (2nd edn), Boulder, CO: Westview Press, pp 189-220. [

SAF (Swedish Agency of Fisheries) (2006) *Regional and local co-management of fisheries*, Göteborg: SAF. [in Swedish]

Sarewitz, D. (1996) *Frontiers of illusion: Science, technology and the politics of progress*, Philadelphia, PA: Temple University Press.

Sawer, M. (1990) *Sisters in suits. Women and public policy in Australia*, Sydney: Allen & Unwin.

Sawer, M. (1996) *Femocrats and ecorats: Women's policy machinery in Australia, Canada and New Zealand*, Occasional Paper No 6, Geneva: United Nations Research Institute for Social Development.

SCB (2011) Press release from Statistics Sweden and Swedish Environmental Protection Agency (www.scb.se/Pages/PressRelease____321510.aspx).

Schattschneider, E.E. (1960) *The semi-sovereign people*, New York: Holt, Rinehart & Winston.

Schelkle, W. (2012) 'A crisis of what? Mortgage credit markets and the social policy of promoting homeownership in the United States and in Europe', *Politics and Society*, vol 40, no 1, pp 59-80.

Schlager, E. (1997) 'A response to Kim Quaile Hill's *In search of policy theory*', *Policy Currents*, vol 7, pp 14-15.

Scott, W.R. (2008) *Institutions and organisations: Ideas and interests*, Los Angeles, CA: Sage Publications.

Scottish Executive (2002) *A plan for action on alcohol problems*, Edinburgh: Scottish Executive.

Secretariat of the Conference on Sustaining Taiwan's Economic Development (2008) *The Minute of the Conference on sustaining Taiwan's economic development: Part 1*, Taipei: Council for Economic Planning and Development. [in Chinese]

Seeleib-Kaiser, M. (2008) 'Multiple and multi-dimensional welfare state transformations', in M. Seeleib-Kaiser (ed) *Welfare state transformations: Comparative perspectives*, Basingstoke: Palgrave Macmillan, pp 210-21.

Seely Brown, J. and Duguid, P. (1991) 'Organisational learning and communities of practice: towards a unified view of working, learning and innovation', *Organization Science*, vol 2, no 1, pp 40-57.

SEPA (Swedish Environmental Protection Agency) (2006) *National strategy for thriving wetlands*, Stockholm: SEPA, Swedish Agency of Agriculture, Swedish Forestry Agency and National Heritage Board. [in Swedish]

SEPA (2012) *Evaluation of the NEQOs 2012*, Report 6500, Stockholm: SEPA. [in Swedish]

SEPA and SAF (Swedish Agency of Fisheries) (2007) *National strategy for stream restoration,* Report 5746, Stockholm: SEPA and SAF. [in Swedish]

SEPA and SAF (2008) *Ecological restoration of streams*, Stockholm: SEPA and SAF. [in Swedish]

SEPA and SFA (Swedish Forestry Agency) (2005) *National strategy for formal protection of forests,* Stockholm: SEPA and SFA.

SER (Society for Ecological Restoration) (2004) *The SER international primer on ecological restoration,* Society for Ecological Restoration International, Version 2, October (www.ser.org/docs/default-document-library/english.pdf).

SFA (2012) *The Swedish Agency of Agriculture and the Swedish Forestry Agency's proposal for a simplified rural development programme,* Report 2012:16, Jönköping: SFA. [in Swedish]

SFI (2013) *Protected forests* (http://protectedforests.com).

SFWF (Seoul Foundation of Women and Family) (2011) *Family survey and policy demand survey in Seoul,* Seoul: SFWF. [in Korean]

Shore, C. (2011) '"European governance" or governmentality? The European Commission and the future of democratic government', *European Law Journal,* vol 17, no 3, pp 287-303.

SIPTU (Services Industrial Professional and Technical Union) (2012) 'SIPTU President says Congress should not meet again with the Troika', Press release, 23 October, Dublin: SIPTU (www.siptu.ie/media/pressreleases2012/fullstory_16665_en.html).

Sjöblom, S. (2009) 'Administrative short-termism: A non-issue in environmental and regional governance', *Journal of Environmental Policy & Planning,* vol 11, no 3, pp 165-8.

Sjöblom, S. and Godenhjelm, S. (2009) 'Project proliferation and governance – Implications for environmental management', *Journal of Environmental Policy & Planning,* vol 11, no 3, pp 169-85.

Skocpol, T. (1992) *Protecting soldiers and mothers: The political origins of social policy in the United States,* Cambridge, MA: Belknap Press.

Skr 2001/02:172 *National strategy for sustainable development,* Stockholm: Ministry of Environment. [in Swedish]

Skr 2001/02:173 *A coherent nature conservation policy,* Stockholm: Ministry of Environment. [in Swedish]

Skr 2005/06:171 *Some fishery policy issues,* Stockholm: Ministry of Agriculture. [in Swedish]

Skr 2009/10:213 *Measures for a living sea,* Stockholm: Ministry of Environment. [in Swedish]

Slater, J. (2008) 'Meshed in web of power', *Times Educational Supplement,* 11 May.

Slattery, L. (2012) 'EU's troika representative denies bailout creates "democratic deficit"', *Irish Times,* 12 October.

Smith, D. (2002) 'Not by error, but by design– Harold Shipman and the regulatory crisis for health care', *Public Policy and Administration,* vol, 17, pp 55-74.

Smith, K. and Hellowell, M. (2012) 'Beyond rhetorical differences: A cohesive account of post-devolution developments in UK health policy', *Social Policy & Administration*, vol 46, no 2, pp 178-98.

Smith, M.J. (2011) 'Tsars, leadership and innovation in the public sector', *Policy & Politics*, vol 39, no 3, pp 343-59.

Smith, M.J. (1993) *Pressure, power and policy*, Hemel Hempstead: Harvester Wheatsheaf.

Social Democratic Party (2006) *Election manifesto 2006* (www.socialdemokraterna. se/upload/Internationellt/Other%20Languages/ElectionManifesto2006.pdf). [in Swedish]

SOU 1997:98 *Protection of forests: needs and costs,* Stockholm: Swedish Environmental Advisory Council, Ministry of the Environment. [in Swedish]

SOU 2005:39 *Forests for all?*, Stockholm: Swedish Ministry of Enterprise, Energy and Communications. [in Swedish]

Spector, M. and Kitsuse, J.I. (1987) *Constructing social problems* (2nd edn), Rutgers, NJ: Aldine de Gruyter.

Spruyt, H. (2002) 'The origins, development and possible decline of the modern state', *Annual Review of Political Science*, vol 5, no 1, pp 127-49.

Squires, J. (1999) *Gender in political theory*, Cambridge: Polity Press.

Squire, P. (2007) 'Measuring state legislative professionalism: the Squire Index revisited', *State Politics and Policy Quarterly*, vol 7, no 2, pp 211-27.

Starr, P. (2011) *Remedy and reaction: The peculiar American struggle over health care reform*, New Haven, CT: Yale University Press.

Steffen, W. (2013) *The angry summer*, Canberra: Climate Commission Secretariat/ Department of Climate Change and Energy Efficiency.

Steinwall, A. (forthcoming) 'Naturalness or biodiversity: conflicting discourses in Swedish protected area management', submitted to *Environmental Values*.

Stern, N. (2007) *The economics of climate change*, Cambridge: Cambridge University Press.

Stewart, J. (2008) 'Shadow regulation and the shadow banking system, the role of the Dublin International Financial Services Centre', *Tax Justice Focus*, vol 4, no 2, pp 1-3.

Stienstra, D. (2012) *About Canada: Disability rights*, Halifax and Winnipeg: Fernwood Publishing.

Stockwell, T. et al (2006) *Alcohol pricing and public health in Canada: Issues and opportunities*, British Columbia: Centre for Addictions Research.

Stoker, G. (1998) 'Governance as theory: five propositions', *International Social Science Journal*, vol 50, no 155, pp 17-28.

Stoker, R.P. (1991) *Reluctant partners: Implementing federal policy*, Pittsburgh, PA: University of Pittsburg Press.

Stone, D.A. (1989) 'Causal stories and the formation of policy agendas', *Political Science Quarterly*, vol 104, pp 281-300.

Stone, D.A. (2000) 'Private authority, scholarly legitimacy and political credibility: Think tanks and informal diplomacy', in R. Higgott, G. Underhill and A. Bieler (eds) *Non-state actors and authority in the global system*, London: Routledge.

Stone, D.A. (2012) *Policy paradox: The art of political decision making* (3rd edn), New York: Norton.

Streeck, W. and Thelen, K. (2005) 'Introduction: Institutional change in advanced political economies', in W. Streeck and K. Thelen (eds) *Beyond continuity: Institutional change in advanced political economies*, Oxford: Oxford University Press, pp 1-39.

Surel, Y. (2000) 'The role of cognitive and normative frames in policy-making', *Journal of European Public Policy*, vol 7, no 4, pp 495-512.

Sutton Trust, The (2013) 'Who we are', London: The Sutton Trust (www. suttontrust.com/who-we-are).

Svantesson, E. (2009) 'Green light for new nuclear power', *Dagens Nyheter* (www. dn.se/nyheter/politik/gront-ljus-for-ny-karnkraft). [in Swedish]

Swedish Government (2009) *Nuclear power: Conditions for transition*, Government Bill 2009/10:172. [in Swedish]

Syal, R. (2010) 'Michael Gove's 25-year-old ex-adviser given £500,000 free schools grant', *The Guardian*, 28 October.

Syal, R. (2013) 'Education civil servants set to ballot for industrial action over cuts', *The Guardian*, 22 January.

Sylves, R.T. (2007) 'Federal emergency management comes of age: 1979-2001', in C.B. Rubin (ed) *Emergency management: The American experience, 1900–2005*, Arlington, VA: Public Entity Risk Institute.

Tahi, B. (1995) 'Biculturalism. The model of Te Ohu Whakatupu', in M. Wilson and A. Yeatman (eds) *Justice and identity: Antipodean practices*, Wellington: Bridget Williams Books.

Tatara, K. and Okamoto, E. (2009) 'Japan: health system review', *Health Systems in Transition*, vol 11, no 5, pp 1-164.

Taylor, G. (2011) 'Risk and financial Armageddon in Ireland: the politics of the Galway tent', *The Political Quarterly*, vol 82, no 4, pp 596-608.

Taylor, M.G. (1978) *Health insurance and Canadian public policy: The seven decisions that created the Canadian health insurance system*, Montreal and Kingston: McGill-Queen's University Press.

Teghtsoonian, K. (2004) 'Neoliberalism and gender analysis mainstreaming in Aotearoa/New Zealand', *Australian Journal of Political Science*, vol 39, no 2, pp 267-84.

Teghtsoonian, K. (2005) 'Disparate fates in challenging times. Women's policy agencies and neoliberalism in Aotearoa/New Zealand and British Colombia', *Canadian Journal of Political Science*, vol 38, no 2, pp 307-33.

Thompson, H. (2010) 'The character of the state', in C. Hay (ed) *New directions in political science: Responding to the challenges of an interdependent world*, Palgrave Macmillan: Basingstoke, pp 130-47.

Torenvlied, R. (1996) 'Political control of implementation agencies: effects of political consensus on agency compliance', *Rationality and Society*, vol 8, no 1, pp 25-56.

Torenvlied, R. (2000) *Political decisions and agency performances*, Dordrecht: Kluwer.

True, J.R., Jones, B.D. and Baumgartner, F.R. (2007) 'Punctuated equilibrium theory: Explaining change and stability in public policymaking', in P.A. Sabatier (ed) *Theories of the policy process* (2nd edn), Boulder, CO: Westview Press, pp 155-88.

Trydegård, G.-B. and Thorslund, M. (2010) 'One uniform welfare state or a multitude of welfare municipalities? The evolution of local variation in Swedish elder care', *Social Policy and Administration*, vol 44, no 4, pp 495-511.

Tsai, P.-Y. (2012) 'The transformation of leave policies for work-family balance in Taiwan', *Asian Women*, vol 28, no 2, pp 27-54.

Tsebelis, G. (1995) 'Decision making in political systems: Veto players in presidentialism, parliamentarism, multicameralism, and multipartyism', *British Journal of Political Science*, vol 25, no 3, pp 289-325.

Uba, K. (2010) 'Who formulates renewable energy policy? A Swedish example', *Energy Policy*, vol 38, pp 6674-83.

UN (United Nations) (1995) 'Women in power and decision making', in *The United Nations Fourth World Conference on Women Platform for Action* (www.un.org/womenwatch/daw/beijing/platform/decision.htm).

USGS (United States Geological Survey) (2006) *Flood hazards: A national threat*, Washington, DC: US Government Printing Office.

van Meter, D. and van Horn, C.E. (1975) 'The policy implementation process, a conceptual framework', *Administration & Society*, vol 6, no 4, pp 445-88.

Vasagar, J. (2011) 'Michael Gove faces questions over department's use of private email', *The Guardian*, 20 September.

Verloo, M. (2001) *Another Velvet Revolution? Gender mainstreaming and the politics of implementation*, IWM Working Paper No. 5/2002, Vienna: Institute for Human Sciences (IWM).

Verso Economics (2010) *The economic impact of Scotch whisky production in Scotland*, Edinburgh: Scotch Whisky Association.

Virtanen, T. (2008) 'Merging and privatising to reach for the top: A new Finnish university of technology, business, and art and design', in T. Aarrevaara and F. Maruyama (eds) *University reforms in Finland and Japan*, Tampere: Tampere University Press, pp 53-76.

Virtanen, T. and Temmes, M. (2008) 'University reforms as a reflection of administrative reforms in Finland: a marathon to the edge of giant leap?', *Köz-gazdaság* 3:3 – Special English language issue, pp 15-36.

Vlassopoulos, C.A. (1999) 'La lutte contre la pollution atmosphérique urbaine en France et en Grèce. Définition des problèmes publics et changement de politique', PhD, University of Panthéon-Assas, Paris II.

Vlassopoulos, C.A. (2000) 'Politiques publiques comparées. Pour une approche définitionnelle et diachronique', in CURAPP, *Les méthodes au concret*, Paris: PUF, pp 187-202.

Vlassopoulos, C.A. (2003) 'L'histoire dans les politiques publiques: un premier bilan', in P. Laborier and D. Trom (eds) *L'historicité dans l'action publique*, Paris: PUF, pp 99-119.

Vlassopoulos, C.A. (2005) 'Car pollution. Agenda denial and agenda setting in early 20th century France and Greece', in M. Armiero et al (eds) *History and sustainability*, Florence: Univercita degli studi di Firenze, pp 252-8.

Vlassopoulos, C.A. (2007) 'Protection de l'environnement où protection du pollueur? L'emprise des industriels sur la politique antipollution', in E. Dockès (eds) *Au cœur des combats juridiques*, Paris: Dalloz, pp 473-87.

Walby, S. (2005) 'Introduction: Comparative gender mainstreaming in a global era', *International Feminist Journal of Politics*, vol 7, no 4, pp 453-70.

Walker, J.L. (1969) 'The diffusion of innovations among the American states', *American Political Science Review*, vol 63, no 3, pp 880-99.

Walker, J.L. (1973) 'Comment: Problems in research on the diffusion of policy innovations', *American Political Science Review*, vol 67, no 4, pp 1186-91.

Wang, S.-I. and Lai, S.-Y. (1997) 'The predicament of childcare and role of the state in Taiwan', in Y.-H. Liu (ed) *Women, state, and care*, Taipei: Fembooks, pp 127-59. [in Chinese]

Wang, S.-I. and Sun, M.-W. (2003) 'The role of Taiwanese government in the child care policy', *National Policy Quarterly*, vol 2, no 4, pp 147-74. [in Chinese]

Washington, S. (1988) 'Great expectations: The Ministry of Women's Affairs and public policy', *Race, Gender, Class*, vol 7, pp 7-16.

Waterman, R.W. and Meier, K.J. (1998) 'Principal–agent models: An expansion?', *Journal of Public Administration Research and Theory*, vol 8, pp 173-202.

Weaver, R.K. (1986) 'The politics of blame avoidance', *Journal of Public Policy*, vol 6, pp 371-98.

Weber, K. and Glynn, M.A. (2006) 'Making sense with institutions: Context, thought and action in Karl Weick's theory', *Organization Studies*, vol 27, no 11, pp 1639-60.

Weber, M. (1925) *Wirtschaft und gesellschaft*, Tübingen: J.C.B. Mohr.

Weber, M. (1947) *The theory of social and economic organization* (translated by A.M. Henderson and T. Parsons), Glencoe, IL: Free Press.

Weible, C., Heikkila, T., deLeon, P. and Sabatier, P.A. (2012) 'Understanding and influencing the policy process', *Policy Sciences*, vol 45, no 1, pp 1-21.

Weick, K.E. (1979) 'Cognitive processes in organisations', *Research in Organisational Behaviour*, vol 1, pp 41-7.

Weick, K.E. (1995) *Sensemaking in organizations*, Thousand Oaks, CA: Sage Publications.

Weick, K.E., Sutcliffe, K.M. and Obstfeld, D. (2005) 'Organizing and the process of sensemaking', *Organization Science*, vol 16, no 4, pp 409-21.

Whelan, K. (2011) *Ireland's sovereign debt crisis*, UCD Centre for Economic Research Working Paper Series WP11/09, Dublin: UCD Centre for Economic Research.

White, G.F. (1945) *Human adjustment to floods: A geographical approach to the flood problem in the United States*, Chicago, IL: Department of Geography, University of Chicago.

Whitfield, S., Rosa, E., Dan, A. and Dietz, T. (2009) 'The future of nuclear power: value orientations and risk perceptions', *Risk Analysis*, vol 29, no 3, pp 425-37.

Williamson, J.B. and Higo, M. (2007) 'Older workers: Lessons from Japan', *Work Opportunities for Older Americans, Series 11*, June, Chestnut Hill, MA: Centre for Retirement Research at Boston College.

Wilson, E. (2006) 'Adapting to climate change at the local level: the spatial planning response', *Local Environment*, vol 11, no 6, pp 609-25.

Wilson, W. (1887) 'The study of administration', *Political Science Quarterly*, vol 2, pp 202-17.

Winter, S.C. (2006) 'Implementation', in B.G Peters and J. Pierre (eds) *Handbook of public policy*, London: Sage Publications, pp 151-66.

Withers, A.J. (2012) *Disability politics and theory*, Halifax and Winnipeg: Fernwood Publishing.

WHO (World Health Organization) (2010a) *Global strategy to reduce the harmful use of alcohol*, Geneva: WHO.

WHO (2010b) *World health report 2010 – Health systems financing: The path to universal coverage*, Geneva: WHO.

Wong, L.-F. and Huang, Y.-M. (1995) 'Research on the development of early childhood education in Taiwan: The implications of day care centre development for early childhood education in Taiwan', *Journal of History*, vol 25, pp 9-38. [in Chinese]

World Bank, The (various years) *World development indicators* (http://data.worldbank.org/indicator/SP.DYN.TFRT.IN).

World Values Survey (1982, 1990, 1996, 2001) Online data analysis (www.wvsevsdb.com/wvs/WVSAnalize.jsp?Idioma=I).

Wu, S.-C. (2006) 'Current childcare services in Taiwan', in Y.-C. Yeh (ed) *Childcare services*, Taipei: Psychological Publishing. [in Chinese]

Yashiro, N. and Oshio, T. (1999) 'Social security and retirement in Japan', in J. Gruber and D.A. Wise (eds) *Social security and retirement around the world*, Chicago, IL: University of Chicago Press, pp 239-67.

Yeates, N. (2002) *Globalisation and social policy*, London: Sage Publications.

Yeates, N. (2007) 'Globalisation and social policy', in J. Baldock, N. Manning and S. Vickerstaff (eds) *Social policy* (3rd edn), Oxford: Oxford University Press, pp 627-53.

York Health Economics Consortium (2010) *The societal cost of alcohol misuse in Scotland for 2007*, Edinburgh: Scottish Government Social Research.

Yoshida, T. (2004) *Why did the accident happen at the YCU? Insights from my personal experience*, Bungei-sha: Tokyo. [in Japanese]

Index

Note: This index is confined to key issues, concepts and authorities for the study of the policy process. Substantive topics and the names of countries have not been indexed; these are generally identifiable from the chapter titles. Similarly expert contributions to the study of the substantive topics, as opposed to contributions on policy theory, have not been indexed.

A

accountability, 101, 105, 109, 114, 120
advocacy coalitions, 13, 16, 55, 59, 130
agenda setting, 7, 8, 30, Part Three, 129, 151, 153, 180, 184, 239

B

Baumgartner, Frank R., 11, 12, 21, 29, 55, 58, 60, 62, 102
Birkland, Thomas A., 72, 89, 91, 101, 102
bureaucrats, 77, 117, 119, 121, 196, 222, 229

C

civil services, civil servants, 8, 24, 48, 82, 106, 130, 180, 181, 182, 183, 187, 188, 198, 226, 240, 247, 248, 289
comparative studies, 6, 11, 15, Chapter 2.2, Chapter 3.4, 66, 72-3, Chapter 6.5
critical junctures, 71, 103
crowded policy space, 71

D

decentralisation, 167, 209
definitions of policy, 129-30
democracy, 6, 139, 141, 274, 277
democratic deficit, 236, 243, 263
devolution, 108, 241, 242, 243-5, 246, 250
diffusion theory, 93-7, 98, 99
discretion, 106, 122, 196
Downs, Anthony, 58, 72
Dunleavy, Patrick, 11, 189

E

elections, 93, 205, 225, 243, 274, 281
European Court, 282-3
European Union, 13, 57, 118, 125, 150, 154, 155, 158, 159, 161, 163, 237, 240, 243, 247, 248, 250, 251, 253, 254, 255, 256, 257, 258, 259, 260, 262, 263, 265, 271, 277, Chapter 6.5
evaluation, 118, 120, 123, 152, 155, 173, 180, 201, 223, 244
exogenous influences on policy change, 13, 30, 59, 185
expertise, 4, 23, 38, 79, 126, 182, 185, 187, 188

F

federalism, federal systems, 11, 73, 75, 98, 141, 145, 146, 196, 236, 239
fiscal policy, 17, 258, 265
focusing events, 72, 89, 96, 97, 99, 100, 101, 114

G

globalisation, globalism, 8, 235, 236-8, 253, 254, 256, 257, 261, 264
governance, 8, 57, 101, 102, 103, 104, 105, 111, 113, 114, 131, 139, 143, 147, 152, 153, 156, 164, 179, 185, 194, 199, 225, 227, 229, 230, Part Six

H

Hajer, Maarten, 236, 241, 250
Hall, Peter A., 6, 12, 14, 17, 20, 45, 52, 55
Hay, Colin, 236-7

Q14

LEARNING
RESOURCES
CENTRE

This book is due for return on or before the last date shown below.

1 2 SEP 2014

- 4 DEC 2019

WITHDRAWN

For enquiries and renewals at
Quarles LRC
Call 01708 462759